VICTORIAN CRUSADERS

Victorian Crusaders

British and Irish Volunteers in the Papal Army, 1860-1870

Nicholas Schofield

with best wishes
Nicholas Schofield

Helion & Company

Helion & Company Limited
Unit 8 Amherst Business Centre
Budbrooke Road
Warwick
CV34 5WE
England
Tel. 01926 499 619
Email: info@helion.co.uk
Website: www.helion.co.uk
Twitter: @helionbooks
Visit our blog at blog.helion.co.uk

Published by Helion & Company 2022
Designed and typeset by Mary Woolley (www.battlefield-design.co.uk)
Cover designed by Paul Hewitt, Battlefield Design (www.battlefield-design.co.uk)

Text © Nicholas Schofield 2022
Images © as individually credited 2022
Maps drawn by George Anderson © Helion & Company 2022

Cover: The Dutch Zouave, Pieter Jong, fighting the red shirts at Montelibretti. Using his rifle butt as a weapon, he is said to have killed 14 of the enemy, by J. Faber, (Zouavenmuseum, Oudenbosch, with permission)

Every reasonable effort has been made to trace copyright holders and to obtain their permission for the use of copyright material. The author and publisher apologize for any errors or omissions in this work, and would be grateful if notified of any corrections that should be incorporated in future reprints or editions of this book.

ISBN 978-1-915070-53-1

British Library Cataloguing-in-Publication Data.
A catalogue record for this book is available from the British Library.

All rights reserved. No part of this publication may be reproduced, stored in a retrieval system, or transmitted, in any form, or by any means, electronic, mechanical, photocopying, recording or otherwise, without the express written consent of Helion & Company Limited.

For details of other military history titles published by Helion & Company Limited contact the above address or visit our website: http://www.helion.co.uk.

We always welcome receiving book proposals from prospective authors.

Contents

List of Illustrations	vi
List of Maps	x
Acknowledgements	xi
Prologue	xiii
1 Risorgimento and Anti-Risorgimento	17
2 The Papal States in Peril	26
Part I: The Battalion of St Patrick (1860)	37
3 The Raising of the Irish Battalion	38
4 The Piedmontese Invasion of Umbria and the Marches	52
5 The Battle of Castelfidardo	61
6 Last Stand at Ancona	70
7 Legacy and Continuity	75
Part II: The Pontifical Zouaves (1861–1870)	85
8 'Z' is for Zouave	86
9 The Failed Revolution of 1867	99
10 The Battle of Mentana	105
11 Reform and Internationalisation of the Pontifical Army	123
12 British and Irish Recruits	128
13 'Far, far from our wild northern home!': Daily Life in Rome	151
14 Endgame: 20 September 1870	166
15 Afterlife	184
Conclusion	195
Appendices:	
I The Cast of Characters	197
II A List of English and Welsh Zouaves	199
III Note on Uniforms	204
IV Orders of Battles – Castelfidardo and Mentana	208
Bibliography	211
Index	218

List of Illustrations

A cartoon illustrating the tense relationship between Pope Pius IX (1792–1878) and Emperor Napoleon III (1808–1873), who tried to balance his dual roles as liberal champion and 'Eldest Son of the Church'. (*Punch*, 8 December 1860, Private collection, author's photograph) — 19

Monsignor Frédéric François Xavier de Mérode (1820–1874), the mastermind behind the reform of the Pontifical Army in the early 1860s. (Private collection, author's photograph) — 29

General Christophe Léon Louis Juchault de Lamoricière (1806-65). (Private collection, author's photograph) — 30

Like the papal volunteers, the British 'excursionists' who fought for Garibaldi came from diverse backgrounds. This picture includes Edward Styles, a recruiting officer, seen wearing his Crimean War medals, and Gabriel Cueto, who unsuccessfully tried to form a Scottish contingent. The striking tartan uniform was never universally adopted. (*Illustrated London News*, 20 October 1860, Private collection, author's photograph) — 46

Troops of the Irish Battalion of St Patrick, wearing their distinctive green uniforms, from a painting by Quinto Cenni (1845-1917). (Private collection, photograph by Ralph Weaver) — 48

Major Myles O'Reilly (1825–1880), commanding officer of the Irish Battalion. (Private collection, author's photograph) — 49

General Enrico Cialdini (1811–1892), commander of IV Corps in 1860, as depicted on the Monumento Nazionale di Castelfidardo. (Photograph: Nicoletta Lampa) — 53

General Georges de Pimodan (1822–1860), the highest profile casualty of Castelfidardo. (Private collection, author's photograph) — 63

A *carte de visite*, printed in Loreto during the 1860s, depicting the battle at its height. The Upper Farm (Casa Serenella) is the building on fire. (Private collection, author's photograph) — 65

The later stage of the battle, as the arrival of Piedmontese infantry and artillery reinforcements drive back the pontifical troops. (Lithograph from *Album Storico–Artistico della Guerra d'Italia*, Torino: C. Perrin, 1860, private collection, author's photograph) — 66

The Sacrario-Ossario dei Caduti della Battaglia, erected on the Castelfidardo battlefield. (Photograph: Nicoletta Lampa) — 67

'Prisoners of the Papal Army': Irish recruits on their way home. (*Illustrated Times*, 17 November 1860, Private collection, author's photograph) — 73

The return of the Irish Battalion in October 1860 attracted large crowds. (*Illustrated Times*, 17 November 1860, Private collection, author's photograph) — 76

A private of West India Regiment, showing the Zouave-style uniform adopted in 1858. Inspired by the French Zouaves, it served to reinforce the divisions between the largely black private soldiers and their white officers, who continued to wear the same uniforms as other British officers in the tropics. (Private collection, author's photograph) — 88

LIST OF ILLUSTRATIONS

The four De Charette De La Contrie brothers: from left to right, Louis (Papal Dragoon), Ferdinand, Athanase and Alain – all three of whom wore the Zouave uniform. Athanase was regarded by many as the unofficial commander of the unit. (Zouavenmuseum, Oudenbosch, used with permission) 90

Joseph-Eugéne Allet (1814-78), the Swiss-born commanding officer of the Zouaves, affectionately known as 'Père Allet'. He was promoted to the rank of colonel on 16 December 1866. (Private collection, photograph: Granddaughters of George Collingridge) 91

The Band of the Pontifical Zouaves. As light infantry, the cornet was used on the field of battle to give signals. (Zouavenmuseum, Oudenbosch, used with permission) 92

Four Zouaves carrying a coffin during the cholera epidemic at Albano in 1867. They pass an ancient monument, on which is inscribed the names of three comrades who died while assisting the sick: Hendricus Peeters, Jacobus van der Meyden and Gijsbertus Johannes van Ophem. (Painting by J. Faber, Zouavenmuseum, Oudenbosch, used with permission) 95

General Hermann Kanzler (1822–1888), pontifical commander-in-chief and minister of arms from 1865. (Private collection, author's photograph) 97

An engraving of Mentana, by the Zouave artist, George Collingridge. (Private collection, photograph: Granddaughters of George Collingridge) 107

An Italian depiction of the fierce fighting at Mentana. (Private collection, author's photograph) 111

French troops advance on Mentana towards the end of the battle. Opponents of the Pope emphasised the decisiveness of their intervention, armed with the new Chassepot rifle. (*La Tribuna*, 3 November 1898, private collection, author's photograph) 112

A popular print of Mentana, published by Pinot & Sagaire. (Private collection, author's photograph) 112

A photograph of Mentana veterans, including Colonel Allet and several of the wounded, taken shortly after the battle at the Dutch Zouave Club near the Piazza Farnese, Rome. They are gathered around a bust of the Pope. (Zouavenmuseum, Oudenbosch, used with permission) 117

Another image of the wounded of Mentana, possibly taken at the Quirinale palace. (Private collection, photograph: Granddaughters of George Collingridge) 118

The Mentana Medal of George Collingridge, with bars for 'Roma', 'Nerola,' and 'Mentana.' (Private collection, photograph: Granddaughters of George Collingridge) 120

A group of Zouaves at the castle of Mentana shortly after the battle. (Zouavenmuseum, Oudenbosch, with permission) 121

Through the winter of 1867, barricades and defences could be seen at strategic spots around Rome, including the Porta del Popolo and Porta San Giovanni in Laterano. (*Illustrated London News*, 23 November 1867, Private collection, author's photograph) 123

Charette, with (to his left) the English Zouave Clement Bishop (1839–1921) at the summer camp at Rocca di Papa, 1868. (Private collection, photograph: Ursula Staszynski) 124

Alfred Collingridge (1846–1867), one of the first English Zouaves, who was mortally wounded at Montelibretti. (Private collection, photograph: Granddaughters of George Collingridge/Susie Gore) 129

Two photographs of Julian Watts-Russell (1850-67). (Private collection, photographs: Granddaughters of George Collingridge) 130

Wilfrid Watts-Russell (1846-79), Julian's older brother and fellow Zouave. (Private collection, photograph: Granddaughters of George Collingridge) 131

A composite image of the Zouave 'Martyrs' of 1867, formed in the shape of a cross, with those who fell at Nerola, Bagnorea, Montrelibretti and Mentana. Alfred Collingridge is right of the central oval, and Julian Watts-Russell can be seen at the extreme bottom left. (Zouavenmuseum, Oudenbosch, used with permission) 132

Emmanuel Dufournel (1840-67), a Zouave from the very beginning, was mortally wounded at Farnese on 19 October 1867. He delighted in shedding his blood through his fourteen wounds for the glory of the Church. (Private collection, photograph: Granddaughters of George Collingridge)   133

George Collingridge (1847-1931) later moved to Australia and became a well-known artist, historian and linguist. In his youth, he had studied under the architect Viollet-le-Duc and the artists Corot and Harpignies. (Private collection, photograph: Winsome Collingridge)   137

A *Vanity Fair* cartoon of Rudolph Feilding, 8th Earl of Denbigh (1823–1892), chairman of the Papal Defence Committee and prominent lay supporter of the English Zouave movement. (Private collection, author's photograph)   138

Alexander Wilson (1855–1901), born in Scotland but settled in Leeds. He worked variously on the railways, with the police and as a rent collector, but it seems his health never recovered from his service as a Zouave. (Private collection, photograph: Kath Bracewell)   139

Charles Woodward (1850–1916), a veteran of Mentana and later the Boer War. His brother had fought with the Franco-Belgians at Castelfidardo. (Birmingham Archdiocesan Archives, OCA/6/3/1/W/38, used with permission)   140

Canon Thomas Wilkinson (1825–1909) and a group of his parishioners who joined the Zouaves; a photograph taken in Rome, July 1869. (Archives of Ushaw College, UC/AJ2/6/2/4281869, used with permission)   145

A large group of Zouaves while on exercises in the *campagna*, 1868. (Private collection, photograph: Ursula Staszynski)   152

This banner, presented by Dutch women in memory of the Battle of Mentana and now kept at Oudenbosch, includes the British royal coat of arms. It was designed by the well-known architect Pierre Cuypers, best-known for the Rijksmuseum and Central Station in Amsterdam. (Zouavenmuseum, Oudenbosch, used with permission)   156

Frederick Tristam Welman (1849–1931), the cricketing Zouave. (Archives of the Archdiocese of Birmingham, OCA/6/3/1/W/11, used with permission)   158

A group of English Zouaves in Rome around Christmas, 1869. Lord Denbigh and Monsignor Stonor are seated. (Private collection, photograph: Kath Bracewell)   162

The papal flagship, *Immacolata Concezione*, built by the Thames Iron Works & Shipbuilding Co., London in 1859. The steam corvette was armed with eight 18-pounders. (*Illustrated London News*, 20 August 1859, Private collection, author's photograph)   172

Italian troops enter the breach at the Porta Pia. (*Illustrated London News*, 8 October 1870, Private collection, author's photograph)   176

General Hermann Kanzler (1822-88), who interpreted papal orders with fluidity and continued the defence of Rome for as long as possible. (Private collection, photograph: Granddaughters of George Collingridge)   178

A staged photograph taken shortly after 20 September 1870, clearly showing the damage to the walls. (Zouavenmuseum, Oudenbosch, used with permission)   179

Daniel Curtin (1837-70), a Zouave originally from County Cork, was wounded on 20 September 1870 and attacked by 'patriots' as he was being carried to a hospital. He suffered a mental breakdown and later died in an asylum. He poses here with a statue of Pius IX. (Private collection, photograph by Granddaughters of George Collingridge)   180

In this cartoon, Pius IX tells Victor Emmanuel II, 'I must needs surrender the sword, my son, but I keep the keys', meaning his spiritual authority. (*Punch*, 1 October 1870, Private collection, author's photograph)   182

Daniel Shee (1846–1912), who, after seeing action with the Zouaves in 1867 and 1870, served for many years as governor of Birkdale Farm Reformatory School, near Southport. (Archives of the Archdiocese of Liverpool, used with permission)	185
The Banner of the Sacred Heart carried by the Volontaires at Loigny. (Private collection, author's photograph)	190
One of the Zouaves who worked with the White Fathers in Africa, the Belgian August Taillieu (1845–1883). (Zouavenmuseum, Oudenbosch, used with permission)	191
The interior of the church at Loigny-la-Bataille as it appeared for Charette's requiem on 21 October 1911. On the catafalque can be seen his uniform, swords and decorations. (Private collection, author's photograph)	192
A French Zouave on his deathbed, dressed in his old uniform. (Private collection, author's photograph)	193
An officer of the Irish Battalion of St Patrick. (Drawing by Ralph Weaver, with permission)	204
The Badge of the Irish Battalion. (Private collection; author's photograph)	205
An Officer of the Pontifical Zouaves. (Drawing by Ralph Weaver, used with permission)#	205
Details of a surviving Pontifical Zouave uniform. (Private collection; photograph by Alan Perry)	207

List of Maps

The Italian Peninsula in 1859. 18
The Piedmontese Invasion of the Papal States, September 1860. 54
The Battle of Castelfidardo, 18 September 1860. 64
The Battle of Mentana, 3 November 1867. 109
Rome in September 1870. The city was divided into four zones, with Kanzler's headquarters at Piazza della Colonna at the centre. 175

Acknowledgements

As a student at the Venerable English College in Rome, I passed the monument to Julian Watts-Russell, an English member of the Pontifical Zouaves, several times each day. As student archivist at the College, I saw my first faded photograph of a Zouave and handled one of their medals. On excursions around Rome and the Campagna with friends – especially Fr Richard Whinder, to whom this book is affectionately dedicated and who perhaps himself should have written it – the Zouaves were often toasted at an appropriate *trattoria* with a *litro* of local *vino*. Living for six months at the Pontifical Irish College, after the English College was closed due to a tragic outbreak of Legionnaire's Disease, I became familiar with the Irish side of the narrative.

Now, more than two decades later, I have finally managed to put pen to paper. Although I began to gather material several years before the outbreak of the Coronavirus pandemic, it became a 'lockdown project', combining my interests in ecclesiastical and military history and providing welcome relief from the ever-changing guidelines and restrictions. I am grateful to Helion for accepting the proposal, especially to my editor, Dr Christopher Brice, for his patience and support, and to the company's proprietor and founder, Duncan Rogers. My gratitude is also due to George Anderson for preparing the maps on behalf of Helion.

Many have helped along the way. I am grateful to the archbishops of Birmingham, Dublin, Liverpool, and Westminster, to the Pontifical Irish College and to Ushaw College for permission to use their archives. I am indebted to various archivists and curators: my colleagues Susannah Rayner and Judi McGinley at Westminster; Naomi Johnson at Birmingham; Neil Sayer at Liverpool; Dr Jonathan Bush at Ushaw; Cezara Petrina at the Pontifical Irish College, Rome; and Noelle Dowling at Dublin, who should be singled out for photographing numerous documents and emailing them to me at a time when travel was impossible. Arno Hommel of the Zouavenmuseum at Oudenbosch in the Netherlands has been invaluable in accessing information and images. It was also good to join him on the trail for the elusive Mrs Stone!

A relative of a parishioner who lives in Castelfidardo, Nicoletta Lampa, kindly took some photographs on the battlefield. And, in the final stages of preparing the manuscript, Ralph Weaver, a fellow 'From Musket to Maxim' author and editor of *The Foreign Corresponden*t (newsletter of the Continental Wars Society), sent some much-needed illustrations and drawings.

British and Irish Archives have only limited collections of relevant documents. It has been a pleasure contacting descendants of Zouaves, who have generously let me use letters, photographs and anecdotes. First mention should go to Winsome Collingridge, granddaughter of George Collingridge, who went to considerable trouble in sharing the rare photographs and other items in the family archive. Sincere thanks to her for sending material from Australia, despite packages getting lost in the post! Heartfelt gratitude goes also to Susie Gore (another link with the Collingridge brothers), Kath Bracewell, John Graham ('Jack') Wilson (RIP), John Blakely Wilson Jnr (RIP), James ('Jim') Nunns, Marj Winter and Dawn Gardham (for Alexander John Wilson), Sylvia Dibbs (for Henry Weetman), Kit Constable Maxwell (great-nephew of the Honourable Walter Constable Maxwell), Ursula Staszynski (great-granddaughter of Clement Bishop), Dr

Julian Watts-Russell (who was able to furnish details about his illustrious namesake), Frances Wood (great-granddaughter of William Ryan) and Angus Hay (himself a great Zouave enthusiast).

Others have provided useful information and generally put up with my obsession: the late Fr Jerome Bertram, Dr Gary Carville, Professor Judith Champ, Mary Jane Cryan, Fr Stewart Foster, Dr Sheridan Gilley, Michael Hammerson, Patrick Hayes, Fr Marcus Holden, Fr William Johnstone, Peter and Dawn Kent, Canon Jonathan Martin, Fergus Mulligan, Alan Perry, Abbot Geoffrey Scott OSB, Dr Joseph Shaw, Fr Gerard Skinner, Greg and Clare Smith, Dr Michael Straiton, Fr Mark Vickers, and Dr Christopher Wright. Special thanks to Dr James Kelly and Professor Michael Questier for looking at the draft; all mistakes are, of course, my own!

Jade Nunn enthusiastically contacted descendants of Zouaves and made the topic part of her MA in Genealogy, while Dan Nunn has assisted on photographic matters. In Uxbridge, Angela Atkins and Dr Samuel D. Seddon - and Frances Atkins and Mikey Atkins too! - have patiently put up with my regular visits to the 'man cave' to 'do Zouaving' and perhaps come to know more about the subject than they ever wanted to!

Nicholas Schofield
Uxbridge, June 2022

Prologue

Liverpool. Friday 14 October 1870, around noon. The steamship *India* anchored in the Mersey after a difficult journey from the Italian port of Livorno, or 'Leghorn' as it was often called by British travellers. The ship was new, having only been launched that February, but it was not designed for luxury travel. The passengers had slept on mattresses on the lower deck and found themselves soaked by the waves penetrating through the hatchways. Although some had admired the beautiful blue waters and picturesque coastal villages of the Mediterranean, food was insufficient, and few had slept during the strong gales on the Wednesday night. All on board must have been relieved to pull into the harbour.

Once anchored, the quarantine flag was briefly hoisted, as required by Customs, and then a steam tug was seen heading in its direction. The eager-eyed standing on the deck might have spotted the distinguished figure of Rudolph William Basil Feilding, Earl of Denbigh, Catholic convert and Chairman of the English Papal Defence Committee.[1] There were others too, including the familiar faces of comrades in arms who had arrived by land a few days previously.

For the *India* had no ordinary cargo. On board were members – ex-members, if one were to be pedantic – of the Pontifical Zouaves, a unit raised in 1861 to defend Pope Pius IX and his Temporal Power. If their faces were melancholic, it was because their cause had just received a crushing blow. Rome had fallen to numerically superior Italian forces on 20 September. The Eternal City was now the capital of the Kingdom of Italy and the Pope a self-declared 'Prisoner of the Vatican'.

The Zouaves had complained of harsh treatment during their brief captivity under the Italians. After being held in Rome, they were taken by train to Civitavecchia and crammed on to a steamer (the *Africa*) bound for Genoa, where the chaplain to the British contingent, Monsignor Edmund Stonor, managed to obtain transport to Liverpool. Dressed in their distinctive grey uniforms with red facings, baggy trousers, short jackets and kepis, the battle-scarred men numbered some 81 English, Scottish, and Irish, and 210 Canadians. Boarding the *India*, Denbigh gave a short address of welcome. There were warm embraces of reunion, news hurriedly exchanged and many cheered when it was announced that some former French Zouaves had recently seen action against the Germans in the war that was unfolding across the Channel.

The British and Irish Zouaves were able to leave the *India* almost immediately. The Canadians, however, were kept on the ship for one more night due to their great number, their chaplain made sure they were all provided for, and the steam tug made several more journeys to the ship with food. The following day the Canadians at last set foot on *terra firma* and marched together up the street, causing much astonishment and curiosity – not only because of their exotic appearance but because of their tired and haggard condition.

In Italy the Zouaves had met with much hostility in recent days but the Catholics of Liverpool resolved to provide them with food and shelter in their homes; indeed, it was seen as an honour to do so. The more well-to-do were able to give lodging to as many as six, others could only host one. A large group was taken

---

1   Based at Newnham Paddock in Warwickshire and ennobled in 1662, the Fieldings claimed to be a branch of the Habsburgs. Their coat of arms featured the double-edged eagle.

to the ancient home of Major Blundell at Little Crosby, others were given hospitality by Colonel Bidwell, a prominent local Catholic, and Mr Sharples at Bishop Eton. As they sat down to hearty meals across Liverpool – their first proper food in weeks – many a tale must have been recounted of recent momentous events, of daily life in Rome, of the beleaguered Holy Father and of past heroism shown at Spoleto, Perugia, Castelfidardo and Ancona in 1860 and Mentana seven years later.

The great hero among them was Daniel Shee, over six feet in height, who was still recovering from his wounds. While out on outpost duty on 14 September he had been cut off and surrounded by a squadron of Italian Lancers. He kept on fighting as they charged him four times. Before being captured, he had killed seven, dismounted two and received nine wounds.

That Sunday, the distinctive Zouave uniform was spotted in Liverpool congregations and references made to their cause from many a pulpit, including the discourse delivered at St Anne's by Monsignor Thomas Capel, one of the country's most popular Catholic preachers. A select party of Zouaves, all from privileged backgrounds, were treated to a banquet at the Adelphi on Ranelagh Place, the city's most prestigious hotel. The veterans, however, came from every stratum of society and the Papal Defence Committee paid the travel expenses for all to return home, along with a gratuity of 10 shillings. It was hoped that those from the lower classes could easily find employment, especially since their experience with the Zouaves would have taught them discipline, hard work and a smattering of French and Italian. The Canadians embarked to New York on 19 October on the Guion steamer *Idaho*. Crowds gathered to cheer them off and they were given papal cockades made from flowers for their hats.[2]

Sadly, not all the returning Zouaves reached their homes. John Perkins of Clapham was taken ill at Genoa and died in hospital soon afterwards. Richard Bentley, a Liverpudlian Zouave, passed away during the voyage and was buried at sea somewhere in the Bay of Biscay. Frederick Woodward, originally from Staffordshire, arrived in Liverpool close to death. He was taken to the house of the Oblate Fathers next to Holy Cross Church where he died at midnight on Monday, 17 October. Liverpool Catholics flocked to his funeral and his burial at Anfield Cemetery, where his body awaits the resurrection within sounds of the cheers of football supporters.[3]

Between 1860 and 1870 over 1,600 British and Irish volunteers travelled to Italy, ready to lie down their lives for the Pope. Most joined two units: the exclusively Irish Battalion of St Patrick in 1860 and, from 1861, the transnational Pontifical Zouaves. It was part of a wider mobilisation, made possible by the mass media, which did much to ignite the culture wars of the nineteenth century and the romantic ideal of the heroic volunteer. The men saw themselves as 'crusaders' and there are striking similarities with the medieval movement. Although Pope Pius IX did not formally declare a crusade and showed at times an ambivalence towards his armed forces, those who volunteered saw themselves as personally responding to his call. They not only fought to defend an Italian territory but the Catholic faith against the enemies of liberalism, revolution, Freemasonry and atheism. In an age of growing nationalism, they fought as citizens of Catholic Christendom and regarded Rome as their spiritual capital. The Pontifical Army had a strong spiritual life and recruits visited churches and shrines in their spare time, as is revealed in their letters and diaries; their expedition took on the appearance, almost, of an 'armed pilgrimage'. Although, unlike the medieval crusades, there was no formal indulgence promising the remission of sins, those who shed their blood for the Crossed Keys were widely considered to be martyrs, giving the highest form of witness to the

---

2   This account is largely based on the report in *The Tablet*, 22 October 1870, p.527. This refers to the Zouaves arriving on 'Friday last, the 15th', which presumably means Friday, 14 October.

3   *Staffordshire Advertiser*, 5 November 1870, p.5.

Faith. 'Endless are the tales told of their noble piety,' wrote Baroness Herbert, 'till one shuts one's eyes, and begin to fancy one-self back again in the time of Godfrey de Bouillon and the Crusaders!'[4]

Although these volunteers have been largely ignored by historians or dismissed as fanatical foreign mercenaries, there is a growing literature on them in French and Italian, with important contributions from Massimo Coltrinari, Piero Crociani, Lorenzo Innocenti, Jean Guenel and Patrick Nouaille-Degorce – to name but a few. In English, David Alvarez has produced an excellent military history of the modern Vatican. On the Battalion of St Patrick there is the classic account by George Fitzhardinge Berkeley, based on conversations with many veterans, and more recent assessments by Donal Corcoran, Emmet Larkin, Ciarán O'Carroll, Anne O'Connor, Mary Jane Cryan, Florry O'Driscoll and others. On the Zouaves the only recent volume in English is Charles Coulombe's *The Pope's Legion*.

This is the first study to look specifically at the British and Irish volunteers of the whole period. Their numbers were admittedly small. The Irish Battalion, numbering around 1,300, was one of several 'national' units raised in 1860 to protect the Pope when his territories were threatened with invasion and insurrection. From 1861, 328 out of 10,920 listed Zouaves came from England, Wales, Scotland and Ireland, constituting around 3 percent of the unit's composition.[5] Nevertheless, what counted was the significance rather than the number of these recruits. The home nations produced two of the 'Martyrs' of 1867, who became household names for many Catholics, as well as several distinguished officers. Their example inspired novels, poems and extensive attention in the press.

To place them into context, this book begins with a summary of the parallel movements of Risorgimento (a term literally meaning 'resurgence') and Anti-Risorgimento in Italy and the United Kingdom, and of the events that led up to the invasion of the Papal States in September 1860. Particular focus is placed on the attempts at rebuilding the Pontifical Army, the setting up of the Irish Battalion and the actions it fought at Perugia, Spoleto, Castelfidardo and Ancona. There was then a second period of reform and international recruitment, despite some opposition at the Vatican. Although some Irish volunteers remained briefly in the Company of St Patrick, British and Irish men joined a glamourous new transnational unit – the Pontifical Zouaves – especially in the late 1860s. Attention is given to the backgrounds and motivations of Zouaves, the networks of recruitment and daily life in Rome, as well as the campaigns of 1867 and 1870, with the important actions at Mentana and Porta Pia. The book concludes by examining the continuation of the cause and the ways that the memory of the papal volunteers was kept alive, even though today they are largely forgotten – or even the victims of a damnatio memoriae in Italian history. For the ease of the reader, appendices include biographical notes on the characters who appear most frequently through the text as well as a working list of the English and Welsh Zouaves, notes on uniforms and orders of battle for Castelfidardo and Mentana.

---

4   Baroness Elizabeth Herbert of Lea, *Mentana; and What Happened Before* (London: J. Atkinson, 1868), p.8.
5   The Zouaves boasted around 125 members from England and Wales, 24 from Scotland and 179 from Ireland.

1

Risorgimento and Anti-Risorgimento

The streets and squares of Italy still bear the names of the heroes who 'made' the nation in the nineteenth century. Rome is no exception. The Piazzale Garibaldi on the Janiculum Hill pays tribute to the charismatic guerrilla leader who defended the short-lived Roman Republic of 1849 and thereafter constantly expressed a desire to complete his unfinished business: 'Rome or Death!' Fiercely anti-clerical, Giuseppe Garibaldi sits on a bronze horse that seemingly offers its backside to the dome of St Peter's below. In his youth, after a failed rising in Piedmont in 1834, he was condemned to death in absentia and fled to South America. Heavily influenced by the gaucho tradition, he adopted its lifestyle and clothing, promoted revolutionary causes and became famous for the red shirts worn by his followers. These are said to have originated in a large supply of woollen shirts intended for the workers of the slaughter and salting houses of Buenos Aires.[1] Offered by a merchant to Garibaldi, they henceforth became inextricably associated with his struggles in particular and revolution in general.

Piazza Mazzini, just north of the Vatican, commemorates the most influential of the many political thinkers and activists who debated the future of Italy following the defeat of Napoleon. Trained as a lawyer, Giuseppe Mazzini was imprisoned for his involvement with the secret society of the Carbonari in 1831 and later founded the 'Young Italy' movement, which included Garibaldi among its members. He dreamt of a single democratic republic, if necessary established through insurrection, but none of his schemes ultimately succeeded. Though he spent much of his subsequent life in exile in Switzerland and London, his presence could be felt across Italy throughout the period of Risorgimento.

Another notable Roman landmark, the Victor Emmanuel monument, commemorates the first modern King of Italy. Despite being acclaimed as such in 1861, he kept the numbering of the House of Savoy, one of Europe's oldest dynasties: thus, he reigned as Victor Emmanuel II. The Kingdom of Piedmont-Sardinia,[2] had been transformed thanks to a series of constitutional reforms and an expanding economy, as well as taking advantage of its strategic position as a crucial buffer between France and Austria. The mid-nineteenth century was indeed Piedmont's 'moment' and the Risorgimento owed much to its highly skilled prime minister, Camillo Benso, Count of Cavour, commemorated in Rome by the Via Cavour, which runs from Termini Station towards the Forum. A late convert to the idea of a united Italy, he never travelled south of Pisa. His first loyalty was to Piedmont, successfully raising its profile on the European stage (especially through its participation alongside the 'great powers' in the Crimean War), investing in its armed forces and even fomenting insurrections that necessitated military intervention to further his aims.

---

1 They were woollen since much of the work was done outdoors or in unheated buildings, and red to hide the blood of the animals.
2 In this book we shall, for the ease of the reader, refer to 'Piedmont' and 'Piedmontese'.

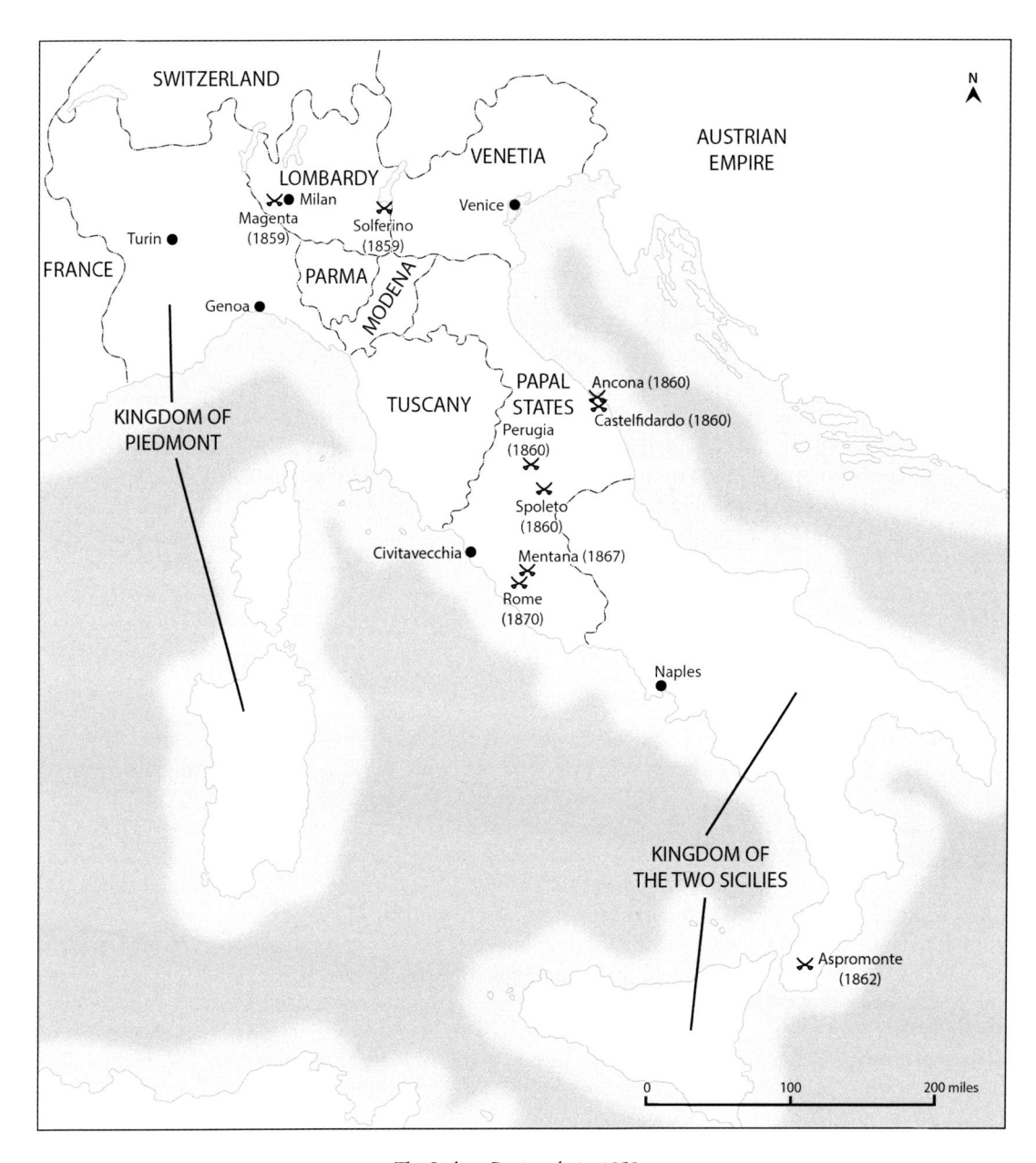

The Italian Peninsula in 1859.

Italian Unification is often seen as an historical inevitability and yet, despite its natural borders, Italy had long been a divided territory. By the 1850s, the peninsula was made up of eight states. The Kingdom of Lombardy-Venetia, which included the great cities of Milan and Venice, was part of the Austrian Empire. There were three independent kingdoms: Piedmont, with its capital in Turin; the Two Sicilies, ruled from Naples by the Bourbons; and the Papal States, spanning central Italy. Added to this jigsaw were the duchies of Tuscany, Parma and Modena, and the tiny republic of San Marino. The Apennine mountains stretching down the centre constituted a major barrier, commerce was hampered by strict tariffs, and the peninsula was further divided by differing histories, customs, dialects and ethnicities. It has been estimated that in 1861 less than 2.5 percent of the peninsula's population spoke modern Italian (essentially the Tuscan dialect). The mother tongue of Italy's first king and prime minister was French.

The long, twisting road that led to Unification was dependent on a series of complex events, wars, accidents, and personalities, and the end was never assured. Most Italians were primarily concerned with constitutional reform and freedom from foreign dominance. That was the crucial point: Italy continued to be the playground of the great powers, as it had been for centuries. Traditionally, Spain, Austria, and France all kept their fingers in the Italian pie, seeing the region as the key to European hegemony and vying with each other to be protector of the Holy See. Spain was no longer in the race and, after 1815, Austria was dominant in Italy, with direct control in Lombardy and Venetia, a substantial military presence and 'networks of diplomatic and dynastic alliances that made Vienna the power behind every Italian throne and every Italian ruler either cousin or client of the Habsburg monarchy'.[3] Austria saw itself as the rightful 'gendarme of Italy', suppressing any sign of popular unrest and upholding the Temporal Power of the Pope.

A cartoon illustrating the tense relationship between Pope Pius IX (1792–1878) and Emperor Napoleon III (1808–1873), who tried to balance his dual roles as liberal champion and 'Eldest Son of the Church'. (*Punch*, 8 December 1860, Private collection, author's photograph)

---

3   John A. Davis, 'Italy's Difficult Modernization', in John A. Davis (ed.), *Italy in the Nineteenth Century* (Oxford: Oxford University Press, 2000), p.9.

Italy was unable to 'make' itself. Much depended on the shifting balance of European power and Unification owed a great deal to the 'foreign' wars of 1859, 1866 and 1870. Despite defeat in 1815, France continued to have the ability to push forward its agenda in the region, especially under the leadership of Napoleon III. A complex figure, full of contradictions, he was judged harshly by many contemporaries: variously called a 'dwarf on the summit of a great wave', 'the Sphinx of the Seine' or simply 'Napoleon *le petite*'. Nevertheless, against the odds, he managed to become president of the Second Republic in the aftermath of the 1848 Revolution and then, from 1852, emperor, making the most of his uncle and namesake's prestige and attracting the support of large sections of the population who looked for a 'saviour' from the perennial threat of war and revolution. He hoped to restore France to greatness, in part by encouraging the formation of new nation-states that would become grateful new allies, including Italy.

Napoleon's role as a liberal champion conflicted with that of sovereign of the 'Eldest Daughter of the Church', conscious that his power partially rested on Catholic votes. Despite his youthful experiences with the Carbonari, Napoleon played a decisive part in defeating the Roman Republic in 1849 and, until 1870 with a brief gap in the 1860s, French troops ensured the protection of the Holy Father in Rome. This military support proved essential, although Napoleon was little trusted by the Vatican, and he continually pushed the Pope to make constitutional reforms and reconsider his temporal power.

Great Britain and the Risorgimento

The creation of Italy, to paraphrase A.J.P. Taylor, depended not only on French armies but British moral approval.[4] Great Britain had long enjoyed a love affair with Italy, or at least an idealised image of it. Educated in the Classics and the glories of Imperial Rome, the well-to-do inevitably included Italy on their travels. There was admiration for the poetry of Dante and the masterpieces of Renaissance art and architecture. Opera, too, was much in vogue and, up until the 1860s, predominantly in the Italian language. It was little surprise that large 'colonies' existed of English artists and writers in Florence, Venice, and Rome.

Yet, combined with this passion, was a distain for the reality – or perceived reality – of Italian life, influenced by a strongly Protestant worldview and the tradition of anti-Catholicism that was at the heart of British identity. The Papal States, with its apparently 'reactionary' clerical government, were viewed with horror as a prime example of corruption and obscurantism – in many ways the antithesis of Great Britain. The Pope was widely considered a sinister, even diabolical, figure who, as recently as 1850, had threatened the liberty-loving English by re-establishing the system of Catholic dioceses and ordinary bishops that had been lost at the Reformation, with an archbishop installed at the very heart of the Establishment at Westminster. Such 'Papal Aggression' led to loud cries of 'No Popery!'.

The Risorgimento filled many with the hope that Italy could be 're-made' – politically based on the British democratic model, which was considered the 'best' in the world, and with the 'darkness' of Popery replaced by the 'light' of Protestant truth. Money was poured into missionary efforts to ensure that the Reformation could reach Italy, as seen in the efforts of the British and Foreign Bible Society and the distribution of thousands of Italian bibles. Despite being officially neutral, the British Government, especially under the leadership of Palmerston, Gladstone, and Russell, supported the work of Italian nationalists and the aims of Piedmont, eager to see a decline in foreign domination over Italy and gain a new ally that held vital access to the Mediterranean, where Britannia ruled the waves.

This enthusiasm could clearly be seen in 1864, when Garibaldi visited England and was feted as a popular hero. Although the Government had stressed that this should be a merely private visit, crowds

---

4 A.J.P. Taylor, *The Struggle for Mastery in Europe, 1848–1918* (Oxford: Clarendon Press, 1954), p.124.

numbering half a million are reported to have hailed him in London; it took his carriage five hours to make the journey from Nine Elms station in Battersea to Stafford House at St James's. He mixed with the likes of the Prince of Wales, the Duke of Sutherland, Palmerston, Russell, and Gladstone. However, the Queen had already left for Balmoral when he visited the royal farms at Windsor, confiding to her journal that she was 'half-ashamed of being the head of a nation capable of such follies'.[5]

The Garibaldi craze led to a well-known biscuit bearing his name, the recipe supposedly inspired by the raisin sandwiches given to his men on campaign. Pubs were named after him, loose-fitting 'Garibaldi blouses' became all the rage and Staffordshire figurines of the hero adorned many a Victorian mantelpiece. When the football club that became Nottingham Forest was founded in 1865, early press reports referred to the team as the 'Garibaldi Reds'.[6] All in all, enthusiasm for both the unification and conversion of Italy have been described as 'the gospel of a generation' and England's 'greatest moral crusade since the campaign against slavery'.[7]

Anti-Risorgimento

Not everyone, however, was enthused with the Risorgimento and by the 1850s Pope Pius IX, Successor of St Peter, had become one of its chief opponents. Part of this obstruction was geographical: the existence of the Papal or Ecclesiastical States, which stretched across the centre of Italy from the Tyrrhenian to the Adriatic Seas, and included the Patrimony of St Peter (Lazio), Umbria, the Marches and Romagna (known as the 'Papal Legations'). Although it had expanded over the centuries, the Papal States dated back at least to the mid-eighth century, when Pepin the Short granted territory to the Pope. The pontiff was not only spiritual head but king; like all rulers he collected taxes, promulgated laws, administered justice, and had an army and navy. It was Europe's oldest kingdom, with a ruler who was regarded as the Vicar of Christ by millions around the globe. Any attempt to 'unify' Italy had to deal with the thorny 'Roman Question'.

Pius IX also posed an ideological obstacle. The traditional narrative of his pontificate describes an open-minded pontiff who became disillusioned and increasingly intransigent after the revolution of 1848, which saw his prime minister assassinated, the papal court exiled to Gaeta and Rome proclaimed a Republic. He had initially shown some sympathy with those who wanted to rid Italy of Austrian influence, though he refused to send his army against a fellow Catholic sovereign. Warm-hearted and full of personal charm, Pius's focus was on religious matters, and he left affairs of state largely to his ministers, especially his Secretary of State, Cardinal Giacomo Antonelli.

During his pontificate the Catholic Church enjoyed a spiritual revival and increasing centralisation and globalisation; however, it was his misfortune to rule over the Papal States at one of the most critical moments in its long history. Pius became increasingly aware that he fought a 'holy war' against liberalism and revolution. After the experiences of 1848, his innate suspicion of revolutionary principles hardened into open distrust. This was nothing new: the imprisonment by the French of both Pius VI (from 1798 to his death in 1799) and Pius VII (between 1809 and 1814) had shown how Popes could easily fall into the hands of hostile powers. The Holy See seemed surrounded by aggressive forces. Ongoing tensions with

---

5   Christopher Hibbert, *Garibaldi and His Enemies* (London: Penguin Books, 1987), p.344.
6   https://www.leftlion.co.uk/read/2018/november/giuseppe-garibaldi-nottingham-forest-freedom-fighter/ accessed 11 June 2020. In 2016 a supporter-driven movement aiming to revitalise the club was set up with the name 'Forza Garibaldi'.
7   John Pemble, *The Mediterranean Passion: Victorians and Edwardians in the South* (Oxford: Oxford University Press, 1988), p.10.

Piedmont concerned not only territorial aggrandisement, but the traditional prerogatives of the Church. Envisaging 'a free church in a free State', Cavour abolished the separate church courts and suppressed 334 of the Kingdom's 604 religious houses in 1855, saving those religious communities who specialised in education and the care of the sick. The law was opposed by the Pope, which excommunicated all those involved.

Throughout his pontificate Pius made a stand for Catholic truth and papal authority in a world that appeared increasingly hostile, as shown in the *Syllabus of Errors* (1864),[8] and the definition of the dogmas of the Immaculate Conception (1854)[9] and Papal Infallibility (1870).[10] The Pope was also becoming an increasingly familiar figure to Catholics. For centuries he had been a centre of ecclesial unity, a name prayed for at every Mass or seen on papal bulls but remained personally distant. Thanks largely to the explosion of the mass media and the opening up of steamship and railway routes to Rome, this all changed in the nineteenth century. The Pope increased his allocutions and encyclicals, aware that he was now speaking to a global audience. Pictures and medals were widely distributed. Visitors to the Eternal City, including curious non-Catholics, could even meet him in audience.

Regarded not only as a spiritual celebrity but a living martyr, attacks on the Pope's temporal power were regarded as sacrilege and the Catholic world was mobilised in response: prayers were offered, signatures gathered on petitions, addresses prepared, meetings organised, bonds purchased, and collections made. In 1849 Peter's Pence, a papal tribute that had originated in Saxon England, was 'rediscovered' and used in many French and Belgian dioceses as a voluntary financial contribution for the Pope; it soon spread further afield.

The Pope increasingly relied on Catholic loyalty beyond the borders of his own territory. This is reflected in a revealing memorandum of Luigi Taparelli, the Jesuit co-founder of the periodical *La Civiltà Cattolica*, prepared for the Pope in the early 1850s. The Pope's kingdom was a polity like no other. To see the Papal States in terms of local issues alone was belittling; the temporal power was an international 'Catholic affair'.[11] At a time when nationalism dominated the European political discourse, the Holy See was stressing the transnationalism of Catholic Christendom, encompassing many peoples and languages, and stretching across the Atlantic. This would have a profound impact on the foreign volunteers who flocked to Rome amid a 'wave of emotion' that brought modern Popes to 'a greater authority in the world-wide Church than any of their predecessors were able to exercise'.[12]

---

8   This condemned 80 modern propositions, including 'The Church has not the power of using force, nor has she any temporal power, direct or indirect' (#24) and 'The Roman Pontiff can, and ought to, reconcile himself, and come to terms with progress, liberalism and modern civilization' (#80).
9   That the Virgin Mary was preserved from the stain of original sin (passed down from Adam and Eve) from the moment of her conception in anticipation of her role as Mother of God. This was the first time a pontiff had solemnly defined a dogma and was a powerful statement of papal authority.
10 That the Pope is preserved from error when formally defining a doctrine '*ex cathedra*' regarding faith and morals to be held by the universal Church.
11 Vincent Vaene, 'The Roman Question, Catholic Mobilisation and Papal Diplomacy', in Emiel Lamberts (ed.), *The Black International, 1870–1878: The Holy See and Militant Catholicism in Europe* (Leuven: Leuven University Press, 2002), p.141.
12 Owen Chadwick, *A History of the Popes, 1830–1914* (Oxford: Oxford University Press, 1998), p.145.

Anti-Risorgimento in Great Britain and Ireland

During the nineteenth century the Catholic Church in Britain and Ireland was experiencing what one of its most eloquent apologists, John Henry Newman, called a 'Second Spring'. Between the reigns of Elizabeth I and George III, Catholics had been forced underground or into exile, unable to worship openly or hold public office, and restricted by a penal code that could result in fines, imprisonment and even death. By the late eighteenth century attitudes were changing: a series of Relief Acts were passed, and Protestant England welcomed 5,500 French clergy in the 1790s, who were seen as refugees from revolution rather than would-be traitors. The Catholic cause was given a further boost by the Union of Great Britain and Ireland in 1800–1801, bringing Irish – and therefore Catholic – questions to the fore in Westminster. Indeed, it was 'the Liberator' himself, Daniel O'Connell, who was an energetic supporter of the Emancipation Act finally passed in 1829. Around the same time, increasing numbers of Catholic Irish immigrants hoped to find the streets of London, Liverpool and elsewhere paved with gold. Meanwhile, a Catholicising movement within the Church of England and a series of high-profile 'secessions' to Rome made some talk of an imminent 'conversion of England'.

Catholicism on British and Irish soil was far from monolithic. There were important differences between England, Scotland, and Ireland, and divergences in opinion and emphasis within the communities. Tensions existed between many 'Old Catholics' (including the families that had kept the Faith alive through 'dungeon, fire and sword', who typically favoured moderation and conciliation) and the growing ultramontane party,[13] numbering many converts who promoted anything 'Roman' and saw the person and office of the Pope as the absolute guarantee of religious truth. The 'Roman Question' was an important factor in these tensions and soon became a touchstone of orthodoxy.

British Catholics were typically dismayed by their compatriots' enthusiasm for the Risorgimento. 'It vexes me to think,' wrote the prominent Catholic convert, Baroness Herbert of Lea, 'how completely one-sided is the picture given in England of the cause of the Roman struggle.'[14] The Archbishop of Westminster, Cardinal Nicholas Wiseman, fervently believed in the necessity of the Pope's Temporal Power. Looking at its long history in 1860, he noted that 'a singular providence has secured this buoyant perpetuity to this feeble sovereignty' and concluded:

> that what are called the 'States of the Church' are truly such: a gift to her, for securing her rightful position in the world, the free union and access of its members to their Head, and the efficient discharge, by that Head, of the function and duties belonging to its office. The Pope is the natural trustee of this inheritance – its administrator – its ruler.[15]

He involved himself in the 1859 General Election, backing the Earl of Derby and criticising Palmerston for his pro-Italian sympathies, even though English Catholics had historically sided with the Whigs. This helped the Tory Party win the majority of seats in Ireland, although Palmerston won the day. The cardinal wrote a memoir of his time in Rome as both a student and rector of the Venerable English College entitled

---

13   Ultramontane means 'beyond the mountains' (that is, the Alps), usually denoting someone in northern Europe who emphatically looked to Rome as the source of authority. In the English context, it was contrasted with Cisalpinism which focused on 'this side of the mountains' and sought accommodation with the British Government to further Catholic Emancipation. Mid-nineteenth-century English Catholicism was polarised into 'parties' with the 'ultramontanes' largely taking precedence.
14   Baroness Herbert, *Mentana*, p.4.
15   Archives of the Archdiocese of Westminster (AAW) Wiseman Papers, Pastoral Letter, 25 March 1860.

Recollections of the Last Four Popes, which stressed the benevolence of papal rule.[16] In a pastoral letter of May 1864 he spoke out against Garibaldi's recent visit to England and was scandalised that statesmen and Anglican bishops should pay homage to a man who represented the atheism of the French Revolution and 'the triumph of reason over revelation': 'Oh, pity, pity, at least, if not worse, that such a spectacle should have been exhibited to England at the time, the moment, when every energy on every hand should be put forth, not to dally with, but to crush the spirit, however embodied, of infidelity as well as disloyalty.'[17]

The most prominent English defender of the temporal power was Wiseman's protégé, Henry Edward Manning, a product of Harrow and Oxford who rose to prominence in the Church of England as Archdeacon of Chichester and became a Catholic in 1851. He soon became a key associate of Wiseman, especially as the cardinal's health declined, and succeeded him as Archbishop of Westminster in 1865. Manning delivered a series of lectures at St Mary of the Angels in Bayswater on 'The Temporal Power of the Vicar of Christ' in 1860 and 1861, which were considered extreme enough to cause concern in Rome, although Manning had a powerful protector in the form of Monsignor George Talbot, one of the Pope's closest confidantes. According to Eamon Duffy, works such as this constituted 'the most sustained and in many ways the most extreme ultramontane political theology in nineteenth century Europe'.[18] Manning saw the potential collapse of the Temporal Power as disastrous; in a letter to his friend, Gladstone, in 1864, he wrote: 'I believe Rome to be providentially the centre of the Christian order of Europe. And I believe that the cry for Rome is not only for its traditions of Empire, but because it is the key of an order which keeps the Antichrist under the feet of truth & grace.'[19] It was part of a cosmic battle. In old age Manning reflected that: 'The special characteristic of this our age, but to speak truly, of that large and powerful faction which has the control of affairs in this modern time, is a tendency to destroy all the old institutions which have life and vigour by reason of a supernatural principle, and then on the ruins, very often indeed with the remains, to erect new structures established upon the dictates of pure, if not always right, reason.' Behind this tendency, he thought, was the spectre of Freemasonry, 'as seen in its true aspect, not as a benevolent association, as it endeavours to appear to be in the eyes of the unwary, but as an institution which seeks to establish upon the ruins of religion a pretended humanitarian Church'.[20]

These views were shared by other clergy and laity, many of them converts, as can be seen in Frederick Faber's *Devotion to the Pope* (1860) and Frederick Oakeley's *The Duty of Maintaining the Pope in his Temporal Sovereignty* (1860). The MP for Dungarvan, John Francis Maguire, produced *Rome, Its Ruler and Its Institutions* in 1856, not only telling the story of the Pope's life but eulogising him as prison reformer, a promoter of material progress and free trade, a patron of the arts and a builder of railways.

In Ireland, the leading ultramontane figure was undoubtedly Paul Cullen, archbishop first of Armagh and then Dublin, and, from 1866, the first Irish cardinal. Residing in Rome between the ages of 17 and 47, as a student, professor and college rector, he had a deep love for the Eternal City and the person of the Pope, enjoying close friendships with both Gregory XVI and Pius IX and, through his contacts, was able to counter English influence at the Vatican. Cullen was largely responsible for shaping modern Irish

---

16 Nicholas Wiseman, *Recollections of the Last Four Popes* (London: Hurst & Blackett, 1860).
17 *The Tablet*, 28 May 1864, p.341.
18 Eamon Duffy, 'Manning, Newman and the Fall of the Temporal Power', in British Embassy to the Holy See (ed.), *Britain and the Holy See: A Celebration of 1982 and the Wider Relationship* (Rome: British Embassy to the Holy See, 2013), p.103.
19 Peter C. Erb (ed.), *The Correspondence of Henry Edward Manning and William Ewart Gladstone, 1833–1891* (Oxford: Oxford University Press, 2013), vol. 3, p.35 (letter of 24 October 1864).
20 AAW Manning Papers, Account of the Vatican Council.

Catholicism. He organised the Synod of Thurles in 1850, which helped unify and reform the Church, and promoted a 'devotional revolution' that stressed Roman rather than Celtic spiritual practices.

Pro-papal feelings could be found on the popular level. Ordinary members of the faithful were encouraged to pray for the Pope and raise money for his defence. When Cardinal Wiseman made his triumphal tour of Ireland in 1858, huge crowds gathered to greet him, not only curious to see the unusual figure of a cardinal, the first to visit post-Reformation Ireland, but keen, through him, to honour the person of the Pope. In 1862 there were riots involving Irish Catholics and English supporters of Garibaldi in Birkenhead and London's Hyde Park.[21]

Other voices within the British and Irish Catholic community were more nuanced. John Henry Newman (a cardinal from 1879) believed that the Temporal Power was not essential for the Church's mission and should never be the litmus test of religious orthodoxy. Nevertheless, he was reluctant to speak openly about his views: 'I am glad,' he wrote to Bishop Moriarty of Kerry in 1866, 'to refer to the words of the Holy Father and the bishops, that "in the present state of public affairs, the Pope's Temporal Power is necessary", and so leave the matter.'[22] Others were less inhibited. Sir John Dalberg-Acton, widely viewed as the leader of the English liberal Catholics and later to be Regius Professor of Modern History at Cambridge, initially defended the temporal power on political rather than religious grounds, since the Pope was a legitimate sovereign. However, he admitted that 'the Church was 700 years without a territory and might be so again for 7,000 years. As things now are it cannot be, but such a state of things might be possible.'[23] Nevertheless, the Anti-Risorgimento had enough proponents in Britain and Ireland to send both alms and arms to defend the Holy Father in his hour of need.

---

21 Sheridan Gilley, 'The Garibaldi Riots of 1862', *Historical Journal*, 16:4 (1973), pp.697–732.
22 Birmingham Oratory Archive BO62-AOO2-DO61, Letter of Newman to Moriarty, 14 November 1866.
23 Josef Altholz, *The Liberal Catholic Movement in England: The 'Rambler' and Its Contributors, 1848–1864* (London: Burns & Oates, 1962), pp.132–133.

2

The Papal States in Peril

On 14 January 1858 bombs were thrown at Napoleon III and his empress as they arrived at a Paris theatre. They escaped unscathed, though eight others were killed. The mastermind behind the attempted assassination was Felice Orsini, a member of Mazzini's 'Young Italy' movement who believed passionately in the Unification of Italy and increasingly saw Napoleon III as one of its chief obstacles. He designed an ingenious bomb: a metal ball with numerous pins sticking out, each filled with mercury fulminate and able to trigger detonate on contact, which was much used by anarchists over subsequent decades and even by the Confederacy during the American Civil War. Subsequently condemned to death, Orsini wrote to the emperor, pleading the cause of Italian unity, and from the scaffold shouted 'Viva l'Italia! Viva la Francia!'

The incident soured relations between France and Great Britain, since Orsini had previously given a series of successful lectures in England and his bombs had been created by Joseph Taylor, a gunsmith from Birmingham, and tested in Sheffield and Devon. The French began to think that her neighbour across the Channel was a refuge for would-be conspirators. Palmerston resigned after failing to pass his Conspiracy to Murder Bill – an attempt to placate the French by making it a felony rather than a misdemeanour to plot an overseas murder within British borders.

Napoleon needed little encouragement to immerse himself in the vexed Italian Question. He had already informally suggested an alliance with Piedmont against Austria. Decisive action would increase his popularity at home, strengthen his international reputation and add fuel to the Bonapartist myth. In July 1858, Napoleon holidayed at the spa town of Plombières-les-Bains and secretly met Cavour, who travelled there on a false passport. The two men spoke of a future war that would remove Austrian influence from Italy and divide the peninsula into four states. Lombardy, Venetia, Romagna and the Legations (the latter two being under papal control) would become part of the Kingdom of Upper Italy, ruled from Turin. Other parts of the Papal States would form, with Tuscany, the Kingdom of Central Italy. The Pope was left with Rome and the Patrimony of St Peter and would be offered the presidency of the Italian Confederation. Finally, in the south, the Kingdom of the Two Sicilies remained as it was, with its borders intact. In return for supporting Piedmont, France would gain Nice and Savoy – a controversial condition, as it turned out, since the former was the birthplace of Garibaldi. The agreement would be sealed by the marriage of the emperor's cousin, Prince Napoléon Jérôme, to the daughter of King Victor Emmanuel.

Napoleon and Cavour carefully watched for an opportunity to force Austria's hand into declaring war. At a New Year reception in 1859, Napoleon told the Austrian ambassador that he regretted that relations were not as good as they once had been. A speech made shortly afterwards by Victor Emmanuel, while opening parliament in Turin, stated that he could no longer remain insensitive to the cries of anguish that could be heard across the peninsula. In meeting the Pope for the first time as the British Government's agent in Rome, Odo Russell[1] was told that 'evil spirits are at work even in my dominions and the late speech of the King of Sardinia is calculated to inflame the minds of all the revolutionary men of Italy'.[2]

The British Government watched nervously, fearing that an all-encompassing European war could break out less than half a century after Waterloo. When France built its first ironclad warship, *La Gloire*, the British Government increased its naval expenditure, one of the fruits of which was HMS *Warrior*, at the time the world's largest and most powerful warship. The perceived threat of a potential French invasion led to the setting up of Rifle Volunteers up and down the country; most localities had a unit, including one in north Middlesex, the 'Barnet Garibaldeans', that clearly looked to the Risorgimento for its inspiration. A Royal Commission on the Defence of the United Kingdom was set up and, following its report, a series of new fortifications constructed across the southeast, especially concentrated around the Solent. Since they never fired a gun in anger, the forts became known as 'Palmerston's Follies'.

Meanwhile, the British and the Russians pushed for a congress to finally resolve the Italian Question. Napoleon seemed to consent to the proposal but then events took on a life of their own. Piedmont provoked Austria by holding military manoeuvres near the border and Austria issued an ultimatum on 23 April. Soon, French troops were making their way eastwards. For the first time, railways were used to mobilise troops and the new invention of the telegraph spread news quickly, focusing the eyes of the world on the campaign and allowing leaders to manipulate public opinion. With the outbreak of war, *The Tablet* noted that it was not only a matter of 'territorial aggrandisement [but] another and violent eruption of that terrible volcano which, at the close of the last century, overwhelmed Europe'.[3]

The 'Second War of Italian Independence', as it became known, lasted just ten weeks (26 April to 12 July 1859), included the bloody battles of Magenta and Solferino, and undermined the stability of the smaller Italian states.[4] The Grand Duchy of Tuscany was one of the first to crumble: the unpopular Leopold II fled to Bologna after pressure was put on him to ally with Piedmont. Modena and Parma quickly followed.

The Holy See was understandably alarmed that its two main protectors were at war with each other. Austrian troops, who had been policing the Papal Legations (Romagna), hurriedly left and in the resulting vacuum there were risings in Bologna and Ravenna. The Papal Arms were torn down at Fano and Senigallia; uprisings broke out in Imola, Faenza, Rimini, Cesena, Forli, Fossombrone, Fano, Foligno, Ancona, Perugia and elsewhere. Pontifical troops were despatched to deal with the unrest: the 1st Foreign Regiment was sent to Perugia, leading Lord John Russell, the British Foreign Secretary, to lament that the Pope had set 'his Swiss wolves upon his poor sheep', surely increasing 'the ill will and animosity of his Roman subjects'. Atrocities and looting were reported: an American family in Perugia saw the innkeeper and waiter at the Hotel de France murdered before their very eyes and such acts of violence stayed in the collective memory as proof that the Pope relied on unsavoury foreign mercenaries.[5] Nevertheless, such intervention saved Umbria and the Marches for the Holy See and demonstrated that, compared to the smaller Italian states, it was a force to be reckoned with. More seriously, however, a provisional government was set up in Romagna,

---

1   Later to become first British Ambassador to the German Empire (1871-84) and Baron Ampthill of Ampthill (1882). His second son, also called Odo, followed in his father's footsteps and served as Envoy Extraordinary and Minister Plenipotentiary to the Holy See (1922-28).
2   Noel Blakiston (ed.) *The Roman Question: Extracts from the Despatches of Odo Russell from Rome, 1858–1870* (London: Chapman & Hall, 1962), p.2.
3   *The Tablet*, 7 May 1859, p.290.
4   Solferino was one of the costliest battles of the nineteenth century, with over 400,000 casualties, while such was the bloodbath of Magenta that it gave its name to a purple-red dye. It is little wonder that one of the fruits of the conflict was the establishment of the International Red Cross.
5   Blakiston, *Roman Question*, p.27. A total of 25 civilians and 27 soldiers lost their lives.

demanding annexation of the province to Piedmont, which was now seen as the main guarantor of order and stability.

Napoleon III himself was placed in a quandary. As Russell noted: '[I]f he protects [the insurrections in the Papal States], how can he keep his word to the Pope? and if he suppresses them by force how can he retain his title of Liberator of Italy?'[6] Such conundrums, combined with the bloodshed at Solferino, the pro-papal leanings of his empress and fear of European reaction, led to a dampening of the emperor's enthusiasm for further conflict. Rather than continue towards the Adriatic and gain Venetia, he negotiated a peace treaty at Villafranca in July 1859.

The plans devised at Plombières were only partially fulfilled. Austria kept hold of Venetia, France gained Nice and Savoy, and Piedmont's power was extended over much of northern and central Italy – the annexation of the duchies and the Legations confirmed by a series of plebiscites in March 1860. There had been further hopes for a congress, but a pamphlet of December 1859 entitled *Le Pape et le Congrès*, hinting at the emperor's acceptance of the Pope's loss of the Legations, quickly led to a diplomatic stalemate and the shelfing of the idea.[7] The Catholic faithful rushed to defend the pontiff and sent loyal addresses. The Pope hit back through allocutions and an encyclical letter, *Nullis Certe*, which stressed the necessity of his Temporal Power.

The Pope's position was indeed perilous. Romagna, the wealthiest and most industrialised of his domains, was lost. Umbria and the Marches were hardly secure, with some of the population showing signs that they wished to follow the example of their northern neighbours. Garibaldi, stationed with Piedmontese troops on the border, expressed the hope that he might mount an invasion but he was quickly called back to Turin. The Pope excommunicated all those who took part or aided in the seizure of his territory and the Piedmontese *chargé de affaires* was dismissed from Rome. Pius hardened in his opposition: no compromise would be forthcoming until his land was restored to him, nor would there be any constitutional reforms. He was reported to have 'taken a profound dislike to the French Emperor', calling him 'a traitor and a liar because he does not fulfil promises made in his private letters during the war and accuses him of secretly encouraging and supporting the revolution in the Legations and in Central Italy'.[8] The Pope expected French troops to be withdrawn from Rome at a moment's notice. He felt let down, also, by Austria, which had withdrawn its troops from the northern provinces of the Papal States and was now weakened by its defeat. There were those who thought that the Pope needed, above all, to be able to fight his own battles rather than rely on foreign princes.

A New Direction for the Pontifical Army

At this juncture a member of the papal entourage, Monsignor Frédéric François Xavier de Mérode, came to the fore.[9] He was able to use his position in the papal household to promote his views on the Pontifical Army. A fervent Legitimist, he saw Napoleon as fickle and duplicitous, and encouraged the Pope to remodel the army, not relying on conscription, which could prove unreliable and unpopular, but on committed

---

6   Blakiston, *Roman Question*, pp.27–28.
7   The same author had produced in February 1859 *Napoleon III et l'Italie*, supported at the highest level and setting forth a vision of the pontiff presiding over a Federal Italy and argued that a reduction of his Temporal Power would strengthen his moral authority.
8   Blakiston, *Roman Question*, p.59.
9   Many English-language books incorrectly refer to Mérode as a cardinal. In 1866, as newly appointed Papal Almoner, he was consecrated an archbishop, and although it was the Pope's intention to name him a cardinal in 1874, he died shortly before the consistory that was to present him with the 'red hat'.

volunteers who would come to fight as nineteenth-century crusaders in defence of the Holy See. It was just what the secular and irreligious age needed, he argued, and might indeed spark off a religious revival. The force of Catholic opinion, too often divided among the nations, would become manifest; with its moral strength and force of numbers, foreign powers would have to take the question of the Temporal Power seriously; and the Holy See would be liberated from its reliance on France and Austria.

The Pope's inner sanctum had becoming increasingly international during the 1850s, reflecting a new reliance on the Catholic world beyond the alps. His household included Gustav Hohenlohe, the son of a German prince; an Anglo-Irish aristocrat, George Talbot, son of Baron Talbot of Malahide; and Louis-Gaston de Ségur, son of a French count and an eminent Russian woman of letters. Mérode fitted in perfectly: his father was a minister of Leopold I of Belgium and his ancestors included medieval crusaders and the Marquis of Lafayette, the celebrated General in the American War of Independence. In his youth, he followed a military career but, bored by peacetime life in the Belgian Army, transferred to the French Army and saw action in Algeria, where he was awarded the *Légion d'honneur* for his conduct at Aydoussa. However, he resigned – some said after killing a man in a duel – and, to the surprise of many, embarked on formation for the priesthood. Ordained in 1849, he briefly served as a chaplain in the Papal Army before catching the eye of the Pope, who appointed him to an honorary position in his household as '*cameriere*

Monsignor Frédéric François Xavier de Mérode (1820–1874), the mastermind behind the reform of the Pontifical Army in the early 1860s. (Private collection, author's photograph)

segreto'. As well as being occupied with everyday duties in the papal court, he was entrusted with specific responsibilities, including the reform of the pontifical prisons.

Pius IX was not a man of war. As early as March 1848 his regime had rejected proposals to reorganise the army and triple its size to 25,000 men. The following month he told his cardinals, many of whom were pushing for war against Austria, that he abhorred the idea: 'I am the Vicar of Christ, the author of peace and lover of charity, and my office is to bestow an equal affection on all nations.'[10] This did not prevent him from moving troops to defend his borders and permit a 'Roman Legion' of volunteers, which, following ambiguous orders and carried along by a surge of patriotism, worked alongside the Piedmontese in operations against Austria.

In 1860, however, the situation was different. The Pope had painful experiences behind him, faced attacks on his own territory and stood increasingly alone. This made him open to Mérode's proposals

---

10   Chadwick, *History of the Popes*, p.77.

and, following his recommendation, he approached one of France's foremost generals to become the new commander-in-chief of the Pontifical Army: Christophe Léon Louis Juchault de Lamoricière. He was a connection of Mérode, the general's wife being a relative. Born in Nantes in 1806, to a family of Legitimist sympathies, he went to Algeria in 1830. His name was closely associated with the French Zouaves, and he was considered their effective founder. He was appointed *chef de battalion* in 1833, lieutenant colonel in 1835 and, after the siege of Constantine at which he was wounded by the explosion of a mine, colonel in 1837. His star continued to rise and in 1845 he became temporary governor-general of Algeria. Lamoricière fought 18 campaigns in North Africa, including the successful expedition of 1847 that led to the capture of Abd-el-Kader, the charismatic leader of the Algerian resistance.

Returning to France, he would probably have had an illustrious career under King Louis-Philippe but the 1848 Revolution changed everything; once, as he tried to calm down the Parisian crowd by announcing the resignation of the 'Citizen King', his horse was shot from beneath him. Had it not been for the protection of some labourers who had served under him in Algeria, he would perhaps have lost his life.

Under the Second Republic he represented La Sarthe in the Chamber of Deputies and was sent on a diplomatic mission to Russia. However, his opposition to Louis Napoleon grew, especially after he declared himself emperor. Lamoricière was among those arrested. After a brief internment in the infamous chateau at Ham, he was sent into exile and his name removed from the list of the French Army. In 1857, after the death of one of his children, he was allowed to reside quietly in France. During this period, he returned to his Catholic faith and was staunch in his piety.

He seemed an ideal candidate as papal commander-in-chief and was first sounded out in the autumn of 1859; 'I think,' he answered, 'that is a cause for which I should be happy to die.' The following March he met with Mérode at Prouzel, where he was living with the monsignor's brother. 'When a father calls upon his son to defend him,' he is said to have replied, 'there is only one thing to be done, and that is to go!'[11] He travelled to Rome via a circuitous route in order to avoid the imperial authorities,

General Christophe Léon Louis Juchault de Lamoricière (1806-65). (Private collection, author's photograph)

---

11   Monsignor François-Nicolas-Xavier-Louis Besson, *Frederick Francis Xavier de Mérode: His Life and Works* (London: W.H. Allen & Co., 1887), pp.126–127.

hiding his African sword, which he regarded as a talisman, in a roll of maps. Despite such precautions, his arrival in Rome led to a protest by the Count de Gramont, the French Ambassador, who threatened to withdraw the French troops from Rome, and much to Lamoricière's distress, the Pope decided to ask permission from the imperial government for the appointment.

Lamoricière had a reputation as one of France's best soldiers, though the years of retirement had led to an obesity that became particularly apparent when wearing uniform: as a result, many surviving photographs of the older general show him in civilian clothing. He could be fiery and blunt in his speech, with one officer remembering him, in a moment of anger, using all the colourful 'African vocabulary' that had not yet been 'purified' by Christian Rome.[12] Nevertheless, with his new appointment, the British press commented that 'the Pope has at last got a real General, who promises to raise for him a real army'. There was, however, some surprise that he was involving himself in Italian affairs; previously in 1849 he had been vocal in his opposition to the French campaign against the Roman Republic in order to restore the Pope to his territory. There were fears, too, that, in the words of one English newspaper, Lamoricière had become 'the hired hangman of a Government of priests' and that 'the sword which for near fifteen years quelled the fiery Moslem is now to keep in awe, and if need be smite, the Christian flock of the Holy Father'.[13]

The Pontifical Army in 1860

On arriving in Rome, Lamoricière worked energetically with Mérode, who had been appointed Minister of War. Troops and garrisons were inspected, and fortifications improved at Ancona, Pesaro, Viterbo and elsewhere. It was decided not to waste energy on units of the Pope's household, including the famous Swiss Guard, which had mainly ceremonial and security duties, or what remained of the navy, which was by now little more than an extension of the papal customs office. The focus was the standing army.

By the end of the eighteenth century, after decades of neglect, the Pontifical Army could justifiably be said to be one of the worst in Europe: 'incapable of offensive operations, ill-prepared for defensive measures, and at best adequate for ceremonial and internal security purposes'.[14] During the French occupation of the Papal States, it had ceased to exist but was re-established with the return of the Pope to Rome in 1814. Despite some improvements, including the establishment of a *Presidenza delle Armi* to coordinate military affairs and a never-realised plan of 1844 to increase the force to 12,679 men, the Holy See survived the revolutionary crises of the 1830s and 1840s thanks to the intervention of Austria and France rather than its own military resources.

After the short-lived Roman Republic of 1849, the Pontifical Army was once again reconstituted under the leadership of Filippo Farina (the Pro-Minister of Arms) and the Swiss General de Kalbermatten. It consisted of two indigenous Line Regiments, two Foreign Regiments (largely made up of Swiss recruits), a regiment both of artillery and gendarmes, a battalion of Cacciatori, two of Sedentari and one each of invalids and discipline. By January 1859 these forces numbered some 15,992. As can be seen, it was made up of indigenous and foreign – mostly Swiss – elements, the latter being considered more reliable in the event of popular insurrection. There was no conscription in the Papal States, partly because of the divided

---

12 Frank Russell-Killough, *Dix Années Au Service Pontifical: Récits et Souvenirs par le Cte Frank Russell-Killough, Ex-Captaine au Régiment de Carabiniers a Pied* (Mans: Typographie Edmond Monnoyer, 1871), p.89 [author's translation].
13 *The Sun*, 14 April 1860, p.8.
14 David Alvarez, *The Pope's Soldiers: A Military History of the Modern Vatican* (Lawrence, KS: University Press of Kansas, 2011), p.7.

loyalties of the people, and foreign enlistment was made on a personal basis rather than through any official diplomatic agreement.

In 1855 a cadet school was established to train officers. However, discipline still left much to be desired and desertions were common. Few men of quality aspired to follow a military career. One of the magazines behind the Belvedere was so cluttered with coach-building and artistic equipment that it was difficult to access the ammunition. The men in many cases were poorly trained, inadequately dressed and armed with old muskets. The artillery consisted of largely obsolete cannon and there was no provision for ambulances or military trains. The command structure was slow and confused, involving too many separate departments. Lamoricière was surprised to discover an army order for marching drill that would take place only 'if the weather is fine'.[15]

Mérode complained that 'introducing reforms in the Vatican is like cleaning the pyramids of Egypt with a toothbrush'.[16] A grave obstacle was Cardinal Giacomo Antonelli, the all-powerful Secretary of State, who, despite replacing Farina ad interim as Pro-Minister of Arms on his death in 1857, showed little interest in the Pontifical Army and put his faith in the power of diplomacy. The differences in opinion revealed the factional in-fighting at the heart of the Vatican. Odo Russell noted in April 1860: '[A] party forming round the Pope of Ultra Catholics who want to turn out Cardinal Antonelli, because they think him too moderate, both in political and religious matters, and because they fancy he may stand in the way of General Lamoricière, through whom they expect to see the Romagna attacked and retaken for the Pope.' On the other hand, the rise to prominence of Lamoricière and Mérode turned some Italians against them, since 'they dread to see the Pope give way to foreign influence which is odious to their national feeling'.[17]

Lamoricière and Mérode had only four months to introduce changes but it is surprising how much they achieved. A cannon foundry was re-established, cavalry stables built, and a riding school opened. A factory was set up to produce ammunition, employing 120 women, which, according to David Alvarez, was 'perhaps the first time in the Papal States that women were employed in anything but household or cottage industries'.[18] New roads were built and a commission set up to examine old ones; 75 miles of telegraph lines were installed and a topographical office was established; army food was improved. Mérode was also aware of the potential of the railways, as was the Pope, in stark contrast to his predecessor who called them 'roads of hell'. In 1856 the first line had been opened between Rome and the holiday destination of Frascati in the Alban Hills. Three years later a new railway linked Rome to Civitavecchia, the first train carrying 240 fishermen, 'each carrying an offering in the shape of a fish for the Papal table' and making the 50-mile journey, much to everyone's astonishment, in a mere three hours.[19] Mérode had further plans to lay down tracks 'to unite the Adriatic to the Mediterranean by way of Florence'.[20]

Experienced and competent officers who shared this vision were needed for the Army. Unsurprisingly many were drawn from Legitimist backgrounds, forming a French military presence in Rome that paralleled Napoleon III's troops already protecting the Pope. The new command structure included George de Pimodan, a French marquis who had been admitted into the celebrated college of Saint Cyr but had left with the advent of the 'July Monarchy' and served with distinction in the Austrian Army, seeing action in

---

15 Jean Guenel, *Le Dernière Guerre du Pape: Les Zouaves Pontificaux au Secours du Saint-Siège, 1860–1870* (Rennes: Presses Universitaires de Rennes, 1998), p.28.
16 Alvarez, *Pope's Soldiers*, p.83. Pope Francis famously quoted Mérode in his Address to the Roman Curia on 21 December 2017, though he substituted 'sphinx' for 'pyramid'.
17 Blakiston, *Roman Question*, pp.99–101.
18 Alvarez, *The Pope's Soldiers*, p.86.
19 *The Tablet*, 9 April 1859, p.226.
20 Besson, *Mérode*, p.138.

Hungary in 1848. Considered as Lamoricière's deputy, he was promoted to the rank of general. Another important addition was Captain Bernard Blumensthil, a Crimean War veteran who promptly resigned his commission in the French occupation force to join the papal cause. He had commanded the artillery at Castel Sant'Angelo and now was able to move up the road to revitalise the Pontifical Artillery. Other highly gifted officers included Colonel Louis-Aimé de Becdelièvre, a Saint Cyr graduate who had fought at Alma and Inkermann; Lieutenant Athanase de Charette, who had served commissions in the armies of Modena and Parma; and Major Théodore de Quatrebarbes, who had known Lamoricière in Algeria.

Foreign Recruitment

The crucial need was for an increase in manpower and the Pope agreed that the Army could initially grow from over 16,800 troops in April 1860 to 20,000, made up of both indigenous and foreign volunteers. Recruitment offices for the latter were set up in Paris, Marseilles, Brussels and Vienna. The Austrian Government took a proactive role in the process, while in other countries it was left to the discretion of local bishops and enthusiastic individuals with the necessary status and wealth.

New units were hurriedly formed: a second battalion of Indigenous Cacciatori and a battalion of Foreign Carabineers, which included some of the Swiss who had left the now defunct Neapolitan Army. Throughout the summer of 1860 volunteers poured in from Catholic Europe; Henry Edward Manning was in Rome that summer and remembered seeing them in the streets and churches:

> There were faithful hearts of every nation gathering round the Holy Father to give their lives for his sake. There were Austrians, full of their inflexible endurance; the chivalrous French; the faithful and fiery Bretons; the devoted Belgians; the heroic, tender-hearted, and fearless Irish. We saw them familiarly. They bore upon them the tokens of a stern manhood with a childlike generosity, the bearing of Christian soldiers, and the joyous docility of sons. They had come from many lands, and their tongues and their speech were many; but they were one brotherhood and one family, in one Church, and under one Common Father, at whose will they came.[21]

The Austrians comprised five battalions of Bersaglieri. The Irish formed a Battalion of St Patrick, as we shall see. The French and Belgians established a battalion of Tirailleurs under Becdelièvre, renamed the Pontifical Zouaves the following year.[22] These included many illustrious names and initially wore a uniform based on the French Chasseurs à Pied. A further group of mounted volunteers became known as the 'Guides de Lamoricière', under the Comte de Bourbon-Chalus, who dressed and equipped themselves – a considerable expense that amounted to around 6,100 francs. Another group assembled under Henri de Cathelineau, grandson of one of the heroes of the Vendee, who called themselves the 'Knights of St Peter' ('Chevaliers de Saint-Pierre') or the 'Crusaders of Cathelineau' ('Croisés de Cathelineau'). They demanded the right to wear a brown waistcoat with a white cross and select their own officers, which Lamoricière refused; they were eventually incorporated into the Tirailleurs.

21　*The Tablet*, 13 October 1860, p.644.
22　By 20 September 1860, they numbered 450 men, divided into four active and one dépôt companies.

Monster Meetings and Peter's Pence

The recruitment process coincided with renewed efforts to promote sympathy and collections for the Pope around the world. Pastoral letters and communications were issued by bishops expressing sympathy for the Pope. In August 1859 the Irish bishops asked for prayers for the Pope as he faced his 'enemies', noting that 'Central Italy, from sea to sea', had 'enjoyed a high civilisation under the mild sway of the Roman Pontiffs' for centuries and, until recently, the princes and peoples of Christendom had 'protected their persons and defended their possessions as well'.[23] They urged the faithful to act on their plea: 'Hold meetings, send forward petitions to Parliament, call upon your representatives to press your claims, … use all legitimate means to put before the empire the justice of your cause.' Large meetings were held across Ireland. Bishop Moriarty reported that the speeches in English were nothing compared to the ones in Irish, one priest asking his audience what they would do if they were carrying arms; 'into the guts of the enemies of the Holy Father', came one response.[24] Over £80,000 was raised and sent to Rome via Monsignor Tobias Kirby, Rector of the Irish College, which acted as a clearing house for donations and recruits. This was a huge amount and a barometer of the support of Catholic Ireland.

Writing from London in September 1859, Cardinal Wiseman was aware that 'while we are enjoying calm and prosperity, he to whom we owe so much, is living in anxiety and affliction'.[25] In a pastoral letter several months later he asked 'who could feel himself, not merely a member of that body whereof he is head, but bound up with him by still closer ties, and not feel and suffer with him'. He appealed for a benevolence for the Holy Father, with collections taking place in all churches that Low Sunday, hoping English Catholics would imitate the enthusiasm of the Irish.[26] It was never seen purely in financial terms but as a spiritual act. Papal loans were viewed in a similar light: 'His Holiness,' wrote the Vicar General of Westminster, 'will regard every effort to promote this Loan as an act of loyal devotion towards himself.'[27]

An English Peter's Pence Committee was established and included Sir George Bowyer, the wealthy convert lawyer and MP for Dundalk, described by *The Times* as 'the avowed representative in the British House of Commons of the Roman Catholic hierarchy';[28] the future earls of Denbigh and Gainsborough; two architects, George J. Wigley and Archibald M. Dunn;[29] and St George Jackson Mivart, an eminent (though controversial) biologist and evolutionist. Such prominent laity, well-connected at home and abroad, took a central role in supporting British recruits in the Papal Army over the subsequent decade.

An interesting English example is the Catholic community of Wednesbury, made up largely of poor Irish immigrants, which sent a donation to the Holy See at the end of 1859. 'Not being, perhaps, without sin ourselves in the matter of obedience to legitimate authority,' the accompanying address admitted, 'we can but wonder that any Italian Catholics should be found who seek to withdraw themselves from him who is above Kings and Emperors.'[30] Fr George Montgomery reported that every member of his flock

---

23 *The Tablet*, 27 August 1859, p.556.
24 Emmet Larkin, *The Consolidation of the Roman Catholic Church in Ireland, 1860–1870* (London: University of North Carolina Press, 1987), p.8.
25 AAW Wiseman Papers, Letter to Clergy, 29 September 1859.
26 AAW Wiseman Papers, Pastoral Letter, 25 March 1860.
27 AAW Wiseman Papers, Letters to Clergy, 25 August 1860.
28 *The Times*, 13 January 1860, p.6.
29 Wigley, who designed the Roman Church of Sant' Alfonso all'Esquilino, helped introduce the charitable Society of St Vincent de Paul to London and died in 1866 after visiting a smallpox victim in Rome. Dunn entered partnership with Edward Joseph Hansom, whose cousin, Joseph Stanislaus, also an architect, joined the Zouaves.
30 *The Tablet*, 24 December 1859, p820.

had contributed in some way to the collection; masses were offered and rosaries prayed; 'with men, also,' he wrote, 'Wednesbury may be said to have aided the Pope, because from it, as the starting-point of their journey, there went to Rome two Irishmen' to join the Pontifical Army.[31] Around the same time, the local theatre hosted a production that raised money for the 'Aid for Garibaldi Fund'. The Staffordshire town was fully engaged in the struggles beyond the Alps.

---

31   *The Tablet*, 13 October 1860, p645.

Part I

The Battalion of St Patrick (1860)

3

The Raising of the Irish Battalion

In January 1860 it was widely reported that the Archbishop of Westminster had promised the Pope an Irish Brigade.[1] On meeting Odo Russell around the same time, the pontiff 'spoke of the Volunteer movement in England and expressed a wish to enlist some Irish soldiers for his own army if he could do so without giving annoyance to Her Majesty the Queen'.[2] It was the not the first time the subject had been broached. The previous July, Cardinal Antonelli had reported that 'the Pope received many letters from Ireland offering him any amount of soldiers for his army'. There were fears, however, not only of offending the British Government, whose diplomatic support could prove invaluable, but that 'the cheapness of wine in Italy … might prove fatal to the Irishman'.[3]

Visiting Rome over Christmas 1859, Sir George Bowyer discussed the subject with Antonelli and assured him that the Irish would indeed lay down their lives for the Pope. He was given the Cross of the Order of St Gregory and caused eyebrows to rise when he wore this decoration at St Peter's over his uniform of Deputy Lieutenant for Berkshire. Meanwhile, Count Charles McDonnell, an Irish-born papal chamberlain and former aide-de-camp to Field Marshal Laval Nugent (a prominent Austrian general in the First Italian War of Independence), was also visiting the Vatican and holding 'frequent confabulations with the Irish Dominican monks of San Clemente', who remained an important communications hub in Rome for the Irish.[4]

As Catholic Europe was being mobilised, it was little surprise that the Holy See viewed Ireland as a potentially rich source of troops; not only was it loyally Catholic, but generations of the Irish had fought for foreign powers. The Battalion of St Patrick (or 'Irish Brigade' as it was often called) was the fruit of the campaign of Catholic Ireland to assist the pontiff in his hour of need. Recruitment was initially coordinated, with Rome's encouragement and with little consultation, by McDonnell, who now made his way from Rome to Dublin. There he met with Alexander Martin Sullivan, editor of the Dublin-based nationalist mouthpiece *The Nation*, who had for some time previously been urging the formation of an Irish Brigade. He reported in his memoir that senior members of the clergy were 'quite started, affrighted, from the use of anything like force or violence even in self-defence'. The journalist was immediately impressed by the Count: 'had he lived in the thirteenth century, he would have been a crusader knight; in 1641 he would have been a Cavalier; in 1745 he would have been at the side of Prince Charles Edward on the fatal

---

1 *The Times*, 5 January 1860, p.8. This seems to have been an unfounded rumour.
2 Blakiston, *Roman Question*, p.84.
3 Blakiston, *Roman Question*, p.44.
4 *Freeman's Journal*, 27 January 1860, p.4.

field of Culloden'.⁵ McDonnell painted a picture of the situation in Rome and asked: 'What will Ireland do for us?' To which, Sullivan replied:

> In the improbable event of the Government allowing volunteers, … you can have thirty thousand men; if, as is most likely, they give no permission but no active opposition, you will probably get ten thousand: if they actively prevent, nothing can be done. … But the chief difficulty will be our own bishops. They will be adverse or neutral. Not one of them believes the little army of Lamoricière can cope with the overpowering odds of Sardinia.⁶

A committee was quickly formed, and the Catholic nationalist press helped whip up pro-papal and anti-British sentiments in encouraging men to take arms:

> At first they [the British] pretended that we did not sympathize with his Holiness in his troubles, but were secretly rather pleased with the proceedings of King Victor Emmanuel and his ministers – a little time, however, disproved that falsehood – then we would give him only shouts and speeches – but not a fraction of such a useful thing to one so circumstanced, as money – well, that story too has been put aside; there now remains but one more of their prophecies to be falsified – that which said Ireland would not send a man to sustain the Pope – shall not that also be proved untrue? What say you, young men of Ireland?⁷

Equally effective was a sarcastic article in the London *Times*, poking fun at the Irish for talking loudly about their sympathy for the Pope but doing nothing in practice to help him. The bishops were indeed divided on the issue. Some, like David Moriarty of Kerry and Joseph Dixon of Armagh, did much to push the cause. The Archbishop of Dublin, Paul Cullen, was also supportive, though he initially expressed some doubts about the expense, the time needed to train recruits and the legality of the project. Others, like Thomas Furlong of Ferns, were open in opposing the project.

Local clergy not only actively encouraged likely candidates in their parishes but wrote them references, helped with passport applications and coordinated travel arrangements. Some even accompanied their 'lads' on all or part of their onward journey. One of these was Fr Timothy Shanahan of St Mary's Parish, Limerick, who measured the height of his recruits by asking them to stand in the doorway between the church and the Town House in Limerick's Athlunkard Street.⁸ The role of the clergy, however, brought criticism. One disgusted Protestant writer asked: '[W]hat is to be said, then, of the Popish priesthood laying aside their sacred functions, and taking to the business of a common press-gang: setting at defiance the Queen's proclamation and the law of the land, to the obedience of which they are pledged?'⁹

All in all, around 1,300 Irishmen journeyed to Rome to fight for the cause, the largest groups of volunteers coming from Cork, Tipperary, Limerick, Kilkenny and Kerry. They came from all levels of society. One recruit, Timothy O'Dwyer of Clonmel, later reminisced that 'there were artisans, labourers, boatmen on the Suir, militia men, disbanded soldiers who had served in the Indian Mutiny, and policemen'¹⁰ – indeed,

---

5   Alexander Martin Sullivan, *New Ireland* (Philadelphia, PA: J.B. Lippincott & Co., 1878), pp.288–289.
6   Sullivan, *New Ireland*, pp.288–289.
7   *The Nation*, 3 March 1860, p.8.
8   Donal Corcoran, *The Irish Brigade in the Pope's Army, 1860: Faith, Fatherland and Fighting* (Dublin: Four Courts Press, 2018), p.61.
9   *Belfast Newsletter*, 20 July 1860, p.3.
10   *Derry Journal*, 31 August 1910, p.6.

20 members of the Cork Constabulary, who thereby gave up their generous salary and pension rights. One large linen-draper's shop in Dublin is reported to have been emptied of assistants, and alongside the many good candidates from Kerry was 'a rowdy gang of about fifteen boys who had been sent out of their parish by their priest because he wanted to get rid of them' and were known as 'The Kerry Boys'.[11]

A handful had previous military experience. Of the officers, one was already in the pontifical service: Frank Russell-Killough, belonging to the Irish Catholic branch of the family that in England was headed by the Dukes of Bedford, had gained a commission in the 1st Foreign Regiment in May 1858, thanks to his family's connections with Monsignor Talbot. Several had come via the Austrian Army, such as Captain Francis O'Mahony of Cork who had served with the Austrian Uhlans at Magenta and Solferino. In Britain, Lieutenant Edward Howley had joined the 10th Hussars; Peter Diamond and Lieutenant Daniel Kiely (a future Zouave) had both been in the Royal Navy; and Thomas Lyons seems to have served in India. Some had been militia men, including Captain James Blackney (Carlow Militia), Lieutenant Michael Luther (Waterford Artillery) and Captain John Coppinger (Warwickshire Militia).

Captain Patrick O'Carroll, a Kildare man formerly of the 18th (Royal Irish) Regiment, wrote that he was encouraged by friends to join up so that the recruits could be drilled and officered by a fellow countryman: 'I immediately resigned a commission in a not undistinguished regiment in Her Majesty's service, feeling that, having, as a loyal subject, worn a sword for my sovereign's defence for many years, I was equally bound, as a sincere Catholic, to draw a sword in defence of the Head of my Church, whose territories were at the time threatened with invasion.'[12]

Interestingly, there was a handful of English recruits. Mr Chambers hailed from Bristol and Henry Woodward was the son of a convert clergyman (whose grandfather had been the Protestant bishop of Cloyne) and brother of a future Zouave, though he was transferred to the Franco-Belgians. A Mr Flood, who had trained at the Royal Military Academy, Sandhurst, and had served for nine years with the British Army in the Tropics and the Crimea, wrote to Dr Kirby in Rome asking to join the Papal Army.[13] A handful of Britons could be found elsewhere in the Pontifical Army, such as the two sons of John Thomas de Selby, the member of a well-established Northumbrian family who served as a papal chamberlain. His eldest son, Robert, became a lieutenant in the Palatine Guard and later progressed to the Foreign Carabineers and his brother, Fauconberg, joined the Guides de Lamoricière and later transferred to the Pontifical Dragoons. Both were striking figures in the Rome of 1860, over six feet in height and towering over many of their contemporaries.[14]

There was further English involvement from the home front. Fr Joseph Meaney of St Anne's, Blackburn, Lancashire, arrived in Rome on pilgrimage, along with a banner made by members of his flock for the use of the Irish volunteers. It bore 'a life size figure of St Patrick on one side on a green silk ground with the Irish national emblems. On the other side it has the Immaculate Conception.' He reported 'a strong and general desire at home and here to join His Holiness'[sic] army' and had already received 'applications from 12 fine active young men'.[15]

---

11 George Fitzhardinge Berkeley, *The Irish Battalion in the Papal Army of 1860* (Dublin: Talbot Press, 1929), p.21.
12 *Freeman's Journal*, 16 November 1860, p.2. Letter written by 'W.C.' from Paris, 13 November 1860 – presumably O'Carroll, who was still in Paris in mid-November 1860 due to illness. See *Freeman's Journal*, 20 November 1860, p.3.
13 Archives of the Pontifical Irish College, Rome, Kirby Papers, KIR/2584, 28 April 1860. Letter of Mr Flood to Monsignor Kirby.
14 *Hull Packet*, 13 July 1860, p.8.
15 KIR/2506, 13 February 1860. Letter of Fr Meany to Monsignor Kirby. The banner was apparently carried into action and kept at the Pontifical Irish College, Rome, until being destroyed by a fire. Fragments are still in the

Nevertheless, although Catholics – especially Irish Catholics – in England participated in the cause, the Irish Church was keen to remain separate. Earlier in 1860, Monsignor Kirby had refused to join the English in presenting a loyal address to the Pope. An opportunity for the Irish to present their own address came in March, when Pius visited the Irish College around St Patrick's Day and wore a shamrock. Kirby's efforts were applauded by many of the Irish bishops. Bishop Patrick Leahy of Cashel told Kirby he was delighted in his victory in the 'battle of the flags'.[16] The Bishop of Waterford, Dominic O'Brien, confessed that 'it has been my opinion for many years that Cardinal Wiseman would like to have the Irish Church at his feet' and 'glad to see our ancient and independent Hierarchy absorbed by England'. It was paramount that 'we should always keep ourselves separated from the English in these public demonstrations'.[17]

Motivations

In March 1860 Bishop Moriarty reported that 'new and big men too are coming in every day to offer themselves for the service of the Holy Father'.[18] What motivated them? This, of course, is a complex question: each case of recruitment was unique and involved many different factors. Most were devout Catholics who wished to uphold the rights of the Church and defend the Pope. By doing so, they could show appreciation for his support for Ireland during the dark years of the Famine. Alexander Sullivan wrote in 1878 that 'of all Catholic nations or countries in the world – the Tyrol alone excepted – Ireland is perhaps the most Papal, the most "Ultramontane"'.[19] An assault on the Pope was seen as an indirect assault on Ireland. According to the historian of the Irish Battalion, George Fitzhardinge Berkeley, 'an attack made on the Papacy represented not merely a blow struck against an institution which he [the Irishman] most revered, but also a change which he feared might indirectly affect his own country by weakening one of the sources of its moral strength'.[20]

One volunteer, Michael J. A. McCaffery, later wrote a long poem on the Siege of Spoleto in which he used crusading language to explain the motivations of many of his comrades:

> 'Twas no dream of martial glory, – though that perhaps were dear;
> 'Twas not to live in story, through many a coming year;
> 'Twas no ambitious wish for power, no tempting of red gold,
> No wiles of syren pleasure that their bosoms brave controlled
> No! – nobler thoughts than wealth, or fame, or power, or pleasure's charm,
> Inspire each lofty hero-heart and nerve each warrior-arm;
> 'Twas the spirit that of old had led the lances of the West
> To redeem from sacrilegious hands the land a Saviour blest.[21]

Alongside matters of faith, however, were other factors: the desire for adventure and travel, Irish pride, and anti-British feeling, especially since the sympathies of the politicians in Westminster were so clearly in favour of the Risorgimento. By fighting a cause dear to the heart of the Protestant British, Catholic Ireland

---
    Archive.
16 KIR/2563, 11 April 1860. Leahy to Kirby.
17 KIR/2530, 5 March 1860. O'Brien to Kirby.
18 KIR/2553, 28 March 1860. Moriarty to Kirby.
19 Sullivan, *New Ireland*, p.280.
20 Berkeley, *Irish Battalion*, p.18.
21 Michael J.A. McCaffery, *The Siege of Spoleto* (New York: P. O'Shea, 1864), p.25.

was making a stand. Moreover, the experience of fighting in Italy would potentially equip the recruits to fight one day for Irish independence. Of course, many pointed out the inherent contradiction of Irish enthusiasm for the papal cause: in defending the Pope, the Irish were fighting Italian nationalists whose hopes for Italian unity and independence from foreign domination were similar to many of the Irish.

Other factors undoubtedly put off recruits: the pay of pontifical soldiers was 2½ pence a day, compared to a shilling in the British Army; middle-class volunteers might have to turn their backs on good jobs and pensions, with no guarantee that they could return after the end of expedition; added to this was the expense and uncertainty of travelling across Europe. Some thought long and hard about the matter, no doubt consulting family and friends. Others made a spur of the moment decision. As volunteers hurriedly signed up, there was confusion about terms and conditions, which caused problems when they reached Italy. One recruit from Limerick confessed that 'up to within a few minutes of the train's departure' he was undecided about what he should do. In the end he was buoyed by the enthusiasm of the others in the group, including Father Shanahan, although the rough crossing to Milford Haven and the lack of funds meant that by the time he reached London he was 'pretty tired of the business already'.[22]

The volunteers took diverse routes to Italy. Sullivan reported that 'deep mistrust of the Emperor Napoleon at first forbade the hazard of sending men through France, and accordingly the route selected was by way of Belgium and Austria',[23] where training was provided around the villages of Glognitz and Schottwein, southeast of Vienna. Others came via Marseilles and Civitavecchia. If some complained of harsh conditions and limited resources, others had a more positive experience. Paul Kenney, a ship's carpenter from Dublin who would see action at Castelfidardo, took a steamer to Liverpool, a train to Hull and then a boat to Antwerp, on which he found everything he needed: 'tea, coffee, meat, brandy, bread and cheese'.[24] There followed an 800-mile train journey from Malines to Vienna, with brief stops at many of the main German cities, including Cologne, where he was much impressed by the large cathedral, 'next in size to St Peter's, in Rome'. After 11 days staying near the Styrian border, the final leg of the journey was made to Ancona. Kenney was accompanied by a 'young nobleman' who 'telegraphed to every town where we were to take refreshment, and when we arrived everything was ready for us'. This was presumably Baron Franz Ferdinand Guttemberg, a Bavarian-born Austrian officer, who spoke excellent English (on account of his well-born English wife) and was deputed with the task of accompanying many of the volunteers through continental Europe. He later joined the Irish Battalion himself and his wife, despite not sharing the soldiers' faith, did much to raise morale and care for the wounded.

Another Dubliner, James McGarry, had to cut his journey short due to ill health, but likewise reported a warm reception as his group travelled through Austrian dominions: '[C]rowds of anxious people thronged to get a peep at the Irlandaise, and every kind attention that could be paid to us was lavished on us.'[25]

The Question of Legality

The papal volunteer movement was viewed nervously by the British authorities. Odo Russell reported on 10 May that he had quizzed Cardinal Antonelli about whether a thousand Irish recruits were about to arrive at Ancona. He was assured that the Holy See 'had too much respect for the laws of other countries' to attempt

---

22 *Kerry Evening Post*, 13 June 1860, p.2.
23 Sullivan, *New Ireland*, p.290.
24 *Freeman's Journal*, 10 July 1860, p.4.
25 *The Nation*, 23 June 1860, p.685.

direct enlistment in Ireland and that any volunteers 'came of their own free will to Italy and enlisted here'.[26] The vision from Antonelli's point of view (even though he was no longer in control of the War Department and Mérode was clearly following his own agenda) was 'to form an army sufficiently strong for all police purposes in the Papal States, so as to make the French occupation cease altogether and free the Papacy from all foreign intervention' – an object he hoped the British Government would look favourably upon and lead it to place no impediments in the way of any individual recruits travelling to Rome.

Nevertheless, there were calls for the enforcement of the Foreign Enlistment Act of 1819, which prevented the enlisting and engagement of British subjects in a foreign service without licence. The *Irish Times* even suggested that all ships passing Gibraltar should be stopped and searched, 'saving these poor people from a miserable fate'.[27] The police kept an eye on the situation and a proclamation from Dublin Castle of 16 May gave a reminder that any breach of the Act was punishable by fine and imprisonment. The issue was discussed in the House of Commons on 25 May. Daniel O'Donoghue, MP for Tipperary, pointed out that support for Garibaldi seemed to be tolerated while that that for the Pope was condemned:

> [T]he Government pursued one course in England and another in Ireland. They seemed to say to the people of Ireland, 'If your actions coincide with our prejudices, you may violate the law with impunity; but, if you do your duty as Irishmen and Catholics, and endeavour to sustain the Pope, we will strain every point to crush the manifestation of your zeal.' [Mr. BOWYER: Hear, hear!] … This repression was an instance of tyranny in its most odious form. … What would be the effect of this Proclamation on Ireland? It would, like all things of the kind, bring forth a crop of informers, transform every policeman in the country into a spy, and subject every man who wished to leave Ireland, no matter what might be his destination, to the intolerable nuisance of having his movements watched.

The Chief Secretary to the Treasury, Edward Cardwell, denied that the Government encouraged any revolutionary interference in Italy and assured the House that the priority was obedience to the law: a statement had been issued throughout Ireland reminding the people what they were prohibited by law from doing but confirmed that no cases had so far arisen with sufficient evidence to warrant a prosecution.[28]

Such measures may have limited the number of recruitments, which never reached Sullivan's optimistic estimate of 10,000, but did not prevent the regular departure of recruits for the Papal States. Enthusiastic crowds often gathered with local clergy to wave off the 'crusaders' at railway stations and quaysides. On 5 June there was a dramatic scene at Drogheda when Sir Thomas Ross of Dardistown Castle, County Meath, arrived with armed police searching for one of the hired men who worked on his farm, who he believed was departing for Rome. This caused a 'sensation' among the crowd; after the man could not be found and 'when the hawsers and chains were loosed which bound the steamer to her berth; and as the paddle-wheels made their first motion, a deafening cheer was raised for the Pope's Irish Brigade'.[29]

The Government was trapped by a number of factors. Recruits were careful to leave British shores as private individuals, under the guise of harvesters, workers, emigrants, or pilgrims, and only officially enlisted once they reached the Papal States. One veteran, Timothy O'Dwyer of Clonmel, told a journalist

---

26 Blakiston, *Roman Question*, p.102
27 *Irish Times*, 18 May 1860, p.2.
28 https://hansard.parliament.uk/Commons/1860-05-25/debates/82cac64c-cf44-4b44-85d2-9eb63, accessed 18 March 2021.
29 *Coleraine Chronicle*, 9 June 1860, p.3.

in 1910: '"Well, now, we didn't enlist at all till we got to Rome. Till then," added Mr O'Dwyer, with a merry twinkle in his eye, "we were just respectable tourists, personally conducted by Fr Sladden of St Mary's, Clonmel."'[30] Bishop Moriarty suggested that it might be safest for the volunteers to travel on a ship hired by the Holy See on the pretext of being employed building railways on papal territory. Indeed, if any problems should occur, the Irishmen could quickly swap their rifles for spades.[31] Field Marshal Nugent, who had recently been appointed titular Grand Prior of Ireland in the Order of Malta, one of the military orders originally established during the Crusades, issued enrolment letters headed with the words '*Gran Priorato d'Irlanda del Sovrano e Militare Ordine di S. Giovanni di Gerusalemmene*' as a further subterfuge.[32] Moreover, Irish enlistment could not be clamped down upon without affecting the parallel gathering of volunteers for Garibaldi, which had the unofficial support of many in Westminster.

Transnational and Ideological Volunteering

The period of the French Revolutionary and Napoleonic Wars is often seen as an important moment in the 'nationalisation' of military service. Previously armies tended to be small in size and professional in nature, fighting in the name of the sovereign and often incorporating foreign mercenaries. However, the values of the French Revolution stressed that the defence of a nation was the common responsibility of its citizens, with a national army that would typically use conscription to build up its numbers. Indeed, in 1793, Clausewitz stated that, whereas in the past war was the affair of the cabinet, now it had 'suddenly become an affair of the people'.[33] Ordinary men and women were becoming increasingly engaged with the armed forces, which were now to be admired rather than feared, and there was heightened interest in the campaigns being fought in the name of 'the people'.

Although a Foreign Enlistment Act was passed in 1819 restricting the joining of armies overseas without licence, Britons continued to fight for foreign powers and causes, and the legislation often remained a dead letter. As many 11,000 may have been involved in the various campaigns for liberation in South America; about a thousand fought in the Greek War of Independence in the late 1820s; British units served in Portugal during the War of the Two Brothers (1828–1834); and during the First Carlist War in Spain (1833–1840) the Foreign Enlistment Act was actually suspended to allow the formation of the 10,000-strong British Auxiliary Legion.

If national armies were a 'modern' development, so too was the advent of ideological volunteering: fighting for a foreign army not simply because of material gain or the desire for glory but because of belief in a particular cause. Simón Sarlin has noted that 'without doubt, the success of this model owes much to the new conceptions of citizenship and heroism forged by the French Revolution, but the attraction of the volunteer force was not exclusive to the revolutionary ideas and ideals'.[34] If British and Irish involvement in overseas military campaigns was typically in support of liberal ideals, the nineteenth century saw numerous counter-revolutionary causes calling international soldiery to arms and reigniting the values of chivalry and sacrifice. The men who fought for the Pope between 1860 and 1870 stood in this tradition, regarding themselves as crusaders in a global 'culture war'.

---

30   *Derry Journal*, 31 August 1910, p.6.
31   Corcoran, *Irish Brigade*, p.62.
32   Mary Jane Cryan, *The Irish and English in Italy's Risorgimento* (Ronciglione: Etruria Editions, 2011), p.34.
33   Nir Arielli & Bruce Collins (eds), *Transnational Soldiers: Foreign Military Enlistment in the Modern Era* (Basingstoke: Palgrave Macmillan, 2013), p.2.
34   Simón Sarlin, 'Mercenaries or Soldiers of the Faith? The Pontifical Zouaves in the Defense of the Roman Church (1860–1870)', *Millars: Espai i historia*, 43:2 (2017), pp.192–193.

This did not prevent them from being dismissed by critics as mercenaries. On the return of the Irish Battalion in September 1860, for example, George Bowyer wrote to the London *Times* to defend them from the slur:

> A mercenary is a man who serves for pay and plunder; but those men enlisted to fight for a sacred principle, to defend the head of the Church and the Vicar of Christ against the assaults of his enemies. If you call them mercenaries why do you not apply the same term to the Englishmen, Poles, Hungarians, &c., who have joined Garibaldi?[35]

If the Irish fought for the Church, other subjects of the Queen, as Bowyer hinted, took up the sword for the nationalist cause. There was a spirit of brotherhood across the nations and shared values, enshrined by the French Revolution, of liberty, fraternity, and equality. There was a sense, also, that the British had a worldwide mission to promote freedom, democracy and liberation from despotic regimes – and, especially in the case of Italy, from popish error and superstition. In the words of Elena Bacchin, 'patriotism was still associated to liberalism and to a need to spread British achievements to the less fortunate nations, while the idea that Great Britain replaced the Roman empire as a bastion of civilisation and progress was also starting to become accepted'.[36] As with the Irish Catholic volunteers, these ideals were combined with the desire for adventure, money, fame and social mobility.

Of Garibaldi's famous 'Thousand', 33 were from Great Britain. Some became household names. Colonel John Whitehead Peard, known as 'Garibaldi's Englishman' and originally a member of the Cornish Militia, was a skilled sharpshooter whose appearance was so similar to the General that he acted as his double. Colonel John Dunne was a Crimean War veteran who commanded his own 'brigade' made up of both British and Sicilian volunteers. Captain Edward Styles was another Garibaldino who wore Crimean War medals and saw action in 1860 at Calatafimi, Palermo and Milazzo. Then there was Percy Wyndham. A true 'soldier of fortune', he had served in the French Navy, the Royal Artillery, and the Austrian Cavalry and went on to fight for the Union Army in the American Civil War. With Garibaldi he commanded a unit which contemporary newspapers sometimes described as 'Wyndham's Zouaves'. Referring to himself as 'Sir' Percy, since Victor Emmanuel had apparently knighted him on a battlefield, he sported a moustache that was two-foot-wide and died in a freak ballooning accident in Burma in 1879.

Such was the enthusiasm following Garibaldi's campaign in Sicily that a British Legion was eventually formed, with Peard as colonel and Styles as a promoter. It was a clear sign of the close link between Great Britain and Garibaldi, for although there were many foreign volunteers fighting for the cause, the British were alone in forming a distinct national unit. While donations were encouraged for the Garibaldi Special Fund, the Central Committee put an advertisement in the press in August 1860:

> A select party of English excursionists intends to visit South Italy. As the country is somewhat unsettled, the excursionists will be furnished with means of self-defense, and with a view of recognising each other, will be attired in a picturesque and uniform costume. General Garibaldi has liberally granted the excursionists a free passage to Sicily and Italy, and they will be supplied with refreshments and attire suitable for the climate.[37]

---

35 *The Times*, 25 September 1860, p.10.
36 Elena Bacchin, 'Brothers of Liberty: Garibaldi's British Legion', *Historical Journal*, 58:3 (2015), p.833.
37 Marcella Pellegrini Sutcliffe, 'British Red Shirts: A History of the Garibaldi Volunteers (1860)' in Arielli & Collins (eds), *Transnational Soldiers*, p.207.

The language was, of course, framed to avoid the requirements of the Foreign Enlistment Act; even Palmerston spoke of the 'excursionists' having a particular interest in the volcanic phenomena of Mount Etna.

LIEUT. CUETO (SCOTCH COMPANY). MAJOR STYLES. SERGEANT SPARKHALL. A PRIVATE.
GARIBALDIAN VOLUNTEERS,—FROM A PHOTOGRAPH BY HERR FEHRENBACHS.

Like the papal volunteers, the British 'excursionists' who fought for Garibaldi came from diverse backgrounds. This picture includes Edward Styles, a recruiting officer, seen wearing his Crimean War medals, and Gabriel Cueto, who unsuccessfully tried to form a Scottish contingent. The striking tartan uniform was never universally adopted. (*Illustrated London News*, 20 October 1860, Private collection, author's photograph)

Over 600 volunteers arrived in October and joined Garibaldi in the last stages of his fight against Bourbon rule in Kingdom of the Two Sicilies. Their reputation was marred by poor leadership and a significant proportion of 'roughs' who, in the words of G.M. Trevelyan, 'considered that they were out for holiday at other people's expense, and though they did not object to the fighting, expected a maximum of food and good quarters and a minimum of discipline'.[38] Their complaints had some justification, for food, equipment and money were all in short supply, but their behaviour was at times unsoldierly. Five volunteers

---

38   G.M. Trevelyan, *Garibaldi and the Making of Italy* (London: Longmans, Green & Co., 1911), p.271.

were imprisoned for raiding a farmhouse and taking animals, blankets and kitchen utensils, while in late November there was a violent confrontation between Italian and British Garibaldians in Caserta. According to one account, 'they stole without shame, mistreated the local people, drank like thugs, got into fights all the time causing a lot of complaints'.[39] Peard himself came under criticism for his violent and drunken behaviour, his mismanagement of funds, and his inexperience as an army officer.

Up to 400 volunteers were recruited in Scotland and promises made that they would form a separate unit or 'Scotch Company of Volunteers', complete with their own variation of red shirt: 'a Royal Stuart tartan uniform'.[40] An attempt was also made to form an Irish contingent, with recruitment based in Belfast. Designed to parallel the Battalion of St Patrick, it attempted to break down the connection between the papal cause and Irish nationhood and create an Irish Protestant voice in the Italian Question. However, the war ended before these plans could come to fruition.

The Irish Recruits in Italy

The papal volunteers headed in a haphazard way to either Rome (via France) or Ancona (via Austria). There was no centralised coordination and insufficient thought was given to how these men would be fed, clothed and trained, and where they would stay. English was not widely spoken in the Pontifical Army and promised commissions could not always be honoured. Initially, however, there was much excitement as the volunteers reached Italy. One of the first to arrive in Rome, Edward Patrick Naughton of Limerick, was overjoyed to be personally presented to the Pope and attend a beatification ceremony at St Peter's. As well as visiting the famous churches, he made a pilgrimage to the Irish College, where the heart of Daniel O'Connell was buried. He was welcomed also to the Venerable English College, where he met Cardinal Wiseman. Naughton wrote that the English and Irish seminarians were equally enthusiastic in the 'holy cause' and dreamed of being 'chaplains in our regiment' or even private soldiers. He took pride in the reputation of his countrymen as fine soldiers and thought the new battalion should be called the 'Knights of St Patrick' or 'The Pope's Own'.[41]

Brimming with Irish pride, the newly arrived 'crusaders' were angered that the battalion's eight companies were assigned to different locations within the Papal States and would never see action together as one unit. They found themselves alongside recruits from all over Europe and, in the words of the *Morning Post*, 'marching to the authoritative "recht links!" of Swiss or Austrian corporals'.[42] Their days were spent on drill exercises and sentry duty. Conditions were harsh, with many sleeping on beds of straw and receiving low salaries. It took Irish stomachs time to become accustomed to the macaroni and one soldier, looking back, complained about 'the almost total absence of potatoes, with which we were all quite familiar'.[43] Whereas the volunteers hoped for an enthusiastic welcome, as they had experienced in Austria, they often encountered indifference and even outright rejection among the inhabitants of the places they were stationed.

They were hurriedly trained and issued with old uniforms – designed to be a temporary measure – and old-fashioned smoothbore muskets. The promised green uniforms with yellow facings, based on that of the French Chasseurs à Pied, never arrived for the majority. Wealthier recruits seem to have had examples

---

39 Bacchin, 'Brothers of Liberty', p.848.
40 Bacchin, 'Brothers of Liberty', p.839.
41 *Tralee Chronicle*, 5 June 1860, p.3.
42 *Wexford Constitution*, 20 June 1860, p.4.
43 Thomas F. O'Malley Baines, *My Life in Two Hemispheres* (San Francisco, CA: Henderson & Co., 1889), p.15.

made by their tailors, earning them the nickname of 'goldfinches' and comparisons with eggs and spinach. However, the lack of uniforms was a serious problem, lowering morale and a sense of national identity. It is reported that workers had left the fields and travelled across Europe in their old clothes, in expectation of a new kit which never arrived. Just as humiliating was the lot of the 'Tipperary giants', over six foot in height, who were given French uniforms that were at least a foot too short.[44]

Troops of the Irish Battalion of St Patrick, wearing their distinctive green uniforms, from a painting by Quinto Cenni (1845-1917). (Private collection, photograph by Ralph Weaver)

The mismanagement that hindered the battalion was caused by poor communication and the differing agendas of Antonelli and Lamoricière in Rome, the Irish ecclesiastical authorities, and McDonnell's Austro-Irish contingent. As McDonnell put it, 'too many cooks spoil all'.[45] First and foremost, there was confusion about who was in command and, for all intents and purposes, there were two separate units in those early months.

---

44 Archives of the Archdiocese of Dublin, Cullen Papers, IE/DDA 274/2/6, 'The Irish in the Papal Service in 1860', manuscript probably written by G. F. E. Berkeley.
45 Ciarán O'Carroll, 'The Irish Papal Brigade: Origins, Objectives and Fortunes', in Colin Barr, Michelle Finelli & Anne O'Connor (eds), *Nation/Nazione, Irish Nationalism and the Italian Risorgimento* (Dublin: University College Dublin Press, 2014), p.85.

Having been given a brief by Rome to make the battalion a reality, it was understandable that McDonnell took it upon himself to make arrangements for supplying arms, uniforms and training. He hoped to give command to Major Fitzgerald, an experienced Austrian cavalry officer who also had the advantage of speaking Irish. Cullen, meanwhile, liaised with the Committee in Dublin and put forward the candidacy of Major Myles O'Reilly, of Knockabbey, near Thomastown, County Louth. Educated at Ushaw, he had entered the Middle Temple and gained military experience with the Louth Rifles. He was not, therefore, a professional soldier – though accounted a stern disciplinarian – and has been described as 'a country gentleman of the genuine type: a man who knew how to direct his own farming operations, who was a keen breeder of prize cattle, who rode to hounds, and in his younger days had kept a half dozen racehorses'.[46] Two years later he would become MP for Longford. A competent administrator, he (crucially) spoke French and Italian fluently, and outlined a series of recommendations, with the help of a Committee member, Canon Laurence Forde, which were published in an anonymous booklet entitled *Notes on the Assembly of Irish Volunteers for the Pontifical Army Who Offer Themselves for the Service of the Holy See*.[47] On a visit to Rome in May, Forde took up O'Reilly's prerequisites, insisting on the necessity of a uniquely Irish unit with homegrown officers and chaplain, and the importance of honouring any promises of promotion made to the volunteers in Ireland. However, Antonelli and Mérode – both with differing priorities – remained vague and non-committal, and there was no attempt to keep McDonnell, now back in Austria, abreast of developments. There were complaints from the Irish Committee that McDonnell was too pro-Austrian and a 'tool' of 'an English or Anglo-Roman conspiracy'.[48]

Major Myles O'Reilly (1825–1880), commanding officer of the Irish Battalion. (Private collection, author's photograph)

O'Reilly set out for Rome on 10 June with his heavily pregnant wife, Ida, a member of the Jermingham family and a direct descendant of the Catholic Tudor martyr, Thomas More. His arrival was delayed, leaving an unfortunate power vacuum. There was confusion also over the appointment of the chaplain:

---

46 Berkeley, *Irish Battalion*, p.23 (footnote).
47 Published in Italian as *Cenni sull'Aggregazione alle Milizie Pontificie dei Volntarii Irlandesi che si offrono al Servizio della S. Sede*.
48 Larkin, *Consolidation of the Roman Catholic Church in Ireland*, p.25. The chief 'conspirators', according to Canon Forde, included Bowyer, Mgr Talbot, Lord Petre and Wallis of *The Tablet*.

although the Irish bishops had their own candidates, the Roman authorities instead appointed a Franciscan, Father Bonaventure McLoughlin.

Volunteers, in the meantime, began arriving in Vienna and, given the lack of leadership, McDonnell and Nugent went ahead in 'appointing' Major Fitzgerald as commanding officer, having gained an assurance from Franz Joseph that he could return afterwards to Austrian service. Fitzgerald subsequently accompanied a group of 500 volunteers, reaching Ancona on 5 July. However, Fitzgerald received no recognition from Lamoricière, who, together with Mérode, stressed that they alone had the right to appoint officers. The Irish meanwhile complained about the false promises made to them at home, offering speedy promotion to encourage recruitment, and Fitzgerald, along with Lieutenant Patrick O'Carroll, were slightly injured in a resulting brawl.

The Pope had initially been prejudiced by racial stereotypes, thinking that the Irish would quickly become drunk on Italian wine. After calling on Cardinal Antonelli in early July, Odo Russell wrote that:

> His Eminence related many anecdotes about the excesses they committed, and said he now understood why I had eight months ago so strongly urged him not to form an Irish Legion, that the Pope as well as himself had not known the Irish character to be so energetic and that he could also now appreciate the difficulties experienced by the British Government in dealing with Ireland etc., etc. ...'[49]

There was undoubtedly truth in these criticisms. The most serious incident occurred at Macerata, where there was a contingent of 260 Irish, including the 'Kerry Boys', some of whom got drunk and on two occasions resisted the guard that came to escort them back to barracks. Stones were thrown, windows broken, and locals asked that the Irish be sent home. Added to this were rivalries among the Irish: one of the officers, Frank Russell-Killough, reported complaints from the Kerry contingent when those from Dublin were given accommodation on the first floor of the Macerata barracks, which was seen as a place of honour.[50] One recruit told a chaplain, 'we came out to fight, and till we meet Garibaldi we must have a spree amongst ourselves'. Russell-Killough himself tried 'to get them into some order' and sent miscreants 'without mercy to the black-hole'.[51]

Paul Kenney, a volunteer from Dublin, wrote about the cheapness of drink while staying in Austria prior to the onward journey to Ancona. However, he also noted 'there are plenty of English spies going about here, with plenty of money to make us drunk and make us fight among ourselves'.[52] Another recruit, signing himself as 'L', wrote:

> Irish are coming here very strong but they don't know what's before them; if they did, they would stop at home. It is not the place people expected at all. There is not a man come here but is quite discontented from the treatment they are getting. ... I don't wish to see any more from my place here. If they do come, they will be sorry. ... Dear father, I'll be home as soon as possible – tomorrow if I could.[53]

---

49 Blakiston, *Roman Question*, p.117.
50 Russell-Killough, *Dix Années*, p.125 [author's translation].
51 Larkin, *Consolidation of the Roman Catholic Church in Ireland*, p.21.
52 *Freeman's Journal*, 10 July 1860, p.4.
53 *Belfast Newsletter*, 24 July 1860, p.4.

The Protestant press seized on such reports to argue the hopelessness of the cause, the poor quality of the troops, and the drunkenness and disorder of Irish Catholics. It is unsurprising that some decided to return home – probably around 290. It was promised, after numerous appeals were sent to the British Consulate, that those who objected to serving in the Army would be sent home at the Holy See's expense.

In late July the Irish troops gathered in Rome for training and aroused much curiosity. Many thought they were Dutch, since '*Olandesi*' sounded much like '*Irlandesi*,' and when a French soldier asked what an Irishman was, he was told 'a kind of Englishman'.[54] Major O'Reilly finally reached the Eternal City and belatedly began his demanding task. Initially without a pontifical uniform, O'Reilly wore on his arrival the uniform of the Louth Militia, making some of the Irish think he was actually an English spy.[55] There were immediate issues to contend with. An aggrieved recruit named Laffan had recently resisted arrest after being spotted walking through the streets in plain clothes; there was an undignified scuffle and the culprit tried to seek sanctuary at the Irish College. It was a minor incident but did nothing to improve the reputation of the Irish in Rome. As O'Reilly arrived at the barracks for the first time, he witnessed one of his men accusing the Franco-Belgians of trying to intimidate the Irish 'with their bayonets' and that they would easily 'sell the Pope and join Garibaldi in the morning'.[56] The aggrieved Belgian pointed his gun but, according to the papers, O'Reilly boomed a command of order, put himself in front of the muzzle and twisted 'the bayonet off like a twig'.[57] Not all the men welcomed O'Reilly with open arms. Fitzgerald was popular as an Irish speaker and a soldier 'with nineteen years practical service in Austria in war and peace, as against the peaceable militia periodical drills of Major O'Reilly'.[58]

Lamoricière saw potential in the Irish and was impressed by their physical stature but realised they needed discipline and drill. He appointed several non-Irish officers to the battalion, such as the Austrian Captain August Boschan, and refused to confirm the commissions of half a dozen candidates, causing further dissension. Some were asked to join the Franco-Belgians for six months so that they could be better grounded in all things military. Three men, Henry Dunne, Eugene McSweeney, and Henry Woodward (an Englishman), took up the offer and would fight gallantly with the Tirailleurs at Castelfidardo.[59] One of the approved officers, James D'Arcy, was aged only 17 and had an uphill task in commanding older men, though he went on to fight with distinction with both the Irish Battalion and the Papal Zouaves.

By August the Irish moved into position. The first two companies under Captains Coppinger and Boschan joined the garrison of Spoleto, which was commanded by Major O'Reilly himself. The third company under Captain Blackney was stationed at Perugia and the fourth, under Captain Kirwan, would march from Foligno with Cropt's Brigade. The remaining four companies meanwhile were sent to the important garrison of Ancona.[60] It would just be a few short weeks before they would receive their baptism of fire.

---

54 *Kilkenny Moderator*, 11 July 1860, p.4.
55 *Derry Journal*, 31 August 1910, p.6.
56 *Derry Journal*, 31 August 1910, p.6.
57 *Dublin Evening Packet and Correspondent*, 7 July 1860, p.2.
58 O'Malley Baines, *My Life in Two Hemispheres*, p.16.
59 *Freeman's Journal*, 29 November 1860, p.3.
60 Berkeley (*Irish Battalion*, pp.22–23) argued that companies 1–4 and 5–8 were essentially two separate corps, seeing little of the other and even being drilled differently: the former according to French methods and the latter English ones.

4

The Piedmontese Invasion of Umbria and the Marches

In May 1860 Garibaldi embarked for Sicily with his 'Thousand', armed with old muskets and dressed in red shirts and grey trousers. The two steamers he had commandeered in Genoa arrived safely at Marsala on 11 May, with the secret support of Piedmont and the discreet protection of HMS *Hannibal* and two British gunboats under Admiral Rodney Mundy, second-in-command of the Mediterranean Fleet. The landing coincided with a rebellion in Palermo; the Neapolitans were defeated at Calatafimi and by early September both Palermo and Naples were under Garibaldi's control. The Royal Family withdrew to the safety of Gaeta, near the papal border. It was no secret that Garibaldi's wish was now to turn his sights on the Eternal City.

The Piedmontese Invasion of the Papal States

Pius IX was understandably alarmed to see the collapse of Bourbon rule and the threat posed to his southern borders by Garibaldi. Napoleon III was aware of Garibaldi's hostility towards his own regime and the complications that a revolution in Italy could pose to his popularity in France. Meanwhile, Cavour – now back in power after a brief absence – was concerned that a Garibaldian invasion of Rome could take events beyond his control and cause a damaging conflict with both France and Austria. In the aftermath of the recent war, he was beginning to think also in terms of national unification rather than simply Piedmontese expansion. Turin needed to seize the initiative. It was decided to enter the Papal States ostensibly to secure order and block a potential Garibaldian invasion. The French Emperor had first, of course, to be convinced. A secret meeting was held at Chambery at the end of August and Napoleon reluctantly agreed to the plan, though he insisted that the pope be allowed to stay in Rome and keep the city and its surrounding area as his territory. '*Faites, mais faites vite!*' ('Do, but do quickly!') he supposedly told General Enrico Cialdini and Luigi Carlo Farini, the Piedmontese Minister of the Interior.[1]

Speed was essential before the might of the Catholic world could leap into action. Cavour started planning a series of insurrections in the papal border towns that could provide a pretext for military action. General Manfredo Fanti was given the responsibility of commanding the invasion force, which consisted of IV Corps (4th, 7th and 13th Divisions) and V Corps (1st and Reserve Division). Comprising some 38,000

---

1 The words echoed those of Jesus to Judas in John 13:27.

men, 2,500 horses and 77 artillery pieces and ready for action as they conducted routine manoeuvres near the borders, they outnumbered the pope's forces three to one.

The Piedmontese Army was the largest and most up to date on the peninsula. It had benefited from a series of reforms, a new system of conscription and combat experience both in Italy and the Crimea. Moreover, following the recent annexation of Lombardy, the central Italian duchies and the Legations, it had grown substantially in size. Its elite light infantry units of Bersaglieri, with their distinctive uniform, had already set a high standard for mobility and professionalism, and by 1860 comprised 27 battalions.

General Enrico Cialdini (1811–1892), commander of IV Corps in 1860, as depicted on the Monumento Nazionale di Castelfidardo. (Photograph: Nicoletta Lampa)

Cialdini's IV Corps was ordered to move along the Adriatic coast as quickly as possible so as to prevent the Pontifical Army from reaching Ancona, where it was assumed it would concentrate its forces and where any reinforcements from Catholic Austria might potentially disembark. V Corps under General Enrico della Rocca advanced on the other side of the Apennines into Umbria, focusing on Perugia and Foligno, and then pursuing Lamoricière – it was unclear at this stage whether he would head for Ancona or Rome, or indeed seek an open battle. A division was to separate from IV Corps and secure Urbino and then move along the Apennines, acting as a connecting link between the two armies and assisting where necessary.

Rome was blissfully unaware of Piedmontese plans and fed with inaccurate intelligence. Antonelli remained confident in foreign protection and believed reports from the French Ambassador that Piedmont had no desire to enter papal territory. Even if the worst were to happen, Napoleon promised to intervene should there be unprovoked aggression. Lamoricière, meanwhile, was aware that he was exposed to attack

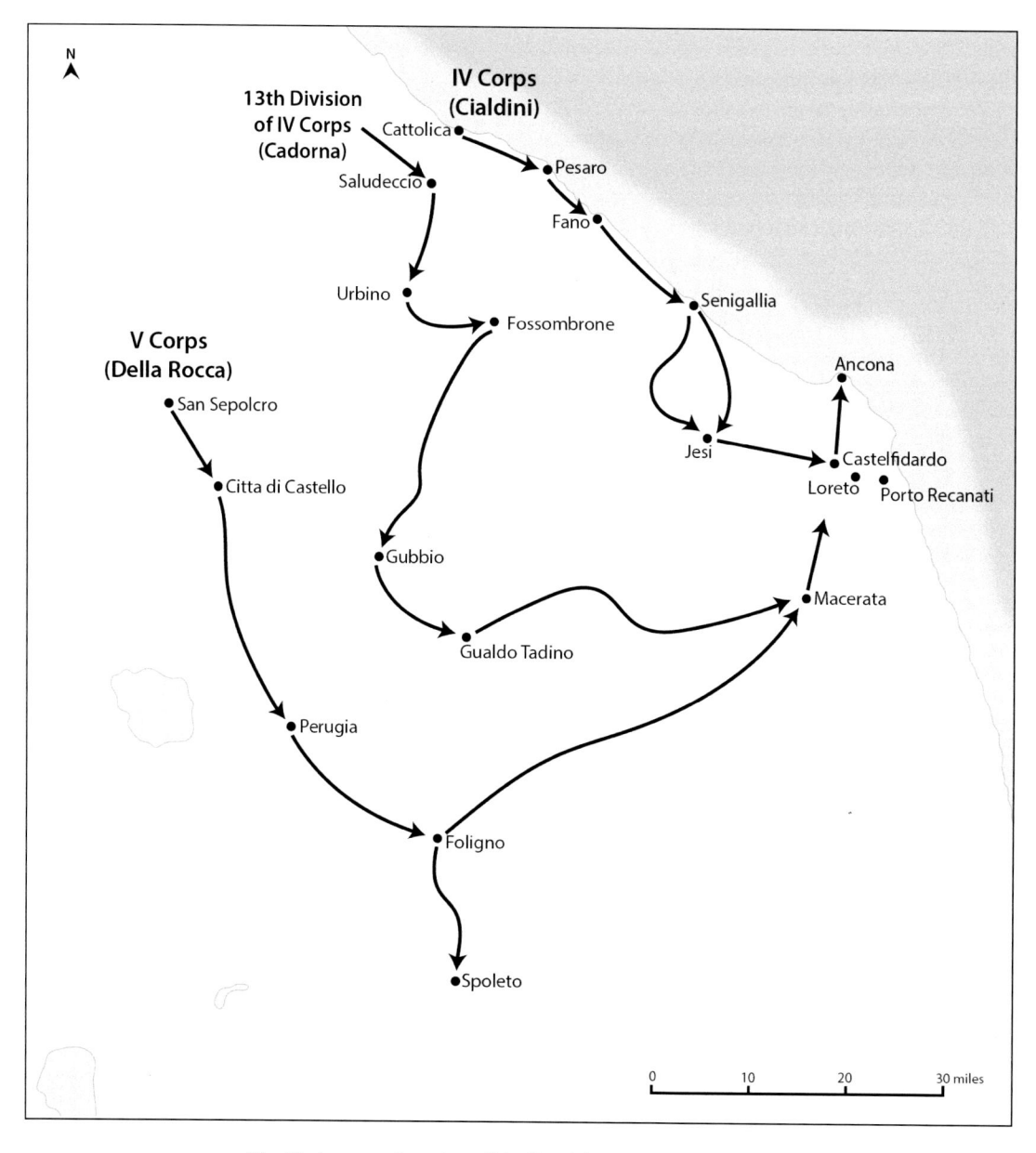

The Piedmontese Invasion of the Papal States, September 1860.

not only from Piedmont in the north but – considered more likely – from Garibaldi in the south and revolutionaries from within. He was forced to divide his limited resources, stationing brigades under General Anton Schmidt at Perugia (3,800 men), General Georges de Pimodan in the area between Narni and Terni (4,300 men), General Raphael De Courten near Macerata (3,800 men) and a reserve under General Cropt at Spoleto (1,900 men).

In the end, the Holy See was taken by surprise. On 4 September 'a small park of siege artillery of 24 pieces' left Genoa by sea for Ancona.[2] From 7 September (the day that Garibaldi entered Naples) revolutionary activity broke out at Città della Pieve, Orvieto, Urbino, San Leo and elsewhere, which the papal garrisons tried to suppress. On 10 September a message arrived for the Pope from Turin, warning that if 'nationalist' insurrections continued to be resisted by the Pope's foreign troops, the Piedmontese Army would feel obliged to occupy and pacify Umbria and the Marche and protect fellow Italians. Such a pretext made it hard for Napoleon to intervene, since he was not only the protector of the Pope but the champion of liberalism. Odo Russell reported that 'a feeling of insecurity has crept over the inmates of the Vatican who begin to fear that the zeal and devotion of the French Ambassador for the Pope and the implacable hatred he professes to the Italians and their aspirations, may have led His Excellency to use language indicating more his own feelings than the future policy of his Government.'[3]

On 11 September 1860 Della Rocca's V Corps advanced from Arezzo into the Papal States towards Perugia, the largest city in Umbria. Papal Gendarmes put up a brave defence at the frontier town of Città di Castello, where they barricaded themselves into the municipal building. Following the Tiber, the men then moved towards Fratto and then, on 13 September, Perugia. IV Corps, meanwhile, made its way from Cattolica towards Pesaro, with Cadorna's 13th Division branching off to secure Urbino. The commander of Pesaro's 1,200-strong garrison, Lieutenant Colonel Giovan Battista Zappi, surprised the Piedmontese with his stubborn defence, despite facing superior firepower and the mutiny of his customs guards. He retreated into the town's fifteenth-century Rocca (fortress) and withstood a heavy bombardment until he was eventually forced to capitulate at 8.00 a.m. on 12 September, though not before 21 of his men had been killed.[4] Advancing southwards, the forces took the port of Fano on 12 September and Senigallia, the Pope's birthplace, the following day. After a short rest, they marched slightly inland to Jesi on 15 September.

Lamoricière faced an immediate disadvantage. Following the information available to him, he had discounted the Piedmontese threat, sent troops to respond to the scattered insurrections and continued to hope in foreign intervention: the French might send reinforcements to Civitavecchia and the Austrians to Ancona – the latter hoping to redeem the defeat of the previous year. With the invasion quickly unfolding before his eyes, his armed resources were now spread thinly across Umbria and the Marches. David Alvarez has noted that, from the pontifical point of view, the campaign 'came at least two years too soon'.[5] There had not been enough time for Lamoricière's army reforms to be implemented; many of the newly arrived volunteers had yet to be trained and equipped properly and the various units were divided not only geographically but linguistically. Commanders sometimes needed translators to communicate effectively. The recent war between France and Austria had showcased the potential of railways to quickly move troops but the Papal States had only recently invested in this new mode of travel and there were no railways in Umbria and the Marche, slowing down mobilisation. There was still the hope that individual units would

---

2   *The Tablet*, 27 October 1860, p.681 (quoting Fanti's report).
3   Blakiston, *Roman Question*, p.126.
4   'The results of this first deed of arms,' reported Fanti, 'were 1,200 prisoners, five cannon, some horses, provisions, and munitions of war.' *The Sun*, 22 October 1860, p.1.
5   Alvarez, *The Pope's Soldiers*, p.94.

do their best to delay the progress of the Piedmontese but the situation for the papal forces was critical. It was imperative to bring the army together and march towards Ancona.

This was easier said than done. One column of papal troops under Colonel Hermann Kanzler, consisting of the 2nd Battalion of the 1st (Indigenous) Infantry, the 1st Foreign Bersaglieri and a section of artillery, had been dealing with unrest in Fossombrone but now faced several attacks from the 7th Division (of IV Corps) as they headed for Ancona. At the village of Sant'Angelo, outside Senigallia, over 150 papal troops were killed, wounded or captured. Nevertheless, Kanzler's remnant managed to withdraw without being pursued and reached Ancona on 14 September, to the cheers of the garrison.

The Fall of Perugia

Della Rocca's V Corps were within striking distance of Perugia, about 90 miles north of Rome. Augustus Hare described the city two decades later as 'crowned with towers and churches at the top of a green hill covered with the utmost luxuriance of vegetation' which boasted fine views of the Tiber valley, 'so unspeakably beautiful towards sunset'.[6] The scene, however, was anything but peaceful on 14 September 1860. Schmidt's brigade stationed in the city had just returned from a few days' diversion at Città della Pieve, where there had been an insurrection, but a combination of poor judgement and ineffective communication meant it stayed longer than was necessary. Lamoricière had ordered units to gather at Foligno but, since Schmidt remained ignorant of this and of the Piedmontese forces nearby, he was ordered to defend Perugia and delay the advance of IV Corps. His troops marched through the night to reach the city and had just arrived when the Piedmontese appeared.

A Piedmontese reconnaissance party under Major Rizzardi found that the city walls were in places deserted. To his surprise, a ladder was let down by sympathetic citizens, for Perugia had a strong element sympathetic with the nationalists, especially after the uprising the previous year and its controversial suppression. Once inside, the Porta Sant'Antonio was opened and three battalions of the 1st Grenadier Regiment, the 16th Bersaglieri Battalion and a section of artillery were let in. Another battalion of Grenadiers was sent towards the Porta Santa Margherita, where the pontifical troops had their first engagement with the enemy. Despite their efforts, this gate also was opened and the Piedmontese began pouring in, forcing Schmidt's men back towards the city centre and the safety of Rocca Paolina.[7]

There was fierce fighting in the narrow streets and, with the arrival of artillery, the beginning of a bombardment of the Rocca. Schmidt's second-in-command, Colonel Lazzarini, retaliated with the fortress guns and a counterattack along the main street, the Corso. This was effective in the short term, but the Piedmontese attack was not stopped. Some papal troops showed a lack of discipline and were only too ready to give in, especially the 1st Battalion of the 2nd Foreign Regiment. However, the defence of the city was increasingly left to individual pockets of soldiers who continued to fire from their positions, despite the hopelessness of the situation.

Among the most conspicuous defenders that day were the Irish, members of the 3rd Company under Blackney. One group could be found in the upper floor of a building on the Corso, firing on the enemy below. Another detachment defended the Porta Sant'Angelo, led by Corporal Francis Allman, a medical student from Cork. He was killed in the street-to-street fighting, as Sergeant Thomas Brophy testified:

---

6   Augustus J.C. Hare, *Cities of Central Italy* (London: Smith, Elder & Co., 1884), vol. 2, pp.236–237.
7   Built in 1543 on the orders of Paul III by Antonio da Sangallo, it had recently been strengthened by Lamoricière.

Poor Allman, whom you knew, fell dead by my side, shot through the heart. He never spoke. Instantly I myself was struck down. My gun was shattered out of my hand, and as I lay on the ground, I was hit again by a ball in the left hip, my trousers torn to atoms, my wound but a trifle; but our company escaped wonderfully, considering it might have been destroyed.[8]

Private Power and Corporal William Synan were also injured, and the detachment became divided. One group took shelter, but the attackers surrounded them both on the lower floor of the building and the upper floors and roofs of surrounding houses. The Irish made a brave stand here but in due course Sergeant Patrick Clooney, a Waterford man who would later lose his life in the American Civil War, was forced to surrender.

After three hours of fighting, a truce was agreed that would last from 10.00 a.m. until 3.00 p.m., allowing negotiations to be held and the wounded to be assisted. The commander-in-chief of the invasion force, General Fanti, met with Schmidt and Lazzarini, but refused to allow the pontifical troops to surrender with honour, marching out of the city with flags and arms. Instead, the men would be allowed to walk away only with their baggage; foreign troops would be repatriated, and indigenous soldiers given the opportunity to join the Piedmontese Army with their current rank. The truce was extended; Fanti threatened to continue the bombardment at 5.30 p.m. if no surrender was forthcoming while Schmidt continued to demand honourable terms. The guns briefly sounded again and, aware that further resistance was useless and that some of his troops had begun fraternising with the enemy in the streets, Schmidt ordered the white flag to be hoisted above the Rocca.[9]

The defeated troops were marched towards Genoa. Sergeant Brophy wrote: '[Y]ou should see the blood oozing out through our shoes and over at the ankles, from streaming down inside our clothes from our wounds.'[10] A total of 37 papal troops lost their lives, in contrast to seven Piedmontese. The loss of Perugia was a blow to Lamoricière; he had hoped the town could be held for a few days as he headed towards Ancona but now the Piedmontese were not far behind. Moreover, it meant that Umbria was effectively lost for the Pope.

The Defence of Spoleto

After Perugia, V Corps went on to secure Foligno and then chase Lamoricière towards Ancona. However, to secure Umbria it was necessary to neutralise Spoleto. General Brignone was sent with the 3rd Grenadier Regiment, the 9th Bersaglieri Regiment, two cavalry units and six artillery pieces (2,400 men).

Spoleto was not seen as a major military target but, with the fall of Perugia, it took on an added significance. Like so many Umbrian towns, it was situated on a hilltop and crowned with a medieval citadel, the Rocca Albornoziana, that looked imposing but was completely unsuitable for the warfare of the 1860s. With no parapet on the roof and a limited number of windows from which the garrison could fire, much depended on holding the outers walls and gates. Nevertheless, the fortress held a strong position and was used as a secure prison up until the 1980s, its later inmates including the would-be assassin of John Paul II, Mehmet Ali Ağca. The spectacular Ponte delle Torri nearby connected the city with Monteluco, a

---

8   *Tipperary Vindicator*, 2 October 1860, p.1.
9   Badly damaged by the bombardment, much of the Rocca was demolished shortly afterwards and replaced by the Piazza Italia. Some parts survive, including the Etruscan Porta Marzio, incorporated by Sangallo into his design.
10 *Tipperary Vindicator*, 2 October 1860, p.1.

wooded summit overlooking the Rocca which in September 1860 provided an excellent vantage point for Piedmontese gunners and sharpshooters.

The garrison of nearly 700 men, under Major O'Reilly, had access to only three cannons, only one of which turned out to be usable. The two Irish companies were keen to fight but inexperienced, poorly trained, lacking uniforms and armed with old muskets. The 25 Franco-Belgians were armed with rifles which had a longer range; otherwise, many of the troops fired their weapons with little effect. After hearing the fate of Perugia and Foligno, O'Reilly feared that the entire V Corps was heading in his direction and asked Rome for instruction: 'If the telegraph conveyed tears,' Mérode replied, 'there would be some of mine on this. I can only say, do your duty. The true reward is not for the stronger.'[11] O'Reilly concentrated his men within the Rocca and waited for the enemy to arrive.

On the night of 16 September, the garrison watched the Piedmontese take their positions. According to Jerome Deady, an Irish Sergeant-Major: 'On the west hill which overlooked the town, a strong force of infantry and cavalry with two batteries of artillery; on the Foligno road another battery, covered by a regiment of Lancers; on the side of the glen beyond the bridge to the south of the citadel, were several columns, one of which we called the battalion of Bersaglieri, or sharp shooters.'[12] For Dubliner M. Dargan, the night before the fight was one of spiritual preparation: 'I myself read the preparations for death and received the holy absolution at twelve o'clock the night before the engagement. We were all expecting to be slaughtered.'[13]

Early on the morning of 17 September Brignone's force arrived and the chief of staff was sent to negotiate with the garrison. O'Reilly met him outside the main gate of the citadel to prevent him seeing the weakness of their position and ignored his pleas to surrender. Some of the women, including Mrs O'Reilly and Frau Boschan, were given safe conduct out of the fortress before the fighting began.

Shortly after 8.00 a.m. the Piedmontese opened fire. O'Reilly wrote: 'Captain de Baye urged that politeness obliged us to reply to the fire of the Piedmontese with our one gun, at least at first. ... [He] took the match and fired the gun himself; it gave a most faint and hissing report as if the cartridge was bad and, as I afterwards heard from General Brignone, the shot fell dead a short way over the town; that was the last cannon shot.'[14] The defenders kept up their fire as best they could. Lieutenant Cronin was considered a good shot and claimed to pick off several artillerymen who were trying to fire a gun that was being brought closer to the Rocca. An Irishman attached to O'Reilly recalled how vulnerable the officers were as they encouraged the men firing from the walls: '[W]e were for some moments a first-rate mark for the enemy's rifles – his uniform, the adjutant's, and mine (I was the only one who wore the new uniform of the [Irish] Brigade) affording a nice diversity of colour for the deadly-aiming Bersaglieri.'[15]

The Piedmontese raised a flag of truce late morning, hoping that the papal garrison would realise the hopelessness of their position. Even the Bishop of Spoleto strongly encouraged O'Reilly to capitulate, but he replied it was duty to continue in his resistance.

The bombardment continued. Several cannon balls went straight through the citadel gate, making round holes, since it was rotten, but 'without shaking it seriously'; one hit an English soldier in the Irish Battalion, Chambers by name, originally from Bristol, and in the words of one of his comrades 'took the whole side out of him'.[16] An Irishman called Fleming, stationed on an exposed part of the wall, was shot

---

11 Alvarez, *The Pope's Soldiers*, p.108.
12 *Cork Examiner*, 31 October 1860, p.4.
13 *Kilkenny Journal*, 27 October 1860, p.2.
14 Berkeley, *Irish Battalion*, p.152.
15 *Tipperary Vindicator*, 5 October 1860, p.3.
16 Berkeley, *Irish Battalion*, p.156.

through the head. His brother, who stood beside him, calmly continued firing, kneeling on the body since it gave him a better view.

Then, around 3.30 p.m., an infantry assault was made against the Rocca's entrance. O'Reilly was ready for this eventuality. The attackers could easily access an undefended outer gate and then advance along a narrow approach road, stretching about 120 yards. In doing so, however, they came under heavy fire from the Irish positioned along the wall and above the inner gateway. Moreover, the one working cannon was within the embrasure of the gate and 23 Franco-Belgians in a nearby house. Further back, against the gate to an inner courtyard, he placed two overturned wagons to act as a barricade for the reserve troops. According to an eyewitness:

> In poured the besiegers into the outer yard. A bloody reception met them there. The Irish had two guns, loaded with grape, planted inside in a position commanding the entrance, and no sooner was the Piedmontese column seen through the smoke of the gateway, than a murderous fire was opened, mowing them down, literally, like corn before the sickle. Again – again – again – the besiegers dashed through the gate; again – again – and again, a perfect hail of grape shot from the two [sic] pieces in the yard, and musketry from the citadel walls behind, met them from the Irish inside.[17]

There was about a quarter of an hour's hand-to-hand fighting as the attackers hacked away with axes at the inner gate, already damaged by artillery fire. At one moment, Sergeant David O'Neill, a veteran of the Crimean War, fired his musket through a small trap; straight in front of him was Captain Prevignano, also a Crimean veteran, who seized the butt of the gun and pushed it away just in time. Seconds later he avoided O'Neill's bayonet thrust. Others were less fortunate: one of the axe-wielding Bersaglieri fell dead against the gate, while Lieutenant Michael Crean of Tipperary was wounded in the right biceps. He showed a courage that would be followed by his son, Thomas, who won a Victoria Cross in the Boer War.

Eventually Brignone ordered his men to withdraw back down the approach road, again under heavy fire. A former Dublin constable, Charles Langley, lost his life at this stage, struck by a ball as he aimed his gun at the enemy. De Baye's cannon fired a second shot as the Piedmontese retired, after which the gunners ran for cover thinking their position now untenable. Some of the Irish reserve, wrongly assuming the Piedmontese had made it through the gate, ran to the guard house for protection, as Captain Coppinger tried to rally them.

The bombardment continued and Brignone asked Fanti if additional guns could be brought into place. Jerome Deady wrote that 'at about 5.00 p.m. you would think hell was in Spoleto, thundering from both sides', looking 'like a world of fire and brimstone'.[18] O'Reilly initially wished to continue resistance but, according to one eyewitness, was asked to surrender shortly after the failed assault on the gate but responded: 'Return and tell your commander that we are Irish-men; and that we hold this Citadel for God and the Pope. The Irish who serve the Pope are ready to die, but not to surrender.'[19]

At 8.00 p.m. O'Reilly requested a truce to tend to the wounded and survey the situation. Despite being outnumbered and under-equipped, the garrison had impressively held the fortress and repelled an infantry attack on the gate. Only three lay dead and ten wounded, compared to 14 Piedmontese dead and 49 wounded. However, supplies and ammunition were running low, there was no sign of relief and the troops,

---

17   *Dublin Evening Post*, 2 October 1860, p.4.
18   *Cork Examiner*, 31 October 1860, p.4.
19   *Dublin Evening Post*, 2 October 1860, p.4.

especially the greener ones, were showing signs of declining morale under the heavy bombardment. Edward Dunne recalled: '[M]y mouth was parched, not merely from the heat, but from biting the cartridges.'[20] Moreover, there was no strong advantage in continuing resistance: the main Piedmontese forces were still chasing Lamoricière and O'Reilly had made a symbolic and respectable resistance.

The following day negotiations were made with Brignone, who wished to leave Spoleto without his reputation in tatters. The pontifical officers were allowed to leave the city with their swords – an important point of honour – and, as far as the Spoleto garrison was concerned, the campaign was over.

---

20   Berkeley, *Irish Battalion*, pp.164–165.

5

The Battle of Castelfidardo[1]

Lamoricière's army of 6,500 men headed towards Ancona as quickly as it could, making stops along the way at Foligno, Serravalle, Tolentino and Macerata. Behind Lamoricière was a second column led by General de Pimodan. The weather was hot and the march exhausting. There was a brief diversion at Porto Recanati on the Adriatic coast, where Lamoricière dropped off a trunk of money to be taken by papal steamer to the garrison at Ancona – an important but time-consuming task.

Meanwhile Cialdini's IV Corps, having marched along the Adriatic by Pesaro, Fano and Senigallia and then inland, had made a circuit around Ancona and by 17 September spread itself in a line from Osimo to Castelfidardo, its left flank on the left bank of the river Musone. The advance was impressive in its efficiency, at one point covering 38 leagues in 28 hours so that the *papalini* could be blocked. The 13th Division, which had separated from the IV Corps in order to reach Urbino, had been making the strenuous efforts to follow the Apennines and reached Gualdo Tadino, just below Monte Penna, when it was ordered to recross the mountain range, reaching San Severino on 19 September. V Corps, which had seen action at Perugia and Spoleto, meanwhile headed for Tolentino, to the southwest of Ancona.

Lamoricière reached Loreto on 16 September. Many of the papal troops would have been excited to see the dome of the famous basilica, under which was the famous Santa Casa (Holy House), where the Blessed Virgin was believed to have received the visitation from the Archangel Gabriel. Less welcome was the sight of the Piedmontese flag flying in the little hilltop town, raised earlier that day after the arrival of a squadron of Lancers. According to a priest at Loreto, tricolours could be found everywhere: 'I never saw a transformation so rapid; the town was in one instant decked with flags, and cowards donned the cockade in the twinkling of an eye. I heard people who had spoken to me in the morning of their love for the Pope cry with all their might – "Long Live Victor Emmanuel!"' Once the Pontifical Army arrived, however, the Piedmontese cavalry retired and 'the banners and cockades disappeared, if possible more quickly than

---

1   Massimo Coltrinari questions the accuracy of the name 'Battle of Castelfidardo'. It actively involved only a small proportion of the Pontifical and Piedmontese forces (19 percent of the IV Corps or 39 percent of the forces positioned between Osimo and the Colle Oro) and it was fought not in the town of Castelfidardo, but around the Colle Oro and Musone valley, near the village of Crocette, all of which lie within the Commune of Castelfidardo. Much of the battlefield is currently located in the Selva di Castelfidardo, a park consisting of woodland. The Piedmontese headquarters, from which the official report was written, was based in Castelfidardo, while the papal forces referred to '*il combattimento di Loreto*', making the link with the famous Catholic shrine. See Massimo Coltrinari, *Il Combattimento di Loreto detto di Castelfidardo, 18 Settembre 1860* (Rome: Edizioni Nuova Cultura, 2008), pp.25–38.

they had appeared, and cries of "Viva Pio Nono! Viva il generale! Viva la Moriciere!" resounded through the air'.[2]

Lamoricière's army bivouacked in the main square, while the fires of Cialdini's camp on the hills of Castelfidardo could be seen in the twilight. Later that evening a small reconnoitring party rode along the Ancona road to assess the situation; they encountered a Piedmontese battery and grapeshot was fired, killing a horse and seriously injuring Mizael de Pas, a Guide, in the arm. He was taken to the Jesuit house at Loreto and then to the hospital run by the Sisters of Charity, where he was able to hear the sounds of the subsequent battle and died on 24 September. He had hoped to train for the priesthood after the campaign and was remembered not only as one of the first French volunteers, but the first to die for the Pope. On his deathbed he repeated, 'How happy I am to have been the first to shed my blood for the Holy See!'[3]

On 17 September Pimodan's brigade, which was following in the rear, joined the bulk of Lamoricière's army. Preparations were made for the battle that seemed inevitable. The papal commander found himself in an unenviable position. His men were tired and hungry from a long march. To advance was to run into IV Corps but to stall would be equally dangerous in that V Corps would shortly arrive. Lamoricière chose to continue towards Ancona using an alternative route. Three columns would ford the river Musone. The left-hand column, led by Pimodan, would cross the river at the Casa Arenici, gather at a collection of buildings known as the 'Lower Farm' ('Casa di Sotto' or 'Casa Andreani-Catena') and then wheel round to face the left flank of the Piedmontese. He would continue uphill to the 'Upper Farm' ('Casa Serenella del Mira') and halt on the summit of the Montoro hill.

The middle column, led by Lamoricière, would cross the Musone further downstream at the Casa Camiletti and then, if necessary, support Pimodan's men from behind. This would allow the right-hand column, made up of reserve artillery, baggage and gendarmes, to get away on the road. The main aim was not so much a large-pitched battle but an attack that would divert the Piedmontese so that the majority of the pontifical troops could speedily reach the safety of Ancona. The historian of the Irish Battalion, George Fitzhardinge Berkeley, wrote that Lamoricière's plan displayed 'an audacity characteristic of his African days' and 'enabled him to throw the whole of his little force – arrayed in two lines of attack one behind the other – against the left-hand point of Cialdini's line, where it was weakly defended'.[4]

Early on the morning of 18 September the army assembled outside the basilica. The preparations for the advance were not only military but spiritual and many made their confession. According to a French priest present at the scene:

> At daybreak on Tuesday there was a scene worthy of the epoch of the Crusades, and which, as a priest and a Frenchman, gave me the greatest consolation. At four o'clock Moriciere, Pimodan, and all the staff-officers, the guides, and the German regiments, the foreigners and natives, all received Holy Communion. I saw the greater number of them prostrate in prayer. ... On the ramparts, towards the north side of the plain, perceiving a movement amongst the enemy's troops, which seemed like a swarm of ants in the distance, the Franco-Belgians said to me: 'Bless me, Monsieur l'Abbe, for we shall never meet again on earth.' And they spoke truly.[5]

---

2 Marquis A. de Ségur, *The Martyrs of Castelfidardo* (Dublin: M.H. Gill & Son, 1883), p.19.
3 Ségur, *Martyrs of Castelfidardo*, p.55.
4 Berkeley, *Irish Battalion*, pp.175–176.
5 Ségur, *Martyrs of Castelfidardo*, pp.22–23. It has been argued, though, that such spiritual preparations delayed the offensive and lessened the chance of surprise. Coltrinari, *Il Combattimento di Loreto*, p.119.

At 8.30 a.m. they set off, carrying the banners kept at Loreto that had been used at Lepanto in 1571, another battle seen as being fought for the survival of Christendom.

The offensive caught the Piedmontese by surprise; many were finishing breakfast and not expecting a fight that day; the general intelligence suggested that the Musone was not easily fordable below Loreto.[6] Hoping to secure the Lower Farm on the other bank, the *papalini* crossed the river as quickly as they could.

Pimodan's men were led by a vanguard made up of two companies of Foreign Carabineers, followed by the remaining companies of Carabineers under Major Jannerat, the 1st Battalion of Indigenous Cacciatori under Major Ubaldini, Becdelièvre's Franco-Belgians and the 9th Artillery Battery, accompanied by around 105 men of the 4th Irish company, under Captain Kirwan.[7] Further behind, in a second section, was Major Giorgi's 2nd Battalion of Indigenous Cacciatori, Major Fuckmann's Austrian Bersaglieri (2nd Battalion), the 11th Battery, two squadrons of Dragoons, a squadron of Guides and a platoon of Ordinance.

At around 9.20 a.m. the first shots were fired between the Swiss and the Bersaglieri, positioned in open order among the reeds. The steep banks and the muddy bed created their own set of problems. Twenty year-old Alfred de la Barre de Nanteuil, a Franco-Belgian, was seen struggling in the midst of the waters: he 'sank, and his shoes remained in the mud; he made several efforts to recover them, but without success, so he was obliged to fight barefoot amidst briers and stones', though he was later able to wear the boots of a fallen Piedmontese soldier.[8] The Irish who were accompanying the artillery pieces worked hard to prevent them from becoming stuck in the river bed.

Despite the surprise attack, the Piedmontese units on the left flank acted quickly. The Bersaglieri

General Georges de Pimodan (1822–1860), the highest profile casualty of Castelfidardo. (Private collection, author's photograph)

---

6   It was fordable in several places downstream from Loreto, and it seems that the papal forces were helped in this by local inhabitants.
7   Martin Kirwan, a former militia man and cousin of Lord Howth. Confusingly, there was also a Sergeant John Kirwan at the battle, ex-Dublin Artillery Militia and police, who, according to a letter from J.P. O'Brien published in the *Dublin Evening Post*, 15 April 1896, p.2, moved to America, served with the 1st New York Infantry and was promoted to 'Captain'. An organiser of the Papal Veteran Association in the United States, he was 'elected' their Captain, a rank that was apparently ratified by the Vatican. Berkeley was not able to locate any surviving members of the company and no eyewitness accounts are extant.
8   Ségur, *Martyrs of Castelfidardo*, p.89.

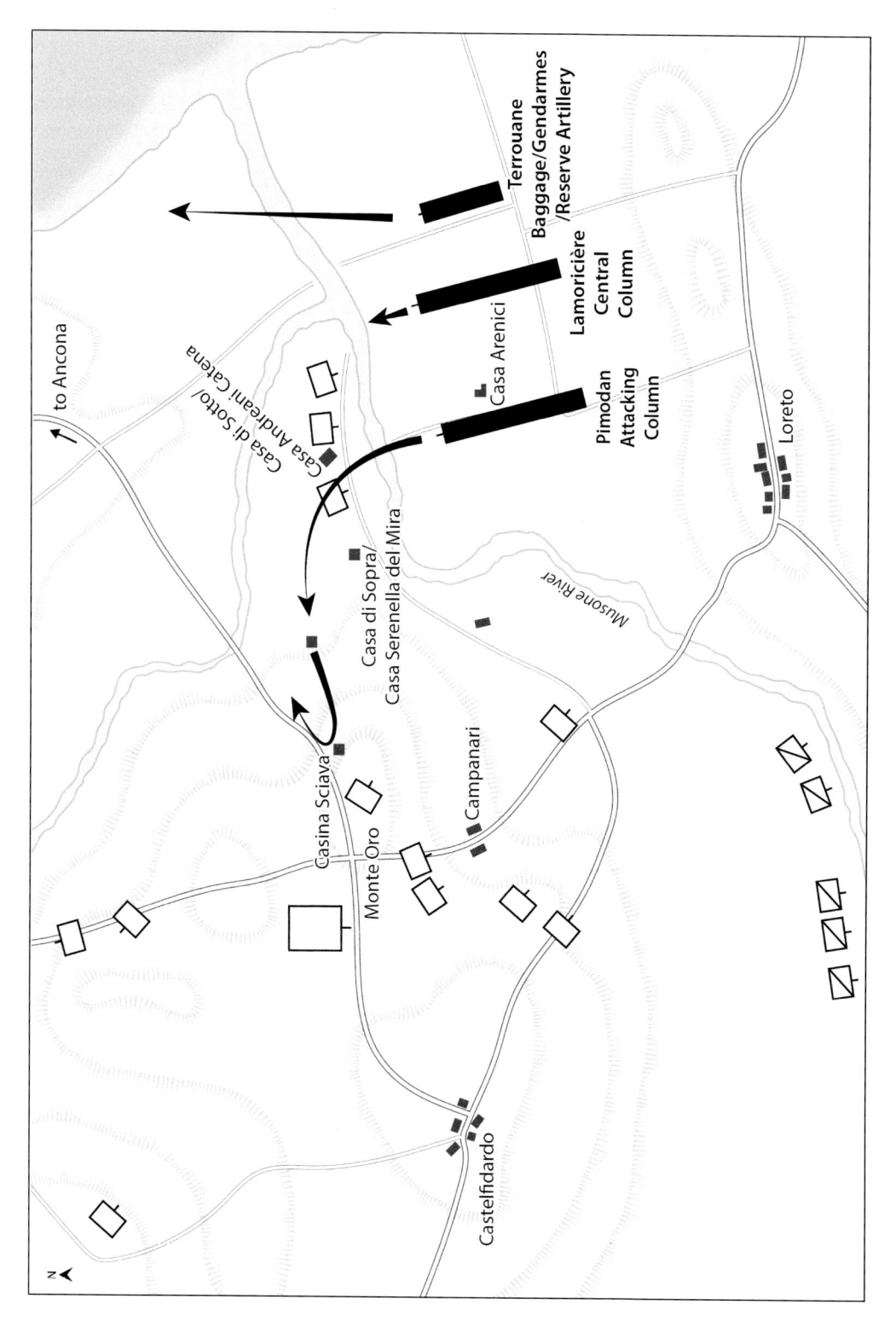

64   VICTORIAN CRUSADERS

The Battle of Castelfidardo, 18 September 1860.

holding the Lower Farm counter-attacked, aiming to push back the advance and capture the cannon that was then being brought across the river. The Irish Company mounted a valiant defence and killed a Bersaglieri officer, Captain Nullo. As the pontifical troops poured onto the banks, the Piedmontese withdrew first to the Lower Farm and then to the Upper Farm.

The early stages of the battle seemed successful for Pimodan. There had been a temporary setback when, due to the 'fog of war', the 2nd Indigenous Cacciatori accidentally fired upon the Foreign Carabineers, leading to the dismissal on the spot of Major Ubaldini and a short delay in the advance. Moreover, the opening shots from the Pontifical Artillery, now safely across the Musone, alerted the Piedmontese command to the unfolding battle. Nevertheless, by 10.30 a.m. the Lower Farm was secured, and preparations made for the next objective: the Upper Farm.

Once again, this needed to happen quickly before Piedmontese reinforcements arrived. The distance was not far but the papal troops had to advance uphill under heavy fire from the Piedmontese, who were protected by the Upper Farm's walls and buildings. Hyacinth de Lanasol, a Franco-Belgian, wrote:

> There was great disorder just then, bullets whizzing around by thousands; the air was actually burning. … We were all in the open country – not a tree to shelter us. Whilst I was loading, one of ours, a Breton named Alfred du Bandiez fell, struck by a ball in the region of the heart, and at the same time I was struck in the left calf. I discharged my musket, and as I could still walk, I advanced to reload it again. I had not gone far when I was struck by a second ball in the same leg, which slackened my pace a little, but did not stop me; but again, as I levelled my gun, a third ball

A *carte de visite*, printed in Loreto during the 1860s, depicting the battle at its height. (Private collection, author's photograph)

struck me in the same leg (it seems the Piedmontese were determined on having this leg), and I fell like a clod of earth.[9]

Pimodan's men had nearly reached the summit of Montoro, crowned by the Casina Sciava, a strong strategic position that could be held for a long period. However, at this moment, two battalions of the 10th Regiment and a battery of guns arrived as reinforcements from Crocette. The Piedmontese mounted a charge and Pimodan did his best to rally his men. As the two sides fiercely fought around the Upper Farm, Pimodan was injured first in the jaw, then in the foot and finally, most seriously, in the chest. He repeated the words, 'Courage, my children, God is with us!' and begged to be given the honour of dying on the battlefield. It was undoubtedly a turning point in the battle, affecting the morale of his troops and the strategy of Lamoricière.

The Irish had hauled at least one artillery piece to the Upper Farm, where they joined in the fierce fighting. Despite being armed with obsolete muskets and exhausted after days of marching, their conduct won praise from Lamoricière. Lieutenant D'Arcy, later to become a significant figure in the Zouaves, was awarded for his gallantry. 'The Sons of St Patrick,' reported Russell-Killough, who was himself stationed at Ancona, 'did not retreat until it was no longer possible to advance.'[10]

The later stage of the battle, as the arrival of Piedmontese infantry and artillery reinforcements drive back the pontifical troops. (Lithograph from *Album Storico–Artistico della Guerra d'Italia*, Torino: C. Perrin, 1860, private collection, author's photograph)

---

9   Ségur, *Martyrs of Castelfidardo*, pp.189–190.
10 Russell-Killough, *Dix Années*, p.163 (author's translation).

The papal troops were eventually forced back from the Montoro to the Upper Farm, part of which was now ablaze. Riding to the Lower Farm to see what was happening, Lamoricière saw Pimodan being carried away mortally wounded. It was perhaps this sight as well as the reluctance to abandon his comrades that encouraged him at this juncture to join in the fray. His objective now shifted to holding on to his position rather than ensuring that as many men and equipment as possible reached Ancona. It would prove to be a fateful decision. He ordered the remaining sections of Pimodan's column that had stayed behind at the Lower Farm to advance forward, while his own central column formed a second line in their place. These included two battalions of the 1st Foreign Infantry Regiment, the 2nd Battalion of the 2nd (Indigenous) Infantry Regiment and a squadron of cavalry.

The central column had hoped to be on the road by now and instead found themselves coming within range of Piedmontese artillery. In the confusion many of the units panicked and fled, despite the best efforts of Lamoricière and his aides. Some of Pimodan's men who were about to advance uphill were themselves affected by the mass desertion, such as the Indigenous Cacciatori, whose comrades were bravely fighting at the Upper Farm.

The collapse of a large proportion of the Pontifical Army would be remembered with anger by those who had continued to fight, including the Franco-Belgians and the Irish, and with glee by opponents of the Pope. At the time it was, of course, a fatal blow to Lamoricière's chances of success. Pimodan's men were isolated and increasingly desperate, especially as further Piedmontese reinforcements arrived. They were forced to withdraw to the Lower Farm, where there was fierce hand-to-hand fighting and a brief

The Sacrario-Ossario dei Caduti della Battaglia, erected on the Castelfidardo battlefield. (Photograph: Nicoletta Lampa)

moment of hope when a battalion of Austrians arrived from the reserve. Many of the men escaped across the Musone, arriving in tatters at Loreto. General Fanti wrote in his report that they were 'compelled to retire in disorder upon Loretto, leaving on the battlefield their artillery, their ammunition carts, arms, and knapsacks without end, which had been thrown away by their soldiers in their flight, as well as all their dead and wounded'.[11] As Mizael de Pas lay on his hospital deathbed and heard of the defeat, he exclaimed 'What a misfortune! What a misfortune!' and 'remained plunged in a mournful silence'.[12] A handful of troops remained at the Lower Farm, defending the wounded who were sheltered there, including Pimodan, and withstanding three assaults. They eventually surrendered and the ailing general died at a Piedmontese aid station that night.

Papal supporters came to speak of a massacre rather than a battle and the fallen as 'martyrs'. Not only Pimodan but many of the noble Catholic youth of France lay dead or dying, their names resembling, it was said, a guest list at a ball in the time of Louis XIV. Alfred de la Barre de Nanteuil, who had lost his boots in the river, was found lying on his back, with his arms extended, his body riddled with bullet and bayonet wounds. Hyacinth De Lanasol, who had been struck three times in his left leg in the advance to the Upper Farm, died of his wounds on 20 October. A former seminarian from Nantes, Joseph Guérin, was found unconscious on the battlefield after being struck in the breast. He was brought to Osimo, where he died seven weeks later and gained a particular reputation for sanctity. 'How happy I am,' he often repeated in hospital, 'to suffer and die slowly for Jesus Christ and his Church!'[13]

Although the pontifical forces claimed to be heavily outnumbered, Emilio Castelli, then working on Cialdini's staff, later argued that, when the size of the Piedmontese forces actually engaged was taken into account, their advantage was only 5:4.[14] Fanti asserted that only 2,525 Piedmontese were engaged in the fighting, though, of course, the presence of a much larger force that could have been called into operation necessarily affected strategy and morale.[15] Official reports state that Lamoricière lost 88 men, with over 400 wounded (around 20 percent of those engaged); Cialdini counted 62 dead and 140 wounded. Irish casualties are estimated to have been between 20 and 30, including Nicholas Furey of Limerick and Eugene McSweeney, both serving with the Franco-Belgians.[16] Such figures perhaps do not do justice to the catastrophic nature of the defeat, especially with the collapse of so many of the papal troops towards the end of the battle.

The problem lay not only in the discipline of the troops. The work of Renato Biondini has stressed the decisiveness of the Piedmontese artillery in the action: not only were they numerically superior but, thanks to recent improvements, the pieces were rifled, in contrast to the old smooth-bore guns used by the papal troops, allowing a greater speed and accuracy of fire.[17] But this was not the only reason for the papal defeat. Lamoricière made a series of major tactical errors. Initially, as his troops advanced to Ancona, he held a slight advantage but the detour to Porto Recanati and then his decision to wait for Pimodan at Loreto proved costly and enabled IV Corps to consolidate their position. On 18 September Lamoricière overestimated the strength of the Piedmontese left flank and might possibly have succeeded in proceeding

---

11 *The Tablet*, 27 October 1860, p.681.
12 Ségur, *Martyrs of Castelfidardo*, p.54.
13 Ségur, *Martyrs of Castelfidardo*, p.215.
14 Anon., *Ai Vittoriosi di Castelfidardo* (Rome: Numero Speciale a Cura del 'Picenum' Autorizzato dal Comitato Pro Monumnto, 1932), p.15.
15 *The Scotsman*, 22 October 1860, p.4.
16 Berkeley, *Irish Battalion*, pp.188–189.
17 Renato Biondini, *I cannoni dell'Unità d'Italia. Le nuove artiglierie nelle campagne militari del 1859–1861* (Ancona: Edizioni Affinità Elettive, 2018).

to Ancona without committing Pimodan's column (already exhausted after days of marching) to a risky offensive. The division of Pimodan's men into two also reduced its effectiveness: Massimo Coltrinari has argued that had Pimodan's column crossed the Musone as a whole, they would have initially had an advantage of 5:1.[18] Then, there was the critical error of sending the central column to support Pimodan when the priority was to get the troops to Ancona.

Lamoricière had not had enough time to form and train his army. The panic of the central column in the latter stages of the battle revealed their inexperience and lack of discipline. Moreover, the aftermath of Castelfidardo revealed substantial divisions within the papal forces. The Swiss caught up in the 'friendly fire' incident after crossing the Musone accused the Indigenous Cacciatori of treachery and jealousy. Moreover, rumours abounded the Pimodan had been mortally wounded not by a Piedmontese bullet but an assassin within the papal ranks, 'specially enlisted … by Culetti, Cavour's notorious agent'.[19]

Lamoricière tried to collect the remnants of his forces and send them towards the safety of Ancona before the route was cut off. Some units disintegrated in the chaos. The Marquis de Chérisey found himself separated from his Franco-Belgian comrades and ended up marching a small group of Swiss and Austrians to Rome. Meanwhile, the survivors who had reached Loreto eventually capitulated and were allowed to march from the town honourably, still bearing their arms, which were then deposited at Recanati. They were treated courteously; a dinner was even held at which Piedmontese and Pontifical officers sat side by side. Within two days many of the former papal troops were homeward bound.

---

18   Coltrinari, *Il Combattimento di Loreto*, p.169.
19   Coltrinari, *Il Combattimento di Loreto*, p.161 (author's translation). This was almost certainly not the case, although the claim was made in many pro-papal sources.

6

Last Stand at Ancona

The Battle of Castelfidardo is often portrayed as the decisive defeat of Pius IX's army that helped unify Italy and yet it was not the end of the campaign. Lamoricière had not surrendered at Castelfidardo and later that day reached the port of Ancona, telling the governor, Colonel de Quatrebarbes, that he no longer had an army. Further survivors reached the port on subsequent days, including the enterprising Lieutenant Uhde who had rescued two guns from the battlefield and found an obliging fisherman to take them to Ancona on his boat, despite the presence of Piedmontese ships on the Adriatic.

Ancona was an important port and the Pope's second city now that Bologna had been lost; until 1859 it had been under Austrian protection and the most likely place for an Austrian army to land. Support from Napoleon III was also expected; shortly after arriving, the French Consul showed a despatch sent him by the Ambassador in Rome indicating that troops were embarking from Toulon and condemning the 'culpable aggression' of the Piedmontese. Lamoricière later reported: 'Yet the prolonged bombardment of Ancona did not bring a single vessel to our aid, not even from those neutral powers who, under similar circumstances, generally send ships to protect their own Consulates and men of their own nations.'[1]

The name 'Ancona' derives from the Greek word for 'elbow', since the harbour is formed by an elbow-shaped promontory, making it one of the few coastal towns where both sunrise and sunset can be seen over the sea. On the highest point of the city was the Citadella, originally built for Clement VII. The magnificent Arch of Trajan was a reminder of the city's ancient past, while a more modern arch had been built in honour of Clement XII who declared Ancona a free port in 1738. Another notable eighteenth-century structure was the Lazzaretto, a pentagonal structure built at the bottom of the harbour for the quarantining of passengers and cargoes. Two stone piers or moles stretched out into the sea, at the end of one of which was a small, fortified lighthouse (*Lanterna*), built in 1784, which had an unrivalled range of fire in three directions. As the Piedmontese approached in September 1860, poles were sunk into the seabed and a large chain stretched across the two moles to prevent enemy shipping from approaching – the last time this well-tried method of defence would be used.

The city's fortifications had in recent months been strengthened, although the work was not yet finished. Despite its imposing location and numerous walls and forts, Ancona was not ready for a nineteenth-century siege. The 129 smooth-bore guns available to Lamoricière were old and out-ranged by the Piedmontese rifled artillery, both on land and sea. When the Austrian garrison had withdrawn the previous year, Cardinal Antonelli turned down the opportunity to purchase 60 pieces of modern artillery since his emphasis was on diplomacy rather than armament. If this offer had been taken up, Lamoricière's hand would have been much strengthened. Nevertheless, the pieces were distributed as follows: Campo Trincerato 29, Cappuccini

---

1 Besson, *Mérode*, pp.154–155.

10, Cittadella 25 (and 2 in reserve), Corte di S. Domenico 4, Lazzaretto 3, Lanterna 12, Lunetta Santo Stefano 5, Molo 4, Montata 6, Monte Gardetto (Cardeto) 10, Monte Marano 5, Porta Pia 6, Ripa 3, Sanità 3 and S. Agostino 2.

The garrison was thinly spread and, with news of the defeats at Perugia, Spoleto and Castelfidardo, demoralised. Included among their number were four Irish companies, under Captains Guttemberg, O'Carroll, O'Mahony and Russell. One company were based at the Citadella and the three others were stationed on the line of defences outside, covering strategic points such as the Lunette Santo Stefano.

Lamoricière was determined to do his duty and make a stand. Ordered to an outpost outside the city walls, Captain Russell recalled the jumpiness of his men, especially at night: 'If one puts oneself in the place of these peasants of only twenty years old, suddenly brought face to face with a real and unceasing danger, and finding themselves five hundred yards from all help, away alone in the middle of the deserted countryside – to say nothing of the burden of individual responsibility which was new to them.'[2] On one occasion the alarm was raised that the Piedmontese were mounting a surprise attack by night until it emerged that the sentry had mistaken falling stars for enemy rockets.

On 19 September, Albert De La Hoyde wrote to his mother in Dublin:

> The town is full of soldiers; they are quartered in the churches, theatres, &c., and many on straw in the streets. … They say the General will have Ancona a mass of ruins before he'll surrender, so we may make up our souls and prepare for our fate. I hope yet to be spared to see again my dear parents, sisters, brothers, and friends; however, as the Turks say, 'God is great, and what will be will be.' The odds against us are terrible; I fear few of us will live to tell the tale.[3]

By this time seven Piedmontese warships (six steam and one sail) had appeared, with supporting craft, on the Adriatic, under the command of Admiral Carlo Pellion di Persano. At first there were hopes that this was the long-awaited Austrian or French fleet, but they started bombarding the port on 18 September. Russell-Killough described how the naval artillery muffled the distant cannons from the battlefield of Castelfidardo and how, as he watched the graceful frigates from his outpost, he had little idea of the 'massacre' taking place just 13 miles away. If it had not been for the contrary direction of the wind and the Piedmontese ships, he surmised, the Ancona garrison might have decisively intervened in the battle and the Irish granted a share in the glory.[4]

The three sections of the Piedmontese Army were finally ready to mount an offensive on Ancona by 24 September: Cialdini's IV Corps, the victors of Castelfidardo; Fanti's V Corps, which had triumphed at Perugia and Spoleto and since then been marching through Umbria on Lamoricière's tail; and Cadorna's 13th Division, acting as a central column. All in all, around 34,000 men stood against the garrison of 5,700. The bombardment continued. According to an account approved by two Irish veterans:

> Imagine the Citadel on the highest part of the cliff – a huge block of massive red-brick bastions, jutting out at strange angles to dominate the town. In it is a company of the Irish who look down all day on the houses and on the soft blue of the Adriatic below, as blue as the sea at Killarney on a fine day, now dotted with frigates and men-of-war, from whose sides come puffs of white smoke as they bombard the batteries in the port, or send a message upwards. From the land, too,

---

2   Berkeley, *Irish Battalion*, p.197.
3   *The Tablet*, 13 October 1860, p.652.
4   Russell-Killough, *Dix Années*, p.159 (author's translation).

it is bombarded; from the ridges of the Umbrian hills which look rather like successive lines of incoming breakers on a rough day. Upon that summit the Irish are at post all day, in the blazing sun. during the first attacks they have leisure to watch the artillery duel beneath them, but as the siege wears on, and the enemy come closer, their own position becomes more and more dangerous; at times they are shelled from three points at once, and then the smoke goes up from the old Citadel as from a cauldron. ... As a general rule the hours drag on slowly under this continuous dropping of missiles, which is not accompanied by great loss of life, but, like all shell fire, is very trying to the nerves![5]

According to the governor, Colonel de Quatrebarbes, the Irish 'greeted each volley with a cheer for Pius IX, and sang in chorus the old ballads of their mountains, and shouted challenges at the Piedmontese'.[6] Nevertheless there were casualties: Daniel Gorman was shot through the shoulder, part of Private Nevin's foot was blown off and Andrew O'Beirne's leg was shattered. When he was taken to the surgeon for his leg to be amputated, he insisted on grasping his gun throughout the procedure, saying 'if I die, anyhow it'll be like a soldier'.[7] The English-born Madame Guttemberg showed much stoicism and tended to the wounded until her husband, a member of the Irish Battalion, insisted that she take shelter until the bombardment was over.

One by one the papal defences were weakened. The outpost on Monte Scrima, south of the city walls, was taken on 24 September. Two days later the village of Pietro della Croce and the important redoubts of Monte Pelago and Monte Pulito were lost. The Irish and Austrian defenders of the Santo Stefano redoubt managed to hold their positions but by this stage the Piedmontese controlled the outlying fortifications and were at the city walls. The morale of the garrison continued to decline; it was increasingly obvious that no French or Austrian force was about to appear. Even Lamoricière wavered in his confidence: 'The sovereigns of Europe may have abandoned Ancona but all the Catholic world is watching Ancona's defenders, and these defenders cannot without dishonour refuse to continue the fight so long as the ramparts and fortifications are intact.'[8]

There was a further blow on 28 September, when a small party of Bersaglieri landed and took the Lazzaretto almost without a fight. Taking advantage of the situation, that afternoon three Piedmontese ships started firing on the harbour defences, especially the *Lanterna*, with its 12 guns. The papal defenders did their best to fight back, even after the rampart and the lighthouse's upper structure were destroyed. In the final moments of the attack the *Vittorio Emmanuele*, commanded by Captain Albini, fired at the *Lanterna*, while still moving, at close range – a feat that was much remarked upon and considered without precedent in naval warfare. The white flag was raised around 5.30 p.m. Only 25 out of the *Lanterna*'s garrison of 150 survived and, as they emerged, an approaching officer thought they 'resembled demons more than soldiers. Their hair and their clothes were burned, their faces blackened and covered with blood and plaster.'[9] The officer in question, Captain Simon de Castella of the 1st Foreign Regiment, rushed to the top of the *Lanterna* and replaced the white flag with a yellow and white one. After making a quick escape, an enemy shell hit the powder magazine and the lighthouse was no more.

---

5 Berkeley, *Irish Battalion*, p.199 (footnote).
6 Berkeley, *Irish Battalion*, p.210. He died in Paris on the journey home.
7 Berkeley, *Irish Battalion*, p.212.
8 Alvarez, *The Pope's Soldiers*, pp.134–135.
9 Alvarez, *The Pope's Soldiers*, pp.134–135.

The guns ceased firing, a recognition of the decisiveness of the moment – the wall to which the great chain was attached had been blown to pieces and the way was now open for the Piedmontese to stream into the harbour. Lamoricière realised that he had lost most of his defences and that his garrison were outnumbered, outgunned and demoralised. Negotiations began for a truce. The Piedmontese insisted on an immediate capitulation and continued the pressure through bombardment until Lamoricière surrendered on 29 September, the Feast of St Michael. The garrison were permitted to march out of the city with full military honours. As the Irish troops were escorted out of the gates, they cried out 'Hurrah for the Pope!' One of the Piedmontese officers was heard to say, 'leave them, they are Irish', causing much mirth among the guards and a redoubling of the Irish cheers.[10]

On 3 October King Victor Emmanuel arrived in Ancona, where he stayed for seven days to bolster his authority. He visited Loreto and spent time with the wounded of Castelfidardo. Meanwhile, the high-ranking pontifical officers were put on board a ship, appropriately named the *Conte di Cavour*, while the rank-and-file were marched from Ancona to Genoa, the Irish under Lieutenant De La Hoyde. The local population often showed hostility: Berkeley recorded in 1914 that surviving veterans still had 'a naïve

'Prisoners of the Papal Army': Irish recruits on their way home. (*Illustrated Times*, 17 November 1860, Private collection, author's photograph)

---

10 Russell-Killough, *Dix Années,* p.195 (author's translation).

expression of surprise at this strange reception by a population whom they had come to defend'.[11] One reminisced that 'the people spat hatred on us'; another, an old farmer, said: 'it was wonderful how the people hated us. The Pope must have been hard on them.'

At Genoa there were further trials as they waited without money, clothing and sufficient food. The Pontifical Government eventually arranged for a French vessel, the *Byzantin*, to transport them to Marseilles, and much kindness was shown by a Piedmontese general whose name, De Boyle, betrayed his Celtic roots. The Irish Committee raised funds for the rest of the journey. In Paris there were reports of the standing ovation of the crowds though the Irish found themselves being plundered for mementoes of the campaign and spoke of 'the tax the Parisians forcibly levied off them, particularly the females – they should have the buttons as souvenirs of the Irish Brigade'. Many of them arrived home with buttonless coats.[12]

For Berkeley, the Siege of Ancona , though 'somewhat tedious' in its narrative, 'will always be remembered because it marks the final passing away of the ancient historic Papal State' and was 'the first siege in which a fleet of steamers used rifled guns for shelling forts'.[13] It was an early victory for what would shortly become the Italian Regia Marina, and even the British naval authorities studied the unique and audacious action that led to the destruction of the *Lanterna*. Reporting to King Victor Emmanuel, General Fanti summarised the impressive victory he had achieved: '[I]n 18 days we won the places of Pesaro, Urbino, Perugia, Spoleto, San Leo, and Ancona. There fell into our hands 28 field pieces, 160 pieces of wall artillery, 20,000 muskets, more than 500 horses, and from 17,000 to 18,000 prisoners, with all the enemy's generals.'[14] Moreover, the victories at Castelfidardo and Ancona enabled the king to personally lead his army southwards, where he met Garibaldi at Teano and went on to besiege Gaeta, the last stronghold of the Bourbons, with the naval support of Admiral Persano. The campaign thus gained for Piedmont not only a large part of the Papal States but also the former Kingdom of the Two Sicilies, which had a lasting impact on the creation of modern Italy.

---

11 IE/DDA 274/2/6, 'The Irish in the Papal Service in 1860', p.9.
12 *Freeman's Journal*, 5 November 1860, p.3.
13 Berkeley, *Irish Battalion*, pp.191–192.
14 *The Tablet*, 27 October 1860, p.681.

7

Legacy and Continuity

Most of the major European powers condemned the aggression of Piedmont. Monsignor Talbot, writing from the Vatican, thought 'the conduct of France and Piedmont is the most iniquitous outrage of all the principles of honesty and justice I have ever heard of. All sense of equity, of justice, of regard for the Law of nations is a dead letter.'[1] However, the British Government, though officially neutral, expressed pleasure at Piedmont's success. On 27 October, Russell sent a despatch to Sir James Hudson, the British Minister at Turin, comparing the House of Savoy's overthrow of the oppressive papal regime to the similar 'liberation' effected in Britain by the House of Orange in 1688. He continued:

> Her Majesty's Government can see no sufficient ground for the severe censure with which Austria, France, Prussia and Russia have visited the acts of the King of Sardinia. Her Majesty's Government will turn their eyes rather to the gratifying prospect of a people building up the edifice of their liberties, and consolidating the work of their independence, amid the sympathies and good wishes of Europe.

Although the Queen prohibited the Foreign Secretary from sending a further despatch, appealing for the cessation of Rome and Venice to the new Italy, the document was widely publicised and apparently reduced Cavour to tears.[2]

Unofficial negotiations were even begun between Piedmont and the Holy See and a memorandum passed to the Pope suggesting that in return for the abolition of the Temporal Power the Church could be granted absolute independence. Pius asked Antonelli to consider the proposal, but it was rejected.

The Homecoming of the Irish

The majority of the Irish volunteers arrived at Queenstown (now Cobh) on the paddle steamer *Dee* on 3 November. The crossing from Le Havre had had its moments of drama, including a fire that broke out near the engine room, but all was calm by the time the Old Head of Kinsale was spotted. The first welcome was provided by cheers from a fleet of fishing boats. There had been some uncertainty about the exact time of the Battalion's arrival and expectant crowds had lined the quay several days previously. However, once word spread that the *Dee* was pulling into harbour, with papal flag flying, 'crowds rushed to all the good

---

1 AAW Wiseman Papers, Talbot to Pattison, 29 September 1860.
2 O.J. Wright, *Great Britain and the Unifying of Italy: A Special Relationship?* (Basingstoke: Palgrave Macmillan, 2019), pp.53–54.

LANDING OF A PORTION OF THE PAPAL BRIGADE AT CORK.

The return of the Irish Battalion in October 1860 attracted large crowds. (*Illustrated Times*, 17 November 1860, Private collection, author's photograph)

points of view along the water's edge, while the windows overlooking the harbour, and many of the heights rising behind the town, were occupied by spectators'. The steamer *Willing Mind* went out with a welcome committee, two bands, clean clothing and packages containing 'an excellent breakfast' for each man. After their recent experiences, it was little wonder that they wore an assortment of clothing:

> Some wore the Zouave red trousers and white leggings, which had been given them in the Papal States, with the long bluish coat, the cut of which reminded us of the uniform coat of the Russian infantry in the Crimean war. Others had red trousers and jackets of many colours, while a great many turned out with frock coats, overcoats &c., having an unmistakeably French style about them, and for which they are indebted to the generosity of the Parisians.

John Francis Maguire, MP for Dungarvan, accompanied by Alexander Sullivan of the Central Committee, gave a speech acknowledging their bravery and defending them from their critics. 'Catholic Ireland,' he said, 'hails you as the champions of a cause dear to her heart.' As the men came ashore on the steam tugs, they were 'seized upon, cheered, embraced and carried about, and the women kissed them, and prayed every blessing upon their heads'. They marched to the Young Men's Society Room on Castle Street and eventually dispersed by train to different parts of Ireland, where there were further celebrations.[3]

---

3   *Freeman's Journal*, 5 November 1860, p.3.

The tone of the Protestant British press was largely critical. The cowardice and desertion of some of the papal troops was laughed at and the whole cause dismissed as hopeless and foolish. *The Times* criticised Lamoricière for being 'beaten upon his own ground, and upon a field of his own choice', proving that 'he is only good to smoke out Arabs and drill Irish mercenaries'. As for the returning Irish, 'the best thing they can now do is to steal back to their homes and hide themselves; they will serve as a warning to their neighbours against temptations by recruiting priests'.[4] They returned to diverse occupations and some helped each other in finding new careers: almost all the members of the Dublin Fire Brigade, newly organised in 1862, were old papal soldiers.[5]

Subscriptions were organised for the returning heroes and in England a Lamoricière Testimonial Fund was opened. Across Ireland there were celebrations. When Major and Mrs O'Reilly arrived at Balbriggan Station, inhabitants illuminated their windows, lit a large bonfire, set off fireworks and drew his carriage along the streets. A banquet was later organised for him at the City Assembly Rooms in Wexford. O'Reilly soon reminded the Holy See of the need for members of the battalion to receive recognition for their loyalty and bravery. He had come across several instances of foreign officers who 'in vain endeavoured to acquire and recollect the, to them strange, names of those who particularly attracted their admiration'.[6] On 12 November the Pope instituted the distinctive '*Pro Petri Sede*' ('For the See of Peter') medal, with its upturned cross of St Peter, for those who had served in the campaign. There was some confusion in the distribution of medals in Ireland, with one batch being sent to John Pope Hennessy, MP for King's County.

On his return to Ireland, Major O'Reilly reflected on his old unit: 'Ireland looked to them as a purely national corps to support the honour of their race' and even those who disagreed with the cause were 'anxious that the military reputation of Irishmen should not suffer in their hands'. Pride was taken in their good conduct. The Piedmontese General Brignone called them 'honourable and brave soldiers' and it was reported that, at Ancona, Lamoricière told his officers that if all the troops at Castelfidardo had fought like the Franco-Belgians and Irish, the battle would have been won.[7]

Catholic Martyrs

For Catholics, the fallen soldiers were martyrs. General de Pimodan was buried at the French church in Rome, San Luigi. The Pope defrayed the funeral expenses, and the epitaph speaks of him being 'wasteful of his great life' for the sake of the Holy See. One of the Franco-Belgians, Paul de Parcevaux, was buried in the basilica of Loreto but, in accordance with his wishes, his heart was taken back to Chateau Tronjoly in western Brittany. After three days resting at the family home, it was borne in solemn procession to the nearby church; on the urn was placed the Cross of the Order of Pius IX, sent him by the Pope as he lay on his deathbed, and a white crown.

The battle was given a further spiritual dimension by the fact that it was fought near the Pope's birthplace of Senigallia and in the shadow of Loreto. The battlefield was considered by some as an extension to the shrine complex. Despite the lack of a monument to the pontifical troops, the Marquis de Ségur recorded that locals would make 'a hasty sign of the cross' as they passed by, saying in a low voice, 'This is the field of martyrs!'[8] While on pilgrimage in 1863, Catherine Straker felt duty bound to visit the battlefield,

---

4   *The Times*, 20 September 1860, p.8.
5   O'Malley Baines, *My Life in Two Hemispheres*, p.18.
6   *The Tablet*, 15 December 1860, p.800.
7   *Cork Examiner*, 14 January 1861, p.4.
8   Ségur, *Martyrs of Castelfidardo*, p.147.

'remembering the heroes who fought there, for St Peter and his See'; it was the eve of the anniversary and she did her best to ignore the patriotic tricolours.[9] When an Irish pilgrimage was organised to Rome in the papal jubilee year of 1893 they stopped at Loreto. The former chaplain of the Irish volunteers, Dr McDevitt, was able to point out to pilgrims 'the very spot where lie "the soldiers and chiefs of the Irish Brigade"'.[10]

In Ireland, the dead were eulogised in sermons and prayed for at requiem masses. The obsequies at Dublin's Pro-Cathedral, attended by no fewer than six bishops, were considered the most magnificent held of their kind since those for Daniel O'Connell in 1847. The requiem at St Michael's Church in Gorey, County Wexford, featured a large catafalque erected before the altar:

> From the four corners of the framework arose aloft and depending four flagstaffs supporting banners of silk in the national colours of the Pontifical States, elegantly decorated and fringed with gold trimming. On one was inscribed in bold and distinct characters, 'Perugia'; on another, 'Castel Fidardo'; on a third, 'Loretto'; and on the fourth, 'Spoleto'. In the centre, rising perpendicularly, and elevated above all, was a Standard, whose lofty summit was tipped with the tiara and cross keys, the arms of the Sovereign Pontiff; and depending from which was a large banner of green, on which was inscribed in silver letters the ever-memorable reply of Ireland's cherished son and his gallant little band to the besieging host, 'The Irish in the service of the Pope can die but not surrender!'[11]

In London, a similar mass was sung at St Patrick's Church in Soho Square, which was seen as the mother church of London's Irish. It was reportedly so crammed that '500 candidates for admission were sent away after every nook and cranny had been filled up'. Cardinal Wiseman sent a message speaking of 'the indignation of all good Catholics at the base treachery to which the Holy Father has been subjected by his own children' and the courage of 'his faithful troops'. His eventual successor as Archbishop of Westminster, Monsignor Manning, preached a fiery sermon that made a link between the fallen soldiers and the medieval martyr, St Thomas of Canterbury, who both died for the Church's sovereignty: 'a common cause should win a common crown.'[12]

Anger was vented towards the politicians who had supported the invasion through diplomatic means. In a sermon in Tuam, Father James Waldron spoke of 'the traitorous conduct of that arch-hypocrite Napoleon, the lawlessness of the infidels of Europe, and the infamous diplomatic trickery of their Anglican and French abettors'.[13] Palmerston and Russell came in for especial criticism. The former was 'famous for his life-long efforts to uproot every Catholic dynasty in Europe'; the second, through his celebrated despatch to Hudson, 'had done more for the Revolution than even an army would have done, by giving all the moral force of this great country to the robberies and villanies of the revolutionists'.[14]

---

9   KIR/1863/279, Straker to Kirby, 28 October 1863.
10 Reverend J. Nolan, *History of the Irish Pilgrimage to Rome; or, Notes on the Way* (London: Burns & Oates, 1893), p.61.
11 *The Tablet*, 13 October 1860, p.652.
12 *The Tablet*, 13 October 1860, p.644.
13 *The Tablet*, 13 October 1860, p.652.
14 *The Tablet*, 1 December 1860, pp.756–757.

The Situation in Rome and Military Reform

With much of the Papal States annexed to Piedmont, Pius IX now found himself with only a third of his previous territory.[15] The invasion of 1860 placed under a spotlight the dangers facing the Holy See. If Rome itself had been preserved, thanks largely to the unreliable protection of France, it was only a matter of time before it would be threatened again. The Pope was more determined than ever not only to regain his lost territory, which had been part of his patrimony for time immemorial, but to hang on to what he still had. Compromise could not be an option.

There was confusion in Rome about what would happen next. The rector of the Venerable English College, Louis English, spoke for many when he wrote to Cardinal Wiseman, 'we are like everyone else, mystified and bewildered'; the French Emperor's intentions were mistrusted and he looked upon it 'as certain that the Piedmontese will have Rome very soon'.[16]

Lamoricière produced a report of the recent campaign and met with the Pope, who thanked him for his services and offered him the title of Papal Count. This he refused, though he consented to remain commander-in-chief and receive the Pontifical Order of Christ. However, he returned to his home in France to recover from the trauma of defeat and declined the offer of a ceremonial sword by Napoleon III in recognition of his leadership. This was not only because of his Legitimist leanings but, as he explained:

> A sword of honour is given to a general for a great victory, for the capture of a strongly defended town by assault, or for having valiantly defended and held a fortress besieged by the enemy beyond the time when resistance seemed possible. Now, as is too well known, I have done nothing of the short. The provinces I was defending have been invaded; the towns taken; our war materiel is lost; and the whole army has been carried into captivity. … But I cannot forget that a General who has done nothing but save the honour of his flag, does not deserve, and cannot receive, any reward.[17]

He continued as commander of the pontifical forces until his death in 1865 but only in name.

There were conflicting schools of thought within the curia as to how matters should proceed. Cardinal Antonelli put his faith in international law and the protection provided by France. There was no point building up a Papal Army that, in itself, could do little to oppose the might of an increasingly united Italy – a point that Castelfidardo seemed to prove. What papal troops there were would be useful in maintaining order within the Papal States and securing the person of the Holy Father.

Mérode, however, favoured a policy of army reform and expansion, despite the odds stacked against him. He set about rebuilding Rome's shattered military infrastructure. He established a military wing in the hospital at Santo Spirito in Sassia (with 500 beds), as well as a school for the soldiers' children, both entrusted to the Sisters of Charity of St Vincent de Paul. Mérode visited the school regularly, knowing many of the children by name and delighting in the workshop where the girls excelled in needlework, using 'a number of sewing machines, the first that had been seen in Rome'.[18] An 'arsenal for military construction' was also established; Mérode wrote in October 1861: 'We have set up two steam-engines which work a vertical saw as well as a circular one, and other machines to work and polish iron. With all

---

15 In 1860 the Papal States was reduced from 17,000 to 5,000 square miles; the population declined from 2.5 million to less than 700,000.
16 AAW Wiseman Papers W3/17/156, English to Wiseman, 10 November 1860.
17 Besson, *Mérode*, p.164.
18 Besson, *Mérode*, p.174.

this we can do a quantity of fresh things, which keep alive our men, develop their intelligence, and enable our little Pontifical Army to pride itself on its progress. Our soldiers feel that the public no longer consider them good for nothing.'[19]

Mérode was comfortable in coming to terms with the demands of modernity. This could be seen not only in his army reforms but in his urban planning, which even won the praise of Hausmann, the celebrated renovator of Paris. Realising that the effective centre of Rome would be shifted eastwards with the opening of the railway station, the Monsignor was quick to purchase real estate in the area and plan its development. In 1862 he bought land outside the Porta Pia to form a camp and field for army manoeuvres, near the site that would see the Pontifical Army's last stand eight years later.[20]

The post-1860 Pontifical Army would be smaller in size. Gone were the two Swiss or 'Foreign' line regiments, the squadron of Guides and the Irish Battalion of St Patrick. The infantry was reorganised into two line battalions and a battalion of Cacciatori, both of which were made up of indigenous troops. The Austrian Bersaglieri were briefly arranged into a battalion which was disbanded soon afterwards. Added to this were a battalion of Foreign Carabineers (raised to a regiment in February 1868), two squadrons of Dragoons (one for indigenous and the other for foreign recruits), artillery, engineers, gendarmes and a reserve force that was rarely mobilised. Of particular interest to this volume are the Company of St Patrick, a small unit which briefly existed as a continuation of the 1860 Irish Battalion, and the Pontifical Zouaves, which came to include recruits from across the Catholic World.

The Company of St Patrick, 1860–1862

Major O'Reilly reported to Rome as soon as he could after the end of the campaign and was granted separate audiences with the Pope, Antonelli and Mérode. The Pontiff hoped that 'as soon as the restoration of possessions of the Church should make it incumbent on him to provide for their defence, he might have a body of chosen Irishmen in his service'. O'Reilly was adamant that the Irish identity of the unit should continue, to the exclusion of all foreigners, and had himself intervened when an attempt was made to introduce Swiss officers of 'an indifferent character'. According to the Memorandum drawn up after his visit to Rome:

> [A]s a nucleus for future reorganisation, a depot exists in Rome, where about thirty men and non-commissioned officers have been allowed to return, with the view of being increased to a company, should the Pontifical Government desire it. Thus, through the knowledge these men will have acquired of the Italian language, and the internal economy of the service, will be obviated in advance every pretext for the introduction of foreigners to the future Battalion of St Patrick.[21]

Some of the Irish bishops were sceptical. Joseph Dixon, Archbishop of Armagh, had 'given up all interest in the Irish Brigade, because until Monsig. De Mérode will understand a little more of the Irish view on the matter it seems to me that it would be a mere waste of words to write or speak about it'.[22] There was a feeling that the immediate danger to the Pope was past and that the French provided protection in Rome.

---

19 Besson, *Mérode*, pp.174–175.
20 This was on the site of the Roman Castra Praetoria; it was often referred to as 'Macao' on account of the vineyard of that name belonging to the Jesuit Novitiate.
21 *The Tablet*, 15 December 1860, p.800.
22 KIR/2909, Dixon to Kirby, 26 February 1861.

Nevertheless, the nucleus mentioned by O'Reilly became the Company of St Patrick on 8 November 1860, initially under the command of Frank Russell of Killough and then Daniel J. Kiely of Waterford, and wearing the striking green and yellow uniforms, with blue collars, promised to the volunteers of 1860. The Company are sometimes wrongly described as 'Irish Zouaves', though it normally served alongside this newly created corps, or even as being part of the Vatican Guard that protected the person of the Pope. The Irish were proud of their close connection with the pontiff and a letter to the *Tipperary Advocate* hoped that 'a stout Irish bodyguard may replace those four hundred Switzers who now pace the corridors and antechambers of the Vatican', who were 'but mercenaries' and at Castelfidardo had allegedly acted as 'traitorous beggars'.[23]

The remaining troops in Rome were proud of their Irish identity and growing reputation. As a sign of gratitude, they were given communion by the Pope at Christmas 1860 and were afterwards served 'not by the household servants but by the princes and peers of the church' with chocolate, coffee and ice cream.[24] Mérode told the Archbishop of Cincinnati, during a visit in 1861, that 'nothing could exceed their bravery in war, their devotion to Religion, or their good conduct at all times'.[25] Those who had been wounded and stayed in Rome became minor celebrities, such as Nicholas Furey, whose leg was amputated after Castelfidardo, and James Power, a humble private, was entertained at a special dinner by a Roman cardinal. He sent his own carriage to collect him and had him carried into the dining room by his servants.[26]

However, there was little opportunity for military action in the months following the campaign of 1860. In a letter of August 1861, the surgeon Philip O'Flynn reported that the company had been on garrison duty in the frontier town of Anagni since February. They were stationed with the Zouaves, with whom they were 'on the best terms of friendship and good feeling; in fact, since our return from Marseilles, we have accompanied them wherever they were sent'. Conditions were pleasant:

> [O]ur men have charge of one of the gates, and are exceedingly well-lodged in a very nice little barrack adjoining their post; they are perfectly free with the inhabitants, who show them on all occasions the greatest possible kindness. … They receive coffee twice a day, and a right good dinner of soup and meat, with whatever vegetables are going. They don't sleep on the ground, as in Spoleto, but actually enjoy the luxury of trussels with sack bottoms, but no paliases, as the weather is too warm. They are furnished with clean sheeting regularly every month, in fact they are as well cared for as the troops of any other army on the Continent.

Pay was augmented by the officers to five baiocchi a day (more than other papal troops) and the men were armed with the Minié rifle, an improvement on the old muskets used in 1860.[27]

The comparative boredom of drill and garrison duty made the opportunities presented by the American Civil War look highly attractive. The Secretary of State William H. Sew pursued a policy of seeking experienced European officers to serve the Union. John Hughes, Archbishop of New York, travelled to the Eternal City with this end in view and met with members of the Company of St Patrick. The Pope seems to have been happy to let his Irish volunteers leave Rome, confident that they would come back to his aid should the situation deteriorate.

---

23 *Kilkenny Journal*, 2 February 1861, p.3.
24 O'Malley Baines, *My Life in Two Hemispheres*, p.12.
25 *Carlow Post*, 16 November 1861, p.1.
26 *Kilkenny Journal*, 23 March 1861, p.2.
27 *Tipperary Vindicator*, 17 September 1861, p.4.

In November 1861, 15 members of the Company sent a group photograph of themselves to Colonel Meagher, the commander of the Irish Brigade fighting for the Union Army. Kiely enclosed a letter, written from Grottaferrata:

> [W]e take the opportunity of congratulating you and our brave fellows for the active part you and they are taking to uphold the majesty and independence of the Stars and Stripes, which has ever thrown its protecting folds over the expatriated sons of Ireland. They owe it their best allegiance, and we say with our whole hearts all honour, and wish success to the men who fight under it. We know it is the anxious desire of the enemies of our race to see it trampled in the dust, but that can never be as long as there are Irish soldiers to fight for its independence.[28]

In March 1862 Myles Keogh and Daniel Kiely both resigned their commissions and arrived in New York in early April. They met another old comrade from Rome, Joseph O'Keeffe, the nephew of the Bishop of Cork. All three were given the rank of captain in the Union Army and almost immediately saw active service. Kiely was seriously wounded leading the charge of the Ohio Cavalry at Port Republic on 9 June 1862 and eventually died of yellow fever in Louisiana. O'Keeffe and Keogh were eventually assigned to the staff of General John Buford; Keogh fought at Antietam, Fredericksburg, Brandy Station, and Gettysburg. After the war he famously gained a captain's commission in the 7th Cavalry and was killed alongside General Custer at the Battle of the Little Bighorn in 1876. It is said that his body was the only one not mutilated on the battlefield because the Indians respected the *Agnus Dei* that was hung around his neck as well as his *Pro Petri Sede* medal, which was taken by Sitting Bull as a memento of his brave adversary. His horse, Comanche, was considered the only U.S. survivor of the battle and at his death in 1891 was given a full military funeral.

Others followed. John Coppinger was wounded at Second Bull Run and Appomattox and eventually placed in command of the 5th New York Cavalry. Michael O'Connell, who had been awarded the Order of Pius IX, was killed at Reams Station while fighting for Corcoran's Irish Legion (155th New York).

Back in Rome, by June 1862 the Company of St Patrick had dwindled to 19 members;[29] on 30 September it was disbanded and a handful of its remaining members transferred to the Zouaves. Dubliner Henry Dunn, Thomas Fulham from Drogheda, William O'Brien of Elphin, James O'Reilly of Letterkenny, Thomas O'Shaughnessy of Kilrush, and Dennis Sullivan all left the Zouaves within a fortnight. Two quickly joined other units in the Pontifical Army: James Barrett transferred as a sergeant to the Foreign Carabineers and James Quirck to the Artillery. Barratt later returned to the Zouaves, as did O'Shaughnessy. The former commanding officer, Frank Russell-Killough, decided to transfer to the Foreign Carabineers, while the surgeon, Philip O'Flynn moved to the Hospital of San Spirito in Sassia. He joined the Zouaves as assistant surgeon in 1866 and was present during the campaigns of the following year, before moving to the Pontifical Artillery.

Five former members of the Company of St Patrick stayed with the Zouaves for a longer period.[30] The most remarkable continuities were James D'Arcy and Albert O'Reilly De La Hoyde, both of whom joined the Zouaves on 1 October 1862, rose to become captains and remained in pontifical service until the bitter end. They became highly respected individuals in the Eternal City. D'Arcy, in particular, was remembered for his 'courtesy and genial manner'; he 'moved in the most refined and elegant circles of Roman society,

---

28 *Morning Chronicle*, 12 February 1862, p.5.
29 *Newcastle Guardian and Tyne Mercury*, 28 June 1862, p.6.
30 Two of them fell ill and died in military hospitals: John Quin and Peter Diamond.

and no man was better known to strangers in the Eternal City. He was an accomplished linguist, speaking French, German and Italian with ease and fluency' and became 'intimately acquainted' with the exiled Neapolitan royal family. His connections led to his selection as an officer under the Emperor Maximilian in Mexico, which accounted for his absence from Rome in 1865 and 1866.[31]

The Irish played an important part in the campaign of 1860, seeing action in the main engagements and attempting to maintain a distinctive national unit in the Pontifical Army in the years that followed. Religious faith was undoubtedly key to the men's motivation but so was the desire to express their national identity in a cause that directly contradicted Protestant English sentiment. However, enthusiasm waned as no major follow-up operations were planned by the pontifical authorities and alternative theatres of military action opened up across the Atlantic. With the demise of the Company of St Patrick, the Irish continued to fight under the crossed keys, though in smaller numbers, and 179 Irishmen joined the Pontifical Zouaves – the most transnational of the units in Mérode's 'new army.'

---

31   *Freeman's Journal*, 30 May 1882, p.5.

Part II

The Pontifical Zouaves (1861–1870)

8

'Z' is for Zouave

The Pontifical Zouaves, the most glamourous and international unit of Pius IX's army, was formed out of the Franco-Belgian Tirailleurs on 1 January 1861. It saw itself as effectively the same unit; many writers confusingly refer to the Tirailleurs as 'Zouaves' and veteran associations celebrated the actions of 1860 as much as the battles of 1867 and 1870. To understand the inspiration behind the new unit, a brief excursus is needed into the origins of the Zouave soldier.

In 1830, in the closing days of Charles X's reign, the French captured Algiers and began to establish a 'Greater France' that would stretch from the Rhine to the Congo.[1] That August, tribesmen from the Kabylie highlands in northern Algeria offered their services to the French Army. They came from the Berber tribes of the Igawawen or Gawawa, called by the Arabs 'Zwawa' or 'Zouaoua', and had a fearsome reputation as mountain fighters.

The veteran French General Bertrand Clausel, who had served under the first Napoleon, organised these tribesmen into a battalion of 'Zouaves' and placed them under French officers. Their number increased and a second battalion raised. Their reputation grew; at the Siege of Constantine in 1837, for example, Zouaves could be seen in broad daylight and under enemy fire dragging to the summit of Mausourah 24-pounder artillery pieces that had become stuck in the mud. The Zouaves became increasingly Frenchified; by 1841, when the Zouaves were reorganised into three battalions, only one company from nine was formed from indigenous troops. The Zouaves became an elite, hand-picked unit of light infantry, the pride of France, while from 1854, African soldiers could join a separate regiment of Tirailleurs Algeriens or 'Turcos'.

The reasons for the popularity of the Zouaves among Europeans were hardly surprising. When Captain George B. McClellan of the United States 1st Cavalry produced a report based on his observations during the Crimean War, he wrote that the Zouaves were:

> the most reckless, self-reliant and complete infantry that Europe can produce. With his graceful dress, soldiery bearing and vigilant attitude, the Zouave at an outpost is the *beau* ideal of a soldier. … Their movements are the most light and graceful I have ever seen; their stride is long, but the foot seems scarcely to touch the ground, and the march is apparently made without effort or fatigue.[2]

---

1   Algeria remained an essential part of French identity until its independence in 1962.
2   Jean Joseph Gustave Cler, *The Zouave Officer. Reminiscences of an Officer of Zouaves: The 2nd Zouaves of the Second Empire on Campaign in North Africa and the Crimean War* (Driffield: Leonaur, 2010), p.iv.

According to one officer: 'They are proud of their uniform, which resembles that of no other corps; proud of their name, of an origin so singular and mysterious; proud of the daring act of gallantry, with which they are constantly enriching the history of their corps; and happy in the freedom which is permitted them, whether in garrison or on the march.'[3]

The uniform was highly distinctive, based on the native Berber dress and adapted for mountain warfare, with short jacket, baggy trousers and fez. It was thought by some to be 'at once the most striking and the most convenient soldier's uniform … well adapted for a hot climate, leaving the chest and limbs perfectly free, it still protects the wearer against sudden changes in temperature'.[4] Their *esprit de corps* bound them closely together like a family; indeed, following the Arab tradition, those messing together referred to themselves as belonging to the same 'tribe'. The commanding officer was known as the 'Father' and, it was said, 'many a simple private in these regiments would refuse to exchange his turban against even the stripes of a non-commissioned officer in any other corps'.[5] They were also depicted as examples of chivalry: on conducting a group of prisoners in Algeria, including women and children, it was reported that 'the brave Zouaves were as tender as sisters of charity, sharing their biscuits with those who were weak, and when their goat-skins were empty, throwing over a she-goat, that the children might drink of its milk'.[6]

Zouaves were among the most decorated French troops during the period and attracted the attention of the world during the Crimean War. Here they proved that they could fight not only in the mountains of Algeria but on a 'European' battlefield. How strange, one British reporter remarked, 'that Frenchmen in oriental uniforms would one day combat by the side of Turks clad like Europeans'. In 1855 a regiment of Zouaves of the French Imperial Guard was formed, cementing their reputation. On the eve of the battle of the Alma, General de St Arnauld famously said, 'of all the soldiers in the world, the Zouaves are the first and the bravest'.[7] It is little surprise that a Zouave is prominent on the Pont de l'Alma, used by Parisians as a water marker when there is a danger of flooding.[8] The French Zouaves saw further action in the Italian campaign of 1859, fighting with great courage at the battles of Magenta and Solferino. As a result of the first of these actions, the 2nd Zouaves, the so-called 'Jackals of Oran', had their eagle decorated with the *Légion d'honneur*.

Despite the defeat of the Napoleonic Wars, the French continued to enjoy prestige in all things military. The Zouaves, seen as exotic, heroic and bohemian, were much imitated around the world. Garibaldi had his Zuavi Calabrese in the campaign of 1860, and three years later Poland saw the formation of the famous 'Zouaves of Death' ('Żuawi śmierci'), taking an oath to seek either victory or death. There were Zouave units, too, in Brazil, Chile, Peru, Spain, and the Ottoman Empire.

News of the gallantry of the Zouaves reached the United States, as could be seen in the reports from the Crimea of Captain McClellan, and over a hundred Zouave units were formed during the Civil War. One of the first to popularise the idea was Elmer E. Ellsworth, who, in 1859, having been inspired by meeting a former French Zouave surgeon, formed a unit from the Illinois State Militia which he called the 'United States Zouave Cadets'. His Zouaves toured the Northern States, challenging all and sundry to drill competitions. Ellsworth quickly became a celebrity and inspired the creation of many other American Zouaves.

---

3   Cler, *Zouave Officer*, p.5.
4   *North Briton*, 25 June 1857, p.4.
5   Cler, *Zouave Officer*, p.7.
6   *North Briton*, 25 June 1857, p.4.
7   Cler, *Zouave Officer*, p.2.
8   *Liverpool Daily Post*, 22 September 1855, p.5.

During the Civil War 'Zoos-Zoos', as they were affectionately termed, were present at every major battle, from the Confederate victory at First Bull Run in 1861 to the Union win at Appomattox in 1865. A French-speaking reporter even commented '*Ils pleut des Zouaves*' ('It is raining Zouaves'). Ellsworth himself formed another unit, called the 'Fire Zouaves' since many of the men had previously been volunteers in the New York Fire Department. He was killed at the very beginning of the war, after cutting down the large Confederate flag that flew over a hotel in newly captured Alexandria, Virginia – the first Union officer to lose his life. 'Remember Ellsworth!' became a popular Yankee cry. Zouave units went on to fight with great distinction. A monument on the battlefield of Antietam (1862) commemorates the heroic charge of Hawkin's Zouaves, with their motto '*Toujours Prêt*' ('Always Ready'). Duryée's Zouaves conducted a similarly ferocious charge at the Siege of Port Hudson, Louisiana in 1863, losing more than a third of their force in the space of an afternoon, while the Louisiana Tigers, fighting for the Confederacy, became known for their skill as 'cannon killers', putting enemy artillery out of action.

The Zouave craze reached Great Britain. There were stories of British troops fraternalising with French Zouaves during the Crimean War, where they were likened to the equally fascinating Highlanders.[9] Zouave jackets became all the fashion and even the great Crimean photographer, Roger Fenton, posed several times for the camera dressed as a Zouave. In the summer of 1856 London concertgoers were treated to the spectacle of Monsieur Jullien's Model Military Band, featuring four trumpeters from 'the 2nd Regiment of the Zouaves, rendered so illustrious by their heroic deeds of daring courage in Africa and the Crimea'.[10] In the publicity, the exotic figure of the Zouave was seen as a model of the 'noble savage': '[O]n the field of battle the Zouaves present a mass of wild and daring men, to whom discipline is apparently unknown, but the piercing note of their favourite trumpets suffices to convert them instantaneously into an invincible phalanx.' Monsieur Jullien hid the fact that, by this stage, French Zouaves were almost entirely European.

PRIVATE OF WEST INDIA REGIMENT IN THE NEW ZOUAVE COSTUME.

A private of West India Regiment, showing the Zouave-style uniform adopted in 1858. Inspired by the French Zouaves, it served to reinforce the divisions between the largely black private soldiers and their white officers, who continued to wear the same uniforms as other British officers in the tropics.
(Private collection, author's photograph)

---

9   *Reynold's Newspaper*, 23 March 1862, p.2.
10 *Sheffield Daily Telegraph*, 17 May 1856, p.1.

It was suggested that the British Army should have a similar regiment:

> Had we regiments like these [wrote one correspondent] in which, if a young man of fair education were to enlist, he would know that if he behaved well and steadily his promotion to a rank of commissioned officer would only be a question of time, would it not go far to fill our local Indian regiments with a better class of men than those who have lately been creating miserable mutinies in Bengal? Would such a corps not prove an outlet for a vast deal of the young and wild blood which at present is something of an incubus on too many families of the middle and upper middle class of our society?[11]

Although no such regiment was formed, the West India Regiment adopted the Zouave uniform at the request of Queen Victoria. This consisted of a red fez with white turban, a sleeveless scarlet jacket with yellow braiding worn over a white shirt, and dark blue breeches piped in yellow. Although the regiment was disbanded in 1927, their full-dress uniform continues to be worn to this day by the bands of both the Barbados and Jamaican Defence Forces.

There were always those who criticised the Zouaves for showing more style than substance, for being little more than showmen in theatrical dress, their reputation vastly exaggerated. Some linked the Zouaves with wild behaviour, as can be seen in the French phrase '*faire le Zouave*', similar to the English 'acting the goat'. The uniforms and tradition of the Zouaves clearly appealed to a world marked by Romanticism and a fascination with all things 'Oriental'. But the popularity of the Zouaves was as much to do with military reality as romantic ideal. Zouave tactics were characterised by speed, mobility and surprise; it was, at its best, reactive. Just as their light, free-flowing uniforms were a far cry from the stiff designs of most of their counterparts, so their formation was a contrast to the traditional lines of infantry now being made obsolete by advancements in armaments and firepower. Typically attacking in speedy advances, dropping to the ground at intervals to fire upon the enemy, and equally skilled in hand-to-hand fighting, they were highly suitable for the new mode of modern warfare. The Zouaves was a military concept that worked, at least on paper, and everyone wanted a share in its success.

The Pontifical Zouaves

It was hardly surprising, then, that some of the foreign volunteers who arrived in Rome to defend the Pope's temporal sovereignty wanted to adopt the heroic tradition of the Zouaves, that 'beau ideal of a soldier'. It was especially apt since General Lamoricière himself was considered the 'First Zouave of France', having had long experience in commanding the troops in Algeria.

The Franco-Belgians were already regarded as Zouaves in all but name. Becdelièvre had realised that their initial uniforms, modelled on the Chasseurs à Pied, were hardly suited to the Italian climate and caused confusion with other units. He pushed for a Zouave uniform, for which permission was eventually gained despite concerns that it was too 'Mohammedan' for Catholic troops or that it unduly flattered Lamoricière. By the time the Piedmontese invaded the Papal States, only the 4th Company of the Franco-Belgians had received the new uniform, created partly through the work of a talented tailor in the 2nd Foreign Regiment, Johann Schuster.[12] Henceforth the Franco-Belgians were often referred to as 'Zouaves'.

---

11   *Bury Free Press*, 30 March 1861, p.31.
12   Born in Bavaria, Schuster transferred to the Zouaves in 1861 and fought in the campaigns of 1867 and 1870. His son became Archbishop of Milan in 1929 and was beatified in 1996 (Blessed Idelfonso Schuster).

When the Pontifical Zouaves were created on 1 January 1861, the continuity between the units was stressed not only by the personnel but the battle-damaged Franco-Belgians' banner, which had been carried at Castelfidardo and was now handed over to the unit.

The Pontifical Zouaves were inaugurated on 1 January, under the leadership of Becdelièvre, now a lieutenant-colonel. On 10 January, 600 Zouaves processed to the basilica of St John Lateran to swear their oath of fidelity to the pontiff:

> I swear before almighty God to be obedient and faithful to my sovereign, the Roman Pontiff, Our Most Holy Father the Pope, Pius IX, and to his legitimate successors. I swear to serve him with honour and loyalty and even to sacrifice my life for the defense of his august and sacred person, in order to uphold his sovereignty and to maintain his rights.[13]

The new unit had their baptism of fire soon afterwards. Italian irregulars had set up a base in a tavern at Passo Corese, about 25 miles northeast of Rome, and taken possession of a bridge over the Tiber and the road to Terni. They taunted the local force of gendarmes with offers of money to desert and boasted that the Piedmontese would soon occupy the area. On 24 January Captain de Chillaz arrived to monitor the situation and was met with revolutionary songs mocking the Pope and his army. That night Becdelièvre marched in a detachment from Monterotondo and, after a brief exchange of fire, easily secured the position.

The action was justified as a necessary defensive operation and a flexing of the Pope's military muscles following the seizure of his territory. However, it angered the French force in Rome, who saw themselves as the Pope's chief protector at the same time as walking in friendship with the government in Turin, and some accused Becdelièvre of being overly aggressive. Due to the resulting tensions, Becdelièvre was relieved of his post as head of battalion on 23 March and departed with a small group of officers.

For a short period, a question mark hung over the continued existence of the Zouaves until Colonel Joseph-Eugene Allet, a Swiss soldier who had served the Pontifical Army since 1832, was appointed the new commanding officer. This giant of a man, affectionately

The four De Charette De La Contrie brothers: from left to right, Louis (Papal Dragoon), Ferdinand, Athanase and Alain – all three of whom wore the Zouave uniform. Athanase was regarded by many as the unofficial commander of the unit. (Zouavenmuseum, Oudenbosch, used with permission)

---

13   Philippe Levillain (ed.), *The Papacy: An Encyclopaedia* (London: Routledge, 2002), p.1644.

Joseph-Eugéne Allet (1814-78), the Swiss-born commanding officer of the Zouaves, affectionately known as 'Père Allet'. He was promoted to the rank of colonel on 16 December 1866. (Private collection, photograph: Granddaughters of George Collingridge)

known as '*Père Allet*', was not, however, the first choice; the charismatic Athanase de Charette was the obvious candidate, but his Legitimist leanings made his appointment imprudent since the Pope still depended on the support of Napoleon III.

Initially, the Zouaves consisted of a battalion of eight companies. On 1 January 1867 – the sixth anniversary of the unit's creation – it was raised to the rank of a regiment, with two battalions of six active companies and a supply or depot company. There were further expansions, with a third battalion being added at the end of 1867 and a fourth the following year.

Zouave Recruitment

A well-organised machine was put into action to obtain recruits for the Pontifical Army: sermons, appeals, parades, religious ceremonies, national and local committees, and publications glorifying the 'martyrs' of Castelfidardo, including novels such as Antonio Bresciani's *Olderico ovvero Il Zuavo Pontificio* (1862). In the early 1860s, enlistment was steady but relatively modest, especially when the long-expected campaign in the aftermath of Castelfidardo never materialised, as can be seen from the following figures:

1861: 1,015	1866: 1,463
1862: 186	1867: 3,274
1863: 217	1868: 1,654
1864: 213	1869: 1,382
1865: 289	1870: 1,227

Enlistments were thus low when the level of threat was seen as minimal, while numbers increased with the departure of the French troops in 1866 and the attempted insurrection and campaign of Mentana in 1867. Moreover, some of those who rushed to Rome in 1870 arrived too late to officially enlist but still regarded themselves as fully fledged Zouaves. All in all, 10,920 individuals joined the Zouaves during its nine-year existence, with figures being complicated by the fact that many re-enlisted.

Given the nature of the cause and the recommendation needed from a priest, it is not surprising that most Zouaves displayed religious motivations. Theodore Wibaux wrote to his parents: 'I tell myself I am not a soldier, but a son of Pius IX. I am obliged to repeat this to myself over and over again, for I always felt an aversion to military life.'[14] Despite the harsh reality of life in barracks, he derived some consolation from living close to the Vatican: 'I can even wish good-night to Pius IX, whose suite of rooms I can see lighted up, and I feel happy in being thus near to him.'[15]

Many French Zouaves saw themselves as continuing the tradition of counter-revolution, which had been inaugurated by the example of the Vendeans and Chouans during the 1790s. They were inspired to fight under Athanse de Charette, the great nephew of one of the most celebrated leaders and martyrs of the Vendée, and many had ancestors who had fought 'for God and King'. Indeed, of the 3,000 French Zouaves, many came from the 'traditional' areas of the west and north, although the cities of Paris, Lyons and Marseilles were also well represented.

Wearing the Zouave uniform was seen as a way of redeeming Catholic France in the eyes of Christendom. Napoleon III's Italian policy was widely viewed as inconsistent and unreliable. Troops of the Second Empire may well have been garrisoned in Rome and Civitavecchia to protect the pontiff, but it was the Zouaves who provided him with unconditional loyalty. Indeed, French Zouaves tended to be Legitimists, who had no desire to join the Army of the Second Empire and saw the Count of Chambord, as the rightful king of France. Charette – himself an illegitimate descendant of Charles X - was in close contact with 'Henri V', as his supporters called him, and Zouaves are recorded as visiting his 'court in exile' at Frohsdorf and Göritz. Many of the Zouaves were therefore fighting not only for the temporal power but the very principle of legitimacy itself: the Pope was a sovereign under attack from a 'sacrilegious king' and a devilish revolutionary; his authority came from God and not from the people. The unit also had close associations with the exiled King of the

The Band of the Pontifical Zouaves. As light infantry, the cornet was used on the field of battle to give signals. (Zouavenmuseum, Oudenbosch, used with permission)

---

14 Reverend C. du Coëtlosquet, *Theodore Wibaux, Pontifical Zouave and Jesuit* (London: Catholic Truth Society, 1887), p.35.
15 Coëtlosquet, *Theodore Wibaux*, p.42.

Two Sicilies, Francis II, who resided in Rome at the Palazzo Farnese and was himself a Bourbon, directly descended from Louis XIV.

Zouaves were often misrepresented as overwhelmingly French, Belgian, and Dutch since, all in all, 25 nations were represented over the unit's brief history. Some names conspicuously leap off the page of the official *Liste*: Abdallah Mustafa of Constantinople, Heahim Chika of Damascus, Albert Puyo of Uruguay, the Chinese Pierre Li-Kou-Win[16] or Faustin Bembo, a Black American. Unsurprisingly, though many Zouaves enjoyed the comaraderie of such a transnational fighting force, there were tensions between the different nationalities and the existence of class and racial prejudices.

It should not be forgotten, either, that recruits included around 200 from the Papal States. Elsewhere in the Pontifical Army, the Dragoons, troops of the Line, Engineers, Cacciatori, Reserve Corps and Gendarmes were largely Italian, as were most of the senior staff. In November 1867 roughly 7,500 out of the total of 12,000 pontifical troops (62.5 percent) were indigenous.[17]

Volunteers came from all sections of society, but the majority of officers (56 percent) were of an aristocratic background. Distinguished names included Prince Rospigliosi, whose family had given the Church several cardinals and a Pope; Prince Salvador Iturbide, grandson of the Mexican Emperor; and London-born Alfonso Carlos, Infante of Spain and Duke of San Jaime, who in later life was the Carlist claimant to the Spanish throne and Legitimist claimant to the throne of France. With their dashing uniforms and noble cause, Zouaves attracted attention from the opposite sex. A Paris marriage broker who visited Rome in 1869 'acquired the conviction that the rich American and English ladies who are staying there only visit the city to get married to the young men of high rank who are to be found among the Pontifical Zouaves' and admitted to being 'in business relations' with several members of the corps.[18] One British reporter thought that the Zouaves consisted of three distinct groups: 'gentlemen or noblemen'; those described somewhat unkindly as 'religious fanatics', whose primary motive was the fighting of a holy war in defence of the Pope; and finally, as in any volunteer unit, 'scamps' – albeit Catholic scamps – who sought adventure and fought for the money.[19]

Indeed, not all recruits were the pious crusaders of Catholic hagiography. Some were clearly unsuited to the military life. In June 1870 a new recruit was 'seized with a fit of madness' and 'fancying himself in battle' began to fire out of the Zouave casino in the Campo de Fiori, killing a passer-by and injuring several others.[20] The military tribunal was kept busy with matters of indiscipline. There were high expectations when Maximin Giraud, one of the visionaries who had seen the Blessed Virgin at La Salette in 1846, joined the Zouaves in 1865 but he was eventually expelled from the corps, apparently because of his drunken behaviour. Others joined the Zouaves for less than noble reasons, as seen in the case of John Surratt, a former American seminarian, suspected of plotting with John Wilkes Booth to kidnap and then assassinate Abraham Lincoln. Following the President's murder at Ford's Theatre in April 1865, Surratt fled to Canada and then Europe, where he joined the Zouaves under the name 'John Watson'. Meanwhile his mother, Mary, was hanged for her involvement in the conspiracy, though almost certainly innocent. Surratt was arrested in November 1866 after being recognised by a French-Canadian Zouave friend while on duty at Sezze. He managed to escape, leaping down a ravine while being escorted by six Zouaves, and was briefly given protection by Garibaldi. His next destination was Alexandria, Egypt, where he was finally arrested by

---

16   He joined the Zouaves after being brought up by a Dutch family and attending school in Oudenbosch.
17   *The Tablet*, 9 November 1867, p.715.
18   *Sheffield Daily Telegraph*, 10 July 1869, p.3.
19   *Birmingham Daily Gazette*, 21 September 1870, p.7.
20   *Manchester Evening News*, 16 June 1870, p.3.

American officials, still dressed in his Zouave uniform. Surratt always proclaimed his innocence; his trial was declared a mistrial and he was released.

The Zouaves were not universally popular with the Roman population, many of whom resented the presence of 'foreign' soldiers in their midst or supported the new Italy. It is perhaps little surprise that they were the victims of abuse and violence. On 16 April 1861, for example, Alfred de Limminghe, a Belgian Count who had joined the Zouaves, was shot shortly after leaving the basilica of Santa Maria Minerva, dying of his injuries the following day. Likewise, in early December 1867 a Spanish Zouave succumbed to an exploding cigar, offered to him by a 'Mazzinian' in the street.[21]

Nevertheless, the Pontifical Zouaves provided heroes for a generation of Catholics. The 1860s saw the construction of a compelling 'legend' around the figure of the Zouave. He was seen not only as a soldier but a crusader, sacrificing his life as a martyr for the Church and an expiation for the sins of the post-1789 world – closely linked to what has been called the 'dolourist Catholicism' of the times, which stressed the value of suffering, penance and reparation.

Brigandage and Cholera

The period between the foundation of the Zouaves in 1861 and the campaigns of 1867 saw an uneasy calm, despite ongoing fears of invasion and insurrection. Most notably, Garibaldi began marching on Rome in the summer of 1862 but was stopped by an Italian army at Aspromonte on 29 August. The action only lasted ten minutes and resulted in Garibaldi being shot in the ankle; he was arrested and retired to his island home of Caprera for the next two years. Nevertheless, it was clear that revolutionaries still posed a real danger to the Pope.

In the absence of active campaigning, the Zouaves spent much of their time on garrison duty in the area around Rome, training exercises and drill. This was, to some extent, deliberate, so that their presence did not unduly irritate Napoleon III, who saw himself as the chief protector of the Holy See. The only experience of action was provided by the 'war of skirmishes and running firefights' against the brigands of the Roman *campagna*. This not only dealt with a threat to public order but 'provided a tough school for the Pope's soldiers' as they marched across the *campagna* 'with full field packs in all weathers, bivouacking on rough ground, living on field rations for days at a time, watching for ambushes, deploying and advancing in the face of the enemy, and seeing comrades fall'.[22]

Brigandage had long been an issue in the Papal States but had now received a new dimension. After the fall of the Kingdom of the Two Sicilies, King Francis II set up his court-in-exile to Rome and, with the help of his supporters and former officers, established guerrilla bands that would attack and disrupt Italian military outposts on the old kingdom's northern border. These bands were tolerated by the pontifical authorities, which even permitted recruitment offices in Rome, Agnani and Velletri. However, as time went on, the brigands increasingly became purely criminal organisations, as likely to attack travellers and tradesmen as Italian soldiers. They were a threat to the internal stability of the Papal States and, especially in the second half of the 1860s, the Zouaves worked alongside the gendarmes in countering their activity. Between 1865 and 1870 just over 700 brigands were successfully hunted down.

In the summer of 1867, the Zouaves were closely involved in the outbreak of cholera in Albano, a popular destination just outside Rome. According to a broadsheet, residents noticed on 6 August 'a dark cloud' coming from the sea, with 'a bad smell as of putrid insects'; 'immediately eighty-six persons at least were

---

21 *The Sun*, 14 December 1867, p.4.
22 Alvarez, *The Pope's Soldiers*, pp.153–154.

struck down by the terrible Asiatic cholera morbus'.[23] As is well known now, the disease was spread not by dark clouds but by contaminated water and food. The pandemic had begun in Bengal and travelled with pilgrims to Mecca, before dispersing worldwide: 90,000 died in Russia in 1866 and, thanks in part to the Austro-Prussian War of that year, it spread across central Europe. In Italy, 113,000 died of the cholera in 1867.

The scenes in Albano were horrific; many panicked and civil government collapsed. The 6th Company of the 2nd Battalion of Zouaves was sent in to keep order and assist the dying. According to one correspondent:

> Everyone took fright and sought to escape; all but a few had lost the presence of mind needed in such an emergency. Foreigners rushed to the railway to make their way to Rome; the carriages were insufficient to contain such a multitude. The inhabitants of the city, leaving their dead in their houses, took flight in the direction of the wood of Palazzuola [Palazzola], intrusting [sic] their house keys to the poor Zouaves, to whom everyone had recourse. These brave young fellows laid aside their carbines and knapsacks, and, listening only to their own generous charitable impulses, transformed themselves into gravediggers, infirmarians, sextons, messengers – everything.[24]

Four Zouaves carrying a coffin during the cholera epidemic at Albano in 1867. They pass an ancient monument, on which is inscribed the names of three comrades who died while assisting the sick: Hendricus Peeters, Jacobus van der Meyden and Gijsbertus Johannes van Ophem. (Painting by J. Faber, Zouavenmuseum, Oudenbosch, used with permission)

---

23   Emma Pearson, *From Rome to Mentana* (London: Saunders, Otley and Co., 1868), pp.274–275.
24   *The Tablet*, 24 August 1867, p.532.

The city was divided into three sections, each under the supervision of a sergeant, and the number of sick and dying was ascertained. The commanding officer 'to give an example to his men, was the first to take a corpse on his shoulder and carry it to the cemetery'.[25] On the first night 90 bodies were thus buried, many of them wheeled in barrows out of the city.

The clergy had their part to play. One Jesuit walked to Albano from the Church of Santa Maria di Galloro but, finding the road through Ariccia closed, climbed down into the valley and up the steep rocks to help the victims. Lodovico Altieri, the Cardinal Bishop of Albano, left Rome with two doctors, paid for at his own expense, and spent three days visiting the sick, giving them material relief and administering the sacraments. He finally succumbed to the disease and died on 11 August; a campaign was later started for his beatification.

Other victims included the Queen Dowager of the Two Sicilies, the Principessa Colonna and two Dutch Zouaves, one of whom contracted the malady after carrying away for burial a body which had been discovered three days after death. The Zouaves impressed many by their selfless devotion. Alfred Collingridge, one of the first English Zouaves, wrote to his parents that 'the coffins and the dead were laying all about in the streets, the inhabitants were afraid to sleep in their houses, but slept somewhere out in the open air, some were found dead the next morning, in some of the houses where the Zouaves went, nearly all were laying dead, and they had to carry them out themselves and put them in the coffins and then take them in a cart to bury them.'[26]

In the words of a Roman broadsheet, 'these are the famous mercenaries of Pius IX, whom the revolutionists would cover with infamy! Oh, blessed are they, for they have the thanks and praises of all who have a human heart in their bosom.'[27] Those who served at Albano were awarded the Cross of the Order of Christ by the Pope.

The September Convention and a New Commander-in-Chief

While the Zouaves settled into a constant rhythm of garrison duty, exercises and campaigns against brigands, there were several important developments that affected the Pontifical Army. Cavour had died suddenly, aged 50, in June 1861 and was replaced by a series of quick-serving prime ministers, each with different approaches to the Roman Question. On 15 September 1864 France and Italy, under the leadership of Marco Minghetti, signed the so-called 'September Convention', in which it was agreed that French troops would be withdrawn from the Papal States within two years and Italy strove to respect the independence of the Pope and the borders of the Papal States as they then stood. Italy also gave up its opposition to the recruitment of foreign volunteers in the papal service and moved its capital from Turin to Florence – not only was the Tuscan city seen as safer from possible Austrian attack, but the move indicated that Italy had given up on its desire for Rome. Although on paper it seemed a compromised solution to the Roman Question, it was opposed by both the Pope, who little trusted in the promised guarantees, and Garibaldi, who still hoped to see Rome as the Italian capital. There were violent riots in Turin, where the population resented the 'demotion' of their city as capital.

The French left the Eternal City in 1866. Those who signed the treaty two years previously could not have foreseen this planned departure coinciding with the war between Austria and Prussia, which resulted

---

25 Pearson, *From Rome to Mentana*, p.278.
26 Anon, 'Pontifical Zouaves: The Collingridge Brothers', *Vatican News: The Journal of the Vatican Philatelic Society*, 6:354 (2012), p.22.
27 Pearson, *From Rome to Mentana*, pp.290–291.

in Venetia being ceded to Italy. Despite reassurances that Rome was safe, the Eternal City was the last missing piece of the Italian jigsaw and without French troops was highly vulnerable.

Meanwhile, the unedifying rivalry between Cardinal Antonelli and Monsignor de Mérode continued, the former stressing the path of diplomacy, the latter following a policy of rearmament. Despite Mérode's best efforts, the military budget was reduced; in 1864 it was half of what it had been five years previously. The vision of a rejuvenated Papal Army was stalled, and numbers of recruits declined as the decisive campaign that had been expected in the aftermath of Castelfidardo never materialised. Mérode was also deeply unpopular; he had made many enemies within the Vatican and was openly critical of the French emperor, so much so that the Pope was several times warned that if French troops departed the Eternal City, it would largely be due to his minister of arms. Pressure was put on the Pope to demand his resignation. The Pope tried to reason that his defects were only 'excesses of his devotion and honesty' and stated that he could not think of separating himself from Mérode.[28] However on 6 October 1865 Pius finally informed him that he was being relieved of his functions as minister, on the pretext of his declining health. The journalist Louis Veuillot said of him, 'he deserves either the prison of St Angelo or the purple. I vote for the purple!'[29] He was eventually made Papal Almoner and titular Archbishop of Melitene and retreated to his Vatican apartments, where he ended his days coordinating the Pope's charitable outreach. The change in personnel coincided with the death of Lamoricière, at his home in Prouzel, near Amiens, on 20 September. The general was buried in Nantes Cathedral, where an elaborate memorial, created by Paul Dubois, was completed a decade later.

With the departure of Mérode and Lamoricière, there was space for new blood. The choice fell upon a German officer in the papal service, Hermann Kanzler. Trained at the military college of Karlsrühe, he had served in the army of the Grand Duchy of Baden between 1840 and 1844 before entering the papal 1st Foreign (Swiss) Infantry Regiment. He rose through the ranks, being wounded during the defence of Vicenza in 1848 and undertaking several secret missions for the Pope during his self-imposed exile in Gaeta. He came to command one of the Italian line regiments in the Pontifical Army and was taken captive at the siege of Ancona in 1860. He then acted as Inspector General of the pontifical troops, before taking up his new post, in which he filled the shoes of both Lamoricière and Mérode. His Italian wife, Laura, was the cousin

General Hermann Kanzler (1822–1888), pontifical commander-in-chief and minister of arms from 1865. (Private collection, author's photograph)

---

28   Besson, *Mérode*, pp.207–208.
29   Besson, *Mérode*, p.212.

of two brothers, Serafino and Vincenzo Vannutelli, who were well-known in curial circles and later became cardinals. The choice of Kanzler was thus one that was approved by Antonelli.

As he presided over his first official reception at his headquarters on the Piazza Pilotta, the press described Kanzler as a good-natured and competent soldier but 'incapable of playing a political part: just the man, in fact, to obey the inspirations of Cardinal Antonelli'.[30] He proved, however, to be no pushover. Like Mérode, he strongly believed in the necessity of a small but efficient professional army, ensuring the security of the Pope's territory. However, he also agreed with Antonelli that international diplomacy was essential and that, in the event of a Garibaldian or Italian invasion, the papal troops would mount the first defence while the support of 'Christendom' was being mobilised through diplomatic channels. His was an attractive personality; he enjoyed close relations with the Pope and knew when to speak and when to keep his own counsel. He could, in other words, build on the work of Mérode while avoiding conflict with the all-powerful Cardinal Secretary of State.

Having served with the Papal Army for over 20 years, Kanzler knew its strengths and weaknesses. Within weeks of his new appointment, he drew up his plans for reorganisation. His approach was that of a realist: the army would be half the size of Mérode's and less of a drain on the fragile papal finances. It would consist of one regiment of line infantry (three battalions), three separate battalions of light infantry (Zouaves and Carabineers), two squadrons of Dragoons, five batteries (each with five guns) of field artillery, in addition to gendarmes, engineers (as of 1866 an autonomous corps), garrison troops (made up of veterans) and the various service and auxiliary units. The army was divided into two brigades: the first looked after the four new Military Zones of Viterbo (under Colonel Azzanesi), Civitavecchia (Lieutenant-Colonel Serra), Tivoli (Lieutenant-Colonel Charette) and Velletri (Lieutenant-Colonel Giorgi); the second, commanded by General Zappi, being responsible for Rome itself.

The departure of the French in accordance with the September Convention led to an increase in foreign volunteers. Frank Russell-Killough, in his memoir of a decade in the pontifical service, gave thanks for this 'diplomatic blunder', since the number of recruits had up until then been falling, morale declining and many papal units feeling without purpose. The departure of the French meant that 'our hopes were renewed with the idea of our responsibility' and the injection of new blood heightened expectations of an imminent 'second Castelfidardo'.[31]

The Pope received a further boost from a new unit, the Antibes Legion, approved by Napoleon on 30 January 1866 and arriving in the Papal States that September. Although originally there was talk of a more international body, it was almost entirely French. Enrolment was for a period of four years and time served in the unit was recognised by the French Army. Many argued that in approving such a corps France was immediately breaking the September Convention. Established by General Dumont at Antibes, near Cannes, it initially took its name from the town though it was more commonly called the 'Roman Legion'. Unlike the Zouaves, many recruits did not join for religious motives, and some were not even Catholic. There were cases of desertion and poor discipline but its members provided the papal cause with valuable military experience and fought well in the campaign of 1867; the following year it was raised to regimental status with two battalions.

---

30 *Leeds Mercury*, 6 November 1865, p.4.
31 Russell-Killough, *Dix Années*, p.395 (author's translation).

9

The Failed Revolution of 1867

The year 1867 saw a worrying deterioration in affairs for the papacy. Those who hoped for Italian unity saw Rome as the final prize and the power vacuum left by the departure of the French as an opportunity. Prime Minister Urbano Rattazzi attempted to make the most of the situation. Money and arms were passed to Garibaldi, aware that the invasion of the Papal States would necessitate Italian intervention. Two birds could thus be despatched with one stone: Garibaldi's destabilising radicalism and the Pope's Temporal Power.

Many supporters discouraged Garibaldi from taking the bait. The memory of Aspromonte was fresh in their minds. Nevertheless, the 'hero of two worlds' spent much of 1867 touring the Italian mainland, making violently anti-clerical speeches and using his contacts with political radicals, exiles and masonic lodges. In September he spoke at the Congress of the International League of Peace and Liberty at Geneva, where, as usual, he was the star of the show, receiving bouquets from enthusiastic young ladies and kissing children who were brought to him. He proposed a list of 'Articles' to the assembly, summarising the Garibaldian 'credo' as it then stood: a union of nations against despotism, the fall of the papacy and a universal religion in which the priesthood was comprised of scientists and intellectuals. His son, Ricciotti, meanwhile visited Great Britain on a fundraising tour 'for the cause of Rome' and included London, Birmingham and Glasgow in the itinerary.

On 24 September, shortly after returning from Geneva, Garibaldi was arrested at Sinalunga, near Arezzo, and taken back to his island home of Caprera. The Italian authorities, who were being carefully watched by Napoleon III, were afraid of what might happen if Garibaldi was not seen to be contained. Garibaldi issued messages stating that 'the Romans have the right of slaves to rise against their tyrants, the priests' and that Italy was seen by the world as 'a Redeemer'. 'Will the arrest of one man,' he taunted, 'terrify Italy into renouncing her glorious mission?'[1] He nearly succeeded in escaping on 2 October but was immediately reconveyed back to his island home.

Meanwhile, bands of Garibaldians began entering papal territory at multiple points: at Grotta San Stefano on 29 September and, the following day, at Canino, Valentano and Acquapendente. The small episcopal town of Bagnorea was captured on 1 October. Pontifical troops responded with efficiency: on 5 October a column of 170 Zouaves and another of 150 Line Infantry, together with two artillery pieces and 20 mounted troops, secured an outpost of Red Shirts in a ruined castle just outside Bagnorea and then, at 11.00 a.m., moved on to the town itself. A letter from one of the Zouaves described the action:

---

1   *The Tablet*, 26 October 1867, p.681.

The enemy occupied the heights round the town but retired before our skirmishers and abandoned the position. We had scarcely gained the heights when a shower of balls rained upon us. The Garibaldians were under shelter in the vineyards, and we were exposed, so, crying Vive Pie IX! En avant les Zouaves! A la Baionnette! we charged and dislodged them and got among the vineyards under the ramparts. The Garibaldians took refuge in a convent and kept up a sharp fire on us from the windows and from the clock tower. We attacked the gate with the butt-ends of our muskets, our lieutenant, though wounded in the arm, dealing formidable one-handed blows with an axe. As soon as the gate was forced we rushed in with levelled bayonets. The Garibaldians threw down their arms and surrendered. We took fifty-six of them and several officers in the convent. As they still held the town, our commander had the cannon pointed against the gate. We got in. The enemy fled. The inhabitants cried, Vive Pie IX! Vivent les Zouaves! White handkerchiefs waved from the windows, and the doors were all thrown open.

It was a morale boosting victory, for the Garibaldians had more than twice as many men. Only one papal soldier was killed (Nicholas Heycamp, a Dutch Zouave who became the first member of the unit to die in action), 30 Red Shirts lost their lives and many others were wounded or taken prisoner. However, many were shocked by the sacrileges reportedly committed in the convent during the Garibaldian occupation: '[T]hey smashed the altars, flung down the sacred relics, and stabbed at the sacred images with their bayonets'.[2]

According to George Collingridge, the English Zouave who later became a distinguished artist, the Red Shirts of 1867 consisted of two elements:

One, the more numerous set, had obtained secret leave of absence from the ranks of the Piedmontese army, and were clad in semi-military, semi-brigand attire; retaining of their former uniform whatsoever appealed to their native inborn sense of picturesqueness and gaiety in point of colour, and, discarding the remainder, either for the sake of assuming a scarlet flannel or silk shirt trimmed with gold lace, or some other fanciful attire, such as velvet jackets and caps, or sombrero hats adorned with waving feathers. The other, the less numerous band of recruits, of a more sinister and brigand type, wore the sombre classical mantle and pointed felt hat, with solitary peacock feather placed cyclopwise, in order to avoid the evil eye.

They may not have been as dangerous as the Goths and Vandals of antiquity but, in his opinion, they were more scheming.[3]

There were also incursions of Garibaldian irregulars to the south of Rome. On 11 October a group attacked Subiaco and took both the governor and bishop hostage. A small group of Pontifical Gendarmes barricaded themselves into the Rocca, where they could fire upon Garibaldi's men and hoist the papal flag. A company of Zouaves under the Belgian Jules-Louis Desclée, who were returning from reconnaissance of the area, then mounted an attack. Desclée, who was subsequently promoted to the rank of captain and eventually returned home to Tournai to help establish a publishing firm famed for its excellence in producing liturgical books, received three sabre wounds. He also shot dead the Garibaldian commander and 15 prisoners were taken. Similar success was seen in Salvaterra, where the insurgents briefly set up a provisional government until being driven out by the *papalini*.

---

2   *The Tablet*, 26 October 1867, p.681.
3   *Evening News Supplement* (NSW), 7 December 1901, p.1, citing 'Vanished Soldiers' by George Collingridge.

Bloodbath at Montelibretti

Up until now, Garibaldi's men hoped their scattered raids would prevent Kanzler from uniting his military resources. The Pontifical Army, well-used to dealing with brigands in the mountainous country around Rome, was able to respond quickly and effectively. A more serious issue was posed by Garibaldi's son, Menotti, who led a larger group of Red Shirts in the Sabine Hills, initially playing cat and mouse with the pontifical troops and withdrawing, when necessary, to the safety of Italian territory.

The number of irregulars steadily grew and on 13 October word reached Charette, the commanding officer of the 3rd Military Zone to the north of Rome, that they were stationed around Montelibretti. An advance company of 90 Zouaves under Arthur Guillemin, a veteran of Castelfidardo who was affectionately called 'Guardian Angel' by his men, made its way towards the village. As an Irish Zouave, Patrick Keyes O'Clery, later noted, 'in this campaign Kanzler and Charette used companies as if they were battalions'.[4] Guillemin was met with fire from outposts of Garibaldians. Dividing the Zouaves into two sections, Guillemin led a bayonet charge through the vineyards and towards the main gate, with the cry *'Vive Pie Neuf!'* He was hit first in the shoulder and then, fatally, in the head. Taking command, the Bavarian Sergeant-Major Joseph Alois Bach, also a veteran of 1860, continued the advance leading to fierce fighting in front of the gate and in the narrow streets.

Many heroes were made that day who would be celebrated in Zouave literature. Pieter Jong, a 'gigantic Hercules', to use the words of the *L'Univers*, from Lutjebroek, North Holland, swung his gun like a club at the Red Shirts, reportedly killing 14. He eventually slumped on his knees, exhausted and bareheaded, to be pierced by a dozen bayonets. One of the first English recruits, Alfred Collingridge, was wounded after being seen with his back to the wall defending himself against six Garibaldians and later died in a makeshift hospital. Urbain de Quelen, of a noble Breton family, who had led the other unit of Zouaves to the left of the village, joined the melee but received fatal wounds. His bugler, a young Roman called 'Mimmi', was hit in his right arm but continued sounding orders.

The Garibaldians fighting in front of the gate eventually withdrew into the village. Bach and his companions barricaded themselves into a house and, despite being heavily outnumbered, managed to resist for several hours. They escaped through a breach in the back wall under cover of darkness. Promoted and decorated for his bravery, Bach was said to have been bathed in the blood of the enemy. Although the rest of the Zouaves had by this stage withdrawn to the safety of nearby Monte Maggiore, the Red Shirts had also departed for Nerola, taking with them some of the wounded Zouaves.[5] Despite the inconclusive result of the encounter, the *papalini* claimed a victory since they had been greatly outnumbered – according to some sources, 13 to one – and, thanks largely to Bach, 'the field of battle and the position both remained in the possession of the Pontifical troops'.[6] Comparisons were even made, somewhat pretentiously, with the stand of the Spartans at Thermopylae.

Charette ordered detachments of Zouaves and the Antibes Legion towards Nerola but, on hearing of this advance, Menotti withdrew most of his men towards the Montorio Romano. Those who were left resisted Charette as best they could on 18 October. Among those present was the Roman correspondent for *The Tablet*, Mrs Stone, who was helping to organise an ambulance for the wounded of Montelibretti. Around 11.00 a.m., 'through the yellowing woods … we distinguished clearly the flash of the Zouave bayonets, the gay uniforms of the Antibes Legion, and the oxen dragging the battery of artillery under M.

---

4   Patrick Keyes O'Clery, *The Making of Italy* (London: Kegan Paul, Trench, Trubner & Co., 1892), p.429.
5   *The Tablet*, 26 October 1867, pp.681–682.
6   *The Tablet*, 26 October 1867, p.682.

de Quatrebarbes'. As the Zouaves and Legionaries attacked, Mrs Stone recalled the Zouaves' 'terrible cry of rage' when Charette's horse was shot from beneath him, though he escaped uninjured. The 'Batterie Quatrebarbes' began firing on Nerola and 'brought down the tri-coloured flag from the castle, and amid a burst of cheering, the company of Zouaves charged up the hill crying "Vive Pie Neuf!"' Having held on for as long as possible, the Garibaldian commander, Major Valentini, raised the white flag and 134 were taken prisoner. Among those present at the action, Mrs Stone was careful to note, were a number of newly recruited English Zouaves: the Watts-Russell brothers, George Collingridge (brother of Alfred) and Oswald Cary, who rivalled 'their French and Belgian comrades in courage and elan'.[7] Charette had hoped to pursue Menotti but Kanzler ordered him to return to Rome, where events were thought to be fast deteriorating. He marched his men to Monterotondo where a train awaited them.

Trouble in Rome

The numerous assaults made across the *campagna* caused considerable alarm in Rome. Of especial concern was the seeming connivance of the Italian government, encouraging the recruitment of volunteers, facilitating their passage on Italian railways, providing arms and funding revolutionary propaganda. Reports abounded that a second Castelfidardo was imminent. It was common knowledge, also, that Garibaldi hoped his attacks on papal territory would result in a popular insurrection in the Eternal City.

Earthworks and barricades were constructed in Rome and plans made to mine strategic bridges, while police and soldiers increased their presence on the streets and squares. Ambassadors left the city for safety and there was talk that even the Pope might be forced to flee Rome, as he had in 1848. The expected insurrection never materialised, largely due to the poor organisation and division of the revolutionaries, and indifference among the Roman populace, but there were enough signs that the danger was very real.

On the evening of 22 October gendarmes raided a villa just outside the city walls and seized 200 rifles; a revolutionary flag was draped over the statue of Marcus Aurelius on the Capitol, until being quickly pulled down; plots to seize the city gasworks and blow up Castel Sant'Angelo were thwarted; and there were skirmishes at the Porta San Paolo and Ponte dei Quattro Capi. Most seriously, bombs were planted in a passage underneath the Serristori Barracks, near St Peter's, which exploded at 7.45 p.m., and 25 Zouaves were killed, mostly members of the regimental band as well as two soldiers who were being disciplined and confined to their 'cells'. The death toll would have been greater had not so many of the Zouaves been dealing with the expected insurrection around the city. Three civilians were also killed, including 6-year-old Rosa Ferri. Romans left floral tributes with blue ribbons, a reference not only to the Zouave uniform but the colour of the dress Rosa had been wearing. Emma Pearson, an English observer with little sympathy towards the papal cause, thought 'it was sad to see the crumbling walls, the dust-covered accoutrements hanging on the pegs, and to think what must have been the horror and agony of that death scene'.[8] Indeed, 'if such acts as this, and flinging Orsini bombs about the streets, were the only efforts of the Roman populace for freedom, I must say, they little deserved it'. The atrocity resulted in a wave of sympathy for the Pontifical Army and, several weeks later, on the battlefield of Mentana, Zouaves are reported to have shouted '*Serristori! Serristori!*' as they attacked the Red Shirts. Further devices were intended to be placed at the barracks of the Antibes Legion at La Cimarra, the Carabineers near the basilica of Santa Maria Maggiore, the Swiss Guard in the Vatican and Castel Sant' Angelo, but nothing came of these plans.

---

7 *The Tablet*, 26 October 1867, p.670.
8 Pearson, *From Rome to Mentana*, p.64.

Efforts were made in subsequent days to clamp down on any remaining revolutionaries. On 23 October there was a skirmish at the Villa Glori, an unoccupied house on Monte Parioli, where a detachment of Foreign Carabineers attacked a group of insurgents who had been planning to enter Rome via the Tiber. Among those killed was Enrico Cairoli, a veteran Garibaldian. Two days later a property belonging to Giulio Ajani on the Via della Lungaretta was raided as a meeting place for plotters and a potential bomb factory. Among those killed in the resulting struggle was Giuditta Tavani Arquati, then pregnant with her fourth child, and her 12-year-old son. The victims were treated as martyrs of liberty and revolution; a piazza nearby now bears Guiditta's name, and a plaque speaks of 'the vile and fierce mercenaries' responsible for the massacre.

Two of the Serristori conspirators – Giuseppe Monti, who had fought against the Austrians the previous year, and Gaetano Tognetti – were captured, tried and, on 24 November 1868, guillotined at the Piazza dei Cerchi, the last public execution in Papal Rome. The two men asked to see Charette, who was moved to tears as he assured them of his forgiveness and that of the whole body of Zouaves. The regiment raised a large sum for the wife and children of Monti. The men died with courage and Joseph Powell, the Gloucestershire-born Zouave who was on duty around the scaffold that day, noted that the condemned men 'showed signs of great penitence'.[9]

Monterotondo

Garibaldi had managed to escape house arrest on Caprera on 14 October and crossed the papal frontier ten days later, joining the column commanded by his son, which by now numbered several thousand. He hoped that three columns could move on Rome – one via Monterotondo, a second through Viterbo on the Tiber's right bank and a third from the southeast. Garibaldi moved his headquarters to the area around Monterotondo, where there was a garrison under Captain Costes of the Antibes Legion. The capture of this stronghold would form the first step in the advance. According to O'Clery:

> Monterotondo is a small city, standing upon a hill, with steep slopes which are in places almost precipitous. The circuit of the town is about a mile round. More than half of this is open, and only capable of defence by lining the garden walls with riflemen and occupying the houses, trusting chiefly to the difficult character of the ground in front to retard and embarrass the enemy. Six hundred metres of the enceinte are closed by an old wall, built in the fifteenth century, and therefore without bastions or any effectual flanking defence. The wall is pierced by three gates, the Porta Romana, Porta Ducale and Porta Canonica. The houses of the suburb are built close up to these gates, and command them. The real defence of the place is the Palazzo, a lofty, square, castellated building, which stands just inside the Porta Ducale.[10]

Early on the morning of 25 October the Red Shirts stormed the three gates, which were ably defended by the garrison. Bernard de Quatrebarbes, the nephew of the governor of Ancona in 1860, brought into action his two cannons, one of which he briefly pushed in front of one the gates. Moving the pieces to different strategic positions, he was hit twice by bullets and died a month later of his wounds. By 7.00 p.m. the red shirts had made no inroads into the town. A final attempt was made and a cart, laden with wood, sulphur

---

9   Joseph Powell, *Two Years in the Pontifical Zouaves: A Narrative of Travel, Residence and Experience in the Roman States* (London: R. Washbourne, 1871), p.79.
10 O'Clery, *Making of Italy*, pp.442–443.

and oil, pushed up to the Porta Romana and ignited. Artillery was then trained at the gate, which soon collapsed, and as the irregulars rushed into the town, avoiding the temporary barricades, the papal garrison retreated to the castle.

The situation of the garrison was highly perilous the next morning: the Red Shirts had managed to penetrate the first floor of the fortress, pontifical ammunition was running low, and there was no sign of reinforcements. The white flag was reluctantly raised and Garibaldi's two sons, Menotti and Ricciotti, complimented Costes on his courageous defence.

Viterbo

Monterotondo delayed Garibaldi's advance and proved that the pontifical troops would be no pushover. It was also becoming clear that there was little enthusiasm for a popular insurrection in Rome. News also reached Garibaldi of a setback near Viterbo on 24 October. Giovanni Acerbi's men were in the area, planning to advance down the right bank of the Tiber in parallel to Garibaldi's column. On meeting several locals, he was assured of the strength of republican sympathy and confidently advanced towards Viterbo, where the pontifical forces under Colonel Achille Azzanesi awaited them. Although the Red Shirts managed to rout an advance guard of Dragoons, they came under heavy fire from a company of Line Infantry at the junction of the Celleno and Quercia roads. The pontifical troops then withdrew to the safety of the city gates and the Garibaldian attempt to enter the city lasted all day, attacking all the gates. By evening ammunition was running low and Acerbi withdrew, although the Red Shirts were able to occupy Viterbo when Kanzler recalled his scattered troops to Civitavecchia and Rome.

Meanwhile, Napoleon III had been alarmed by recent occurrences and felt that the Italian Government, by implicitly supporting the Red Shirts, had undermined the September Convention. As a result, a French expeditionary force was despatched, landing at Civitavecchia on 29 October and triumphantly parading down Rome's Corso a few days later. They numbered some 22,000, under General Pierre Louis de Failly, a veteran of the Crimean War and an imperial favourite. According to an official notice, the troops had been sent 'to protect the Holy Father and the Pontifical throne against the armed attacks of revolutionary bands'.[11] In meeting with Kanzler, Failly advised a cautious approach, hoping that his mere presence in Rome would shake the morale of the Red Shirts and leave the Pontifical Army to concentrate on any necessary operations around the *campagna*. He was also anxious to avoid any direct confrontation with the Italian forces, whose intentions as they moved around the frontier were unclear. Kanzler, however, favoured a more offensive approach, taking the opportunity of the failed insurrection and the arrival of the French to deal with the Garibaldian threat once and for all.

---

11   *London Daily News*, 5 November 1867, p.5.

10

The Battle of Mentana

The great set piece of the 'Agro Romano' campaign of 1867 was fought near Mentana on Sunday, 3 November. The town was two miles southeast of Monterotondo, which had become Garibaldi's base since its capture on 25 October. Two days later he sent a proclamation to his 'Roman Brothers':

> Having conquered the enemy we are in sight of the old matron of Rome. Some miles only divide us. In a few days the undaunted soldiers of liberty will rapidly traverse them to give the last blow to the tyranny which has oppressed us for centuries. Hold yourselves ready for the supreme trial – prepare by every means for the destruction of the Sbirri [papal police]– it is the right of the slave. This time it is you who will give to the world the new era, the initiative of truth and progress.[1]

With the enemy only 12 miles away from the Eternal City, Kanzler was keen to take swift action and show the world that the defence of papal territory was not the sole preserve of the French. His military creed emphasised the importance of the offensive. 'An army is as good as its aggressive spirit,' he wrote, 'a minute of daring is worth more than many months of study, the most beautiful and convenient defence is called attack.'[2] This doctrine was put into action at Mentana. He convinced the newly arrived Failly that an advance on Monterotondo was the best way forward, with the French operating as a reserve.

The troops gathered early at the Campo Pretorio on the morning of 3 November, near the recently opened temporary railway station of Termini, so-called because it stood near the Baths (or Thermae) of Diocletian. The weather was cold and wet, and the torches illuminated the impressive ruins, with the basilica of Santa Maria degli Angeli beside them. Rome itself was in the state of siege; since late October the five main gates were closed, barricaded with sandbags and heavily guarded.

The forces at Kanzler's disposal, drawn primarily from the Rome-based 2nd Brigade, totalled 2,923, with a reserve, largely drawn from the French Expeditionary Force, numbering 2,500. Joining Kanzler's staff were such luminaries as Don Alfonso de Borbone, brother of the exiled King of Naples; Major Ungarell; and Captains de Maistre, Bourbon-Chalus and Maumigny. The Papal Ambulance, made up of around 60 doctors and nurses, was augmented by volunteers from abroad. These included the English aristocrat and writer Mrs Katherine Stone, Dr Charles Ozanam (who left an account in *Une Ambulance a Mentana*) and a small group of Sisters of Charity of St Vincent de Paul.

---

1 *London Daily News*, 5 November 1867, p.5.
2 Attilo Vigevano, *La Fine dell'Esercito Pontificio* (Rome: Stabilimento Poligrafico per l'Amministrazione della Guerra, 1920), p.129.

In the aftermath of the battle, there were debates about each side's numbers and quality of troops. Menotti Garibaldi himself claimed the Papal Army was larger than had been officially stated by Kanzler, heightening the sense of papal aggression and the needless slaughter of the Pope's compatriots. Papal supporters stressed the barbaric 'otherness' of the Red Shirts and claimed it was a well-fought and necessary battle, narrowly averting a disaster for Rome. The role of the French was also deliberately downplayed by Catholic writers, while those sympathetic to Garibaldi pointed to the decisive intervention of the French Chassepots.

The number of Garibaldians is uncertain. Menotti Garibaldi later stated that his father had 8,000 men at his disposal but that desertions (occasioned in part by the failed insurrection in Rome) and the need to secure other strategic points in the area meant that the number at Mentana may have been between 4,500 and 4,800. Kanzler himself thought he was facing 10,000.[3]

Contrary to many popular depictions, the Garibaldian forces contained seasoned and professional elements. Although obsolete muskets were used by some, Dr Ozanam, on examining the battlefield the following day, noted that many Red Shirts had Italian rifles, Swiss carbines, revolvers, and even rudimentary weapons such as an explosive bullet that caused terrible wounds. Some were seasoned fighters, who had been with Garibaldi on previous campaigns, and others had held commissions in the Italian Army.[4]

Garibaldi's volunteers had differing motives and experience. The Ukrainian co-founder of the Theosophical Society, Madame Helena Blavatsky, claimed to have been present at the battle: 'I went with friends to Mentana to help shooting [papists] … and got shot myself.' When she met her future biographer, Henry Olcott, seven years later she made him feel 'in her right shoulder a musket ball still embedded in the muscle, and another in her leg'.[5]

There were several Britons present among the Red Shirts. When Emma Pearson watched the Garibaldian prisoners being escorted into Rome the following day, she noticed that 'one or two had English Crimean medals'.[6] The newspapers contained accounts of an Englishman, 'Scholey', who joined the Garibaldians, not out of any sympathy for the cause but in order to test his collection of 'eight carbines of the best and most elegant make'. He positioned himself behind a large tree and, with the help of a servant who loaded the guns and took technical notes, fired on the papal troops. He shot ten of them and earned the nickname of 'The Man Killer'; it was even rumoured that he was responsible for two of the most high-profile Zouave casualties of the day: De Vaux and Watts-Russell. 'Scholey' was eventually hit by a bullet in the wrist and taken to a hospital in Rome; the wound became infected, and he died shortly after his 'homicidal hand' was amputated and without the comforts of religion. 'At this conjecture,' it was reported, 'his mother arrived from London. "Your son is dead," said one of the infirmarians to her. "Ah!" said she quietly: then I must get his photograph taken.'[7] Reality may have been exaggerated here for the purposes of a moral tale about an unrepentant deathbed and stories of Scholey's idiosyncratic sharpshooting skills sound similar to those told about 'Garibaldi's Englishman', Colonel Peard, but it underlines the diverse nature of Garibaldi's forces.

Many of the volunteers were young, poorly disciplined and lacking in previous military experience. Nevertheless, at Mentana they were in a strong defensive position and the Roman *campagna*, with its

---

3   Alvarez, *The Pope's Soldiers*, p.183.
4   Charles Ozanam, *Une Ambulance a la Bataille de Mentana* (Paris: Imprimerie Adrien La Clere, 1868), pp. 19, 29.
5   https://www.theosophical.org/publications/quest-magazine/3617-blavatsky-and-the-battle-of-mentana, accessed 1 March 2020. Theosophy is a philosophical movement, established in 1875, with numerous influences (including Hindu, Buddhist and Neoplatonic).
6   Pearson, *From Rome to Mentana*, p.146. These were not necessarily British veterans.
7   *The Tablet*, 11 January 1868, p.11.

fortified villages and hilly terrain, suited Garibaldi's favoured style of guerrilla warfare based on skirmishes and ambushes.

The March towards Mentana

The papal troops set off at 4.00 a.m. on 3 November, proceeding through the Porta Pia into the countryside, following the ancient Via Nomentana northeast out of Rome. Their uniforms stuck to their skin, shoes became full of water, equipment weighed down on them – though, confident of a short campaign, they carried supplies for only two days. Since the paper cartridges were dampened, hand-to-hand combat would be important in any fighting that day. The French followed behind, setting off at 5.30 a.m.

At the Ponte Nomentana over the Aniene,[8] with its picturesque medieval tower, three companies of Zouaves (3rd, 4th, and 5th Companies of the 2nd Battalion) under Major de Troussures were sent to the west up another ancient road, the Via Salaria. In case of an attack, they would advance on the enemy's flank and cause a valuable diversion.

Meanwhile, the Red Shirts were passing through the Mentana area. Their departure from Monterotondo had been delayed because of the need to distribute new shoes to some of the men. Garibaldi had initially appeared uncertain of his tactics and doubted the intelligence he received that the advancing Papal Army included a French contingent. He eventually ordered the advance towards Tivoli, where there was a strong Red Shirt presence, in the hope of avoiding a direct encounter with his foes. The result, paradoxically,

An engraving of Mentana, by the Zouave artist, George Collingridge. (Private collection, photograph: Granddaughters of George Collingridge)

---

8   Sometimes called the Teverone.

brought him closer to them and the reluctant decision was made to quickly take up position around the walls and in the buildings of Mentana, as well as in advance positions along the Via Nomentana.

It was a Sunday and when the main papal column stopped for rest and refreshment at 11, mass was offered in a wayside chapel dedicated to St Anthony Abbot at the Casale Capobianco, a farm complex and *osteria* situated on a crossroads. After 90 minutes or so confirmation reached Kanzler that the Red Shirts were a short distance away. There was a general air of expectation of a great, perhaps decisive battle. The Irish Captain Russell-Killough of the Foreign Carabineers wrote that 'for the first time, perhaps, since the beginning of the campaign, our hearts were joyful; a sort of general presentiment told us that this day, which seemed to be sad and rainy, would end in a brilliant way'.[9] As the troops rested in three lines on a large meadow, smoking, drinking coffee and enjoying their rations, and news arrived of an imminent engagement, Russell-Killough remembered the sun began to show through the dark clouds.

The troops scrambled into battle order, with final prayers being said by the chaplains and last-minute checks being made on ammunition and equipment. The Dragoons went ahead to scout for the enemy and form a protective screen, along with the avant-garde of three Zouave companies (1st, 2nd, and 3rd Companies of the 1st Battalion); the main papal column continued along the road with the French behind, acting as a reserve.

At last, the papal troops caught sight of Mentana, the Roman 'Nomentum', which gave its name to the road.[10] It was a typical Sabine town, famed for its olive oil and a meeting between Charlemagne and Pope Leo III in November 800. At its heart was the old *castello* and the Palazzo Borghese. When the English Catholic convert, Lady Herbert of Lea, visited in September 1868, she thought it 'perfectly glorious', with 'its old walls and buttresses and crenelated towers' making it look 'as if it had remained untouched since the Middle Ages'.[11] According to the American writer F. Marion Crawford:

> As the rider approaches Mentana the road sinks between low hills and wooded knolls that dominate it on both sides, affording excellent positions from which an enemy might harass and even destroy an advancing force. Gradually the country becomes more broken until Mentana itself appears in view, a formidable barrier rising upon the direct line to Monterotondo. On all sides are irregular hillocks, groups of trees growing upon little elevations, solid stone walls surrounding scattered farm-houses and cattle-yards, every one of which could be made a strong defensive post. Mentana, too possesses an ancient castle of some strength, and has walls of its own like most of the old towns in the Campagna, insignificant, perhaps, if compared with modern fortifications, but well able to resist for many hours the fire of light field-guns.[12]

A Papal Dragoon by the name of Arduino was the first to come across a small group of Garibaldians as his troop scouted ahead. He fired at them and in riding back towards his officer came under a hail of bullets. The battle had begun. The early stages of the fight were centred around the area to the south of Mentana, where Red Shirts had occupied strong defensive positions on the high ground and woods on either side of the road, establishing outposts at several strategic points. These had to be dealt with first before the village itself could be secured. These included, most notably, the Vigna Santucci, a large stone farmhouse on the right of the road, surrounded by a walled vineyard and outbuildings. On the other side of the road,

---
9   Russell-Killough, *Dix Années*, pp.439–442.
10 The name 'Mentana' was a corruption of 'Nomentum' and the later 'Civitas Nomentana'.
11 Herbert, *Mentana*, p.3.
12 F. Marion Crawford, *Sant' Ilario* (London: Macmillan & Co., 1895), p.202.

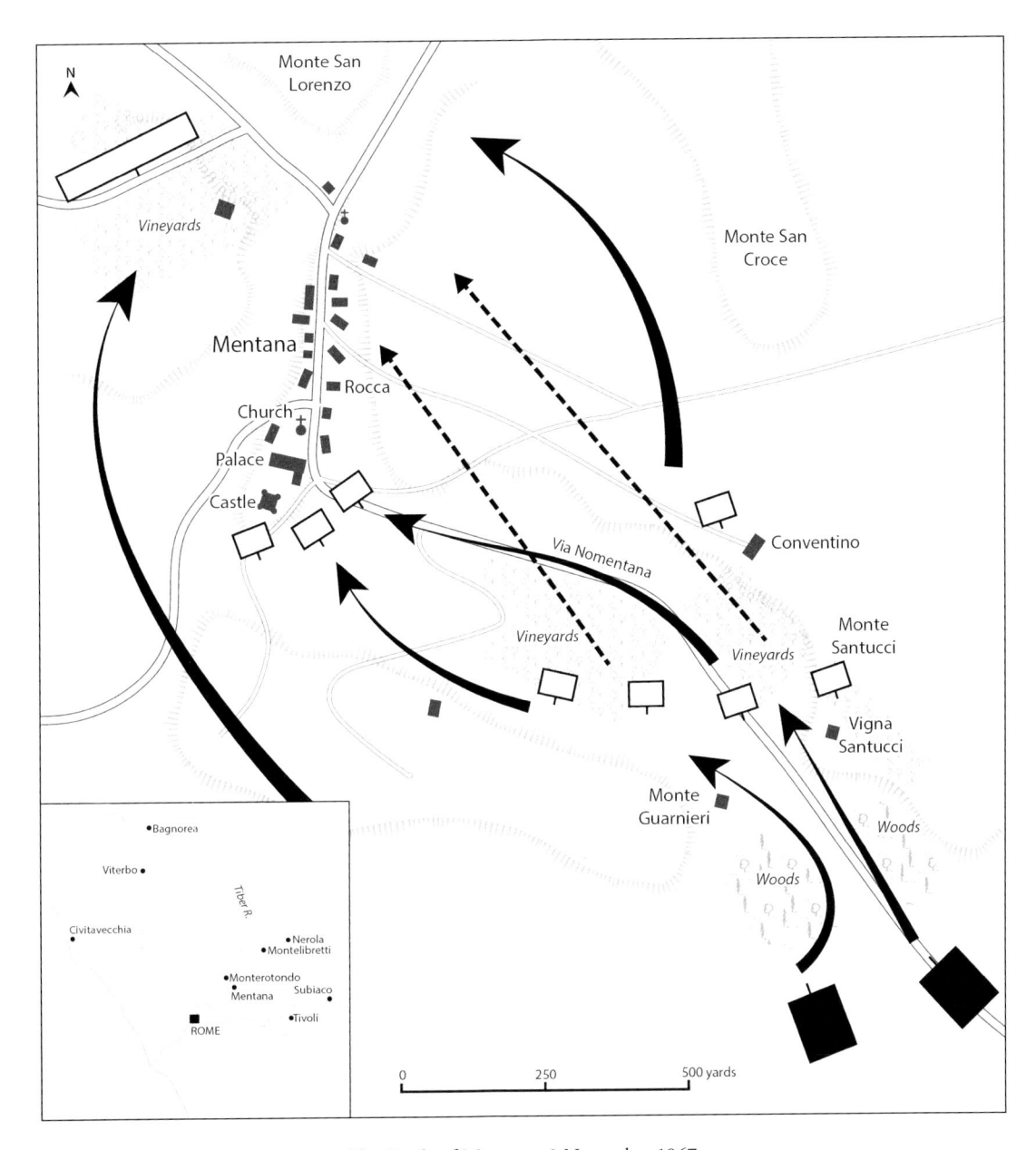

The Battle of Mentana, 3 November 1867.

Garibaldians took positions along the Monte Guarnieri, using the walls, vegetation and contours as natural cover as they awaited the advancing Franco-Papal forces. Further behind, also to the right of the road, was a second line clustered around an abandoned seventeenth-century *conventino*, once the home of Capuchin friars.

The Zouaves were ordered forward, supported by the Foreign Carabineers. According to Ozanam, the Zouaves, many of them French Legitimists, had wanted to be in the vanguard so that they could demonstrate to their compatriots in the Imperial Army their courage and loyalty to the cause.[13] The 3rd Company of Zouaves under Captain Alain de Charette (a veteran of Castelfidardo and the younger brother of the colonel) moved up the main road and forced some of the enemy to move back into the hills. The 2nd Company under Lieutenant Jean Thomalé made directly for the Vigna Santucci, where they encountered heavy fire. Colonel de Charette came forward with reinforcements, telling his men to drop their packs and charge. It was now that he uttered his famous words: 'Forward Zouaves! If you won't go, I'll go alone!' ('*Si vous ne me suivez pas, j'irai tout seul!*'). Meanwhile, the 1st Company of Zouaves under Lieutenant Numa d'Albiousse advanced up the Monte Guarnieri on the left, where Garibaldians were firing upon the papal troops.

In these early stages of the battle, Captain Arthur de Veaux was a conspicuous casualty. Much was made of the fact that the fatal bullet pushed his Castelfidardo Medal, with the words '*Pro Petri Sede*' ('For the Chair of Peter') into his heart. It seemed to encapsulate the cause for which the papal troops were fighting.

The main thrust of the Zouaves' attack proved initially effective. The Garibaldians fiercely defended their ground, firing on their enemy from behind trees, walls, and haystacks. They were gradually driven back one by one into the safety of the Vigna Santucci and the *papalini* advanced tree by tree, building by building. Kanzler stationed himself and one of his guns at a farmhouse on a nearby hill, with a clear view of the Vigna Santucci, to support the attack.

The Zouaves continued their assault on Santucci and, still under heavy fire, smashed down the door with axes and rifle butts. Charette was present in the midst of the combat, though much alarm was caused when he fell to the ground, his horse ridden with three bullets. Many Red Shirts were taken prisoner and, once the building was secured by the Zouaves, it was used as a base by Ozanam and the Sisters of Charity, who worked tirelessly in cramped conditions. 'You could not turn around,' wrote the doctor, 'without hitting a broken limb, a bleeding wound!'[14] Medical treatment was combined with the care of souls and special attention was given to the injured Red Shirts, that they might make their peace with God.

Kanzler also moved his headquarter there and, with the first objective taken, set his sights on the town itself. Several papal and French guns were moved to the nearby heights, which had an excellent view of Mentana, while another piece was moved further along the road, 500 metres away from the walls.

By 2.00 p.m. the papal troops were in a strong position and the offensive continued, under cover of the newly placed artillery. The Zouaves advanced towards the town, supported by the Antibes Legion on the left and the Foreign Carabineers on the right. The Garibaldians were soon driven from the *conventino* but the attack began to falter outside the village walls under intense fire from the buildings and castle.

Just after 2.00 p.m., Garibaldi surprised Kanzler by mounting a counter-attack on both flanks – the Legion and Dragoons on the left held their ground but the Carabineers on the right were pressed back, with their commander, Lieutenant Colonel Simon Castella, seriously injured. An ordinary soldier, Count Victor de Courten, who had retired from the Papal Army after nearly 30 years of service as lieutenant colonel

---

13 Ozanam, *Une Ambulance*, p.10.
14 Ozanam, *Une Ambulance*, p.22 (author's translation).

An Italian depiction of the fierce fighting at Mentana. (Private collection, author's photograph)

in 1861 and recently enlisted again as a private, was forced to take temporary command. It was a critical moment, for if the Red Shirts broke through, both the *conventino* and Vigna Santucci risked recapture.

Kanzler ordered the Antibes Legion to move to the right to support the beleaguered Carabineers; only two companies could be freed but this managed to restore the balance in favour of the Papal Army. However, there would be little opportunity for the pontifical troops to draw a sigh of relief. At 3.30 p.m. a second counter-attack was launched. Kanzler's men were increasingly fatigued after the long march and several hours of fierce combat, and ammunition was running low. Moreover, the detachment under de Troussures that had separated from the main army at the Ponte Nomentana had not yet reached Mentana.

Kanzler decided to call upon French support. He had hoped that the action could be won without recourse to this option and it seems that the French, perhaps following the orders of Napoleon himself, were content to observe the battle from afar and not take a leading initiative. Indeed, Polhés was slow to react to the request and Kanzler is supposed to have threatened complaining to the European powers about the treachery of the French.[15]

---

15   Alvarez, *The Pope's Soldiers*, p.188.

French troops advance on Mentana towards the end of the battle. Opponents of the Pope emphasised the decisiveness of their intervention, armed with the new Chassepot rifle. (*La Tribuna*, 3 November 1898, private collection, author's photograph)

A popular print of Mentana, published by Pinot & Sagaire. (Private collection, author's photograph)

The French appeared on both flanks of the pontifical forces, carrying their new breech-loading Chassepot rifles. It was an essential moment in the battle, dealing a grievous blow to Garibaldian morale; any counterattack would now surely be useless. Garibaldi left the scene late afternoon, leaving command in the hands of his son, Menotti. A mortally wounded Zouave from the Pas-de-Calais, Henquenet, described on his deathbed seeing the great man, dressed characteristically in red shirt, red cap and white feather, looking firm and determined but staying distant from the combat around him.[16] Kanzler quipped that he had turned his famous war cry of 'Rome or Death' into 'Run for your lives!' Garibaldi was later arrested at La Spezia, a railway station just outside Florence, and after three weeks imprisonment taken back to the seclusion of his island home.

Some Red Shirts fled into the countryside but enough were left to continue the defence of Mentana. Two papal guns were brought within 100 metres of the walls of Mentana by Captain Daudier, a veteran of Castelfidardo, though many of the gunners and their horses were felled by enemy fire and there was a real chance that the guns could be captured. Count Bernardini came forward with new horses and pulled the pieces back to safety, though he was killed in the process.

Kanzler commanded a final push, sending two battalions of the French 59th Regiment and a battalion of Chasseurs towards the main gate, but the Garibaldians held on, firing onto the troops from windows and barricades. Zouaves and Legionnaires came to their support and many acts of bravery were later recounted. However, it was now early evening and, as the light dimmed, Kanzler decided to pause the offensive and wait until the next morning. His troops camped for the night, with strong advanced posts to prevent any further counter-attack.

With superior resources and key objectives already taken, Kanzler was in a strong position. Nevertheless, there were many challenges to overcome. The troops were exhausted and hungry; another day of fighting was expected since Mentana was still occupied, and there were fears that the Italian forces gathered near the border might intervene. Supplies of food and drink were limited; when the owner of the Vigna Santucci went to draw water two miles distant, he found that the source produced only yellow liquid mud. The night was cold and windy and there were few blankets for the men to use.

The wounded were tended by the ambulances as best they could. Ozanam claimed that it was the first time that religious sisters were seen on a battlefield, within firing range, 'their white cornettes shining in the midst of the cannons, which they almost touched'. Medical equipment was largely lacking and many of the wounded still lay on the battlefield: their exposure to the plummeting temperatures in many cases worsened their state. Ozanam, who argued that soldiers should have basic first aid training and carry bandages with them, thought that what a soldier feared the most was the thought of being:

> abandoned at the bottom of a ditch, at the corner of a wall, stretched out on the cold, bare ground, losing all his blood, his voice too muffled to be able to cry for help, while the dark night reigns everywhere, the rain is falling, the wind is blowing and twenty paces away he may perhaps hear the only last friend who might be interested in him moving away with his regiment.[17]

The end came more quickly than expected. Early on the Monday morning a Garibaldian approached with a white flag and asked to speak with Kanzler. Russell-Killough of the Foreign Carabineers expected to see a colourful character in 'the obligatory felt hat, red shirt, tie fluttering in the wind, wide trousers tucked into rustic boots, belt with a conspicuous buckle', but was disappointed in the blindfolded bourgeois figure

---

16 Ozanam, *Une Ambulance*, p.14.
17 Ozanam, *Une Ambulance*, p.22.

being led towards the headquarters, with a black overcoat and 'a tie knotted with care!'[18] His request that the Garibaldians depart Mentana with their arms and baggage was turned down, but they would be escorted to the borders of the Papal States, where their weapons, ammunition and equipment would be left behind.

Meanwhile, fresh supplies reached the troops from Rome, including much needed water. Dr Ozanam had brought with him a large supply of cans produced by Liebig's Extract of Meat Company, founded only the previous year. In just a few minutes 180 cups of broth were produced at the Santucci, a 'culinary wonder' that much impressed Mrs Stone.[19] Prominent Roman families sent their carriages to help collect the wounded and they were taken not only to Santo Spirito in Sassia, Santa Trinita dei Pellegrini, and Sant'Agata but various makeshift hospitals; even a section of the papal palace at the Quirinale was handed over for their use. Kanzler reported over 1,000 Red Shirt casualties, while Garibaldian accounts mention 150 dead and 206 seriously injured. On the pontifical side, 30 were killed and 103 wounded, while only two French soldiers lost their lives and 36 were wounded.

The triumphant forces entered Rome on 7 November, escorting their prisoners. Reports of the reaction of the crowds differ. Lady Herbert exclaimed 'never was there such a reception from a grateful and joyous people. And yet there are men in England who will tell you that the Romans are weary of the Papal Government and wish in their hearts for Garibaldi and a United Italy.'[20] The *Tablet* reported that windows were filled with spectators and balconies draped with cloths and autumnal flowers; 'the Zouaves came first and were cheered again and again by the crowd'.[21] Other claimed that the cries of the crowd were focused on the French troops: 'Long live the Emperor!' A Protestant observer, Miss Pearson, noted a 'dead silence': 'not a hat was lifted, no viva greeted the conquerors. … The monks and priests alone were going about with a nasty smile upon their faces: it was the first day that we had seen many of them, hitherto they had kept studiously within doors.'[22]

In the days that followed, many travelled to see the bloody scene; omnibuses even advertised 'To the battlefield and back, a scudo'. Miss Pearson went with some companions: 'the whole plateau was covered with epaulettes, cartouch boxes, caps, belts, shoes, bayonets, broken musket stocks, &c., and we picked up what reminiscences we chose', including 'half a photograph of a lady, evidently Dutch, and taken at Breda'.[23] She was offered a fine linen shirt collar with an English maker's name stamped on the back of it for two baiocchi but declined since it was covered in blood. The dead were being buried by soldiers and local residents, many of whom had taken shelter during the battle in the woods and local caves.

Also to be seen on the battlefield were the Fratelli D'Alessandri, Don Antonio and Paulo Francesco, pioneering papal photographers. Their iconic shots of the undulating battlefield, littered with debris and dead Garibaldians, were included in the French journal *L'Illustration*, while CdVs of heroic (and sometimes wounded) Zouaves were widely distributed, proclaiming far and wide the papal victory. New technologies played their part in promoting the papal cause.

---

18   Russell-Killough, *Dix Annés*, p.460 (author's translation).
19   Ozanam, *Une Ambulance*, p.26. The same company produced the OXO cube in 1899.
20   Herbert, *Mentana*, p.26.
21   *The Tablet*, 23 November 1867, p.737.
22   Pearson, *From Rome to Mentana*, pp.143, 147.
23   Pearson, *From Rome to Mentana*, p.156.

Mentana: A Forgotten Battle

The Battle of Mentana has been largely overlooked by historians and dumbed down by contemporaries. 'As a political event,' wrote *The Times* correspondent, 'very little importance can be attached to the battle'; it was merely 'an affair of mathematics' since the victors had the greatest number of troops and the best arms.[24] The Pope was accused of massacring Garibaldi's volunteers. For the English observer, Miss Pearson, 'it was terrible to think of the Chassepot rifles, used against such boys, and by order of the Vicegerent of Christ upon earth'.[25]

Many were indeed disquieted that the pontiff had shed the blood of so many of his fellow countrymen. The size of the Pontifical Army seemed disproportionate to the actual population, and there were fears that the Papal States could become a military regime like Prussia. Odo Russell reported to Lord Salisbury that at the beginning of 1868 defences and earthworks were being constructed outside the walls of Rome and that 'France tends to make of Rome a fortified city and of the Pope a military despot'.[26]

The Garibaldian dead were treated as martyrs. Italian writers have seen Mentana as a necessary sacrifice on the road to national unity. The Red Shirts were compared to the heroic Spartans, outnumbered and defeated at Thermopylae in 480BC. A large and elaborate monument, the *Ara dei Caduti* (Altar of the Fallen), was eventually erected over the mass grave of the dead, with the words 'Rome or Death' inscribed on the side, and in 1905 the Museo Garibaldino was opened, interpreting the battle from the 'Italian' point of view.[27]

Such sympathy was shared by many across Europe. At his home in Guernsey, Victor Hugo produced 326 verses in three days on hearing news of the battle, attacking the ferocity and hypocrisy of the papal forces:

> Young soldiers of the noble Latin blood,
> How many are ye–Boys? Four thousand odd.
> How many are there dead? Six hundred: count!
> Their limbs lie strewn about the fatal mount,
> Blackened and torn, eyes gummed with blood, hearts rolled
> Out from their ribs, to give the wolves of the wold
> A red feast; nothing of them left but these
> Pierced relics, underneath the olive trees,
> Show where the gin was sprung–the scoundrel-trap
> Which brought those hero-lads their foul mishap.
> See how they fell in swathes–like barley-ears!
> Their crime? to claim Rome and her glories theirs;
> To fight for Right and Honour;–foolish names!

In England, Francis Palgrave celebrated the 'Lion-hearts of young Italy' in his poem 'Mentana', and Algernon Charles Swinburne wrote sonnets celebrating the battle on its first, second and third anniversaries. There

---

24 *The Times*, 12 November 1867, p.8.
25 Pearson, *From Rome to Mentana*, p.146.
26 Blakiston, *Roman Question*, p.349. A. Vigevano has calculated that there was one soldier per 53 inhabitants.
27 The museum was refurbished for the 150th anniversary in 2017, with the addition of a multimedia display, and the website speaks of the need to 'reflect' on the Garibaldian ideals behind the battle: freedom of peoples, the social dignity of every person, constitutional rights, the need for a homeland with common roots and shared values. https://www.mugamentana.it/ilmuseo/, accessed 19 August 2019.

were popular demonstrations too: Bonfire Night fell two days after the battle and one commemoration in London's East End featured figures of Garibaldi about to strike the Pope with his sword alongside Guy Fawkes.

Despite the small scale of the action, the consequences of Mentana were considerable. It was a disaster for the Italian Government, who were shown to be two-faced and conspiratorial. Once again, it was France that rushed to protect Rome from the revolutionaries rather than the King of Italy. Lord Clarendon dismissed Victor Emmanuel as 'an imbecile' and 'a dishonest man who tells lies to everyone'.[28] The Queen's Speech, shortly after the battle, acknowledged that Garibaldi's volunteers acted 'without authority from their own Sovereign' but expressed the hope that, now he had accomplished the objective of defending Rome, Napoleon 'will find himself enabled, by the early withdrawal of his troops, to remove any possible misunderstanding' between France and Italy.[29]

Mentana showed that the Red Shirts were hardly invincible and that, despite their undoubted courage, they were poorly trained and disciplined. The battle led to division within the Italian left, with some distancing themselves from Garibaldi and Mazzini, and declaring the former 'dead'. Though no one knew it at the time, Mentana was, in many ways, Garibaldi's Risorgimento swansong. He would have no further military involvement in the Unification of Italy and it would be Italian troops who breached the walls of Rome in 1870. Garibaldi seems to have been disillusioned not so much by his defeat but the betrayal of the Italian Government. After Mentana, he remained in seclusion on Caprera for three years, resigned as a parliamentary deputy and became 'an outspoken critic of the monarchy and the political system in liberal Italy'.[30]

For France, it was a mixed blessing. Napoleon's support for the Pope won him the approval of French Catholics and was a reminder, once again, of the supposed invincibility of the French Army – a myth that would prove fatal in the war with Prussia that broke out three years later. However, in the light of the September Convention, the involvement of the French weakened relations with Italy and deprived France of a potentially useful ally during the crisis of 1870–1871. In a speech before the French Senate, Eugène Rouher, seen by many as the '*vice-empereur*', famously said that the French would 'never' ('*jamais!*') allow Rome to be taken by the Italians. The following day, Napoleon congratulated him on his speech but noted that in politics one should never say 'never'. France was increasingly seen as the enemy of Italian Unification and this perspective was one reason why Italy allied with Germany and Austria in the years leading up to the First World War.[31]

Most Catholics, meanwhile, saw Mentana as a resounding triumph. Thomas Nulty, co-adjutor Bishop of Meath, told Kirby: 'Thanks be to God that the Garibaldians have been so soundly thrashed, that the Pope's soldiers have proved themselves heroes, and that the grand old Pope still retains his ground in spite of all his enemies.'[32] The same day, Manning wrote to Talbot at the Vatican that 'it seems to me that two good things have come: the infidel revolution has thrown off its mask and the Catholic world had made itself felt'.[33] Rumours circulated in the press about what a Garibaldian victory might have entailed:

> Five hours' pillage was to have been allowed by the Garibaldian army. The church and convents were to have been sacked, the priests massacred, the nuns insulted. Hundreds of barrels loaded

---

28 Lucy Riall, *Garibaldi: Invention of a Hero* (London: Yale University Press, 2007), p.351.
29 *The Tablet*, 23 November 1867, p.738.
30 Riall, *Garibaldi*, p.351.
31 Chadwick, *History of the Popes*, p.166.
32 KIR/1867/405, Nulty to Kirby, 6 November 1867.
33 AAW Manning-Chapeau Papers, Manning to Talbot, 6 November 1867.

with shot were found; and pour comble, a well-made guillotine, with ax, rollers, pulley, and all, en regle, was among the moral forces discovered in the search for arms.[34]

Talbot himself believed similarly: 'Rome has had a most providential escape from being sacked, and us all from being massacred.'[35]

Such was the paranoia that even Odo Russell's apartment in the Palazzo Chigi was searched by 'an officer and about 30 men in plain clothes'. They had been in the cellars looking for 'a mine or of Garibaldian arms supposed to be concealed there'. Russell was away in Florence at the time and understandably indignant, although none of his papers were confiscated. In meeting Antonelli for an explanation, he was told of the extraordinary measures necessitated by fear of insurrection and shown one of the dreaded 'Orsini bombs', which was 'the size of a large orange and so covered with copper caps as to blow up wherever they fall'. There were fears that the Palazzo Chigi, among others, had been undermined with explosives.[36]

A photograph of Mentana veterans, including Colonel Allet and several of the wounded, taken shortly after the battle at the Dutch Zouave Club near the Piazza Farnese, Rome. They are gathered around a bust of the Pope. (Zouavenmuseum, Oudenbosch, used with permission)

---

34 *The Tablet*, 23 November 1867, p.737.
35 AAW Manning-Chapeau Papers, Talbot to Manning, 13 November 1867.
36 Blakiston, *Roman Question*, pp.345–346.

Another image of the wounded of Mentana, possibly taken at the Quirinale palace. (Private collection, photograph: Granddaughters of George Collingridge)

The dead and wounded of Mentana were celebrated as heroes. On 8 November Pius IX was present at a requiem mass held in the Sistine Chapel, during which he was overcome with tears. He visited the wounded in the Roman hospitals, comforting those who came to defend him and including the Garibaldians on his itinerary. At Castel Sant'Angelo he visited 200 Red Shirt prisoners and is reported to having addressed them with his well-known wit and charm: 'Here I am, my friends: you see before you the vampire of Italy, of whom your general speaks. What! you all took arms to attack me, and you find only a poor old man.'[37]

The aftermath of the battle led to a wave of sympathy and enthusiasm among British and Irish Catholics. Requiem masses for the dead were celebrated in many churches. At London's Pro-Cathedral, 'the altar, the pillars, the throne and the pulpit were all draped with black velvet edged with gold lace' and before the sanctuary stood a large catafalque with candlesticks at each corner. Archbishop Manning alluded to the medieval crusades:

> [I]f it was an act of Christian chivalry to defend the frontiers of Christendom why is it not both Christian and chivalrous to defend its head and centre. [After all,] Rome is not the capital of Italy. It is the capital of Christendom; God has made it and man cannot unmake it, and all Christian nations have a right in it. [Thus,] the unity of Christendom will not make way for the unity of Italy.[38]

---

37 *The Tablet*, 16 November 1867, p.722.
38 *The Tablet*, 16 November 1867, pp.728–729.

St James' Hall was one of London's premier Victorian concert halls, with frontages on both Piccadilly and Regents Street, and an interior that echoed both Italianate and Moorish influences. The following year Charles Dickens was to host a series of sell-out 'Farewell Readings' at the venue but in December 1867 it was the turn of a large Catholic meeting. It was reported that 'almost every conceivable inch of superficial space in the building was occupied by one of the most influential assemblages that has for a long time assembled within the walls of a London assembly hall for a purely Catholic object'.[39] Among the many clergy present were Archbishop Manning of Westminster and Bishop Grant of Southwark; leading laity included the Earl of Denbigh, and Lords Petre and Arundell. The aim of the meeting was 'to sympathise with the Holy Father on the outrage and sacrilege which have been levelled against his sacred person and his sacred office'. As he opened proceedings, Manning presented some of the essential arguments:

> First, it is to deny that Rome is the capital of Italy (loud applause), and to affirm that it is the capital of Christendom (cheers); next, to deny that the so-called Italian nationality should absorb the patrimony of the Church (cheers), and then to affirm that the patrimony of the Church is sacred, and ought to be guaranteed by Christian Europe. Further, we are to affirm that it is the duty of every Christian Power to protect, if needs be in war, the Head of the Christian world.

The inconsistency of the British Government's position was highlighted: '[L]et England be consistent, let her equally oppose revolution in Italy and rebels in Ireland.' A resolution was passed to invite 'all Christians of every nation to rally round the throne of the Vicar of Christ, to assert his rights, and to aid him, by every means at their command, to defend his States, the common inheritance of the whole Catholic Church'.

Mentana meant that the life of the Papal States was extended – for three years, as it turned out, though the Catholic world hoped it would be longer – and confidence instilled in the papal cause. There was pride in Kanzler's achievement and a lessened sense of dependence on France. The reprieve allowed the Pope to make several important gestures to stress his authority. The eighteenth centenary of the martyrdom of St Peter and St Paul had already been celebrated that June, attended by over 500 bishops and 130,000 pilgrims. In April 1869 the Pope celebrated his golden jubilee of priestly ordination – a more intimate occasion but 'there was scarcely accommodation left even for a mouse'.[40] Most importantly, in December 1869 a General Council of the Church was convened in Rome, going on to solemnly define the dogma of papal infallibility. Had it not been for Mentana, it is unlikely that such a council would have met at this time.

There were hopes, also, that the Pope would regain the provinces lost to him over the previous decade. Shortly after Mentana, Napoleon III suggested an international conference to settle, once and for all, the Roman Question. Pius accepted the invitation on condition that the principle of legitimate right and justice be acknowledged and the territories 'robbed by the Piedmontese Government' restored.[41] Nothing came of the proposal.

The Pope quickly approved the striking of a medal to commemorate the Mentana campaign: a Greek cross with a central medallion and a blue and white ribbon. The obverse had papal keys and the words '*Fidei et Virtute*' ('With faith and courage'), and on the arms of the cross 'PIUS IX PP 1867'; the reverse showed

---

39   *The Tablet*, 7 December 1867, p.773.
40   *The Tablet*, 17 April 1869, p.801.
41   Blakiston, *Roman Question*, p.347.

the Cross of Constantine, a laurel wreath and the words '*Hinc Victoria*' ('Hence victory').[42] A cantata on the battle was composed by Rosati and a monument to the fallen pontifical soldiers unveiled in the Campo Verano Cemetery in June 1870, beside the basilica of San Lorenzo where Pius himself would be buried eight years later. Designed by Virginio Vespignani, it showed an armoured knight holding the papal flag and kneeling before St Peter and handing him his sword.

'*Les Chassepots ont fait merveille!*': *A Reconsideration*

The most common interpretation of Mentana is that the papal forces were only triumphant because of the intervention of the French with their new breech-loading rifles. As General Failly famously put it, 'the Chassepots did wonders' ('*Les Chassepots ont fait merveille!*'), suggesting the ineffectiveness of the pontifical offensive. The London *Times* even doubted Garibaldian reports that the brunt of the attack had been from the *papalini* since their uniform 'differs in nothing but the cockade from that of the French troops, on whose pattern it was organised'.[43] As far as Talbot was concerned, the victory was indeed a French one: '[I]f our army had been armed with the best rifle in existence, and France had not interfered, Rome would have been sacked and all of us massacred. It was Almighty God and his saints who freed Napoleon to send his troops to Rome against his will.'[44]

The bolt-action breechloading rifle with needle ignition had been designed by Alexandre Chassepot and adopted by the French Army in 1866.[45] Mentana was its first test in action. On paper it signified an important advancement in firepower and was far superior to the Prussian Dreyse. Up to 15 rounds could be fired per minute and it reach a distance of 1,200 metres. An English observer with the Germans during the War of 1870–1871 noted that 'the immense distance that a Chassepot ball sometimes strays is notorious'. It made two distinct noises: 'when in its most dangerous flight it makes a prolonged and musical ping as it passes you' while 'when nearly spent the ping is changed into a whistle'.[46]

The Mentana Medal of George Collingridge, with bars for 'Roma,' 'Nerola,' and 'Mentana.' (Private collection, photograph: Granddaughters of George Collingridge)

---

42 Eight bars existed for the medal: AQUAPENDENTE, BAGNOREA, MENTANA, MONTE-LIBRETTI, MONTE-ROTONDO, NEROLA, VITERBO and ROMA.
43 *The Times*, 12 November 1867, p.8.
44 AAW, Talbot to Manning 13 November 1867.
45 When the rifle's developer met the Pope in December 1868, 'His Holiness jocularly observed that M. Chassepot's name made a great noise in the world' (*Morning Post*, 24 December 1868, p.5).
46 Hon. C. Allanson Winn, *What I Saw of the War: A Narrative of Two Months' of Campaigning with the Prussian Army of the Moselle* (London: William Blackwood & Sons, 1870), p.80.

Nevertheless, the accuracy of the rifle could be affected by its vicious recoil and its tendency to foul the barrel with gunpowder after constant use. Its effectiveness was also limited by the nature of the battlefield of Mentana, which was characterised by uneven ground, full of vines, trees and walls. The enemy was largely unseen, barricaded into buildings and shooting through windows. Many of the French troops would have been inexperienced in the use of this new weapon. One of the Garibaldians, Augusto Mombello, later wrote in his memoir that the Chassepot shots were largely 'badly directed' and 'exceeded the target by a third in height' or else they hit the ground 'raising dust and stones'. Moreover, 'in the jagged terrain of small hillocks and hollows the long range is worth much less than the precision of the shot'.[47]

Further evidence of the limitations of the Chassepot was provided by a physician, Dr Gason, who attended to many of the wounded and whose observations were eventually reported in *The Lancet*. At previous trials of the rifle in Lyons, using dead horses, the 'disproportionate size of the exit as compared with the entrance wound' was noted, revealing the damage potentially inflicted by the bullet. However, the experience at Mentana seems to have been different. There was little difference in size between entry and

A group of Zouaves at the castle of Mentana shortly after the battle. (Zouavenmuseum, Oudenbosch, with permission)

---

47 Lorenzo Innocenti, *Per il Papa Re. Il Risorgimento Italiano Visto Attraverso la Storia del Reggimento degli Zuavi Pontifici, 1860/1870* (Perugia: Casa Editrice Esperia, 2004), p.84 (author's translation).

exit wounds; compared to the muzzle loaders, long bones were more frequently fractured and there was less effusion of blood beneath the skin; 'the immediate effects of the chassepot were more fatal, but the ulterior effects less fatal and severe'. The majority of wounds were in the upper part of the body, which implies that the inexperienced French infantry were firing too high.[48] The Chassepot was, nevertheless, a cutting-edge weapon which clearly startled contemporaries with its fearsome possibilities. Mentana remains an important moment in the development of nineteenth-century firepower.

The intervention of the French at Mentana came at a critical moment. However, this was only after the pontifical troops had borne the brunt of the offensive amid hours of intense combat, summed up by the English Zouave, George Collingridge: '[I]t was a terrible fight. … [W]e, the Papal Zouaves, used the long blade bayonets, while Garibaldi's troops lunged with their three-cornered spike bayonets. But we won the day. … I will carry a bayonet scar on my knee to my grave as a memento of that day of slaughter.'[49] The myth of the Chassepot at Mentana allowed supporters of Garibaldi to hide their defeat behind the veneer of technological progress. Credit must be paid to Kanzler's achievements both in crushing the insurrection in Rome and winning on the battlefield.

---

48 *The Lancet*, 26 September 1868, pp.421–422.
49 *Australian Star*, 10 November 1908, p.1.

11

Reform and Internationalisation of the Pontifical Army

In the aftermath of Mentana, Rome remained on a war footing. Through that winter the barricades could still be seen at the gates, and fortifications were constructed on the Aventine Hill. 'The Belvedere court of the Vatican became an arena for trials of strategic skill, the conflagration and rescue of mimic fortresses,'

Through the winter of 1867, barricades and defences could be seen at strategic spots around Rome, including the Porta del Popolo and Porta San Giovanni in Laterano. (*Illustrated London News*, 23 November 1867, Private collection, author's photograph)

wrote one observer, 'the Borghese Villa, for mock fights and assaults of bulwarks.'[1] For fear the tricolour might be illegally hoisted, it was prohibited 'to ascend up to the lantern and descend into the crypt of St Peter's, to mount the corkscrew stairs in the columns of Trajan and Marcus Aurelius; and (still more annoying to the eager tourist) the prohibition to ascend the tower of the Capitol, whence is enjoyed the finest panorama of the city and her environs'.

For Kanzler, Mentana had been a triumph and the army enjoyed a surge of morale. If the Garibaldians could be defeated, then surely the wider war against all the enemies of the pontiff and 'true religion' could be won. Kanzler energetically continued his army reforms, which now seemed fully vindicated. All aspects were covered. The medical service was improved, logistics expanded, and a board was set up to monitor army hygiene. With the experience of the Mentana campaign in mind, an equipment train was established, initially made up of 117 men, 151 horses and 68 wagons of different types. Given the proven threats to the States of the Church, military funding was increased to such an extent that between 1867 and 1869 more spending was provided than in the previous six years combined.[2] In 1868 the Zouaves grew to five battalions and was given full regimental status.

Much attention was given to the training of troops, with weekly rifle practices and regular exercises. In his letters home Joseph Powell, an English Zouave, described a sham fight behind Tre Fontane on the Via Ostia, in which the Dragoons executed a 'magnificent cavalry charge', and the tir or rifle practice: 'we are mustered into ranks by daybreak, and then march out to the Farnesine Meadows. … It takes two hours at least for the whole company to fire the requisite number of shots.'[3]

Charette, with (to his left) the English Zouave Clement Bishop (1839–1921) at the summer camp at Rocca di Papa, 1868. (Private collection, photograph: Ursula Staszynski)

---

1 *Union Review* (1871), pp.75–76.
2 Alvarez, *The Pope's Soldiers*, pp.209–210.
3 Powell, *Two Years in the Pontifical Zouaves*, pp.76, 86.

In the summer the Army held several intensive weeks of training and mock battles in the Alban Hills to the south of Rome, in which the Pope took a keen interest. In August 1868, for example, he visited one division while training at Hannibal's Camp, near Rocca di Papa. A temporary structure was erected for the celebration of mass, including an image of the barque of St Peter made from 'platted barks of trees and coloured canvasses', rising from which was the figure of Our Lady and the Zouave banner. On either side of the ship was a dragon, 'representing Italy, which seemed to be struggling to destroy it, but was restrained from doing it injury'. The troops slept in tents but were inventive in constructing wooden 'day-houses', some of which had two stories.[4] Rocca di Papa was an excellent choice of location and several degrees cooler than Rome. However, when exercises were held there the previous month, proceedings were affected by appalling weather. As the Pope stood at the altar, rain pierced the roof of the makeshift chapel and a red umbrella was held over him; moreover, 'the white linen for the altar was retained in its place by the weight of bullets and the host was placed under a glass clock stand to prevent it being carried away by the tempest'.[5] After blessing the troops, he left the field, which had become nothing less than a quagmire, and 'could only proceed by catching at the rifles of the soldiers'.

Armaments were also improved. Initially, the Papal Army of the 1860s used a variety of firearms with no standardised ammunition, including old-style muzzle-loading muskets. Change was necessitated by the speedy developments in small arms during the period, as clearly demonstrated by the use of the Chassepot at Mentana. Batches of new rifles started arriving from the end of 1868, largely funded by the Papal Committees around Europe. These were Remington breech-loaders, variants of the Remington M1867 made under licence from the American gunmaker by Westley Richards in Birmingham and the Belgian firm of Nagant in Liege. Fitted with a rolling block, it boasted a cutting-edge design and had won a medal at the previous year's Imperial Exposition in Paris. The English Zouave, Joseph Powell, wrote that it was 'very simple, light, and a breech-loader, and we are able to fire very rapidly with it'. He spent three weeks training with the rifle and used a new manual, *Theory of Rifle Shooting*, with the hope that excellence in marksmanship would earn him promotion.[6]

A further 10,000 muskets were adapted into breech-loaders for the indigenous troops, half of which were produced by the Vatican Arsenal and the other half being Tabatière rifles from France, converted from the old Miniés. When the supply of the new rifles was delayed, Kanzler considered accepting the offer of the French Government to purchase 20,000 Chassepots at cost price, which worked out cheaper than the Remington while ensuring that all papal troops used the same guns and the same bores. However, it was decided to stick with the original contract since many members of the committees were 'not warm partisans of the Napoleonic Government'.[7]

Kanzler even purchased a primitive machine gun, invented by the American F.S. Claxton and made in Liege, which had six horizontal 25mm guns that could fire 80 shots a minute. In the words of David Alvarez, this made 'the papal army the third in Europe (behind the British and French armies) to deploy rapid-fire weapons'.[8]

The final years of Papal States therefore paradoxically saw the Pontifical Army at its peak. Discipline was excellent and motivation generally high, with most officers boasting recent combat experience both in 1867 and the campaigns against brigandage. The late 1860s saw a flood of volunteers: '[T]he Pope's army,'

---

4   *The Sun*, 25 August 1868, p.8.
5   *Edinburgh Evening Courant*, 10 July 1868, quoting the *Pall Mall Gazette*.
6   Powell, *Two Years in the Pontifical Zouaves*, pp.99, 108. The Remington 'pontificio' model boasted the crossed keys and tiara stamped on the stock.
7   *Morning Post*, 23 December 1868, p.5.
8   Alvarez, *The Pope's Soldiers*, p.210.

wrote Odo Russell a few weeks after Mentana, 'is being rapidly increased, and every ship from France brings recruits for the Zouave and Antibes Legion to Civitavecchia.'[9] There was a clear desire to emulate the example of the heroes of 1867 and the expectation of future battles. Moreover, the hope that the restoration of the Pope's lost territories was imminent meant that troops would soon be needed 'to occupy Umbria, the Marches and Romagna'.

Zouaves from the Netherlands were particularly numerous.[10] Despite Catholics making up just over a third of the population, over 3,000 volunteered for pontifical service. Like England and Wales, Dutch Catholics had been recently granted a restored hierarchy of diocesan bishops, the first since the Reformation, with the archbishop based in Utrecht, a city known for its Protestantism. This had led, in 1853, to anti-Popery demonstrations and the fall of the government.

Nevertheless, the period saw, on the Catholic side, an increase in religious vocations and church activity. The number of Zouave recruits can be explained not only by the strength of this resurgent Catholicism but by its politicised and well-organised nature. Dutch society was distinctive for its *verzuiling*, or pilarisation: Catholics and Calvinists, socialists and liberals each constituted a self-sufficient 'pillar', with its own set of churches, political parties, schools, hospitals, welfare agencies, scouting associations, social clubs and so on.

The clergy did much to coordinate the movement that sent volunteers to Rome, including Cornelius de Kruyf, an Augustinian in Amsterdam who became known as the 'Father of the Zouaves'. Oudenbosch in North Brabant became a central point of recruitment. Not only was it well-connected, with excellent road, railway and water links, but its pastor for over 40 years, Willem Hellemons, worked tirelessly for the cause, supported by his assistant, Brother Bernardinus. Here volunteers gathered and caught trains that took them to Marseilles and ultimately a steamer to the Papal States. The ultramontane sympathies of Hellemons can still be seen in the magnificent basilica he begun in 1865, with a facade modelled on St John Lateran and a dome and interior inspired by St Peter's, albeit on a smaller scale.

The North American Dimension

Two Canadians from Montreal fought with the Zouaves at Mentana: Alfred La Rocque (who had studied at Stonyhurst, the Jesuit school in Lancashire) and Hugh Murray; both were seriously injured. In subsequent months appeals were made across the territory and the Bishop of Montreal suggested that each Catholic should contribute 25 cents, making a potential diocesan contribution of some CAN$100,000. A central committee was set up in Montreal, with La Rocque, now invalided out of the Pontifical Army, acting as treasurer, and recruitment began. Concerns were expressed that this process was illegal; after all, Canada was at peace with Italy and strenuous efforts had previously been made to prevent Canadians from fighting in the American Civil War. Nevertheless, as in the United Kingdom, the Foreign Enlistment Act remained a dead letter and it was even argued that it did not apply since Italy and the Papal States were not technically at war.

On 18 February 1868 a colourful 'demonstration' was held for the first contingent of 133 recruits in Montreal's parish church of Notre Dame, before an estimated congregation of 15,000. The men wore their Zouave uniforms, lovingly made by nuns, and were presented with their colours, bearing the papal tiara and arms of Canada, complete with maple leaves and beaver. They responded with a resounding 'yes' to the question posed by Bishop Bourget: 'Will you brave children of religion and the country take your oath

---

9 Blakiston, *Roman Question*, p.347.
10 There were Dutch Zouaves from the early 1860s, but two thirds of recruits joined after Mentana.

to do nothing during the noble crusade on which you are about to enter, which might make blush your faith and your land, of which you desire to be the ornament and the glory in the eyes of stranger nations.'[11]

There was music, including Rossini's overture to *L'Italiana in Algieri* (appropriate given the Algerian roots of the Zouaves), and a hymn which celebrated Montreal as the 'Rome of the New World'. The printed text of the bishop's lengthy discourse was arranged into 23 sections and included a survey of the threats faced by the Church down the centuries and reference to the 'providential mission of the Canadian people', opening with the words: '[T]he whole earth is a vast battlefield and human life is a continual war.'[12] Bourget's devotion to the Eternal City was such that, like Fr Hellemons in Oudenbosch, he built a cathedral based on St Peter's.

On arriving in Rome the following month, the Canadian Zouaves marched with colours flying to the Vatican, where the Pope saluted them from a window of his palace. Their presence would introduce Canadian ways into Rome: one of their most surprising legacies was the game of lacrosse, hitherto unknown in Italy. There was hope that a Canadian battalion of Zouaves could be set up, with their own officers and barracks, 'a little Canada on the banks of the far away yellow Tiber', their number exceeding that of a lukewarm Europe.[13] Although the number making the transatlantic journey impressed many, it was never sufficient, in the eyes of Kanzler, to merit a separate unit.

The response of the United States was less enthusiastic. Charles Carroll Tevis, a convert to Catholicism who had trained at Westpoint and fought with the Turks in the Crimean War, the Union Army in the American Civil War and, more recently, the Fenian Army, offered to recruit an American battalion of Zouaves.[14] With the help of the *Freeman's Journal* of New York, an enthusiastic promoter of the papal cause, appeals were made for recruits. It was even suggested that if every Catholic parish donated US$100 in gold every year, a unit of 1,000 troops could be funded. However, many of the American bishops showed coldness and even hostility to the proposals, perhaps because of fears that fighting for the Pope would throw doubt on the patriotism of American Catholics. As in Great Britain, Catholics were often seen as 'foreign', largely made up of immigrants, and politically subversive, especially since the papacy was perceived to have favoured the Confederacy during the Civil War. As already noted, the Zouaves had been tainted in American eyes by its brief connection with John Harrison Surratt, whose mother had been hanged for her involvement in Lincoln's assassination. A number of individual Americans signed up, from both the north and the south, and Tevis was appointed a Papal Chamberlain in February 1868 for his loyal efforts, but the American contingent never matched that of its northern neighbours.

---

11 Edouard Lefebvre de Bellefeuille, *Le Canada et les Zouaves Pontifcaux. Memoires sur l'Origine l'Enrôlement et l'Expédition du Contingent Canadien à Rome, Pendant l'Année 1868* (Montréal: Typographie du Journal 'Le Nouveau Monde', 1868), p.64.
12 Lefebvre de Bellefeuille, *Le Canada et les Zouaves Pontifcaux*, p.64.
13 Howard R. Marraro, 'Canadian and American Zouaves in the Papal Army, 1868–70', in *Canadian Catholic Historical Association (CCHA) Report 12* (1944–45), pp.89-92.
14 According to *The Irishman*, 7 March 1868, p.14, Tevis was 'a remarkably handsome, intellectual-looking man. His wife – his second – is a Jewess of great beauty and an immense fortune, and all admit him to be as brave as a lion.'

12

British and Irish Recruits

A handful of British and Irish recruits served with the Pontifical Zouaves in its early years. The first, according to the official matriculation list, was Joseph Wells of London, who joined the Pontifical Army in 1860 as a Crusader of Cathelineau, quickly moved to the Franco-Belgians, saw action at Castelfidardo, and transferred to the newly formed Zouaves in February 1861.[1] As already noted, several members of the Irish Battalion transferred to the Zouaves in 1862. Veterans of the 1867 campaign included two sets of brothers, Alfred and George Collingridge, and Julian and Wilfrid Watts-Russell, as well as Charles Woodward, Daniel Shee and Oswald Cary (a cousin of the Collingridges).

Alfred Collingridge and Julian Watts-Russell: English Martyrs for the Nineteenth Century

Crucially, two English Zouaves were included among the fatalities of 1867. The first, Alfred Collingridge, was originally from Godington, Oxfordshire, and one of the first English Zouaves: he had left the Institute Notre Dame in Auteuil, where he hoped his studies would lead to his entry into the Jesuits, and enlisted on 19 May 1866 – the same day as John Herbert Dalton of Liverpool.[2] It is recorded that 'he hoped to go to Heaven by the direct road of martyrdom, by dying on the battlefield, as a soldier, as he had formerly wished to die, as a Priest, tending the sick'. At Montelibretti, he was seriously wounded and, along with five others, taken by the red shirts to a chapel at Nerola which had become a makeshift hospital. There he was eventually visited by Mrs Stone, Monsignor Stonor and his brother George, who had only recently joined the Zouaves and happened to be in a company arriving in the area. Alfred is reported to have said: 'The Lord has given me the favour I asked – to die for the Holy Father. Oh yes, may God accept of my death and my blood for the triumph of the Holy Church and for the conversion of England!' Expressing sentiments similar to those recorded in many other Zouave hagiographies, he became 'the first of the victims of Catholic England for the cause of the Holy See' and, on hearing of his death, his father expressed the regret that he could not take his son's vacant place.[3] George wrote home on 23 November reporting he

---

1 Wells also appears as 'Charles' and left the Zouaves on 1 July 1861.
2 Little is known about Dalton; he is not recorded as having been awarded the Mentana Medal and was ejected from the unit on 1 January 1868.
3 *The Tablet*, 26 October 1867, p.681; Valerian Cardella, *Giulio Watts-Russell, Pontifical Zouave* (London: John Philp, undated), p.53; N. Nuyens, *Gedenkboek der pauselijke Zouaven* (Roermond: Henri van der Marck, 1892), p.238. Alfred was buried at Nerola and a window was later erected to his memory at the beautiful Catholic Church of the Holy Trinity, Hethe (Oxfordshire).

was now in possession of some of his personal effects, including a 'medal rosary' and the money he was saving for a new watch, and that 'he is now a saint in heaven praying for us, our family must be happy to have such a martyr for the church of Jesus Christ'.[4]

The second English 'martyr' of 1867 had a particular reputation for holiness: Julian Watts-Russell ('Giulio'), of the 2nd Company of the 1st Battalion of the Zouaves, was killed in the later stages of Mentana by a bullet that pierced his right eye. Aged only 17 and ten months, he was subsequently presented as the ideal Zouave. Watts-Russell ticked a number of boxes. He was young and belonged to a *nouveau riche* family, based at Ilam Hall near Ashbourne, Staffordshire. The estate had been brought in 1809 by David Pike Watts, a wealthy brewer and vintner. In 1816 it was inherited by his daughter, Mary, who married Jessie Russell, a devout Anglican who served as MP for Gatton and High Sheriff of Staffordshire, who rebuilt the house in the neo-gothic style.[5]

Their second son, Michael, was educated at Eton and Christ Church and ordained in the Church of England. He became Rector of Benefield, Northamptonshire, near the second family home of Biggin Hall. In 1845 he became a Catholic, along with his wife and children, and as a result was excluded from his father's will. By the time of Julian's birth in 1850, the family lived in Florence; the baby was baptised by the archbishop himself, Cardinal Piccolomini. Their life was itinerant, flitting between Kensington, Florence, Venice, Rome (where the boys enrolled in the Collegio Nobili) and Vouvray, near Tours. They also considered starting a new life in Australia.

Alfred Collingridge (1846–1867), one of the first English Zouaves, who was mortally wounded at Montelibretti. (Private collection, photograph: Granddaughters of George Collingridge/Susie Gore)

The Watts-Russells were deeply religious. Maria, mother of Julian, died of consumption in 1851 and on her deathbed appeared to see 'an angel who was eagerly waiting to conduct her into the presence of God'.[6] Michael was a friend of other converts such as Frederick Faber, Edward Caswall and John Henry Newman and, in later life, was ordained a priest of the Archdiocese of Westminster, spending his final years residing at the French shrine of Lourdes. When he was told of his son's death, he exclaimed that 'if he had ten sons,

---

4 Anon., 'Pontifical Zouaves: The Collingridge Brothers' in *Vatican News. The Journal of the Vatican Philatelic Society*, 6: 354 (2012), p.22.
5 The name was changed to 'Watts-Russell' by Royal Licence.
6 Cardella, *Giulio Watts-Russell*, p.18. For Julian, see also Richard Whinder, 'Julian Watts-Russell and the Papal Zouaves', in Nicholas Schofield (ed.), *A Roman Miscellany: The English in Rome, 1550–2000* (Leominster: Gracewing, 2002), pp.109–121.

Two photographs of Julian Watts-Russell (1850-67). (Private collection, photographs: Granddaughters of George Collingridge)

he would be willing that they should all be thus gloriously sacrificed in so holy a cause'.[7] Of the other children, one became a Carmelite nun at Darlington and another a Passionist priest.

The young Julian possessed all the masculine qualities that were expected in the mid-nineteenth century. As a student at Ushaw College, the Catholic school and seminary near Durham, 'he was so fond of amusement and bold adventures that he not unfrequently got into "scrapes"' and was particularly influenced by nautical tales. He wrote a story in which he described himself sailing to Australia in a little boat and on one occasion escaped the college with a companion, turning their coats inside out as disguise and carrying only two shillings between them. They hoped to reach the nearest seaport and embark on 'some strange adventure' but lost their way and were brought back to the college, tired and hungry. A letter written from his worried father is preserved in the Ushaw archives. After news of his death reached his alma mater, it was proudly said 'Giulio ran away from Ushaw, but he did not fly before the muskets at

---

7   *The Tablet*, 17 March 1894, p.416.

Mentana'.⁸ He and his brother had considered a military career and an Austrian connection offered them commissions in the Imperial Army at the time of Austro-Prussian War but were put off due to the Foreign Enlistment Act.

His deep piety spread even into the military sphere, especially 'his holy custom of reciting an *Ave* to the Blessed Virgin, whenever he fired, for the poor soul whom his shot might send into eternity'.⁹ A South American Zouave who was with Julian at Mentana described him as 'an angel of vengeance' as he charged with fixed bayonet, bareheaded since a bullet had knocked off his cap.¹⁰ This perhaps summed up the nineteenth-century ideal of the Zouave, combining soldiery courage with deep piety.

A manuscript book of devotion was found on his body, including the lines: '*Anima mia, anima mia/ Ama Dio e tira via*' ('My soul, my soul, be this thy song/Love, love thy God and speed along'). This was much quoted and, translated into French, used by the Canadian Zouaves as their motto. It formed the chorus of the 'Song of the English Zouaves': 'Love God, oh my soul, love Him alone/And then, with light heart, go thy way.'¹¹

Another key element was his virtuous life and his youthful purity. Indeed, it is interesting that throughout Zouave literature 'there was never mention of a fiancée, or even a girlfriend at home or a possible love interest in Italy'.¹² The majority of Zouaves went on to marry and raise families in later life. However, for the purpose of their service in defence of the Pope, they were presented as models of purity, like the early Roman martyrs.

The body of Julian Watts-Russell was initially buried in the cemetery at Monterotondo. Shortly afterwards it was recovered by a friend, the Chevalier Geneste, and brought to Rome, where it was embalmed and lay in state in a private house near St Mary Major, dressed in his Zouave uniform, with 'a wreath of white roses', a crucifix and a palm

Wilfrid Watts-Russell (1846-79), Julian's older brother and fellow Zouave. (Private collection, photograph: Granddaughters of George Collingridge)

---

8 Cardella, *Giulio Watts-Russell*, pp.25–27.
9 Cardella, *Giulio Watts-Russell*, p.59.
10 Cardella, *Giulio Watts-Russell*, pp.58–59.
11 Ushaw College Archive UC/P9/22/12, letter from Mother Drane to John Walker, 1 January 1869. In 2011 Colin Mawby set the 'Song' to music, at the request of the Latin Mass Society, and it is sung during the annual walking pilgrimage to Walsingham. Information from an email from Dr Joseph Shaw, Chairman of the Latin Mass Society, 6 April 2020.
12 Thomas Buerman, 'Lions and Lambs at the Same Time! Belgian Zouave Stories and Examples of Religious Masculinity', in Jan De Maeyer, Leen Van Molle, Tine Van Osselaer & Vincent Viaene, *Gender and Christianity in Modern Europe* (Leuven: Leuven University Press, 2012), p.113.

A composite image of the Zouave 'Martyrs' of 1867, formed in the shape of a cross, with those who fell at Nerola, Bagnorea, Montrelibretti and Mentana. Alfred Collingridge is right of the central oval, and Julian Watts-Russell can be seen at the extreme bottom left. (Zouavenmuseum, Oudenbosch, used with permission)

to symbolise martyrdom. Many came to pay their respects and exclaimed 'What an angel he looks!'; some kissed his body and took away the evergreens that surrounded him. On 9 November he was solemnly received at the English College by the Rector, Father O'Callaghan. The requiem was celebrated the following day in the presence of Monsignors Stonor and Talbot, as well as many of his Zouave companions. Some of the students at the college had known Watts-Russell at Ushaw. His brother, Wilfrid, could not help saying that 'the funeral had left upon him the impression of a *Festa*'. The body was viewed one last time before being placed in its leaden coffin and taken to the cemetery at Campo Verano; 'that sweet smile on the innocent face, and that suppleness of the whole body, assured them that he slept the sleep of peace'. The blood-stained uniform was sent back to his father in England to be treasured as a 'family relic'.[13] The Carmelite nuns of Darlington (a community that included his sister, Catherine Ellen) produced 'a small picture of the field of Mentana, in which that town is represented in the distance, and Giulio's soul as winging its flight from the field of battle to Our Lady, by her to be presented to her Divine Son'.[14]

Julian was also remembered at Mentana. His heart, which had been removed during the embalming process, was buried there and in 1869 a monument erected, with a cross in the shape of the Mentana medal. On the inscription Julian was described as 'the youngest who fell on the field of victory and the nearest to the gate of Mentana'.

The cult of the dead Zouave had many similarities with the cult of the saints: the martyr's palm, the viewing of the body that reportedly remained fresh and supple, the relics and pictures that were distributed, the shrines that were erected. It also bears comparison to that of other Zouaves who fell in the campaign. Urbain de Quelen's death at Montelibretti was seen in continuity with his forebears who had fought in the Crusades; the family motto was: 'There are always Quelens to defend honour and right.'[15] In a letter to the *Universe*, comparison was made between the angelic smile seen on Arthur De Veaux's face, not a drop of blood staining his uniform, with the corpse of a red shirt lying nearby on the battlefield of Mentana, 'bathed in blood, with damnation written on his face'.[16]

Most extraordinary was the precedent set at Castelfidardo by Joseph-Louis Guérin, a young Breton seminarian at Nantes who joined the Pontifical Army in 1860. Technically he was not a Zouave, since the unit

Emmanuel Dufournel (1840-67), a Zouave from the very beginning, was mortally wounded at Farnese on 19 October 1867. He delighted in shedding his blood through his fourteen wounds for the glory of the Church. (Private collection, photograph: Granddaughters of George Collingridge)

---

13 Cardella, *Giulio Watts-Russell*, pp.3–5, 71–72.
14 Cardella, *Giulio Watts-Russell*, p.79.
15 *The Tablet*, 9 November 1867, p.705.
16 *The Tablet*, 16 November 1867, p.722.

had not yet been founded, though there are images of him in the distinctive uniform. Although initially he had joined the Crusaders of Cathelineau, he transferred to the Franco-Belgian Tirallieurs and was seriously wounded in the chest at Castelfidardo, a bullet puncturing his lung. He was taken to the convent at Osimo, which had been made into a hospital, where gangrene set in and he died in agony on 30 September, aged 22. In February 1861 his body was brought back to France and buried at the ecclesiastical cemetery of La Barberie. Pilgrimages were organised to his grave, novenas recited and relics eagerly distributed. The Abbé Allard, who had personally known the young seminarian, published a hagiography within a few months of his death. Even the Pope had an image of the young 'martyr' placed near the chapel in his summer residence at Castel Gandolfo and there was talk of his impending beatification.

Many miraculous healings were claimed; 30 alone in 1861. One of the most famous occurred in Rome in March 1863, when Guérin appeared in the Zouave uniform to a blind 15-year-old girl, the niece of the parish priest of San Rocco. She told him that she had been praying to be healed of her blindness and he told her to keep on praying. Two days later, in the early evening, he appeared again and said: '[Y]our prayers are answered; get up and see.' The girl could indeed see and soon identified the man in her vision when she saw an image of Guérin. The popular cult that surrounded Guérin continued in France until the 1950s and in 2014 his tomb was restored by the diocese of Nantes. It spread across the Channel; writing from Brussels in 1862 while his wife was ill, Major O'Reilly asked Kirby for an image of Guérin: '[H]e was a most pious youth and we have been praying to him'.[17]

The Jesuit priest, Valerian Cardella, referred to Watts-Russell as the 'Guérin of England' and noted how his friend, the Chevalier Geneste, who helped with the arrangements for his funeral, had been intimately involved in Guerin's obsequies. Watts-Russell had heard him speak of the French hero and 'had often kissed the medal of the ancient Image of our Blessed Lady of Spoleto, which Guerin had brought from that place on his march to Castelfidardo, and which he had left with Signor Geneste as a souvenir of his death-bed'.[18] Like Guérin, Collingridge and Watts-Russell were seen as martyrs. Fr Cardella confessed that he had never offered a Mass for Julian's soul since he considered him already in heaven. Archbishop Manning recalled:

> I remember bidding farewell to Julian and Wilfrid Watts-Russell, in their Zouave uniform, on the Piazza Farnese in July [1867]. I little thought then of the duty of veneration I am fulfilling now. If it be true that *Causa facit martyrem*, the cause makes the martyr, this noble disciple and soldier of Jesus Christ has won a martyr's crown.[19]

The translator of a Flemish Zouave novel, *The Double Sacrifice*, published to promote the papal cause in the English-speaking world, noted that critics had accused Pio Nono of bathing his banners at Monterotondo and Mentana in the blood of Italian boys:

> They *were* bathed, in good truth, in the free, pure blood of our English boys, who gave the flower of their bright and beautiful lives for the defence of the Vicar of Christ – true and worthy successors of the *flores martyrum* on whom S. Philip's eyes rested in wistful tenderness, when they

---

17   KIR/1862/176, O'Reilly to Kirby, 10 October 1862.
18   Cardella, *Giulio Watts-Russell*, p.71.
19   Cardella, *Giulio Watts-Russell*, Preface.

came to Rome to be trained for the gibbet and the axe, and to make their blood the seed of a harvest which is now beginning to whiten the fields of our long barren and desolate land.[20]

The Zouave volunteers were thus compared to the young men who trained at the English College, Rome, in the sixteenth century and were greeted by St Philip Neri, who resided at the church opposite, with the words '*Salvete flores martyrum*' ('Hail! Flower of the martyrs'). Many of them returned to England to face a martyr's death. Martyrdom in the nineteenth century took on a different guise, but it was martyrdom nevertheless.

The victory at Mentana and the heroic witness of two new English 'martyrs' resulted in an increase in British and Irish recruits. There was a sense of urgency, even prior to the campaign: '[W]e have not a man or a rifle too many. It is no question now of an idle garrison life. The Pope's flag is in the field, and the question may be decided in a month from this time.' The Roman correspondent of *The Tablet* gave instructions for would-be Zouaves:

> All that is necessary is to bring a letter from the bishop of the diocese or the parish priest and arrive in Rome, the quickest route being by Paris and Marseilles, and as a direct service for bringing the volunteers is organised it is only necessary on reaching Marseilles to ask at the railway station of the Chef de Gare the way to the Bureau d'Expedition du Zouaves Pontificaux, and every facility of speed and price is immediately given. The Pontifical Consulate is of course in direct communication with Rome and will furnish all directions on arrival at Marseilles.[21]

The Question of Motivation

Why did they join the Pontifical Army? The subject of motivation is a complex and problematic one for the historian and, of course, each individual had his own unique circumstances. In their memoirs and letters, Zouaves often stressed what they thought others wanted to hear, maintaining silence on other, more mundane or personal factors. Nevertheless, it is clear that their Catholic faith and devotion to the Pope were a major factor for many. There was a widespread fear of revolution, the work of the Freemasons and secret societies, and the spread of liberalism, all stemming from the 'anti-Christian' principles that had been spread through the Enlightenment and French Revolution. The English Zouave, Joseph Powell, thought these 'subversive of all government' and resulted in 'liberty and license; fraternity; atheism; and a belief and worship of the goddess Nature'.[22] Contemporary events were interpreted apocalyptically, and action was needed urgently. Some even had a hope of martyrdom: a comrade recalled that John Archdeacon 'expected the martyr's crown' and seemed 'fully prepared, if not more fully prepared to receive it than any other Zouave I ever knew'.[23]

Added to this was a desire to defend the Pope, who was seen through his tribulations as a living martyr, and his temporal power, regarded as a guarantee of his authority. This was considered a common cause for

---

20 Rev. S. Daems, *The Double-Sacrifice; or, The Pontifical Zouaves. A Tale of Castelfidardo* (Baltimore, MD: Kelly, Piet & Co., 1870), p.vi.
21 *The Tablet*, 19 October 1867, p.365.
22 Powell, *Two Years in the Pontifical Zouaves*, p.15.
23 W.J. Jacob, *My Personal Recollections of Rome: A Lecture, Partly Delivered on the 9th of February 1871, at the Town Hall, Pontypool* (London: R. Washbourne, 1871), p.78.

all the faithful: if Rome was the Pope's capital, then all Catholics were its citizens. As Manning had argued at the Mentana requiem, it was an error that 'the highest and ultimate unity on earth is a unity of a nation' since there was a higher unity 'in which the welfare of all nations is bound up – the unity of the Christian world'.[24] The Papal Volunteers were fighting for their 'nation' of Christendom just as much as the 'Italians' were for theirs.

The religious motivation of recruits was ensured by the requirement that each man provide a letter of recommendation from his priest. 'I beg of the clergy,' wrote one English promoter,

> that they will be most careful to give certificates to those only on whom they can thoroughly depend – men with an undivided heart, who are content to fight for the holy cause in whatever capacity it shall please their superiors in Rome to place them. … Let them weigh well, if the cause of the Holy Father is so dear to their hearts that it outweighs the patriotic feelings that at present fill the breasts of most of their countrymen. If they are not imbued with this spirit, let them remain at home.[25]

Priests were even urged to write a separate letter so that their signatures could be checked with those on the letters of recommendation.

Yet, within the transnationalism of the Pontifical Army, there was great pride that a soldier's own nation was part of the common fight. During the Siege of Rome, William Jacob, originally from Cardiff, was aware that he was 'the sole representative of St David in the Pontifical army. If I could have got it, I certainly would have worn a leek in my kepi on the memorable day of the Porta Pia. … When dragged through the Via Babuino as a prisoner, I thought of my countryman, Caractacus, and consoled myself with the reflection that I was not the first Welshman led through Rome as a captive.'[26]

British and Irish recruits had their 'national' reasons to fight for the cause. There was gratitude for Pius' restoration of the hierarchy in England and Wales in 1850 and his support for Ireland during the Famine. There was a hint in some sources of reparation for past wrongs: in her poem, 'Vicisti!', Mrs Stone, a keen supporter of the Zouaves, wrote of 'the task of expiation' for 'the sacrilege of ages' – namely the Protestant Reformation.[27] Moreover, English recruitment may have been influenced by the militarisation of Victorian society, which saw 'unprecedented adulatory attitudes towards Britain's professional soldiers', who were no longer 'brutal and licentious soldiery' but 'thin red 'eroes', as well as a 'civilian imitation of military organization, discipline, and paraphernalia' and 'the diffusion of military sentiments and rhetoric in general'. Such developments had gained a Christian veneer, with popular biographies detailing how Victorian soldiers combined 'devout piety with distinguished military service'. The 1860s saw the composition of hymns that displayed a forthright Christian militarism, such as 'Onward Christian Soldiers' and 'Fight the good fight', though these were not initially part of the Catholic canon.[28]

From an Irish perspective, as in 1860, there was the same contradictory dynamic of protecting the Pope in order to protect Ireland and its ancient faith. Yet, support for the pontiff implied a denial of the Italian right to fight for their own nationhood, despite the fact that many Irish Catholics hoped for a loosening of

---

24   *The Tablet*, 16 November 1867, p.728.
25   *The Tablet*, 11 January 1868, p.26, letter of Mary C. Kavanagh.
26   Jacob, *My Personal Recollections*, p.74.
27   Katherine Mary Stone *Our Flag: A Lay of the Pontifical Zouaves and Other Poems* (London: Burns & Oates, 1878), p.45.
28   Olive Anderson, 'The Growth of Christian Militarism in Mid-Victorian Britain', *English Historical Review*, 86:338 (1971), pp.46–47.

the bonds with Great Britain. There was a close connection between the two causes: when Father Thomas Roche of Enniscorthy in County Wexford wrote introducing two recruits, Charles and Bartholomew Teeling, he noted 'they bear a historic name and the blood of martyred patriots runs in their veins' – as important an attribute, it seemed, as their piety and good character.[29]

For some Irish, serving the Pope was an attractive alternative to joining the British Army. Charles Edward Lynch wrote to Monsignor Kirby at the Irish College in 1863 that he had been nominated for a commission but was reluctant to take it up since 'firstly I have a great dislike to England and the English, secondly to live on my pay in the English service I should be continuously on foreign service perhaps in India or some bad climate, and the thirdly the want of religion and morality in the army is quite disgusting'.[30]

There were other attractions to serving with the Pontifical Army, including worldly advantages beneficial to those leaving Catholic schools and colleges. Two years of service provided training and discipline that could be useful for a future career and the experience of living abroad and learning some Italian and French would be valuable life skills. George Collingridge, a budding artist, used his spare time to study the old masters in the galleries and paint studies of the Roman *campagna*, like many a grand tourist. His brother, Alfred, who was also a talented artist, had initially hoped to continue his studies in any spare moments and asked his parents to send him Latin and Greek dictionaries and grammars.[31]

There was also a rare opportunity for travel and adventure, with many of the expenses being met. Volunteering for service overseas was a radical 'break with dull daily routine' and could be 'seen in the context of the Romantic exaltation of adventure as well as the search for different forms of sociability, in this case in martial and mostly male societies'.[32] William Jacob's *Recollections* featured lengthy descriptions of the Vatican and other sights. Joseph Powell's memoir, *Two Years in the Pontifical Zouaves*, included the subtitle 'A Narrative of Travel, Residence and Experience in the

George Collingridge (1847-1931) later moved to Australia and became a well-known artist, historian and linguist. In his youth, he had studied under the architect Viollet-le-Duc and the artists Corot and Harpignies. (Private collection, photograph: Winsome Collingridge)

---

29 KIR/1867/336, Roche to Kirby, 17 September 1867. Charles Teeling never joined the Zouaves and instead entered the engineering profession. See KIR/1867/355.
30 KIR/1863/168, Lynch to Kirby, 16 June 1863.
31 Typescript of Alfred Collingridge's letter to his parents, Velletri, 26 September 1866, given to the author by Susie Gore.
32 Ferdinand Nicolas Göhde, 'German Volunteers in the Armed Conflicts of the Italian Risorgimento 1834–70', *Journal of Modern Italian Studies*, 14:4 (2009), p.466.

Roman States'. Alongside accounts of life in the corps and the campaigns of 1867 and 1870, there are descriptions of beautiful scenery, a boating trip on Lake Bolsena, splendid papal ceremonies and sites of antiquity. Such excursions were facilitated by the two-thirds discount papal soldiers enjoyed on railway fares. Despite the limitations of army service, Zouaves were able to follow in the tradition of the Grand Tour and, in having personal contact with the Holy Father and visiting the churches of Rome, continue in the footsteps of generations of pilgrims.

There was a tremendous diversity in ages and backgrounds. Most recruits were in their late teens or twenties – it was, in many ways, a cause that was particularly attractive to the young and, once they reached the Papal States, many wore beards to hide their youthfulness. There were more mature recruits, however: William Brennan, a Londoner who had spent some years as a 'colonist' in Australia, joined at the age of 45, and Jacob Hinde, a former Church of England clergyman and one of the few Welsh Zouaves, was 52.

The Catholic Aristocracy and the Zouave Movement

The Zouaves claimed to be marked by equality: '[E]veryone enters the ranks,' explained Powell, 'no matter what his station in life may be, so that we number a prince and men of noble blood amongst the privates, as well as a good many of high family, and a great admixture of the middle classes.'[33] Promotion was technically possible for anyone, though in practice it was reserved for those who were proficient in French.

The French members of the Pontifical Zouaves contained a large number of nobles, especially from Brittany and the Vendée. The British Catholic aristocracy and gentry were also represented, though not in such large numbers. The Papal Defence Committee, which helped organise the logistics and financing of recruitment, included such illustrious names as the Earls of Denbigh and Gainsborough, and Lords Arundell, Herries, Langdale, and Petre. The Marquess of Bute, one of the richest men in the country, also became interested in the Zouaves after his conversion to Catholicism in 1868. During his visit to Rome at the end of the following year he appeared in group photographs with them and 'liked to watch the Zouaves at rifle-practice in the Borghese

A *Vanity Fair* cartoon of Rudolph Feilding, 8th Earl of Denbigh (1823–1892), chairman of the Papal Defence Committee and prominent lay supporter of the English Zouave movement. (Private collection, author's photograph)

---

33   Powell, *Two Years in the Pontifical Zouaves*, p.54.

Gardens, visited the officers on guard at the Colosseum and elsewhere, and entertained them once at a famous supper of which the recollection long survived in the corps'.[34]

A handful of recruits were drawn from these aristocratic families. Oswald and William Vavasour grew up at Hazlewood Castle in Yorkshire, where their family had lived since the reign of William the Conqueror; on a clear day (it was said) both York Minster and Lincoln Cathedral could be spotted from the crenelated tower and the Catholic mass had been celebrated without interruption through the vicissitudes of the Reformation in the little Chapel of St Leonard. Their cousin, the Honourable Walter Constable Maxwell, a friend of the Marquess of Bute, was the son of Lord Herries of Terregles, whose ancestor, the Jacobite Earl of Nithsdale, had managed to escape the Tower of London the day before his execution in 1716 by exchanging clothes with his wife's maid. Another kinsman in the Zouaves was Arthur Joseph Stourton, whose grandfather, the 19th Baron Stourton of Allerton Castle, was celebrated for having written down the memoirs of Mrs Fitzherbert, the secret wife of George IV, which she dictated to him.

Oswald Petre, born in New Zealand but later returning to England, was the nephew of the 12th Baron Petre of Ingatestone and Thorndon Hall in Essex. The English Zouave chaplain, Monsignor Edmund Stonor, was the son of Lord Camoys of Stonor Park, the co-founder of the Henley Regatta. Frederick Welman belonged to a well-known Somerset family based at Poundisford Park and Norton Manor. Although it was his father who had brought them into the Catholic faith, they were already well-connected: Frederick was a cousin of the Earl of Gainsborough and had recently gained a Stonor brother-in-law.

The Catholic aristocracy also acted as an example and encouraged those in their locality to support the cause. Alexander Wilson of Leeds is said to have been encouraged to join the Zouaves by William Vavasour.[35] Likewise, Henry Charles Weetman grew up on his father's farm in Wiltshire and may have been encouraged in his intentions by the Arundell family, who lived nearby at Wardour Castle.

Alexander Wilson (1855–1901), born in Scotland but settled in Leeds. He worked variously on the railways, with the police and as a rent collector, but it seems his health never recovered from his service as a Zouave. (Private collection, photograph: Kath Bracewell)

---

34 David Hunter-Blair, *John Patrick Third Marquess of Bute, K.T.* (London: J. Murray, 1921), p.88.
35 https://ajwpapalzouave.blogspot.com/, accessed 5 November 2020.

The number of well-born Zouaves was necessarily small: the great Catholic families had dwindled over time and, for many, serving Queen and Country was seen as a more promising option for those with a military disposition. Some may have been touched by residue 'Cisalpinism', which viewed excessive devotion to Rome and the Papacy with suspicion. Nevertheless, there were enough volunteers from the old Catholic families to show a marked continuity with the values and traditions of their forefathers and the potency of the inter-connections among the Catholic aristocracy and gentry.

In addition to these were recruits from wealthy backgrounds, such as Clement Vansittart, belonging to a family of Dutch merchants who had settled in England in the early eighteenth century. His mother, along with three aunts, became Catholic in 1845, which led to estrangement from her husband, Reverend Charles Vansittart, the Rector of Shottesbrooke, Berkshire, a notable divorce case and a move to Italy. Indeed, a number of Zouaves came from British families who lived on the European mainland and thus had a heightened awareness of the movement of papal volunteers: not only the Vansittarts but the Watts-Russells, Collingridges, and Coventrys. George Collingridge later admitted that having received his education in Paris, he counted himself a Frenchman and proudly bore his battle scars as 'emblems of his French fighting past'; indeed, he was attracted to the Zouaves as he saw them as 'the most reckless soldiers in France'.[36]

Other recruits had close associations with the clergy. John Errington was the nephew of the famous archbishop, the *bête noire* of Cardinal Wiseman, while James D'Arcy, a veteran of the 1860 campaign who carried the Zouave banner at Mentana, was the great-nephew of the Vicar General of Waterford, and had two priest uncles. The Vavasour brothers had an uncle who was a canon in the diocese of Leeds and Walter Constable Maxwell's uncle was a Jesuit.

Clement Bishop and Francis Mandy were both seminarians at Oscott when they joined the Zouaves in early 1868; the former returned to seminary after his service but was never ordained. Alfred Collingridge was studying in France with the intention of becoming a Jesuit

Charles Woodward (1850–1916), a veteran of Mentana and later the Boer War. His brother had fought with the Franco-Belgians at Castelfidardo. (Birmingham Archdiocesan Archives, OCA/6/3/1/W/38, used with permission)

---

36 *Australian Star*, 10 November 1908, p.1.

when he joined the Zouaves in 1866. His family boasted a bishop among its ranks and his brother, Charles, was ordained, serving for a time in Australia (he was a chaplain to the New South Wales Contingent that took part in the Suakin Expedition of 1885) and in the diocese of Westminster. Though he did not follow his brothers into the Zouaves, 'much of his leisure was devoted to literary work in English and French, chiefly in vindication of the rights of the Holy See to independence and temporal power'.[37]

Others were converts to the Catholic faith: Charles Woodward, James Coventry and the Watts-Russells were all sons of former Anglican clergymen. Jacob Hinde had been ordained and served as curate of Llandinam, then in Montgomeryshire, before 'crossing the Tiber'. John Kenyon, the grandson of Baron Kenyon and nephew of the Church of Ireland Archbishop of Armagh and Primate of All Ireland, was received into the Church just before volunteering in 1870 and was disinherited as a result.

Only a handful of volunteers already had some military experience. A Lancashire recruit writing home in March 1868 mentions a 'Major L.', 'a capital companion' who had spent nine years in India.[38] Arthur Stourton initially joined the 20th (East Devonshire) Regiment of Foot and then moved to the 78th Highlanders (Ross-shire Buffs), serving as Ensign and Lieutenant. His elder brother, Marmaduke, held a commission for many years in the 63rd (West Suffolk) Regiment of Foot and died while on duty in Pietermartizburg in 1879. Arthur Combes of Dorchester had also served as a lieutenant. Others were part of the Victorian tradition of amateur soldiers: John O'Donnell, for example, was a Captain in the 64th Lancashire Rifle Volunteers.[39] Zouaves from the upper classes normally had relatives who held military commissions, which, combined with a deep Catholic piety, may have encouraged recruitment: Clement Vansittart, for example, had an uncle who was killed in the Second Opium War of 1859 and two others who were officers in the Coldstream Guards and the Life Guards. The father of the Irish Zouave Bartle Teeling had served with the British Auxiliary Legion in the First Carlist War in Spain.

The majority of Zouaves belonged to the professional and working classes. Among the ranks were sons of lawyers, farmers, writers, millers, upholsterers and carpenters. Both Philip Duke and John O'Donnell were sons of well-known doctors; Joseph Hansom's father was a prominent architect who gave his name to the Hansom cab; and Ernest Burchett the son of an artist with links to the Pre-Raphaelite movement. The Collingridges were yeoman farmers in Oxfordshire and Philip Vassar, a convert, grew up on a Norfolk farm of 70 acres. A number were Oxbridge graduates. The Zouaves were thus more socially diverse in rank and file than any contemporary unit in the British Regular Army.

Despite claims of equality among the English-speaking Zouaves, there was a definite distinction between gentlemen and those of a humbler birth: an unofficial officer class. According to Father William Delany,

---

37   *The Tablet*, 3 August 1907, p.178. The Suakin Expedition was the first time an Australian colony deployed a military contingent overseas and constituted the Australian Army's first battle honour. Another brother, Arthur Collingridge, painted *The Embarkation of the Sudan Contingent at Circular Quay, Sydney, 3 March 1885*, now displayed at the Australian War Memorial, Canberra.

38   *Preston Chronicle*, 4 April 1868, p.2. This could be Ralph Fitzgibbon Lewis, who was wounded in the Indian Mutiny with the 86th (Royal County Down) Regiment, though he does not appear in the matriculation list of Zouaves. The *Morning Post* (24 December 1868, p.5) mentions Major Lewis as serving with the Zouaves and, in a letter from Fr Charles O'Connor to Mgr Moran (?) of 30 September 1868, he is mentioned as acting as Charette's secretary, presumably because of his linguistic abilities. IE/DDA 333/3/5.

39   This unit, known as the 'Liverpool Irish' or even the 'Catholic Brigade', was founded in April 1860. As a result of the Cardwell-Childers army reforms it became the 5th (Irish) Volunteer Battalion in the King's (Liverpool Regiment), which, as we shall see, had several prominent connections with former Zouaves.

gentlemen who have private resources are, of course, not at all dependent on the barracks allowances. They may have private apartments, can go to balls, parties, &c., dine where they please. Their accoutrements are cleaned and kept in order by some poorer Zouave, who takes in compensation their barracks allowance. In a word, they have almost none of the privations or hardship of soldier's life.[40]

Such arrangements could cause friction: Walter Constable Maxwell reported that he had fallen out with Oswald Petre, 'a desperate fellow', over accommodation that was too expensive and consequently moved to another room, which was in the same building as Frederick Welman, though he complained there was no sitting room to share. His cousin, William Vavasour, had to intervene with the landlady since, he confessed, 'my Italian prevents me drawing up any agreement myself'.[41]

In early 1868, Perceval Mitchell narrowly avoided court martial by taking advantage of this system of independent living. He apparently

> deserted his barracks, went to the Hotel de Roma where he lived in grand style for five weeks and ran up a bill for more than 500 francs. The landlord then finding he had no money turned him out and sent the bill to Monsignor Stonor. Mitchell went back to the barracks but the same day or next deserted again and went to the Hotel de la Minerve where under a false name he stayed for ten or twelve days. One day, however, he was recognised by his sergeant and arrested. Mitchell knocked down the sergeant in the street, burned the sergeant's face with his cigar to make him leave his hold and get away.[42]

On a happier occasion, Monsignor Stonor hosted a special dinner at Spilmann's restaurant to celebrate the Queen's Birthday in 1868, to which he 'convoked 18 of the most aristocratic English Zouaves'.[43] There were also occasions when all were able to participate; 60 marked St George's Day 1869, shortly after being received in audience by the Pope, at the Café de Paris, at which the health both of the Pope and Queen was drunk and the boisterous singing of the National Anthem astonished the Romans.

Networks of Recruitment

In December 1867 three youths from Worcester left for Rome: Henry Swift, Joseph De Courcy and James Dunn. The first of these had been an inmate of the Worcester Workhouse and subsequently found employment with a Catholic baker in the city; shortly afterwards he was received into the Church. This led to the Board of Guardians intervening, especially when one of the three men returned home complaining of the food and conditions: 'I did not like the living nor the people with whom I had to associate.'[44] There were suspicions that the three youths had been forcibly enlisted and that they were under 18. The fact that one of the lads, despite his limited education, had written at the top of a letter from Rome the Latin

---

40 IE/DDA 333/3/VI/2, Fr William Delany S.J., 'The Irish Zouaves 1867–68'.
41 UDDEV-60-30-52, letter from Maxwell to his father, undated.
42 IE/DDA 333/3/VI/2, Delany, 'The Irish Zouaves'. There were complaints that Mitchell escaped punishment and was allowed home on leave while an Irish Zouave, John Walshe, was sent home in disgrace for a less serious offence.
43 *The Tablet*, 13 June 1868, p.372.
44 *The Scotsman*, 1 February 1868, p.7, quoting the letter of Dunn.

abbreviation 'A.M.D.G.' seemed proof that they were not acting on their own volition.[45] The local priest, Father Waterworth SJ, was called in by the Board of Guardians to give an explanation.

The priest understood that the boys had decided to travel to Rome after 'seeing the statement in the paper that Major Gordon was going to Rome and a pastoral of the Bishop referring to the soldiers who had gone out to support the Holy See'. He believed that they were over 18 and reported that he himself had dissuaded them from joining the army, since they all had 'good situations in the city'. However, he promised to make enquiries on their behalf and wrote to 'a certain nobleman upon the subject, who replied that in consequence of the operation of the Foreign Enlistment Act it would not be well for him to have anything to do with it, but told him that he knew of a person in London who would give him the information he wanted'.

Despite his reluctance to support their decision, he gave them £1 each and one of them a greatcoat for the journey. He insisted that they gained parental permission: Mrs Dunn wished her son 'God speed' while De Courcy's mother wanted her son to return since 'he contributed to the maintenance of an invalid brother and herself'.[46] Mr Longmore of the Board of Guardians, in justifying his involvement in the matter, presumably spoke for many when he stated: 'I hold that every Englishmen has a right to interfere when he sees lads set out of the country to the join the army of the most despotic power in Europe.'[47]

The case of the Worcester recruits, though exceptional, highlights a number of important factors encountered by many British and Irish Zouaves. The influence of family was essential. The Collingridge brothers were joined by their cousin, Oswald Cary; Oswald and William Vavasour by their cousin, the Honourable Walter Maxwell Constable. The two Holtham brothers, sons of a Worcester tailor, and the three Keens brothers of London likewise all volunteered.[48] Peer influence could also be decisive. When Donat Sampson arrived in Rome in 1867 to study art, he met a fellow Irishman, Bartle Teeling, who had just arrived to join the Zouaves. He induced 'his new-found friend to lay aside his pencil and his palette and they both marched off to the depot'.[49] Recruits often left for Rome in small friendship groups, as in the case of the Worcester recruits or James Kinsella and Frank Stanley, whose departure from Crewe was announced in a local paper in September 1868.[50]

The Role of the Clergy and Catholic Colleges

Great Britain had no Catholic universities and so lacked the 'Academic Committees for the Support of the Papal Army' that were established in Germany to disseminate the latest news from Rome, collect money and promote enlistment. Nevertheless, the Catholic colleges – many of them consisting of both school and seminary – had an important role to play, at least informally. All provided recruits, although their numbers were always small.

By the first half of 1868 Oscott College, near Birmingham, had produced Clement Bishop, Francis Mandy, Oswald and Walter Vavasour, Frederick Welman and Charles Woodward; another old boy, Randolfo Gabrielli-Wiseman, nephew of the cardinal, had several years earlier joined the Papal Artillery. St Cuthbert's College, Ushaw, near Durham, could boast not only of the Watts-Russell brothers but William

---

45 Standing for '*Ad Maiorem Dei Gloriam*' ('For the greater glory of God').
46 *Worcester Journal*, 18 January 1868, p.8.
47 *Worcester Journal*, 15 February 1868, p.7.
48 Their maternal grandfather was an officer in Louis XVI's guard exiled to London during the French Revolution.
49 *The Tablet*, 2 January 1915, p.25.
50 *Congleton and Macclesfield Mercury*, 12 September 1868, p.1.

Johnson and Francis Newsham. Stonyhurst, the Jesuit college outside Preston, had already provided Alfred La Rocque, a Canadian student, in February 1867, and the following year the names of William Vavasour, Walter Constable Maxwell and Benjamin Holtham were added to the list. St Edmund's, Old Hall Green in Hertfordshire produced Bernard Charles Molloy and Upholland claimed Alfred Renaud.[51]

When news reached Ushaw of the death of Julian Watts-Russell at Mentana in November 1867, there was an explosion of enthusiasm among the boys, many of whom would have remembered him: 'Julian's photographs are amongst us,' wrote one. 'I fancy a couple of hundred will be amongst us next week. Two young fellows, who have given up studying for the Church, left here yesterday with the intention of starting for Rome.'[52] The boys arranged a raffle to raise funds to provide the necessary uniforms, donating gold pins, college prizes, prayer books and other valuables as prizes. Parents had, of course, to be persuaded and superiors may have shared the same concern aired by the Belgian bishops, who feared that the minor seminaries might easily be emptied and the papal cause would become a *bambineria*, merely one for children.[53]

Oscott College took pride in its Zouaves. At the annual dinner of the Oscottian Society in 1869, the president, James Spencer Northcote, paid homage to two alumni present who had joined this 'honourable corps'. Charles Woodward had already seen action at Mentana, while Frederick Welman was ready to do so and, judging from 'the way he had wielded the cricket-bat, there could be no doubt but that he could handle the rifle or the sword with equal efficiency'.[54] Such recruits are likely to have been inspired by the Romanità of Northcote, who had lived in Rome shortly after his conversion in 1846 and wrote a scholarly work on the archaeology of the catacombs.

Away from the colleges, many clergy took a prominent role in drumming up recruitment among their flocks; not all were as ambivalent as Father Waterworth in the case of the Worcester youths. A notable example was the convert, Canon Thomas William Wilkinson, a future bishop of Hexham and Newcastle, who looked after a large area of County Durham and established missions at Wolsingham, Crook, Tow Law and Willington. This was virgin territory for the revived Catholic Church. At Wolsingham he started with a chapel in a hay loft and a school in the stables below; over 22 years he built three permanent churches and founded schools and convents. He had a great devotion to the Pope and his parishioners were generous in their contributions to Peter's Pence. Six young men from his congregation 'fired with their pastor's spirit, went out to Rome to join the Papal Zouaves and to shed their blood, if necessary, for the sacred cause'.[55] When Wilkinson visited his men in Rome in July 1869, the Pope personally presented him with a silver medal of the Mentana monument at the Campo Verano 'as an acknowledgment of his services'.[56]

When William Jacob published a lecture on his experiences as a Zouave, he dedicated it as a tribute to Father Elzear Torreggiani, an energetic Capuchin friar who had been born not far from the battlefield of Castelfidardo and served the Welsh Catholics around Pontypool. His forthright views on the Temporal Power undoubtedly helped to inspire Jacob to join the Zouaves at the beginning of 1870.[57] In the Midlands mission of Wednesbury, Father George Montgomery sent regular donations to the Irish College throughout

---

51 Molloy is not mentioned in the official *Liste* but is described in several sources as a Zouave. See his obituary in *The Edmundian*, July 1916, p.90.
52 Cardella, *Giulio Watts-Russell*, p.87.
53 Buerman, 'Lions and Lambs', p.109.
54 *The Tablet*, 31 July 1869, p.282. Welman had recently completed 14 months service as a Zouave.
55 *The Tablet*, 7 January 1899, p.24. These included James Quinn (originally from Ireland) and Bernard Riley.
56 *The Tablet*, 17 July 1869, p.216.
57 This picturesque area had several Zouave connections. The opening of the Pontypool friary was sponsored by the Earl of Denbigh and the friars also served the mission founded at nearby Dan-y-Graig in 1869 by Godfrey

Canon Thomas Wilkinson (1825–1909) and a group of his parishioners who joined the Zouaves; a photograph taken in Rome, July 1869. (Archives of Ushaw College, UC/AJ2/6/2/4281869, used with permission)

the 1860s. In April 1867 he wrote to Monsignor Kirby announcing that he was sending a recruit, Thomas Ahearn, 'at the expense of myself and some of my flock', thus fulfilling a promise he had made the previous year in an address his parishioners had sent to the Pope.[58] Sadly, Ahearn did not last long and a few months later the priest wrote bemoaning the conditions of 'my poverty-stricken and degraded people', which made further recruitment impossible, and sending £1 'to pay for a few cartridges for the Pontifical Zouaves'.[59]

When a French church was opened near Leicester Square in 1868, it is perhaps little surprise that the head of the mission, Father Charles Faure, showed an interest in the movement. During the heady days of 1870, the address was used for applications to the Papal Army. A member of the Marist Order, he was well-placed to use his connections across the channel.

The bishops themselves officially made few explicit remarks on recruitment; they had to act carefully given the restrictions of the Foreign Enlistment Act and, as we have already noted, displayed different levels of active support for the Temporal Power. The Archbishop of Westminster was the most outspoken in the Pope's favour. At the Mentana requiem, he had spoken of how the bloodshed of battle 'calls with the voice

---

Radcliffe, brother-in-law of Mrs Stone, the great friend of the Zouaves (who was herself buried in the cemetery there).
58 KIR/1867/139, Montgomery to Kirby, 15 April 1867.
59 KIR/1867/369, Montgomery to Kirby, 11 October 1867.

of a trumpet upon the youth of all Catholic peoples': 'We may trust that their places here will be filled up tenfold – a hundredfold – that the manhood and chivalry of Catholics in all nations will spring forward with a new energy of devotion and close around the person of Pius IX.'[60]

Archbishop's House in London, then situated at 8 York Place, acted as a discreet clearing house for applications from recruits: when Monsignor Stonor, the chaplain to the English Zouaves, visited London in September 1868 he invited potential applicants to contact him at that address.[61] Privately, Manning gave encouragement to recruits: in the spring of 1869, for example, he visited the rectory at Saffron Hill and blessed 20-year-old Jeremiah Crowley as he prepared to leave for the Papal States, remarking that 'to be a soldier for the Pope was the next best thing to being a priest' – a sentiment that greatly pleased the young man.[62]

In Dublin Cardinal Cullen was at first reluctant to encourage another 'movement' of mass Irish recruitment, after the logistical problems and disappointments of 1860. In the midst of the 1867 campaign, he rejoiced that 'the Zouaves have covered themselves with glory' and promised Kirby the usual addresses and subscriptions, but sounded a note of caution: 'There are many here who would go out as volunteers but the expense is great and probably they would not agree with the French and the Belgians, so it is as well to let the great numbers go from the countries where French is spoken, so that the army may not have discordant elements in it.'[63] Irish recruits in the late 1860s never matched the enthusiasm of 1860; in many ways, it was now England's opportunity to demonstrate loyalty to the Holy See.

Lay Involvement: Major Gordon and the Papal Defence Fund

The Worcester recruits had been inspired by the news that Major Gordon was organising a contingent to Rome. William Fletcher Gordon belonged to a longstanding Catholic and Jacobite family from Banffshire and served for many years in India. In 1860 the Pope created him a Knight of the Order of St Gregory the Great in recognition of 'his bravery in the field and for the assistance generally afforded by him to the Christian community' during the Indian Mutiny; four years later he retired from the 1st Bombay Fusiliers.[64] Moved by the Pope's plight in 1867 and believing that plentiful recruits could be found in Scotland, he began to gather men, with the help of the Glasgow clergy and his nephew, Charles Menzies Gordon of Greenock. Meetings were held, articles placed in the press and a suggestion made that each of Glasgow's 120,000 Catholics contribute a penny to the cause.

Within a few weeks the first group of recruits was ready to make the journey to Rome. Thanks to its links with one of the priests in Glasgow, Father Moreau, the Belgian Committee offered to cover their expenses from Paris to Rome, while money was raised for the journey to Paris. Charles Gordon himself covered the expenses of 40 recruits. Testimonials were hurriedly gained from parish priests and, for those under 21, parental consent. The *Glasgow Free Press*, the organ of the Catholic Irish in Scotland, suggested that there was frustration at the low level of English recruitment and so 'the brave Irish fellows of Glasgow flung themselves into the breach … to become defenders of the holiest cause that can engage the minds of men'.[65]

---

60 *The Tablet*, 16 November 1867, p.729.
61 See, for example, *Liverpool Daily Post*, 7 September 1868, p.7.
62 *The Tablet*, 5 June 1869, p.20.
63 KIR/1867/391, Cullen to Kirby, 24 October 1867.
64 'A Banffshire Leaders of Zouaves', *Transactions of the Banffshire Field Club*, 26 February 1914. <https://banffshirefieldclub.org.uk/PDFs/BOOK_9/Banffshire_Field_Club_Transactions_1910-1914_-_1914_A_Banffshire_Leader_of_Zouaves_WM.pdf>, accessed 2 May 2022.
65 *Glasgow Free Press*, 18 January 1868, p.4.

The *Weekly Register* reported the 50 Highlanders passing through London en route to Paris: '[A] finer set of young fellows it has rarely been our lot to see. Forty-seven of the number were upwards of six feet high; the youngest of them seemed to be about 20, the oldest not more than 28.'[66] Although they were reported to be sons of West Highland farmers, they were largely Irish immigrants living in Glasgow. The journey did not go smoothly: their large number caused the suspicion of the authorities before leaving English soil, there were reports of ill treatment after Father Moreau left them at Paris and of drunkenness at Marseilles. By January 1868 125 Glasgow Irish had gathered in Rome and there were hopes that a papal Highland Brigade would be formed: 'the Pope's Own Highlanders' or 'the Pope's Scottish Guard'.[67] This was not to be and, as we shall see, many of the recruits did not fare well in Rome and quickly returned home.

Major Gordon made another decisive contribution to the cause by helping set up the 'Papal Defence Fund' or 'St Peter and St Michael's Fund' at the London Joint Stock Bank in October 1867, acting as secretary and using his London club as the correspondence address (Stafford Club, 2 Saville Row). The Fund was administered by leading members of the Catholic laity, including members of the aristocracy and Sir Robert Gerard, Aide-de-Camp to the Queen; Sir George Bowyer, MP for Dundalk; Sir Charles Clifford, previously the first Speaker of the New Zealand Parliament; and Henry Matthews, later to serve as Home Secretary under Lord Salisbury.[68]

Established in part to counter the British fundraising campaign for Garibaldi, the Fund differed from Peter's Pence in that it specifically financed the military needs of the Pope. These included the provision of breech-loading rifles, though those who preferred could donate to the sick and wounded. The Fund also covered the expenses of the British volunteers and the practicalities of recruitment. Presumably, the 'certain nobleman' to whom Father Waterworth addressed his letter was one of these and, thanks to his contact, the three Worcester boys on reaching Paddington Station were met by 'a gentleman', who took them to Victoria Station.

Information about enlistment appeared in the press. In September 1868 Monsignor Stonor published the following in several newspapers:

1. All who enter the Papal service must do so as privates, no foreign grade being accepted.
2. The term of enlistment is for 2 years or 6 months. If the latter the sum of 60 francs must be paid down.
3. It is advisable to take a small an amount of clothes as possible to Rome, a few flannel shirts and socks being most needed.
4. Those who have means of their own will find that 1 or 2 francs a day are quite sufficient to supply any extra food or wine they may require.
5. The rations of the men are the same as those of the French army and the pay, deducting all expenses, 3 sous a day.
6. The Committee of the Papal Defence Fund have added 3 sous a day of extra pay to all English and Irish Zouaves who may require it, besides a weekly allowance of tobacco.
7. The expenses of the journey for Rome is about £6.
8. Before entering the service all must have a letter of recommendation from one of the Committee and also a testimonial of good character from their parish priest.[69]

---

66 *Dundee Courier*, 26 November 1867, p.2.
67 *The Sun*, 9 December 1867, p.4.
68 *Evening Standard*, 1 November 1867, p.7.
69 *Chelsea News and General Advertiser*, 26 September 1868, p.7.

Indeed, the Risorgimento and Anti-Risorgimento continued to be fought out in the press. Thanks to the abolition of taxes and the introduction of new technologies, cheap papers could be accessed in every part of the country, reporting international events and representing every shade of opinion. The London *Times* was particularly vocal in criticising the Pope's band of 'mercenaries', as it had in 1860, while the Catholic press publicised the plight of the Holy Father and news of 'our boys' in Rome. Donations for the Papal Defence Fund could be sent to the offices of *The Tablet* and lists of subscribers regularly published, while the *Universe* even arranged for Christmas puddings to be sent to the Zouaves in Rome.

Support came from every section of the community. In November and December 1867 lists of recent subscriptions for the Fund were headed by many distinguished names giving substantial sums – the Dowager Duchess of Argyll, Baron Weld, Lord and Lady Stourton, Lord Lovat, Lord Stafford, Count de Torre Diaz, the Scott Murrays and Bedingfields – and went on to include laity, clergy, whole congregations, 'Mrs Stapleton's Servants' (£3), 'Two Little Children' (10s) and 'A Protestant Lover of Justice' (£5). By the end of 1867 over £3,200 had been raised.

Donations could be given for particular purposes: in December 1867, for example, the boys of the Oratory School, Edgbaston, raised over £18 for the Pope's wounded soldiers. Another popular cause was the purchase of rifles, including 'three breech-loaders for his Holiness' from Fr Henry Browne and the congregation of Saints Peter and Paul, Ribcheste. The people of the Fylde likewise donated funds for three Chassepots at £4 each: '1st rifle, bought by 32 souls, at 2s 6d; 2nd rifle, by 16 souls at 5s each; 3rd rifle, by 4 souls, at £1 each.'[70]

Such offerings were seen as a worthy cause:

> [H]ow many are there amongst the immense number of Catholics in England, who, not being able to render any other assistance, will at least present the Pope with a rifle? The sum is not large, and would not be thought much of were it required for the comfort and convenience of our own homes. And is not Rome the home of all Catholics; is it not the asylum to which all who are oppressed and heavily laden fly for refuge?[71]

There were misgivings about such gestures in the corridors of the Vatican. After Mr Mullins, the gunmaker who initially supplied rifles to the cause was granted a papal audience shortly before Mentana, Monsignor Talbot reported to Manning that 'the Holy Father received him coldly'. Rifles were not a priority because 'his reliance was on God, and the present muskets were good enough for all his purposes'. Talbot was more encouraging, giving Mullins letters of approval for his campaign so that the Papal Army had the best possible equipment. However, Talbot thought that the English were far too practical, having 'more faith in Snider or Chassepot rifles than in God and his saints'.[72]

Obstacles to Recruitment

There were concerns regarding the extent of recruitment. Charles Menzies Gordon thought that

> we are disgracing our country by leaving to Frenchmen, Dutch, and Belgians, the honour of fighting in a cause that is common to us all, and certainly we must appear contemptible in the

---

70 *The Tablet*, 30 November 1867, p.765.
71 *The Tablet*, 13 April 1867, p.234, letter from 'An English Catholic'.
72 AAW Manning-Chapeau Papers, Talbot to Manning, 13 November 1867.

eyes of our Protestant countrymen, who, if their dearest interests were outraged as ours are, would not display the same apathy. There is surely pluck enough amongst us to change the present state of matters.[73]

Another asked: '[S]hall it be said that amongst the descendants of that army of martyrs and heroes whose blood has watered this island and who have laid down their lives in defence of their faith, and the spiritual supremacy of the Sovereign Pontiff, none can be found to emulate their noble example?'[74] After the campaign of Mentana, 'our own half-dozen English volunteers' reminded one correspondent of 'the solitary Englishman amongst the Knight Templars at the siege of Rhodes'.[75]

Ultimately, the Zouaves were a heroic but atypical response to the complicated Roman Question. If no more than 3,000 Frenchmen joined the corps, it could not be expected that there would be a similar number of British recruits. There were distinctively English reasons for the limited recruits. One correspondent thought the principal obstacles were the 'non-existence of conscription, primogeniture and the almost universal business habits of our people'.[76] For Monsignor Talbot, writing from the Vatican, the English character was naturally opposed to Roman authority. Catholics had been 'corrupted by the Protestant atmosphere' and displayed a 'utilitarian narrow-minded spirit'.[77] Indeed, 'the English Episcopate and almost all the Old Clergy are as insular, national, narrow-minded, Anglo-Gallican, Anti-Roman as they well can be and have only been checked and kept down during the last twenty years by the talent, the power, the influence and the high position of Cardinal Wiseman'.[78] This strongly pro-Roman attitude was continued by Manning, his successor at Westminster, but many clergy took a more ambivalent approach to the Vatican.

Undoubtedly, there was a nervousness in taking the extreme step of joining the Pontifical Army when only a decade or so previously England had been consumed in cries of 'No Popery' following the restoration of Catholic dioceses and bishops. English Catholics were keen to show they could be faithful Catholics and loyal British subjects at the same time. This was an ongoing tension, felt as much by Elizabethan Catholics as their Victorian successors. Father Henry Formby suggested in the *Weekly Register* at the beginning of 1868 that the small number of recruits was because of 'the confusion and ignorance in the minds chiefly of English and Scotch Catholics as to what constitutes true loyalty to a civil power'.[79] Yet, fighting for the Pope could be seen to imply disloyalty to the Queen – a fear only encouraged by the association between Irish Catholics and revolutionary movements such as Fenianism.

Moreover, the risk of legal action under the Foreign Enlistment Act remained, as it had in 1860. Although it was normally considered a dead letter, problems could be caused. In 1863 Merseyside shipbuilders were commissioned to build three vessels for the American Confederacy. Although one ship was detained before it could cross the Atlantic, the other two undertook attacks on Union merchant ships. The CSS *Alabama*, built by John Laird, Sons & Co., became the Confederacy's most infamous raider, until she was sunk by the USS *Kearsarge* just off the French coast at Cherbourg in 1864. In June 1863 five of the ship's builders stood trial for outfitting a ship for warlike purposes for a foreign force, in breach of the Foreign Enlistment Act. They were found not guilty but in 1872 the British Government paid over US$15 million in damages

---

73 *The Tablet*, 15 June 1867, p.376, letter from Charles Gordon.
74 *The Tablet*, 13 April 1867, p.234, letter from 'An English Catholic'.
75 *The Tablet*, 9 November 1867, p.715, letter from 'Papalino'.
76 *The Tablet*, 16 November 1867, p.731.
77 AAW Manning-Chapeau Papers, Talbot to Manning, 13 November 1867.
78 AAW Wiseman Papers W3/20, Talbot to Patterson, 15 February 1861.
79 *Glasgow Free Press*, 1 February 1868, p.4.

to the United States. The affair, which at one stage might even have resulted in the relinquishing of the Bahamas or Canada as compensation, showed that the legislation was not entirely inactive. Indeed, it was reported that as the Glasgow Irish volunteers were waiting in London for their steamer to France, en route to Rome, 'they were scattered about the low coffee-houses, to evade the provisions of the Foreign Enlistment Act'.[80]

In other countries, enlistment in the Zouaves carried heavy burdens. In the Netherlands it resulted in loss of Dutch citizenship, although permission to join the Pontifical Army was normally given to those who requested it; French recruits were also threatened with the same penalty; and foreign recruitment was likewise banned by Article 111 of the Prussian criminal code. As in 1860, British and Irish recruits were careful to leave home as tourists or seeking work abroad; enlistment only formally took place once in the Papal States.

Further obstacles were provided by the critical attitude of many peers – recruits are reported to have 'left amidst the jeers if not the curses of their fellow workmen'[81] – and the practical hurdles of linguistic difficulties, harsh conditions and poor pay. A Roman correspondent knew of one English Zouave in the summer of 1868 who had earned £3 a week at home and now had to make do with sevenpence in the same period. Although life could be comfortable for those with personal wealth, those from poorer backgrounds invariably struggled.

Nevertheless, the relatively lukewarm response in Ireland gave English Catholics an opportunity to prove their worth. A well-connected lay committee and strongly pro-Roman Church leaders, led by Manning, discreetly encouraged recruits. The events of 1866 and 1867 in Rome gave English Catholics a proximate cause for direct intervention. Not insignificantly, the British Government's enthusiasm for Italian affairs was gradually dampening. It could not afford to ignore the opinion of Catholics, who made up around 20 percent of the United Kingdom population, and, indeed, the new Italy had so far been a disappointment to English liberals. Piedmontese expansion and the reduction of the Pope's Temporal Power had not prevented a succession of domestic crises and scandals. If 1860 had been Ireland's moment for bearing arms for the Pope, conditions were ripe in the late 1860s for greater English involvement.

---

80 *The Atlas*, 23 November 1867, p.7.
81 *The Sun*, 31 August 1868, p.4.

13

'Far, far from our wild northern home!': Daily Life in Rome

The journey to Rome was the first part of the adventure. Joseph Powell, who has left us the most detailed account of a British Zouave, travelled from the Cotswolds to London in March 1868, where he received his passport, had a doctor's examination and collected 'letters of introduction to parties to Rome' from an agent, Captain Mullins. He then caught a train from London Victoria to Newhaven, where he boarded the steamship for Dieppe. Though he travelled alone, he met 'a very kind young Frenchmen' in London who accompanied him as far as Paris. 'I get on pretty well with the language,' Powell excitedly reported, 'though I cannot yet understand much French spoken by natives.'[1] There were stops at Rouen and an opportunity to see the main sights of the French capital: '[T]he river Seine and its bridges are very beautiful, especially by gaslight.' His onward train journey was with a Zouave sergeant and five French recruits. There was a moment of elation when the Mediterranean was spotted for the first time, but at the busy port of Marseilles he 'began to experience some of the difficulties of being entirely amongst foreigners.' Another steamer was then caught for Civitavecchia; onboard accommodation was 'very rough – a good breaking in for my future life.' At last, setting foot on papal territory and being taken to the barracks, he was 'warmly received by the English and Irish recruits.' He felt at home and liked 'the grey uniform very much.'

The journey was not without its dangers. On 7 May 1869 the *General Abbatucci* sank after colliding with a Norwegian brig just off the coast of Corsica. On board were substantial offerings to the Holy See in the form of money and recruits: among the would-be Zouaves who perished was Jeremiah Crowley from London's Saffron Hill, who was consequently described in the Catholic press as a 'martyr', as well as a young man by the name of O'Donoghue.[2]

On arrival in Rome, the volunteers officially enlisted, presenting their letters of recommendation and associated paperwork. The Zouaves were not the only option for service. The Pontifical Dragoons were seen as more appropriate for those who were well-to-do and with appropriate skills of horsemanship; the pay was better, but most officers were Italian. William Vavasour transferred to the Pontifical Dragoons in June 1868 before returning to the Zouaves three months later. Likewise, the Foreign Carabineers in November 1868 boasted five English members, though its other members were predominantly Swiss and German.[3] The Artillery was also considered a worthy option, though its term of service was five rather than two years: '[T]hey receive a large bounty, have good pay, wear a handsome uniform, and number some

---

1 Powell, *Two Years in the Pontifical Zouaves*, pp.45–48.
2 *The Tablet*, 5 June 1869, p.20; *Advocate (Melbourne)*, 10 July 1869, p.11.
3 A recruitment centre for this unit was set up at Pontarlier on the French–Swiss border.

A large group of Zouaves while on exercises in the *campagna*, 1868. (Private collection, photograph: Ursula Staszynski)

aristocrats among the rank and file.'[4] All in all, advised an Irish recruit, it was best to 'enter the Zouaves in the first instance, and then see for himself the advantages and disadvantages of joining any other branch of the service.'

Often there was an opportunity for a papal audience: a few days after arriving in Rome in May 1866, Alfred Collingridge wrote that he was about to 'receive the Pope's blessing and the medal he gives to all the Zouaves', dressed in his new regimentals (of which he promised to send a photograph).[5] The new recruit, who normally lacked military experience, first spent time in a depot to be trained. Powell, for example, was sent to the Torlonia barracks, near the Vatican: '[O]ur time is divided between drill, duty, such as picket, guard, keeping our clothes in order, cleaning our arms, belts, &c, making up our knapsacks, with our overcoats, tent, rug rolled round; then we march out with all our kit for inspection by the lieutenant, who remarks if even a buckle is out of place.'[6]

The discipline was strict and Powell soon found himself in the *salle de police* for a minor infringement of the rules; nevertheless, in those early weeks he was able to visit the catacombs, participate in the splendid ceremonies of Holy Week and see the Pope pass by in procession: 'I think it would be difficult to imagine

---

4   *Dublin Weekly Nation*, 15 May 1869, p.13.
5   Typescript of Alfred Collingridge's letter to his parents, Rome, 22 May 1866, given to the author by Susie Gore.
6   Powell, *Two Years in the Pontifical Zouaves,* p.51.

how a *man* could be a better representative of the Lord.'[7] By July he was ready to join the 2nd Company of the 1st Battalion and found both the life and the food while on duty in the Roman *campagna* much more agreeable.

Linguistic problems continued to be an issue for many recruits. A Lancashire Zouave spent his evenings lying on his bed studying the French drill that an English corporal had written out for him. Occasionally the lack of comprehension could be used to his advantage. One morning, after seeing his name down for 24-hour guard duty, he returned to bed since he felt tired and subsequently missed 'guard parade'. When a corporal ordered him to peel potatoes, 'I pretended not to understand him and turned over to sleep again'.[8]

It was not an easy life. Lady Herbert revealed her aristocratic background when she wrote admiringly of the Zouaves:

> It is one thing to lead gallantly a forlorn hope, – to fight even with incredible bravery against superior numbers, – to be everywhere victorious by sheer personal courage and pluck! It is another, to sit down day after day in a miserably dark and dirty cantonment in a petty provincial town, without beds or bedding, mixed up with men of a much lower class, and without any of the comforts, and few even of the necessaries of life.[9]

Alfred Collingridge wrote: 'I find that a soldier's life is very hard, the living is not very grand but I think it is good, the fatigue will be great but the open air of the country strengthening.'[10] His artist brother, George, later reminisced that 'we were ironically called mercenaries when we enlisted, because we could make £10 a week at wood-engraving, and with the Zouaves we were paid only 2½d. every five days. The Australian soldier, with his 6s. a day, had the remuneration of an Eastern potentate in comparison.'[11]

Without private means, life was austere. One English volunteer wrote in March 1868:

> Our rations are poor certainly, but it cannot be helped, as our Holy Father is so poor he cannot afford at present to give better. We get up at five o'clock in the morning for a cup of coffee; at half-past ten a tin of soup with a little meat in, about four ounces in weight. (The same quantity of flesh meat is not required in Italy as in more northern climes; besides the wine supplies the deficiency.) At half-past three in the afternoon we get another tin of either potatoes by themselves (but got up in a tasty manner), beans and oil (des haricots), or rice (e.g. pillaw). I cannot take the oil and beans, so I go to a café, and get something there. (An English Zouave should have about £20 per annum over and above his pay, to meet these deficiencies. Most fathers who have sons there allow it. And this will in a great measure explain the discontent of those who could not afford this. Such should not be sent out until the committee can make some other arrangements). Those who wish to come here and serve, must know how matters stand, and not come expecting good dinners, &c. Our beds are jolly ones; true we have no feather beds; but we have a sheet fastened to two good poles (a hammock), then comes a good mattress, two sheets, a tent cover, a good double blanket, and half a blanket. Each of us has one to himself: they are raised about three feet from the ground. … Let anybody come that can get a good character, but nobody else. …

---

7   Powell, *Two Years in the Pontifical Zouaves,* p.50.
8   *Preston Chronicle,* 4 April 1868, p.2.
9   Herbert, *Mentana,* p.7.
10 Typescript of Alfred Collingridge's letter to his parents, Rome, 22 May 1866, given to the author by Susie Gore.
11 *The Sun,* 18 May 1919, p.9.

Several English snobs came out here and stayed for a few weeks, and then went back jolly quick. They were a lot of softs.[12]

Powell likewise reported in September 1868 that 'some of Englishmen – some on account of ill-health and some for other causes – have lately felt the barrack life too hard for them, and have gone. ... I know also that many who have already served in the Zouaves would return, were there any prospect of a campaign against the Garibaldians.'[13] An Irish Zouave who returned home in 1869 wrote to the *Dublin Weekly Nation* to put off would-be recruits:

> A respectable young man, or one who respects himself, has no business whatever in the Papal service, where he is subjected to the slightest whim of a 'funchenaire' corporal. He is on duty frequently in the worst weather, and, when completely saturated with wet, has no resource but to 'grin and bear it', as the government serves him out with only one uniform, whilst oftentimes he has to wear it till it is literally in rags on him! ... When our countrymen can make up their minds to hear every second word addressed to them accompanied by a curse, and to be called 'pigs' by men immeasurably their inferiors, I will no longer caution them.[14]

Links were made with the British community in Rome. The Venerable English College, the English seminary in Rome, was a home away from home for many, especially since some of the students were familiar faces from schooldays. A Zouave reported in March 1868 that:

> [T]he rector of the English College took some of us out for a day's fun, and didn't we enjoy ourselves? What a jolly dinner we had. We tasted good English beef again, and we did eat it with a relish. It isn't bad getting those invitations, is it? There is only one fault I can find, and that is that they are too much like angels' visits, very few, and far between.[15]

Joseph Powell went to Vespers and Benediction at the college, since they were 'sung as in England'.[16]

Zouaves, as we have seen, were not always popular figures among the Roman populace. William Brennan wrote to his brother in Australia that the Romans probably had 'a poor opinion of some of our chaps' for as soon as they were paid 'than away they go like mad men'.[17] Sometimes they experienced the hostility of the local population because of what they stood for: in March 1868 three English Zouaves, along with a German, were assaulted as they returned to barracks.[18] Nevertheless, there were opportunities to damage any strained relations. An English Zouave, Herbert Duke, came to the rescue when a Roman shop caught fire. The firemen hesitated when it became apparent that a barrel of gunpowder may have been nearby. Duke, who was helping with the pumps, 'darted through the crowd and into the burning house, whence he

---

12   *The Tablet*, 28 March 1868, p.203.
13   Powell, *Two Years in the Pontifical Zouaves*, p.76.
14   *Dublin Weekly Nation*, 18 May 1869, p.13. Fr Charles O'Connor believed the writer was Henry Kerr. IE/DDA 333/3/28, letter to Mgr Moran, 6 June 1869.
15   *The Tablet*, 28 March 1868, p.203.
16   Powell, *Two Years in the Pontifical Zouaves*, p.49.
17   *Advocate (Melbourne)*, 29 February 1868, p.13.
18   *Preston Chronicle*, 28 March 1868, p.3.

emerged in a few minutes, blackened with the flames through which he had had to pass, and carrying the powder-barrel on his shoulders!' His bravery was credited for saving a block of houses from destruction.[19]

When two of the first English Zouaves enlisted on 19 May 1866, they were part of a group of nine: of these, one was killed in action (Alfred Collingridge), another died in what was officially reported as an accident (falling at night from a fourth-floor window of the Serristori barracks) and a third succumbed to cholera. More Zouaves died from illness than battle wounds: all in all, 476 men died while wearing the grey uniform, of whom only 89 died in action or as a result of wounds. A further 36 died after violent assaults or accidents, but the vast majority who died (78 percent) succumbed to illness.[20] On 1 August 1868 Thomas Mitchell, a Londoner, died of the dreaded 'Roman fever' (malaria) caught while on duty at Ceccano, south-east of Rome: '[H]e was never very strong,' wrote Powell, 'and had suffered from fever soon after arriving.'[21] Powell himself was confined to the hospital of Santo Spirito at the end of 1868 due to pleurisy. He was bled and had leeches applied, and was impressed by the kind Sisters of Charity, the piles of books and newspapers to read, visits from friends and chaplains, and daily mass celebrated in the dormitory. Some Zouaves returned to Britain after the completion of their service with damaged health. Three English Zouaves died as they journeyed home after the capture of Rome. Alexander John Wilson of Leeds is believed to have contracted malaria during his time in Rome from 1868 to 1870 and years later, in the 1901 Census, is still listed as an 'invalid through ague'.[22]

Improvements were made to the Papal Medical Service throughout the 1860s although, in times of action, it was under-resourced and relied heavily on volunteers, including well-born ladies such as Madame Kanzler and Mrs Stone. There were also questions regarding the professional rigour of the medical personnel: despite his years of dedicated service in the Papal Army from 1860, it was only in 1869 that the Irish surgeon Philip O'Flynn was granted leave to go to Louvain and obtain his diploma.[23]

Esprit du Corps

The English and Irish Zouaves had a strong sense of their national identity and there were initial hopes to form a distinctive battalion. The Honourable Mrs Kavanagh dreamt of raising an English battalion of Zouaves, dedicated to Our Lady of Victories. Residing in Bruges, she used her links with the Belgian Zouave Committee, 'to whom the battalion will be presented, and who will take charge of them to Rome'.[24] Though this battalion never materialised because the Vatican did not approve of battalions organised on ethnic lines or unauthorised recruitment agents, Mrs Kavanagh did produce two banners for the men. The English, Irish, Scottish, and Canadian volunteers were presented with them in a ceremony at the English College at Pentecost in 1868. The flag

> displays in the centre the figure of Our Lady of Victories, beautifully embroidered on a ground of white silk, and on either side a Papal Zouave, on bended knee, with his musket and sword-bayonet

---

19   *The Tablet*, 19 June 1869, p.89. There may be confusion here with the English Zouave Philip Duke.
20   Guenel, *Le Dernière Guerre du Pape*, p.265.
21   Powell, *Two Years in the Pontifical Zouaves*, p.70.
22   https://ajwpapalzouave.blogspot.com/2019/01/the-papal-zouave.html, accessed 8 December 2020.
23   Jean Guenel, 'Service de santé, morbidité et mortalité dans le regiment des zouaves pontificaux en Italie (1861–1870), *Histoire des Sciences Médicales*, 29:3 (1995), p.264.
24   *The Tablet*, 13 June 1868, p.377. She later admitted: 'I sent out four or five [recruits] with the few pounds I was able to collect, and was then told that only certain authorized persons forming a committee could be permitted to send volunteers to the Pope's army.' *The Tablet*, 27 August 1870, p.267.

clasped between his arms. Around are the scrolls, Pro Sede Petri, and Sancta Maria Victrix. Above are embroidered in gold and colours, the English arms and mottoes, below the arms of Pius IX, surmounted by the cross-keys and tiara, and at the lower extremity the arms of the family of the donor. Precious stones on raised gold are set in a deep border of blue velvet which goes round the whole, and from the edge of which hangs a heavy gold fringe. At the top of the pole is an embossed brass decoration, consisting of an open laurel-wreath surmounted by a cross, in the centre of which is a large amethyst; and underneath the garland on a cross bar the motto ROMA.

A second lighter banner was made in waterproof silk, 'designed to be carried into the field'. Interestingly, the men present included Dragoons as well as Zouaves, including one of Mrs Kavanagh's sons (William Vavasour).

This banner, presented by Dutch women in memory of the Battle of Mentana and now kept at Oudenbosch, includes the British royal coat of arms. It was designed by the well-known architect Pierre Cuypers, best-known for the Rijksmuseum and Central Station in Amsterdam. (Zouavenmuseum, Oudenbosch, used with permission)

This sense of shared identity could be seen also in the song produced for the British Zouaves by Mother Francis Raphael Drane, the influential convert, writer and Prioress of St Dominic's Convent, Stone. She had been asked to compose the piece by a Zouave in 1868. 'Set to a famous tune', the chorus of 'Love God, O my soul, love Him only/And then with light heart go thy way' was based on the motto of the 'little Ushaw Saint, Julian Watts Russell'.

> We come from the blue shores of England,
> From the mountains of Scotia we come,
> From the green, faithful island of Erin, –
> Far, far from our wild northern home.
> … If 'tis sweet for our country to perish,
> Sweeter far for the cause of today;
> … Though the odds be against us, what matter?
> While God and Our Lady look down,
> And the saints of our country are near us,
> And angels are holding the crown.[25]

As with any military unit, friendships developed among the men. Powell typically spent his evenings with his close circle of five English Zouaves either at the Caffè Luigi or in the dormitory, where they sat on adjoining beds and held their 'parliament': '[T]he subjects are various, the discussions generally interesting and very animated, but the conclusions not always unanimously accepted.' Clement Bishop, in particular, was considered 'an excellent disputant'.[26]

An Italian intelligence officer observing the Zouaves in August 1870 reported that 'officers and men treat each other with the greatest familiarity, and at the café you will see soldiers of all ranks at the same table'.[27] Such *esprit du corps* was kept alive by its senior personnel – the fatherly Allet and the sociable Charette, who invited a selection of men to his dinner table each evening – and by the cercles or clubs. There was an officer's mess in a building formally used by Benedictine nuns, which featured 'a large representation of the Cross of Mentana wrought into shape out of weapons'.[28] However, the cercles were normally arranged on national grounds: a Dutch Zouave Club on the Piazza Biscione and a Canadian one at the Arco della Ciambella, which boasted a stuffed beaver, the first to be seen in the Eternal City.

The English, Scots, and Irish Zouaves had use of a reading room from the beginning of 1868 near the Church of Sant' Antonio dei Portoghesi. A more spacious club was opened at 91 Piazza della Valle in December 1868, thanks to the generosity of the Papal Defence Committee and substantial donations by Catholic grandees such as the Duke of Norfolk. It consisted of a reading room with a small library and the latest newspapers; a billiards room (with a table donated by the Vansittart family); a sitting room with chess and draught boards; a chapel; a dining room where, for a small fee, food could be ordered to supplement the meagre rations; and accommodation for those returning to Rome while being quartered in the country. This was 'supplied gratis to those who, having been in hospital, are well enough to leave that place, at the same time not sufficiently recovered to return to their military duties'.[29] There were special occasions, such

---

25 Ushaw College Archive UC/P9/22/12, letter from Mother Drane to John Walker, 1 January 1869.
26 Powell, *Two Years in the Pontifical Zouaves*, p.75.
27 Alvarez, *The Pope's Soldiers*, p.213.
28 *Evening Freeman*, 7 March 1870, p.1.
29 *The Tablet*, 22 January 1870, p.110, William Vavasour.

as the 'tea party' on the evening of St George's Day 1869 with 'an Ethiopian entertainment, jokes by Bones and Pompey, and concluding by a farce of the "Sublime and Ridiculous"'.[30] The Zouave Club undertook an important role in distributing the allowance of 3 sous and tobacco provided through the fund and was used as a postal address by many friends and relatives. A member of the corps was assigned to the club to look after its day-to-day running. Open each day until 10 p.m., it was also the home of the assistant chaplain, Father Gurdon. One of the Zouaves acted as its secretary.

Powell noted that 'none of the cercles are exclusively opened to one nationality' and often used the Canadian, French and Belgian clubs – the latter being particularly good for its beefsteak – but 'every one feels most at home in the company of his own countrymen'.[31] The Zouaves were, indeed, a transnational corps and bonds of friendship transcended ethnicity and language.

Cricket matches were another distraction, normally played against other English residents at the Piazza di Siena, the sports ground in the Villa Borghese. In March 1868 there was a cricket match between 'All England in Rome' and 'All English Zouaves'; 'a very heavy rain stopped the play, or there is no doubt the Zouave score would have shown a most triumphant result in the second innings'.[32] Among the opposition, wrote a Lancashire Zouave, was a certain 'Mr F.', who, 'together with his wife, a young lady of 24, is very kind to the Zouaves. … During the match Mrs F. drove up in her carriage and pair with two large hampers of provisions of every description and bitter beer, … and after the match Mr F. entertained us all at dinner'.[33]

The matches, which brought together the English community in Rome, were the idea of Monsignor Stonor, who was 'anxious to get up some active amusements for the English Zouaves'.[34] The captain of the Zouave Eleven was Frederick Tristam Welman, who had been a keen cricketer at Oscott. Described as 'a splendid type of manhood, graceful and active with his bat', he had 'a minute knowledge of all the points in the game'[35] and went on to play 65 first class matches as a wicket keeper for Middlesex, Somerset, and Surrey.

Frederick Tristam Welman (1849–1931), the cricketing Zouave. (Archives of the Archdiocese of Birmingham, OCA/6/3/1/W/11, used with permission)

---

30 Powell, *Two Years in the Pontifical Zouaves*, p.98.
31 Powell, *Two Years in the Pontifical Zouaves*, p.75.
32 *The Tablet*, 21 March 1868, p.185.
33 *Preston Chronicle*, 4 April 1868, p.2.
34 Powell, *Two Years in the Pontifical Zouaves*, p.153.
35 *Tamworth Herald*, 12 March 1932, p.2.

Another highlight was provided by the carnival, just before the beginning of the penitential season of Lent. There was a race of riderless horses down the crowded Via di Corso, and 'the spectators on both sides do their best to increase the speed of the animals to the utmost'.[36] There was a wide variety of costumes and ladies on the balconies of the houses threw confetti onto passers-by: 'tall hats are considered fair game' and there were regular 'battles of confetti'. English Zouaves 'received several bouquets from the ladies' and 'threw others in return'.

English versus Irish: Issues of Nationality in a Transnational Army

At the beginning of 1868 many of the Irish recruits newly arrived from Glasgow were dismissed and sent home. Their presence en masse had led to the emergence of tensions, complaints and anti-Irish prejudices among the authorities. The well-to-do Zouaves resented sharing their barracks with these rough 'unwashed adventurers' and there were fears that they would be ill-disciplined and drunken soldiers. Most importantly, they were suspected of being members of the Fenian or Irish Republican Brotherhood, which campaigned for an independent Ireland through armed revolution. From the English Protestant point of view, any form of Irish nationalism was open to accusations of Fenianism and in Rome, Irish Republicans were quickly equated with Red Shirts; Pius IX even told Odo Russell that he considered the Fenians to be 'the Garibaldians of England'.[37]

The year 1867 had seen a Fenian rising against British rule in parts of Ireland as well as attempts to release Fenian prisoners in England. A prison van was attacked in Manchester on its way from the courthouse. As a result, a police sergeant lost his life and three of the culprits were hanged at Salford Gaol on 23 November. The following month Clerkenwell Prison was bombed, causing the deaths of 12 and leading *Punch* to publish a cartoon on 'The Fenian Guy Fawkes'. To observers in Rome, comparisons were made with the recent atrocity at the Serristori barracks.

According to a memorandum written by Father William Delany, who acted as an unofficial chaplain to the Irish recruits, the crisis began when the newly arrived men became disillusioned with their conditions:

> Those already in uniform were in some instances lodged simply in rooms with Dutch and Frenchmen, and were therefore necessarily leading for 20 hours of the 24, often for the whole day, what was practically a life of solitary confinement. Again, they did not understand the orders given them; and yet were at times put into prison for not fulfilling their orders.[38]

They disliked the bread and bean soup, which appeared to be 'a favourite repast with the Dutch', and on several occasions 'found a worm in the meat'. Some had to wait weeks to receive arms and uniforms, even though French recruits received theirs almost immediately. When, shortly after Christmas 1867, they were paid a lower allowance than expected, they assumed this was another injustice and refused to accept it. There was, apparently, a valid explanation for the difference in pay but linguistic barriers prevented them from understanding the explanation given and their stubborn refusal was seen as a 'military revolt'.

Around the same time, a requiem was organised at the Church of Sant' Andrea della Fratte for the recently executed 'Manchester Martyrs' by Mr O'Connor, a former Zouave, who worked as a clerk at Piale's Library on the Piazza di Spagna. He had led the authorities to believe that the mass was being

---

36 Powell, *Two Years in the Pontifical Zouaves*, p.85.
37 Blakiston, *Roman Question*, p.351.
38 IE/DDA 333/3/VI/2, Delany, 'The Irish Zouaves'.

offered for three soldiers who had been killed at Mentana. As Rachel Busk, the Roman correspondent of the *Westminster Gazette*, explained:

> The church had been already prepared for the service in question; but as it was pretty well known that only one English Catholic was killed at Mentana, a doubt was suggested in time to investigate the matter, when the nature of the design was discovered, and the demonstration, of course, stopped. It has led further to the discovery of an unsatisfactory spirit in a certain number of the lately-arrived Irish recruits.[39]

O'Connor had asked for the support of the rector of the Venerable English College, Henry O'Callaghan, who alerted the English Zouave chaplain. As a result, the Irish Zouaves were confined to their barracks that day, even though they claimed that they had known nothing of the mass. A number were sent home and many others left in protest over the following weeks – around 100 in total, their expenses being covered by papal funds. O'Connor himself was banished from the Papal States.

A London-born Zouave, Samuel Muggeridge, told Delany that some deserved to go but others were innocent of the suspicions of Fenianism. Indeed, as far as the Irish were concerned, the crisis was a result of an English plot involving Stonor, Talbot and others. Stonor had expressed his opinions to Delany on the matter: the Irish, he thought, were 'hard to discipline and clannish' and feared that 'any sort of Irish corps, or even an Irish company' would mean 'the Fenian chiefs would send over an agent to win them to the Fenian cause, and then have at the end of their two years' service, so many trained soldiers ready for the first call against the English Government'.[40] Charette even threatened to resign if greater care was not taken in the future over the 'quality' of recruits and declared: 'I would not have a battalion of Irish for all the gold in the world.'[41] 'One cannot suppose,' a writer commented, 'a commanding officer of Legitimist principles and high Catholic sentiments would be much delighted that a number of Fenians had enlisted in his regiment.'[42]

The numbers returning to Ireland increased and, as Delany explained, 'every man that went home was a new proof in the eyes of some that the Irish were an unreasonable, discontented, ever complaining, ungenerous set'.[43] In Glasgow, the clergy, shocked by events, organised a public meeting and sent a protest to Cardinal Antonelli.

In Rome, attempts were made to pacify the disillusioned volunteers, who claimed that 'Irish *money* was very welcome at Rome but that Irish *men* had little justice to expect them'. Promises were made to put them into companies under Captains D'Arcy and De La Hoyde, although Charette, believing in the divide and rule principle, told them sternly: 'I may put three or five or seven – up to 20 together, but never more.'[44] The Irish also received a sympathetic interim chaplain in Father Charles O'Connor of the American College.

As 1868 went on, the dust settled, and Monsignor Stonor sent a pacifying statement to the newspapers stating that the presence of Fenianism among the Zouaves had been overstated. 'Several of our volunteers,' he explained, 'left their homes without being fully aware of the nature and exigencies of the military service

---

39 Busk, Rachel H. [published anonymously as 'Roman Correspondent of *The Westminster Gazette*'] *Contemporary Annals of Rome: Notes Political, Archaeological and Social* (London: Thomas Richardson & Son, 1870), p.296.
40 IE/DDA 333/3/VI/2, Delany, 'The Irish Zouaves'.
41 IE/DDA 333/3/VI/2, Delany, 'The Irish Zouaves'.
42 *Falkirk Herald*, 20 January 1868, p.7, quoting the *Daily Post* correspondent.
43 IE/DDA 333/3/VI/2, Delany, 'The Irish Zouaves'.
44 IE/DDA 333/3/VI/2, Delany, 'The Irish Zouaves'.

here in Rome.'[45] At the summer camp near Rocca di Papa, 'a tea-fight for the English and Irishmen' was organised 'near the edge of the precipitous rocks hard by the camp fountain', which, Powell reported, was attended by 'most of the fellows' and was 'a very pleasant social evening together'.[46]

Nevertheless, tensions continued between the national committees that supported the English and Irish Zouaves. There were fears that the English were trying to take control of Irish funds and Father O'Connor categorically stated that he would have nothing to do with the English reading room.[47] He took it to himself to give out tobacco and a small allowance to his men, just as the English club did.[48] When summoned at the beginning of 1869 by Archbishop Manning to explain why he would not work with the English, he stated he would only answer to Cardinal Barnabò, Prefect of Propaganda Fide (the congregation in charge of the missions, under which Britain and Ireland were still placed).[49] Likewise, when the Irish were invited to join the devotions to the Blessed Virgin Mary at the English Club in May 1869, they were actively discouraged from attending by the Irish Committee, and the Irish resisted attempts to amalgamate the national committees.

The Irish were keen to assert their national distinctiveness and avoid any hint of English superiority. When the Papal Army went on manoeuvres at Rocca di Papa in the summer of 1868, one of the temporary 'streets' between the tents was named by them 'O'Connell Street'.[50] In 1869 a small Irish reading room was at last opened and a reception was attended by Colonel Allet and Archbishop Manning.[51]

Religious Life

Given the nature of the cause and the fact that a recruit needed the recommendation of a priest, it is no surprise that the spiritual life was at the heart of the corps. There were regular prayers, devotions, and masses (including formal 'military' masses); pilgrimages were frequently made to the city's numerous sanctuaries; many joined a Conference of St Vincent de Paul, a group that combined prayer with work for the poor. In Lent troops undertook a retreat and there were red letter days, such as the annual requiem for the fallen of Mentana, the feast of St Patrick for the Irish or that of St George, when the English Zouaves attended mass at the Church of San Giorgio in Velabro and venerated the saint's relics. In his account of the final days of Papal Rome, Eugène de Gerlache, a Zouave chaplain, described taking a group of 50 Zouaves to sing Vespers (evening prayer) under the trees of the Villa Medici and hearing their confessions before battle. Moreover, their weapons consisted not only of Remington rifles, 'each soldier armed himself with a medal of the Blessed Virgin, with a scapular, a rosary, and a little red cross distributed by the fathers of the institute of St Camillus'.[52]

'Go into a church at early morn,' wrote an Irish reporter at the time of the Vatican Council, 'or in the gloom of the *Ave Maria*, and so sure as you do, either kneeling in rapt devotion before the altar of the Blessed Sacrament, or away in a little nook where a lamp is burning in front of a Madonna, you are sure to find a Zouave upon his knees, and praying as intensely as if the decision of the Council depended solely

---

45 *Glasgow Evening Citizen*, 25 January 1868, p.3.
46 Powell, *Two Years in the Pontifical Zouaves*, p.79.
47 IE/DDA 333/3/7, O'Connor to Mgr Moran?, 9 November 1868.
48 IE/DDA 333/3/8, O'Connor to Mgr Moran?, 20 November 1868. He was able to do this thanks to the money raised by the Irish Ladies' Papal Defence Fund.
49 IE/DDA 333/3/10, O'Connor to Mgr Moran?, 6 January 1869.
50 *The Sun*, 25 August 1868, p.8.
51 IE/DDA 333/3/19, O'Connor to Mgr Moran?, 27 February 1869.
52 Eugenius de Gerlach, *The Last Days of the Papal Army* (Birmingham: D. Kelly, 1870), p.14.

upon his favours.' Zouaves could be found at almost every church function, whether it be at St Peter's or elsewhere, so much so that they were called by one wit 'The Inevitables'.[53] Joseph Powell's first taste of this was in St Peter's at Easter 1868:

> After entering the Basilica we formed into line on either side of the nave … ; we were about six hundred in number (Zouaves) … we were all armed, and our duty was to keep a passage clear for the procession. After some few preparations, the procession came in from the Vatican. A more magnificent one can hardly be imagined; first came the senators and suite, most brilliantly attired, then the servants bearing the hats of the Cardinals, the different Religious Orders, and the secular Clergy, including the Canons of St Peter's, next the Bishops, the Cardinals attended by their gentlemen, and then the Holy Father borne aloft on the Sedia Gestatoria, attended on either side by the Noble Guard in their full dress uniform; as he passed between our lines the commands of 'Portez armes,' 'Presentez armes,' 'Genou à terre' were given, and we presented arms, knelt on one knee, and saluted him with our right hands, and received his blessing. I saw him perfectly, the sight was a striking one, the face most benignant and yet so noble.[54]

A group of English Zouaves in Rome around Christmas, 1869. Lord Denbigh and Monsignor Stonor are seated. (Private collection, photograph: Kath Bracewell)

---

53 *Evening Freeman*, 7 March 1870, p.1.
54 Powell, *Two Years in the Pontifical Zouaves*, pp.49–50.

Such experiences strengthened the bond between the recruit and the person of the Pope; through their correspondence it also increased this devotion at home.

The chief chaplain to the English Zouaves was Monsignor Edmund Stonor, a member of one of England's most venerable Catholic families. Despite their Catholicism, many Stonors served in the royal household: the Monsignor's sister-in-law, for example, was the favourite Bedchamber Woman of the future Queen Alexandra as Princess of Wales.[55] Stonor was described as 'very precise, with an upright bearing and a ruddy face'[56] and his 'great kindness' to the Zouaves is memorialised in a silver inkstand presented to him in 1871, now kept at Stonor Park.

His assistant was Father Anselm Bertram Gurdon, who also belonged to the well-to-do family at Assington Hall in Suffolk. Educated at Winchester, where he was accounted a 'good shot' and all-round sportsman, he was ordained for the Church of England before being received into the Catholic Church in 1856 and joining the London Oratory. He was a skilled preacher and remembered for 'his warmth of heart and generosity, his vivid imagination and cultivated tastes, his tender piety and ardent faith.'[57] Father William Delany, recently ordained in 1867, and Father Charles O'Connor acted as chaplain to the Irish Zouaves, as we have noted. Such chaplains provided valuable support to the volunteers and kept up their morale and religious motivation.

Women and the Defence of the Pope

The Risorgimento was largely worked out in the public sphere by men. Nevertheless, on both sides of the spectrum, women were able to participate in a significant way through their enthusiasm, their writings, their practical works and even their efforts on the battlefield. If they could not join the Pontifical Army, Catholic women did much to promote the cause on the home front. Of primary importance was the role of the mother in encouraging her son to fight for the Pope. Zouave literature contains many examples of this maternal sacrifice, often in contrast to the irreligious father figure who tries to prevent his son's departure.

Women also desired to be involved in the struggle. Even communities of religious women, such as the Poor Clares of Amiens, referred to themselves as 'Pontifical Zouaves'. Bernadette Soubirous, the visionary of Lourdes, told a papal official who was visiting her convent in 1868 that they were 'soldiers of duty, Zouaves of prayer' and eight years later wrote to the Pope that she was 'your Holiness' little Zouave.'[58] Another saint of a slightly later period, the Carmelite Thérèse of Lisieux, wrote in 1896: 'I feel as if I've got the courage to be a Crusader, a Pontifical Zouave, dying on the battlefield in defence of the Church.'[59]

Beyond the convent walls, women were actively involved in fundraising and practical support. The Irish Ladies' Papal Defence Fund was set up in Dublin in 1868, with the encouragement of Cardinal Cullen, to support the material needs of the Irish Zouaves – a cause, it was felt, that 'recommends itself naturally to female piety and tenderness of feeling. … [After all,] you cannot, with the chivalrous Zouaves, shed your blood in the cause of religion and of God, but you can by a trifling sacrifice find means to supply

---

55 Stonor was heavily involved in Edward VII's visit to the Vatican in 1903.
56 *Westminster Gazette*, 29 February 1912, p.4.
57 *The Tablet*, 19 August 1899, pp.304–305.
58 Carol E. Harrison, 'Zouave Stories: Gender, Catholic Spirituality and French Responses to the Roman Question', *Journal of Modern History*, 79:2 (2007), pp.293–295.
59 Thérèse of Lisieux, *Story of a Soul: The Autobiography of Thérèse of Lisieux* (Washington, DC: ICS Publications, 1996), p.192.

that sustenance without which the most devoted cannot maintain the combat.'[60] Supporters included the Marchioness of Londonderry, the Countess of Porterlington, the Countess of Granard and the Lady Mayoress of Dublin.

Another enthusiastic voice, already alluded to, could be found in Mary Constantia Kavanagh, a granddaughter of Thomas Weld, the widower who became a priest and later a cardinal. Two of her sons from the first marriage joined the Zouaves: Oswald and William Vavasour. In the months after Mentana, she was active in drumming up English recruits and, as we have seen, dreamt of raising a specifically English Zouave battalion. When her banners were presented to the English Zouaves at Whitsun 1868, Stonor paid tribute to her support, stating that if there had been several other ladies who had done as much, many of their difficulties in Rome would have been overcome.[61]

For the privileged few, there were limited ways of being more actively involved: as volunteers with the military ambulance or as journalists, often present on the battlefield (a new departure for women in the nineteenth century). Madame Kanzler herself was auspicious in tending the wounded at Mentana and was applauded when the victorious Army returned to Rome. Her most famous English counterpart was Katherine Mary Stone, an enigmatic figure in many reports and misidentified by some journalists as American. Her roots were unmistakably English: the daughter of Anthony George Wright, who inherited the Sussex estate of Burton Park from a relative and added to his name that of 'Biddulph', a distinguished Catholic family, and Catherine Dorothy Scrope, of the same family as a fifteenth-century Archbishop of York.[62] She was also a cousin of Monsignor Stonor.

Mrs Stone, who had separated from her husband in the mid-1860s, lived for a time in Rome, writing as Roman correspondent for *The Tablet*, and acted as an 'angel of mercy' at Nerola and Mentana. Stonor commented on the 'joy and consolation it was for those who were wounded and dying on the field to have the tender cares of one who was faithful to them to the last, and whom he had himself seen on the battle field braving every danger, holding up the head of the dying and whispering words of piety and encouragement to those in the agony of suffering.'[63]

It was reported that after hearing that six Zouaves wounded at Nerola, including Alfred Collingridge, were being held by Garibaldians in a makeshift hospital nearby, she was given power of attorney by Colonel Allet and immediately set out to assist them. The figure of a lone English lady wrapped in her brown shawl and travelling through such dangerous territory must have been striking. She was interrogated by Italian troops near the border and eventually managed to seek out Menotti Garibaldi, who was eating at the table. 'Sir,' she said, 'I have travelled all over Europe, I have lived in all kinds of polite societies, and I never saw a man address a woman with his hat on. That custom is probably a new one, and forms part of the manners that you bring us.'[64] The *papalini* commonly accused Red Shirts of uncivilised, barbaric behaviour; other accounts state that Mrs Stone was immediately given liberty to tend to the wounded and that her large supply of linen was used to treat friend and foe alike. The Menotti story, however, tells us something of her formidable character. Mrs Stone later wrote of her experiences on the battlefield of Mentana in her poem 'Our Flag: A Lay of the Pontifical Zouaves':

---

60 *Dublin Weekly Nation*, 11 July 1868, p.5.
61 She first married William Vavasour and, after being widowed in 1860, married Maurice Kavanagh.
62 Richard Scrope (c.1350–1405) was executed after his involvement in the Northern Rising against Henry IV and is considered by many to be a saint.
63 *The Tablet*, 13 June 1868, p.377.
64 *Kendal Mercury*, 2 November 1867, p.3. See also the account, taken from the narrative by Padre Franco, in Nuyens, *Gedenkboek der pauselijke Zouaven*, p.226.

Have you ever kept a night watch,
    Comrades dear, on tented plain,
When the moon's wan light shines paler
    On the faces of the slain?
When from the dying battle
    The far-off thunders rolls,
And the ghostly wind is laden
    With the flight of parting souls?
… Have you heard the last dear message
From the cold and quivering lips,
While the loving heart still lingered
On the verge of life's eclipse?
… Then you know how fared the sleepless,
How the awful night hours sped
On the field 'twixt mirk and morning –
'Mid the dying and the dead.[65]

There were many other female supporters of the Zouaves, including Elizabeth Maria Lowther Winchester, whose death in November 1868 was attributed to her fatigues during the hot summer and whose funeral was attended by most of the English in Rome; and Rachel Busk, correspondent for the *Westminster Gazette*, folklorist and aunt of the Zouave, Clement Vansittart.

Ladies such as these were included in Benjamin Disraeli's 1870 novel *Lothair*, partly set in the Rome of 1867, which speaks of 'the Roman ladies and their foreign friends' showing 'the greatest spirit and the highest courage at this trying conjuncture'; 'they scarped for lint for the troops as incessantly as they offered prayers to the Virgin'.[66] After being injured at Mentana, where he fought for Garibaldi, the protagonist is nursed back to health by the Catholic Clare Arundel, 'the superior of the sisterhood of mercy, that shrank from no toil, and feared no danger in the fulfilment of those sacred duties of pious patriots'. They also formed a Catholic counterpart to the likes of Jessie White Mario, originally from Gosport in Hampshire, a prolific writer who married an Italian patriot and was present as a nurse in many of Garibaldi's campaigns, even assisting the surgeon who extracted the bullet from the hero's ankle at Aspromonte. Often overlooked by historians, the devotion and practical support of such women both at home and in Rome were an essential part of the volunteer movement.

---

65 Stone, *Our Flag*, pp.26–27.
66 Benjamin Disraeli, *Lothair* (London: Oxford University Press, 1975), p.245.

14

Endgame: 20 September 1870

On 18 July 1870 the Vatican Council promulgated the Dogmatic Constitution *Pastor Aeternus*, solemnly defining the dogma of papal infallibility. Approved by all but two of the bishops present, it was based on a long established understanding of papal authority but was open to differing interpretations which caused heated discussion across the world. Indeed, ever since the convocation of the Council, concerns had been expressed by monarchs and statesmen alike: many saw infallibility as a step backwards and rumours abounded that the doctrine presumed the Pope's right to depose sovereigns. Within the Church, a vocal party of ultramontane bishops actively drummed up enthusiasm, including Archbishop Manning of Westminster. The day of the definition was marked by thunderstorms; lightning struck St Peter's, which was variously interpreted, depending on one's viewpoint, as divine approval or condemnation.

Meanwhile, war clouds loomed. On 19 July France declared war on Prussia. It had serious repercussions for the Holy See, which still regarded, for good or for bad, Napoleon III and his troops as its main military and diplomatic support. Without this protection the Holy See would be vulnerable not only to revolutionaries but to Italian aggression; it had only been a decade since the Piedmontese entered papal territory on the pretext of preventing Garibaldi from reaching Rome. The government in Florence gave assurances that the September Convention would be respected but this did little to reassure the Roman authorities.

The order was finally given on 26 July for the French troops to withdraw. Many expected this regardless of the war, since Napoleon had warned that the definition of papal infallibility could endanger the ongoing retention of French troops. Pius IX, after reading the emperor's letter announcing the news, is reported to have said: 'Tell the Emperor I have no fear. If he abandons Rome to the Italian forces, I shall not hesitate to go into exile; and Europe and not the Papacy will be the sufferer. "I trust in God, not in man.".'[1]

There was growing concern around the Catholic world for the security of the Pope and a rush of volunteers for his army. In England, *The Tablet* asked: '[W]hile the youth of Germany are glowing with military ardour to face the chassepots and mitrailleuses – while the men of France from city, bourg, and village, are hastening to the standard of their God-forsaken Emperor, is there no generous fire burning in the breasts of the Catholic men of England?'[2] Lord Denbigh wrote excitedly that 'now "the dogs of war" are unchained' and 'the revolutionists are up to their old tricks again', it was incumbent on English Catholics 'to come forward and show of what stuff they are made of'.[3] Ex-Zouaves were encouraged to return to the colours. Mary Kavanagh appealed:

---

1 *The Tablet*, 6 August 1870, p.174.
2 *The Tablet*, 13 August 1870, p.194.
3 *The Tablet*, 20 August 1870, p.235.

Where are all those Catholic young men who wrote to me formerly from all parts of the United Kingdom, professing so deep a devotion to the Holy See? Now is your time. Arise! Hasten to Rome furnished with passports and arms if possible. Range yourselves around the Holy Father.[4]

A further option lay in the Urban Guard or Pontifical Volunteers of the Reserve, which had originated in the scare of 1867 and been formally set up in February 1869 to patrol the city and its walls. Intended for those of independent means, no military oath was required and uniform optional. By September 1870 they numbered around 500 and included those of different nationalities.[5]

Joseph Powell, remembered being with Sergeant Shee, who was on leave of absence, at Swindon station and hearing of the declaration of war between France and Germany: '[T]his news occasioned us some very deep reflections, for we both at once saw the possibility of another raid upon Rome.'[6] Shee returned to his post in Rome and Powell hoped to give up his business in order to travel Romeward.[7] Keyes O'Clery, an Irish Zouave, departed from London's Cannon Street a few weeks later. Passing through Paris, 'the thought forced itself on my mind that at that moment the two great cities of the world – Paris and Rome – were both threatened with a siege', one 'the capital of luxury and fashion', the other 'the citadel of religious truth'.[8] Another welcome returnee was Wilfrid Watts-Russell, brother of the 'Martyr' of Mentana, who made 'the greatest of sacrifices in leaving a beloved wife to offer his sword a second time for the Church'.[9]

The Eternal City began to be deserted. The Council was suspended, and the bishops returned home. The early days of the war saw disastrous defeats for the French: Wissembourg (4 August), Spicheren (5 August) and Wörth (6 August). Catholic writers viewed events with a grim satisfaction:

> Scarcely had the French flag ceased to wave over the Pontifical territory than it had retreated before the conquering hosts of Prussia, and the sovereign to whose personal initiative the betrayal of the Pope was owing, was defeated in his own territories, and obliged to confess that his cause was nearly a lost one. … At every angle of the streets [in Rome], in the churches, at the doors of the cafes, eager groups were to be seen discussing the intelligence, and one word, one phrase, was heard on all sides, '*E la mano di Dio*' ['It is the hand of God'].[10]

The Italian government meanwhile considered its options. Victor Emmanuel had dreams of leading his army against Prussia, in alliance with France. Along with his prime minister Giovanni Lanza (already the eighth to hold that office in the new Kingdom of Italy), he realised that the September Convention bound Italy to respect the independence of Papal Rome. However, there were many radical voices around him, hoping he would take advantage of the situation and make Rome his new capital. Fears were expressed once again that a revolution in the Eternal City would not only complicate matters for the Pope but also lead Victor Emmanuel to lose his throne. Radicals were indeed at work; Mazzini had returned to Italy from his English exile and was arrested in Palermo in mid-August. Of course, just as insurrection was seen as a

---

4   *The Tablet*, 27 August 1870, p.267.
5   *The Tablet*, 20 August 1870, p.235. See also Piero Crociani, *L'Ultimo Esercito Pontificio* (Rome: Stato Maggiore dell'Esercito, 2020), pp.28–29.
6   Powell, *Two Years in the Pontifical Zouaves*, p.240.
7   Powell gave his notice on 8 September and three Zouave friends also declared their intention to join him, but Rome fell before they could set out. Powell, *Two Years in the Pontifical Zouaves*, p.255.
8   *Evening Freeman*, 19 October 1870, p.4.
9   *The Tablet*, 3 September 1870, p.301.
10 *The Tablet*, 20 August 1870, p.237.

threat, it might be also a justification for action. Risings could be secretly engineered and, in the light of the departure of the French and the September Convention, Italy could claim to be the protector of the Holy See. The King hoped that the Pope would agree to his troops occupying his territory, while maintaining his spiritual authority. Moreover, once the pontifical forces realised they were clearly outnumbered, then this process could surely be achieved with little or no bloodshed.

Reports reached Kanzler by mid-August that Italian forces had been detected near the borders. In seeking an audience with the Pope on 20 August, he was disappointed to find that his master downplayed the threat of invasion, trusting that God would provide and instructing that, in the unlikely event of action, his troops should offer no resistance and withdraw to Rome. Cardinal Antonelli, meanwhile, explained the movements of Italian troops in terms of internal security and continued to put his faith in diplomacy and assurances of foreign protection, if not from France then at least from Austria or even from Protestant Prussia.

The rest of Europe watched nervously. In London, Archbishop Manning feared that the fall of Papal Rome would signal a return to the revolutionary horrors of 1793: '[W]e have already a political conflict in all countries, we should then have also a religious conflict, that is the history of Ireland reproduced over all Europe.'[11] He corresponded with Gladstone about the need to 'exercise a high office of providence in being at hand to prevent excesses' and protect both British nationals and the Pope, who 'may be in personal danger from the revolution and the conspiracies which are working upon Rome'.[12] HMS *Defence* was consequently sent towards Civitavecchia to stand by, arriving at the port on 23 August. The Foreign Secretary, Lord Granville, was clear that, if the request be made, 'His Holiness should be received on board Her Majesty's ship and entertained with all possible respect'.[13] Even his temporary residence on Malta or another British territory might be considered. Manning sent news of this confidential arrangement to the rector of the English College, who acted as agent of the English bishops in Rome. Gladstone recorded that Manning dared not communicate directly with the Pope as he 'would undoubtedly blurt it out to those around him, & they are not to be trusted & would trade in it with France or Austria'.[14]

The main motivation, of course, was not support for the papacy *per se* but a concern that the fall of the Temporal Power could destabilise international politics. Added to this was a desire to attract Catholic votes, which counted for up to 20 percent of the United Kingdom electorate. In sending the *Defence*, the British Government appeared to offer support to the beleaguered Pope, while at the same time, as one historian suggests, discouraging the Catholic powers from intervening themselves and therefore assisting the work of unification by potentially taking away one of its main obstacles.[15]

The French defeat at Sedan on 2 September and the abdication of the emperor drastically changed the situation and, with the September Convention null and void, opened the floodgates for Italian intervention in Rome. The Italian Government received petitions from a series of towns in the Papal States, including Viterbo and Frosinone, requesting annexation. An envoy, Count Gustavo Ponza di San Martino, was sent to the Vatican to negotiate, Prime Minister Lanza hoping that the Pope 'will not reject in these times, full of menaces for the most venerated institutions and for the peace of nations, the hand which is loyally

---

11 Peter C. Erb (ed.), *The Correspondence of Henry Edward Manning and William Ewart Gladstone, 1833–1891* (Oxford: Oxford University Press, 2013), vol. 3, p.222, Manning to Gladstone, 14 September 1870.
12 Erb, *Manning and Gladstone Correspondence*, vol 3, pp.217–218, Manning to Gladstone, 15 August 1870.
13 British Parliamentary Papers 1871. LXXII. Rome. No. I. *Correspondence Respecting the Affairs of Rome, 1870–1871* (London, 1871), p.4, Earl Granville to the Lords Commissioners of the Admiralty, 20 August 1870.
14 Erb, *Manning and Gladstone Correspondence*, vol. 3, p.219, Gladstone to Granville, 20 August 1870.
15 O.J. Wright, *Great Britain and the Unifying of Italy: A Special Relationship?* (Basingstoke: Palgrave Macmillan, 2019), pp.192–193.

stretched out to him in the name of religion and of Italy'.[16] The Count brought with him a letter from the king, written 'with the affection of a son, the faith of a Catholic, the loyalty of a king, the spirit of an Italian' but beneath the diplomatic niceties was a stark ultimatum. Aware that a revolutionary storm was threatening the twin pillars of 'the Monarchy and the Papacy', Victor Emmanuel stated his intention to replace the vacuum left by the French with Italian troops to ensure good order and the Pope's own security. However, there were references to the 'national aspirations' of the people and thinly veiled hopes that bloodshed would be avoided. He was particularly keen that Rome should be freed of the foreign volunteers then gathering to defend the Pope: '[T]he state of feeling among the populations governed by your Holiness, and the presence among them of foreign troops come from various places with various intentions, constitute a hotbed of agitation and evident dangers for all.'[17] According to a draft agreement, Rome would become part of Italy but the Pope would retain all prerogatives of sovereignty, including the right to have ambassadors, full jurisdiction over the Leonine City (the area around St Peter's) and an annual endowment. The English representative in Rome, Henry Jervoise, reported there was even 'some idea that he should retain a strip of territory on the right bank of the Tiber, as far as Ostia, where the Italian Government would engage to construct him a port'.[18]

At his meeting with the Count on 10 September, Pius insisted that there were not yet any revolutionary disturbances in Rome; Garibaldi was safely on his island home of Caprera, Mazzini behind bars in Gaeta and the Pope's troops (numbering over 12,000) well able to maintain internal security. The Italians were acting as the aggressor and there was no guarantee that future administrations would respect the terms of such an agreement. During the heated interview, the pontiff lost his temper, crying: 'Fine loyalty! You are all a set of vipers, of whited sepulchres, and wanting in faith.'[19]

The ultimatum was firmly rejected. The Pope continued, as best he could, his duties as both bishop and king. On 11 September he went to the Piazza dei Termini to inaugurate the Acqua Marcia-Pia, a new aqueduct using an ancient Roman source and bringing water to the fast-expanding development around the railway station – a reminder of the urban expansion of his pontificate, thanks largely to the vision of Monsignor de Mérode.[20] It would be the pontiff's last visit outside the city walls.

Meanwhile, the Italian forces prepared to move into papal territory. General Raffaele Cadorna[21] had been placed over an 'Corpo di Esercito di Osservatione nell'Italia Centrale' (soon renamed the 'IV Corpo d'Esercito de Operazione') and concentrated the 11th, 12th and 13th Divisions, totalling 30,000 men, in the area south of Spoleto around Narni, Terni, Rieti and Magliano. General Nino Bixio commanded the 2nd Division that was stationed near Orvieto, and General Diego Angioletti's 9th Division was to the south of Rome at Arce and Isoletta, both numbering 10,000 men.

Kanzler was clearly outnumbered but did what he could. The city had been divided into four zones: the first, under Colonel Allet, covered the Vatican, Trastevere and Janiculum; the second under Colonel Perrault of the Roman Legion included much of the historic centre; the third under Colonel Lepri of the Dragoons comprised of the regions of Monti and Quirinale; and the fourth, commanded by Colonel

---

16 *Correspondence Respecting the Affairs of Rome, 1870–1871*, p.27, Lanza to San Martino, 29 August 1870.
17 *Correspondence Respecting the Affairs of Rome, 1870–1871*, p.36, translation of the King's letter to the Pope, 8 September 1870.
18 *Correspondence Respecting the Affairs of Rome, 1870–1871*, p.38, Jervoise to Granville, 11 September 1870.
19 Raffaele De Cesare, *The Last Days of Papal Rome, 1850–1870* (London: Archibald Constable & Co., 1909), p.444.
20 Indeed, the main street he envisaged linking this part of Rome to the centre was eventually built, being called Via Nazionale rather than Via Nuova Pia (or, as some dubbed it, Via de Merode).
21 His son, Luigi, who saw action in the 1870 campaign with the 2nd Regiment of Artillery, would become Italian Chief of Staff during the first part of the First World War (until 1917).

Jeannerat of the Foreign Carabineers, included the Campidoglio and Aventine. Kanzler hoped to effectively keep order within the different zones and move troops quickly to strategic points. He saw the area around the Vatican, with Castel Sant'Angelo and the Leonine Walls, as a possible final line of defence and aimed to ensure that the road to Civitavecchia was kept open in case the Pope needed to escape.

Aware that the walls of Rome, a large proportion of which dated back to antiquity, were highly vulnerable and, in David Alvarez's words, 'more suited to repelling medieval spearmen than withstanding the fire of siege artillery', he ordered the use of barricades and sandbags.[22] One English ecclesiastical student wrote to his mother:

> [T]here is a very great extent of wall, and, considering the small number of our artillery, it will be a very difficult thing indeed to oppose the enemy with as many guns as they can bring against us, particularly as we hear that the Italians are very strong in artillery. Besides this, in some places the walls are most awfully weak, and apparently it would require small cannonading to make a breach, whereas, in other places, it would be almost impossible to make a breach.[23]

Some gates were entirely closed with masses of earth. The gap in the walls at the Tre Archi, through which the railway line passed, was placed under careful surveillance given its strategic importance. Bridges across the Tiber were fortified, and pontoons constructed between the Ripa Grande and the foot of the Aventine Hill to increase mobility within the city. The 150 pieces of artillery – most of which were smoothbore – were spread across the city as evenly as possible, and gardens, woodland and even vineyards that adjoined the walls were cleared to maximise firepower and visibility.

Kanzler realised that any successful campaign depended on surprise and playing off the five Italian divisions to prevent them uniting. During an audience on 10 September, Kanzler was once again ordered to avoid any direct confrontation near the borders and pull troops back to Rome. At a time when France and Germany were at war, the Pope had no desire to cause further bloodshed or to hand on a legacy of hatred and bitterness. A withdrawal to Rome, moreover, would force the Italians to attack the city, which would surely cause an international reaction. The General underlined the Army's desire to fight and his fear that the Italians would literally walk into Rome ('*un pubblico passeggio*') but was told 'we choose to surrender. Not to die is sometimes the bigger sacrifice.'[24]

Resistance at Civita Castellana

On 11 September, the Italian 13th Division crossed the papal frontier and occupied Orte, 37 miles north of Rome. The four Papal Gendarmes present retreated after a brief exchange of fire. The following morning the 12th Division moved towards Civita Castellana, where there was more serious resistance. The 5th company of the 4th Battalion of Zouaves under the Belgian captain, Zénon de Résimont, and numbering around 100 men, occupied the town, along with gendarmes and a company of 71 disarmed soldiers from various units who were held there as a result of disciplinary offences. When news reached them of the proximity of the enemy, barricades were hurriedly raised and detachments placed at strategic locations, including a *convento* on the main road beyond the walls.

---

22   Alvarez, *The Pope's Soldiers*, p.220.
23   *The Tablet*, 1 October 1870, p.430.
24   Alvarez, *The Pope's Soldiers*, p.223.

The Italians came under heavy fire and there were a handful of casualties, much to General de la Roche's annoyance since the defence of the town seemed futile. The papal forces, on realising the size of the enemy, including three batteries of artillery, withdrew to the safety of the Renaissance fortress. A white flag eventually appeared after 45 minutes of fire and the papal troops marched out with the honours of war. The bombardment could be heard across the *campagna*. A student wrote from the English College villa at Monte Porzio, over 40 miles away, that a friend had come into his room at 11.00 a.m. 'saying that fighting was going on in the direction of Soracte and that the fellows on Tusculum [a nearby summit] had heard the cannonading on all morning. On going out to the Parish Church only heard one shot. So it has begun!'[25] The London correspondent of the *Daily News* spoke to one Irish Zouave at Civita Castellana, who expressed his disappointment that he had not died for the Pope, and saw some of the men selling their revolvers at 10 francs each.[26]

Towards Rome

The 13th Division, having taken Orte, moved on to Viterbo on 12 September, where the handful of Papal Gendarmes quickly surrendered. Colonel de Charette and his garrison had slipped away to Rome and managed to escape the Italian Lancers that were sent in pursuit. Meanwhile Angioletti's 9th Division advanced from the south and easily took Frosinone, one of the main initial objectives. As the Italians marched towards Rome, plans were also made to organise an insurrection within the Eternal City which would be seen to justify Italian intervention. However, the 'popular' rising failed to materialise due to a lack of enthusiasm and the effectiveness of the city's internal security.

As the advance parties of the 11th and 12th Divisions reached the outskirts of Rome, there was a skirmish near Sant'Onofrio on 14 September between a squadron of Lancers and a picket of Zouaves under Sergeant Shee. The *papalini* at first mistook the Lancers for Papal Dragoons, who were patrolling the area, but then realised they were being attacked. Shee was later feted for his heroism; a seminarian at the English College recalled hearing the story from his lips:

> A day or two before the *Venti Settembre*, he was out patrolling the road north beyond Monte Mario when he descried a reconnaissance of Piedmontese lancers pricking along towards them. Fourteen or twenty men against eight. He at once lined his men across the road with orders to fall back in fours each side of the road, line the fences and re-load after firing from the line. The lancers charged and Shea's men fired, emptying five saddles. The lancers swept by spearing nothing. Back they came, and five more saddles were evacuated. Then Shea ordered his men home to report and stood alone to face the third charge of the remainder. He shot one man dead, bayonetted a second who lanced his thigh as he came. 'I was nearly smothered in his blood, and it felt quite hot,' he said. Then he pulled a third off his horse, and got a down cut of a sabre which knocked him out. His zouave cap had saved his life, but he woke in Viterbo lying on straw in a flat cart with his head aching horribly.[27]

The Lancers were defeated, and the Zouaves took the unhorsed lieutenant back to Rome as a prisoner.

An English traveller catching a night train from Civitavecchis to Corneto wrote:

---

25   *The Venerabile*, 3:4 (April 1928), p.322.
26   *Daily News*, 21 September 1870, p.6.
27   *The Venerabile*, 5:4 (April 1932), p.375, quoting the reminiscences of John O'Connor.

[M]y attention was attracted by a line of fires blazing steadily, but with unequal lustre, through the darkness, which there was no moonlight to dispel. The more vivid and ruddy of these fires were on board the war ships advancing against Civitavecchia. The nearer and paler lights were from a bivouac of the troops on their march to that city.[28]

It was Bixo's 2nd Division heading for the papal port, where there was a garrison of 1,400 men (including four Zouave companies), 173 guns and the papal flagship *Immacolata Concezione*, built in London 11 years earlier. There was potential for a stiff resistance as the Italians lined up their forces and their warships appeared off the port. Realising the odds were against him, the Pope, at Antonelli's insistence, ordered a surrender. There was reluctance to do this and Colonel Serra, the Spanish commander of the garrison, was torn between satisfying military honour and following instructions. After several hours of indecision, and persuaded to avoid wasteful destruction, he surrendered without a fight on 15 September.

On arriving at Civitavecchia two days later, Keyes O'Clery saw with concern 'the hated Piedmontese flag' and observed from a safe distance the several hundred Zouaves who had been taken prisoner. With Kenyon, an English veteran who had made a similar journey, he managed to visit some of the prisoners of war.

The papal flagship, *Immacolata Concezione*, built by the Thames Iron Works & Shipbuilding Co., London in 1859. The steam corvette was armed with eight 18-pounders. (*Illustrated London News*, 20 August 1859, Private collection, author's photograph)

---

28 *Union Review* (1871), p.83.

The Last Days of Papal Rome

Most of the operational Papal Army had fallen back to Rome by 14 September: around 8,000 infantry, 500 Dragoons, and 750 artillerymen. The Italian forces paused outside the walls as various messages were sent between the Italian and Papal Governments. Kanzler rejected a letter from General Cadorna, once again claiming that his forces had come only to conserve order: 'His Holiness desires to see Rome occupied by his own troops and not by those of another Sovereign.'[29]

Rome had officially been in a state of siege since 12 September. Residents were encouraged to remain within their homes although curiosity led many to walk around the fortifications. Some viewed the hostilities as a spectator sport. William Kirkham, a student at the English College, recorded excitedly in his diary on 18 September: '[T]he Papal troops have had a few skirmishes in which they killed about 30 Bersaglieri: one shot at the Porta Pia bowled over 8 Lancers at an Osteria not far from S. Agnese's.'[30] The following day, an attack was widely expected, since it was the tenth anniversary of Castelfidardo, and Kirkham reported that 'rifle bullets were flying about our ears like angry wasps on the Lateran steps'. This did not deter him and his friends from taking out the college telescope, which they lent to Colonel Charette to train his guns on a house occupied by Italian troops half a mile away. The English seminarians had got to know many of their compatriots in the Zouaves; some had been at school together. Kirkham even bought them 'a whole lot of cigars at the Custom House' and, along with other students, wanted to volunteer for ambulance work alongside them. The rector refused to give permission, although seminarians at the Propaganda and North American Colleges seemed to have got their way.[31]

On reaching Rome in the final days before the attack, Keyes O'Clery recognised familiar faces on the walls, including 'Mr Edmond de la Poer, M.P., Major Lewis, and Captain Coppinger, who are on guard, rifle in hand'.[32] Though they do not appear to have been attached to any unit of the Pontifical Army, these names are significant. Two had held commissions in the British Army while Edmond de la Poer was Liberal MP for County Waterford from 1866 to 1873.[33] Born in 1841 as Edmond Power, the surname was changed to 'de la Poer' in 1863 to reflect his Anglo-Norman ancestry and in 1864 he became a Papal Count. Judging from his correspondence with the rector of the Irish College, he had first shown interest in the Papal Army in 1862, as had his brother, Raymond, a few years later. In July 1870 Edmond wrote to Kirby saying that, despite his parliamentary responsibilities, he was essentially free until March and thought he 'cannot better pass the time than in the service of His Holiness'.[34] Though he did not formally enter the Zouaves, as he wished, the *Tipperary Free Press* reported that 'the young Member for the County Waterford was in the midst of the fire, … perilling his life like a brave Irishman and a good Catholic'.[35] It is remarkable that a sitting Member of Parliament, fighting for the defence of the Pope's temporal sovereignty, gun in hand on the walls of Rome, did not cause more public attention at the time.[36]

---

29 *Correspondence Respecting the Affairs of Rome, 1870–1871*, p.41, Kanzler to Cadorna, 16 September 1870.
30 *The Venerabile*, 3:4 (April 1928), p.325.
31 *The Venerabile*, 3:4 (April 1928), pp.324–325.
32 *Evening Freeman*, 19 October 1870, p.4.
33 Ralph Fitzgibbon Lewis was wounded in the Indian Mutiny with the 86th (Royal County Down) Regiment and Dudley Coppinger served in the 54th (West Norfolk) Regiment. Lewis went on to act as governor of Brisbane Gaol. For Coppinger, see *The Tablet*, 18 March 1871, p.336.
34 KIR/1870/139, Poer to Kirby, 28 July 1870.
35 *Tipperary Free Press*, 21 October 1870, p.2.
36 See his obituary in the *The Tablet*, 4 September 1915, p.308. After resigning as MP, De La Poer briefly considered a religious vocation and went on to serve on an ambulance during the Third Carlist War. He served as Lord

On 19 September the Pope left the Vatican for what would be the last time. Kirkham bumped into the Zouave, Oswald Vavasour, who told him that the Pope had arrived at the Scala Santa, the staircase believed to have once formed part of Pontius Pilate's Praetorium and ascended by Christ before his crucifixion. They rushed back to witness this historic occasion: the Pope 'prayed very hard and went up on his bare knees asking God to have pity on his beloved *cittadini*'.[37] It was a pious gesture and a powerful one, for the Pope was publicly associating Christ's passion with his own.

Among the Italian generals who were assembling their men outside the ancient walls, one name above all struck terror in the hearts of the pontifical troops: Nino Bixio, who had reached Rome after receiving the surrender of Civitavecchia. Now fighting for the King of Italy, he was one of Garibaldi's longest serving collaborators, having taken part in the capture of Rome in 1849 and the 'Expedition of the Thousand'. He was also known for his radical opinions. Keyes O'Clery later recalled his own hurried journey to Rome, falling in with the advancing Italians and apparently hearing Bixio observe that the destruction of the Zouaves, 'those pet lions', was inevitable.[38] The General quickly became the focus of the fears and aggression of the *papalini*, whipped up by his well-publicised threat that he would throw all the cardinals into the Tiber and the fact that his banner showed what looked like a severed head (though it was, in fact, that of the Italian hero and poet, Dante). Even the Pope, who had a serene confidence that the Italians would not dare to enter the city, is said to have turned pale when he heard that Bixio was approaching. Moreover, rumours abounded that the Eternal City faced not only the Italians but the Red Shirts, some of whom were apparently spotted by anxious observers.

XX Settembre

In the early hours of 20 September 1870 those stationed at the Porta Pia, Porta Salaria and Tre Archi noticed continuous sounds and faint lights in the darkness. The Italians were preparing for attack. At 4.40 a.m. the Pontifical Army was ordered to their battle positions and quickly took the initiative. Some 30 Zouaves under Lieutenant Paul van de Kerkhove established an advance post at the Villa Patrizi, just beyond the Porta Pia, and fired on the Italian artillery; the 5th, 6th and 8th Batteries of the 9th Artillery Regiment had set up their guns nearby, around the Villa Albani. There were several casualties. In response, the 35th Bersaglieri of the 12th Division attacked the Villa Patrizi. The Zouaves stood their ground until forced to withdraw after the Italians entered the building through a breach blown open by engineers. This allowed the beginning of an intense bombardment of the section of city wall between the Porta Pia and Porta Salaria, which was considered particularly weak; by 6.30 a.m. one Zouave counted 210 hits. The four papal guns deployed in this area could do little against the 52 enemy pieces. It was not long before the walls began to crumble, and gaps were filled with mattresses, carts, timber, and haystacks. Captain De La Hoyde commanded one of the Zouave companies nearby and, in the words of his comrade, Bartle Teeling, fought 'like a true Irishman'.[39]

The Porta Pia, of course, had a powerful symbolism: originally designed by Michelangelo for Pius IV, not only did it bear the current Pope's name but had the previous year been restored by him, with the help of his architect Virginio Vespignani. It was also the gate through which the papal troops had marched on the

---

Lieutenant and High Sheriff of County Waterford and was a founder member of the British Association of the Sovereign Military Order of Malta in 1876. In 1881 he married the Hon. Mary Monsell and had six children.
37 *The Venerabile*, 3:4 (April 1928), p.326.
38 *Evening Freeman*, 19 October 1870, p.4.
39 *Dalby Herald and Western Queensland Advertiser*, 3 December 1870, p.3.

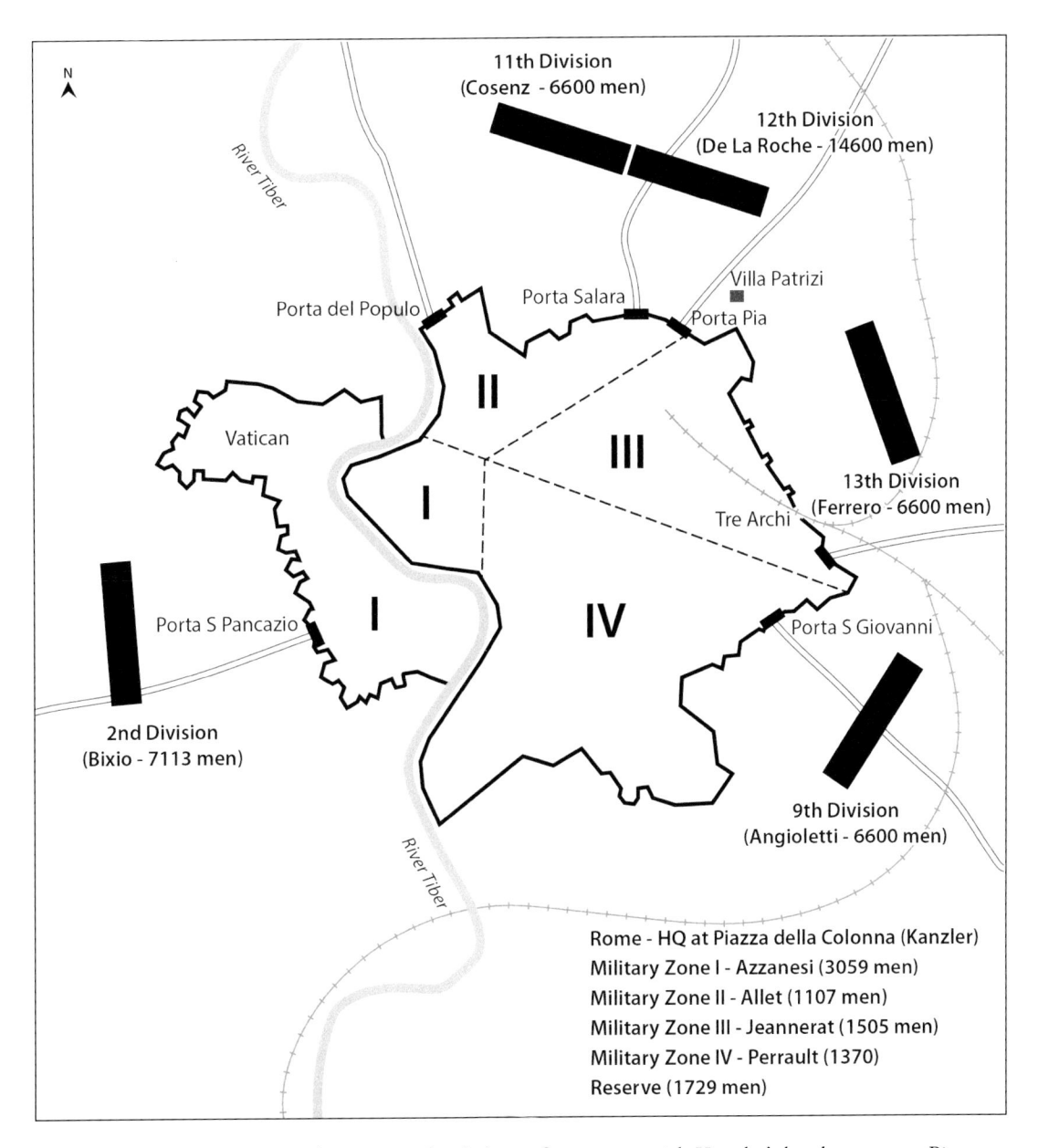

Rome in September 1870. The city was divided into four zones, with Kanzler's headquarters at Piazza della Colonna at the centre.

ITALIAN TROOPS STORMING A BREACH IN THE CITY WALLS AT THE VILLA BUONAPARTE.

Italian troops enter the breach at the Porta Pia. (*Illustrated London News*, 8 October 1870, Private collection, author's photograph)

way to Mentana three years before and then returned victorious. Just within the walls, also, was the Villa Paolina Bonaparte, a reminder of the French presence which had for so long delayed the Italian advance on Rome.

This was not the only sector that saw action. At the Porta Pinciana, to the north, there was an attack from the 35th Infantry Regiment and 21st Bersaglieri; there were heavy exchanges of fire at the Tre Archi and Porta San Pancrazio, near the Vatican Gardens (although the Italians were keen to avoid an international outcry by damaging the area around St Peter's). At 8.00 a.m. the Italians attacked the wall between the Porta Pinciana and Porta del Popolo but were held back by a training company of Zouaves and a company of Line Infantry. Pressure was also being put on the walls near the Lateran by the 9th Division; under heavy fire many of the defensive positions were destroyed and the gates unhinged. Charette did his best to fight back: his troops were deployed behind a second line of defensive barricades and the pontifical Claxton Gun lay in readiness in the Porta San Giovanni. This could have easily become the point of entry for the Italians but there was no desire for a bloodbath and the aim was to distract and demoralise the papal defenders.

Within the Apostolic Palace, the Pope celebrated mass early, to the background sound of artillery fire, and nervously awaited news. The corridors became thronged with concerned prelates, aristocrats, and diplomats, while the Pope's personal guards – Noble, Swiss and Palatine – were ready to fight in his defence. Ordinary Romans themselves were endangered. About 8.30 a.m. on 20 September 1870 Kirkham was standing at his window on the top floor of the English College, when he was 'startled by a shell hitting an opposite house a little to the right and bursting on the roof. The inhabitants on the balcony rushed in with a shriek.'[40] The community were ordered to gather on the ground floor and then in the cellars: 'we could hear nothing else but heavy explosions and the rattling of stones and broken glass', including one shell that led to 'bricks falling and windows crashing into the garden'.

Visitors were caught up in the drama of events. David Hunter Blair, who would later win fame as a writer and abbot of Fort Augustus, a Benedictine abbey in Scotland, had just finished at Eton and was touring Italy. The 16-year-old found himself alone 'at a most critical moment in the history of both Rome and Italy' and resolved to help the wounded, working closely with a red-haired Scottish seminarian near Porta San Sebastiano: '[W]e were provided with strong wheelbarrows stuffed with hay, and in these we were engaged for at least two hours wheeling wounded soldiers (and some dead ones) into a neighbouring convent.' It was one of the hottest summers on record and all concerned were exhausted. In later years he remembered with affection the kindly nun who had put 'two big ripe oranges into my pocket as were going to and fro.'[41]

The wounded were tended not only by the army ambulances but by volunteers, including Mrs Hassett and Mrs Coppinger, 'our Irish ladies', who were 'always to be found near the Zouaves with baskets of refreshments, &c, to cheer and nourish them while making trenches and raising earthworks'. At the Porta Pia they assisted those who had fallen 'in spite of shot and shell, old bricks, mortar, dust, &c that surrounded them.'[42] Likewise, when Daniel Curtin, a Zouave from County Cork, died from his wounds shortly afterwards, Miss Winter is named as being 'assiduous in her attention to him to the very last.'[43]

The English Zouave chaplain, Monsignor Stonor, stood at his post amid the bursting shells, as did Mrs Stone. On hearing the Italian guns starting to fire, she jumped out of bed and rushed through a 'shower of balls' to her ambulance near Porta Pia. Once there:

> I found the doctor had just been dreadfully wounded (Dr Heiler, a Swiss) and had one leg carried off. We had just got into order again with an Italian doctor, when in came a great big shell; and another thing all red hot (I don't know what they called it) took the roof off and made a great hole in the farther side of the wall of this stable we were in, and carried off half the hand of a gentleman of the ambulance, – so that we had to retreat under a '*feu d'enfer*' across the piazza dei Termini by the railway, carrying our wounded as well as we could to the villa Strozzi and thence sending them on to [the hospital of] Santo Spirito.[44]

At 8:30 a.m. it was reported that the breach at Porta Pia was complete and that the Italians might enter at any time. There was hesitation about what should happen next. Kanzler met with his Committee of Defense at the Palazzo Wedekind on the Piazza Colonna; they reluctantly agreed that Rome would have to capitulate. There is some debate about what orders Kanzler had indeed received. It seems that Antonelli favoured an immediate, bloodless surrender, while the senior military personnel wished to defend the city for as long as possible. The Pope took a middle course, ordering on 14 September a token, demonstrative resistance to show that he was the victim of Italian aggression. In his original communication, the Pope ordered Kanzler to 'open negotiations for surrender at the first shots of the cannon.' Kanzler and his colleagues, driven by

---

40 *The Venerabile*, 3:4 (April 1928), pp.326–327.
41 David Hunter-Blair, *In Victorian Days and Other Papers* (London: Longman, Green & Co., 1939), pp.180–86.
42 *Evening Freeman*, 25 October 1870, p.4.
43 *Cork Examiner*, 17 November 1870, p.3.
44 Erb, *Manning and Gladstone Correspondence*, vol. 3, p.232, account of Mrs Stone, 21 September 1870, sent by Manning to Gladstone.

their military expertise, honour and desire to defend the Pope, interpreted the order with fluidity but came to realise that once the breach had been made there was no option but to surrender. At the last minute, Zappi pleaded a final re-evaluation of the situation. There were reports of light casualties, high morale and the prospect of a counter-attack but eventually at 9:35 a.m. Kanzler ordered the white flag to be hoisted. According to the memoirs of his son, Rodolfo Kanzler, the text of the Pope's original order was changed on 21 September and backdated two days to save face, so that the order read: '[O]pen negotiations for surrender after the wall is breached.'[45]

The ceasefire was greeted with fury. A seminarian wrote to his mother that 'the rage of the Zouave officers at hearing this was so great, I thought some of them would have gone raving mad. Some put away their swords, threw themselves upon the hedges of box and cried for disappointment.'[46] Charette tore up the order but followed it dutifully at his position near the Lateran; at the Porta Pia, Major de Troussures told the Dragoon who issued him with it that he needed confirmation from a higher-ranking officer. Wilfrid Robinson, stationed with the Zouaves near Santa Croce, remembered being surprised when the bugles sounded and a white banner was hoisted over the Lateran basilica: '[W]e used some rather strong words about it. We hope the recording angel has blotted them out!'[47] For O'Clery:

Nothing could exceed the anguish and disappointment of the Zouaves when they heard of the capitulation, but the very principle of the organisation taught them that obedience to the wishes of the Holy Father was their first duty. In thus yielding at his command, they made for him the highest sacrifice to which the actual shedding of their blood was of far less moment as was manifest when the gallant hearts which fell during the attack were envied rather than lamented by their comrades; for the Pontifical Zouaves the martyrdom of Castelfidardo was an infinitely greater triumph than the victory of Mentana.[48]

The Pope himself ordered the white flag to be flown over St Peter's so that all could see it; nevertheless, there was a significant delay in many sectors and the troops around Tre Archi were 45 minutes in stopping fire.

Amidst the confusion, the Italians around the Porta Pia – namely the 12th and 34th Bersaglieri and battalions of the 39th and 41st Infantry Regiments – advanced towards the breach. In a moment of pathos, the papal troops sang their regimental song and, crying '*Viva Pio Nono*', fired on the

General Hermann Kanzler (1822-88), who interpreted papal orders with fluidity and continued the defence of Rome for as long as possible. (Private collection, photograph: Granddaughters of George Collingridge)

---

45 Crociani, *L'Ultimo Esercito Pontificio*, pp.87–88.
46 *The Tablet*, 1 October 1870, p.430.
47 *The Tablet*, 23 February 1929, p.251, Wilfrid Clavering Robinson.
48 *Evening Freeman*, 19 October 1870, p.4.

approaching enemy. William Jacob, the sole Welshman among the volunteers, wrote that 'we kept a regular fire from the walls upon the enemy as they approached':

> [O]ur men, especially the Irish, were then just in the tune for fighting: so we could not and would not give up when we heard the 'cease firing' sound. After the breach was made, and the 'cease firing' had sounded, many an Italian had to go to his account. The Irish fellows could not be stopped firing. One Egan (a noble fellow, some six feet one inch high) would not hear of giving up; he couldn't understand such a thing: 'Faith , and didn't we come to fight for the Pope?' We were, however, at last obliged to give up, as the few we had opposite the breach were utterly in adequate to the thousands who poured in upon us.[49]

As the Italians flooded through the breach and the orders to ceasefire repeated, the papal guns were eventually silenced.

A staged photograph taken shortly after 20 September 1870, clearly showing the damage to the walls.
(Zouavenmuseum, Oudenbosch, used with permission)

---

49   Jacob, *My Personal Recollections*, p.70.

The papal defenders claimed that the Italians had violated the law by entering the city before an armistice was signed, while the Italians were incensed that their men had been fired upon by the Zouaves after the ceasefire. The defenders near the Porta Pia were dealt with severely. According to Jacob: '[T]he officer in command of the Bersaglieri threatened to shoot us for having kept on fighting after the cease firing had sounded. For about a quarter of an hour we were kept there in suspense, every moment expecting to be shot. While in this unenviable state of mind I smoked two cigars and said Hail Maries all the time between each whiff.'[50] He was taken, with his comrades, to stables near the Piazza del Popolo, where they were held overnight. As they were marched through the streets there were called '*Briganti, Assassini*', and Italian soldiers 'gave us a prick with their bayonets, and, in some cases, even attempted to brain us with the butts of their rifles.'[51] The Porta Pia itself was badly damaged: the statues of St Agnes and St Alexander were decapitated, though the image of the Blessed Virgin remained unscathed.

The rest of the pontifical troops fell back to the Vatican, still armed, to await further orders and defend the Pope if necessary. Many spent the night on St Peter's Square. It was something of a bitter-sweet reunion with old comrades:

> Collected in groups about the fires, which were lighted near the fountains, were Zouaves, their faces half hidden in the deep hoods of their Arab manteaux; dragoons wrapped in their white cloaks, their brazen helmets gleaming in the fitful blaze; legionaries, carabiners, soldiers of the line, and gendarmes – all discussing in subdued but earnest tones the disaster of the morning.[52]

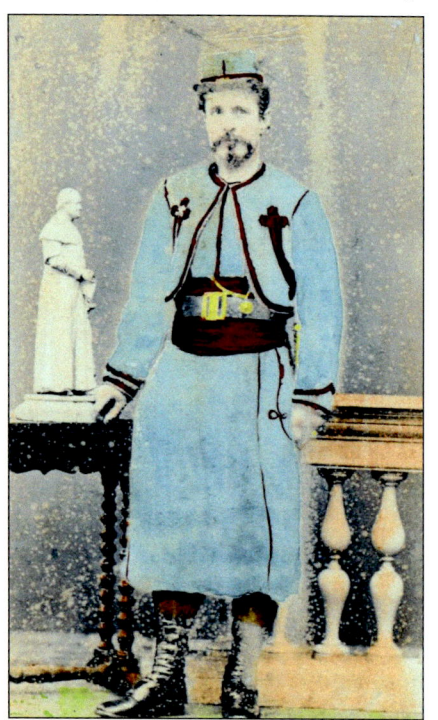

There would be a final parade on 21 September, an emotional scene imprinted on the memory of Wilfrid Robinson:

> The order to march was about to be given, but officers and men murmured. All eyes were turned towards the palace of the Vatican. Should we not see once more our beloved Holy Father? A window opened. The well-known White Figure appeared. For many minutes our cries of *Vive Pie Nono!* rang out. Then we presented arms and knelt, and Pius IX blessed us. Seemingly overcome with emotion, he sank back and we left him to be the Prisoner of the Vatican.[53]

Panic returned to the streets of the Eternal City, just as it had three years previously. Stonor thought that 'for two days no

Daniel Curtin (1837-70), a Zouave originally from County Cork, was wounded on 20 September 1870 and attacked by 'patriots' as he was being carried to a hospital. He suffered a mental breakdown and later died in an asylum. He poses here with a statue of Pius IX. (Private collection, photograph by Granddaughters of George Collingridge)

---

50 Jacob, *My Personal Recollections*, pp.71–72.
51 Jacob, *My Personal Recollections*, p.73.
52 *Evening Freeman*, 19 October 1870, p.4, Keyes O'Clery.
53 *The Tablet*, 23 February 1929, p.251.

one is safe', especially once the prisons were flung open and general disorder ensued.[54] Mrs Stone feared that Rome would soon be under 'the reddest of red republicans': '[W]e have no police, no rule, no law, … and unless we have a gun boat up the Tiber, no one of the Catholic English residents is safe.' She had searched the bastions for the body of one of the Pope's slain defenders and 'had to fight nearly with a horrible mob for his remains, to give them decent burial at the Cappucini [sic]. … I don't know what gave me strength to take him away, but I felt as if I had the body of a martyr with me.'[55] Rumours abounded of revolutionaries carrying around the heads of Zouaves and Gendarmes on bayonets. The seminarian Kirkham wrote:

> There were a lot of murders committed, no lights in the streets, and I saw a long procession going down the Monserrato [the street on which the College was situated] with torches, the dregs of Rome with camp followers of the Italian Army, any amount of women with them, waving swords and singing 'Viva Garibaldi' and other such like songs. It all reminded me of what I had read of the scenes during the French Revolution.'[56]

The British institutions in Rome made sure the Union Jack flew outside their buildings and asked the authorities for assurances of protection.

In agreeing the terms of the capitulation, Cadorna objected to Kanzler's reference to the Pope being forced to yield to violence so that further bloodshed could be avoided. The Italian commander stressed that he had tried to negotiate a peaceful entry into Rome and that military action had been necessitated by Kanzler's stubbornness. Nevertheless, Rome (with the exception of the Leonine City around St Peter's) was handed over to the Kingdom of Italy, the defeated pontifical troops were accorded the honours of war and the foreign volunteers repatriated at the expense of the government. Despite the heavy bombardment of the city, the Pope had avoided the bloodbath he had feared: 32 Italians were killed, with 145 wounded, while the Pontifical Army suffered 12 dead and 47 wounded.[57] The pioneering Claxton gun was dismantled and eventually displayed at Turin's Museo Nazionale dell'Artiglieria. Many of the weapons were either re-used by the Italian Army or sold off. After the battle of Dogali in January 1887, when an Italian battalion was routed by the numerically superior Abyssinians, it was found that many of the latter's rifles had formerly belonged to the Pontifical Army, causing some to rejoice that the weapons had at last been used, as a form of retribution, to wipe out an Italian force.[58]

Many of the British and Irish volunteers were taken by rail to Civitavecchia and by steamer to Genoa, where, with the help of Monsignor Stonor, passage was arranged home. However, letters in *The Times* complained of harsh treatment. Writing from the safety of the Adelphi Hotel, Liverpool, seven ex-Zouaves protested that 'as soon as we had laid down our arms, [we were] thrust into prison, fed on bread and water for 24 hours, kept under lock and key for six days, and exposed to all the hardships which fall to the lot of ordinary prisoners.'[59] William Chilton wrote that after being taken at Civita Castellana, he and his companions were moved to Spoleto, where they were refused permission to attend mass, and then

---

54 *The Tablet*, 1 October 1870, p.429.
55 Erb, *Manning and Gladstone Correspondence*, vol. 3, p.232, account of Mrs Stone, 21 September 1870, sent by Manning to Gladstone. The dead soldier was 'Maurice de Guy', though he does not appear in the official list of Zouaves.
56 *The Venerabile*, 3:4 (April 1928), p.327.
57 Alvarez, *The Pope's Soldiers*, p.248.
58 *Advocate (Melbourne)*, 7 June 1913, p.24. Some of the rifles were reportedly used by the troops of Haile Selassie against Mussolini in 1935.
59 *The Times*, 18 October 1870, p.6.

to Leghorn, where for 13 days they were 'fed on nothing but bread and water' and slept on 'a very small quantity of straw, which was never changed.'[60] It was argued, though, that the ex-Zouaves had been locked up for their own protection and they were not prisoners, since they were on their way home. *The Times* went as far to suggest that they 'deserved this and worse ... as a punishment for their arrogant behaviour towards the military authorities to whose keeping they were entrusted.'[61] Emotions remained high on both sides of the political spectrum.

ITALY IN ROME.

Papa Pius (*to* King of Italy). "I MUST NEEDS SURRENDER THE *SWORD*, MY SON; BUT *I KEEP THE KEYS!!*"

In this cartoon, Pius IX tells Victor Emmanuel II, 'I must needs surrender the sword, my son, but I keep the keys', meaning his spiritual authority. (*Punch*, 1 October 1870, Private collection, author's photograph)

---

60 *The Times*, 11 November 1870, p.5.
61 *The Times*, 7 November 1870, p.9.

Rome transitioned into the new capital of Italy. In 1870 it had not yet expanded to its current proportions: sheep and goats could still be found grazing in the Forum and the population numbered only 200,000. What mattered was its symbolic importance. The King of Italy was now truly heir to the splendours of Ancient Rome and had not only crushed the perceived corruptions of the Papal States but could bask in the prestige of the Eternal City. However, reports of enthusiastic crowds greeting the triumphant Italians served the purposes of propaganda but in many cases were exaggerated; indeed, the appearance of Italian flags at people's windows is likely to have been stage-managed, since the tricolour had been formerly banned within the Papal States. The British representative, H. Clarke Jervoise, reported that much of the popular enthusiasm was produced by the 'hordes' who accompanied the Italian troops and when the Romans themselves joined in the cheering it was often as the result of fear.[62]

As with any change of regime, there were spontaneous outbursts of popular resentment against the old order and the Pope's foreign volunteers took the brunt of attacks. There were numerous examples of 'Zouave-phobia' in the weeks following 20 September. A missionary bishop, with a long black beard, was attacked on the Tiber Island because he was suspected of being a Zouave in disguise. Religious houses were searched for hidden Zouaves. A particularly ridiculous instance was provided by a large grey hen kept at a refuge for poor old women on the Via dei Pontifice. Because of its colour it was named 'Zouave' and when it went missing one day the cry was heard 'the Zouave has run away!' This was overheard by patriotic locals who reported it to the authorities and led to a speedy visitation from the police, who looked under every bed and even behind the altar in the chapel.[63]

Nevertheless, the Italians were keen to restore order and stamp their authority on their new capital. A plebiscite was held on 1 October to show the 'will' of the Roman people and calm international opinion. It was, for the times, a rare case of universal male suffrage but the result was in little doubt and the fact that there were only 46 opposing votes (against 40,785) immediately raises the historian's eyebrow. Although some groups, in particular the middle classes, welcomed the new regime, there were plenty who had strong reservations. The 'black' aristocracy, still loyal to the Pope, withdrew from society. Many resented the higher taxes, rising property prices and the arrogance of those from the 'north'. Not every Roman had a sense of a new Italian-ness.

---

62 Dora Dumont, 'The Nation as Seen from Below: Rome in 1870', *European Review of History*, 15:5 (2008), pp.481–482.
63 *The Tablet*, 22 October 1870, p.525.

15

Afterlife

Most of the English-speaking Zouaves arrived in Liverpool on 14 October 1870. Received warmly by the Catholic population, they quietly returned to their homes over the following days. There were no parades or public homecoming celebrations. In Ireland there were some individual moments of public enthusiasm: a Zouave, still dressed in his uniform, stopped at Mallow in County Cork and 'received a great welcome from numbers on the platform' and was treated to dinner before continuing his journey to Tralee.[1] Another was officially welcomed home at a public meeting held at St Mary's, Belfast.

It could be a challenge to find jobs and the Papal Defence Committee did its best to help. A letter to *The Tablet* in December 1870 lists 12 unemployed former Zouaves, eight of whom were looking for employment as clerks; one had only Protestant relatives who refused to have anything to do with him. Their ability to speak French and Italian was stressed as an advantage.[2] A final burst of fundraising was launched to the cover the costs of transporting the Zouaves home and providing them with clothing at Genoa.

Former members of the Zouaves entered many different professions. The long-serving Captain Albert O'Reilly De La Hoyde moved to Kensington and was employed by the Indian Mail Service. Henry Vrain worked at Cardiff's Bute Dock and Benjamin Holtham rose to become stores superintendent of the Cardiff Railway Company. Ambrose Keens is listed in 1871 as a 'factory packer' and his brother Christopher a 'photographic colourer'. Some Zouaves tried to earn a living together. Ernest Burchett and Philip Duke are listed as working together as tobacconists in Holborn in 1871. Daniel Shee, the hero of 1870, became governor of Birkdale Farm Reformatory School, near Southport in Lancashire, where his old comrade, Francis Newsham, was the medical doctor.

At the other end of the social scale, John Kenyon inherited Gillingham Hall from an aunt in 1889, and William Vavasour succeeded his uncle as baronet in 1885, although by 1907 he faced bankruptcy and was forced to put Hazlewood Castle up for auction. Several former Zouaves were elected to Parliament, representing Irish constituencies. Two were MPs for Wexford, John Talbot Power (1868–1874) and Patrick Keyes O'Clery (1874–1880), while Bernard Charles Molloy represented first King's County (1880–1885) and then the Birr Division (1885–1900). Described in 1888 as 'one of the finest-looking and best-dressed men in Parliament' and 'by profession a lawyer but by liking an engineer', Molloy took a keen interest in mining and made frequent trips to South Africa, Australia and New Zealand.[3] Added to these parliamentarians were former members of the Battalion of St Patrick: Major Myles O'Reilly was elected as Member for the Longford Division (1862–1879) and helped establish the Home Rule League, and Jeremiah Sheehan, who

---

1   *Cork Examiner*, 10 November 1870, p.2.
2   *The Tablet*, 17 December 1870, p.779.
3   *Pall Mall Gazette*, 12 June 1888, p.1.

Daniel Shee (1846–1912), who, after seeing action with the Zouaves in 1867 and 1870, served for many years as governor of Birkdale Farm Reformatory School, near Southport. (Archives of the Archdiocese of Liverpool, used with permission)

had been badly injured during the Siege of Spoleto, sat for East Kerry (1885–1895).

Some emigrated overseas. Clement Bishop taught for many years in Trinidad, Oswald Petre settled in California, and Reginald Durrant ended his days in New Jersey. The Honourable Walter Constable Maxwell spent a period in the 1870s as a rancher in Kansas, part of an (ultimately unsuccessful) English 'colony' set up by George Grant with younger sons of the aristocracy specifically in mind. There, in the prairies of the Midwest, Maxwell and his companions lived a lifestyle that incorporated cricket clubs, horse races, hunts and other aspects of English life. Meanwhile, George Collingridge became a noted artist and writer in Australia, where he founded the (Royal) Art Society of New South Wales. He wrote an important work on the discovery of Australia and enthusiastically promoted Esperanto.

There was indeed a strong scholarly and creative streak. Some former Zouaves published their experiences as memoirs – including Joseph Powell's *Two Years in the Pontifical Zouaves*, with illustrations by Collingridge, and W. J. Jacob's *My Personal Recollections of Rome*, which originated as a lecture at Pontypool's Town Hall – or fiction, such as Wilfrid Clavering Robinson's *Under the Cross Keys*, Bartle Teeling's *My First Prisoner* and George Collingridge's *Tales of the Papal Zouaves*.[4] Patrick Keyes O'Clery wrote two substantial volumes of history covering the Risorgimento.[5]

Ernest Sellon lectured in literature and became a Fellow of the Linnean Society, and Jacob Hinde (later Lloyd), who seems to have left the Catholic faith, published several works on Welsh genealogy. Joseph Hansom followed his father into the architectural profession and included among his designs the Catholic church in Bognor Regis. He was also an enthusiastic antiquarian and instrumental in the foundation of

---

4   Joseph Powell, *Two Years in the Pontifical Zouaves: A Narrative of Travel, Residence and Experience in the Roman States* (London: R. Washbourne, 1871); W. J. Jacob, *My Personal Recollections of Rome: A Lecture, Partly Delivered on the 9th of February 1871, at the Town Hall, Pontypool* (London: R. Washbourne, 1871); Wilfrid Clavering Robinson, *Under the Cross Keys* (publication details unknown); Bartle Teeling [writing as 'The Governor'], *My First Prisoner* (London: Roxburghe Press, undated); George Collingridge, 'Tales of the Papal Zouaves', *Austral Light* (Melbourne) (1899).

5   *The History of the Italian Revolution. First Period: The Revolution of the Barricades, 1796–1849* (London: R. Washbourne, 1875) and *The Making of Italy, 1856–1870* (London: Kegan Paul, Trench, Trubner & Co., 1892).

the Catholic Record Society, which is still the United Kingdom's premier association of Catholic history. William Ryan, meanwhile, designed a number of buildings both in England and Ireland and, according to family tradition, helped procure marble for the new Westminster Cathedral.[6]

Some remained soldiers. Perhaps the most astonishing military continuity was a former French Zouave, Arthur Dumas, who had responded to the Pope's call in 1867 and was finally killed near Clery on the Somme in September 1916. He had been wounded at Mentana and this, according to a report at the time of his death, was 'to be followed by nine other wounds in nearly fifty years of continual fighting.'[7] Several Anglo-Irish Zouaves also continued their military career. Before returning to London to qualify as a lawyer, Bernard Molloy found himself serving in the Franco-Prussian War as an Officer d'Ordonnance in the Army of the East. William Vavasour acted as Major in the Yorkshire Hussars and Benjamin Holtham served as a member of what became the 3rd Volunteer Battalion of the Welch Regiment and is reported to have never missed the annual camp over a period of 28 years.[8] His brother Samuel joined the 40th Regiment (2nd Somersetshire) of Foot in 1872 but was medically discharged three years later while serving in India.

Charles Woodward, a veteran of Mentana, became Colonel in the 4th (Militia) Battalion, King's (Liverpool Regiment). He saw action at the battle of Tel-el-Kebir in 1882 and the Sudan Campaign of 1885. The Honourable Walter Constable Maxwell, after returning from Kansas in 1880, obtained a commission in the same battalion and was promoted to captain in 1883. On 6 January 1902 he sailed for South Africa, serving as the second-in-command during the Battalion's service in the Boer War. On retiring in 1905, he was granted the honorary rank of lieutenant-colonel. The prominent Irish Zouave, Bartle Teeling, also saw service in the Boer War with the 3rd Battalion, Royal Irish Rifles, having previously been captain in the Longford Militia and 8th Battalion, the Rifle Brigade.

Others followed religious vocations. All in all, five former Zouaves became bishops, including Charles Menzies Gordon, who had recruited many of the Scots-Irish Zouaves. Joining the Society of Jesus in Rome in 1869, at the relatively mature age of 38, two decades later he was appointed Vicar Apostolic of Jamaica. John Archdeacon, who enlisted at the beginning of 1870, was ordained for the diocese of Clifton in 1877 and worked in several missions, including Salisbury. Both the widowed father and the brother of Julian and Wilfrid Watts-Russell were ordained priests – the former became one of the first English priests to be based at the French shrine of Lourdes.

Many Zouaves were awarded papal decorations, knighthoods and titles, and some continued their service to the Holy See as Papal Chamberlains, an honorary lay role involving short periods of duty at the Vatican. These included John Kenyon, Walter Constable Maxwell, Bernard Molloy, Patrick Keyes O'Clery and Bartle Teeling.[9] The latter, through his contacts, gained a place for his son, Luke, in the Pope's Noble Guard in 1914. When he joined the Royal Field Artillery the following February he became 'the only officer of the British Army who was also an officer of the Pope' and was eventually killed just before the Armistice of 1918.[10]

---

6   Information from his great-granddaughter, Frances Wood.
7   *Hartlepool Northern Daily Mail*, 20 September 1916, p.4.
8   *Stonyhurst Magazine* (February 1917), p.1847.
9   O'Clery was created a papal count in 1903.
10   *The Tablet*, 7 December 1918, p.654.

Continuation of the Cause

The capitulation of Rome did not silence the cause of the Zouaves. Meetings were organised and associations formed to show support for the 'Prisoner of the Vatican', 'Peter in Chains'. In Rome, feelings remained high, and Catholics were forbidden to engage in public life under the new regime. When Wilfrid Ward arrived at the English College in 1877, his fellow students still regarded Victor Emmanuel as a 'robber king' and 'victorious brigand'; 'for us it was still a time of war,' he recalled, and there were occasional brawls in the streets between English seminarians and 'Garibaldians'.[11]

In England and Scotland, a 'Protest' was sent by '2,000 Catholics of the upper classes' and by 26 December 503,347 signatures had been added to a 'Filial Address' to the Pope, offering 'to pray for You … and never to cease to labour, by all means permitted to conscience and honour, until once more we can gather round You, ruling in your own free City, Bishop and King of Rome and of the States of the Church'.[12] A large meeting was held at St James' Hall on 9 December 1870, with the Archbishop of Westminster in the chair. Despite the thawed snow on the streets, the venue was packed half an hour before proceedings commenced. It resolved that the 'violent occupation of the City of Rome' was sacrilegious, that it constituted an attack on the liberty of the Church and the 'dispositions of Divine Providence', and that it violated not only papal sovereignty but 'the rights on which all Civil States are founded'. Arguments touched 'the ground upon which her gracious Majesty can claim the continued allegiance of her faithful subjects' and one speaker speculated 'with exceeding humour' how the English would have treated Garibaldi and Mazzini 'if these two patriots had chosen Ireland, instead of Italy, for the field of their labours' – a comparison often used by Catholics over the previous decade.

In Dublin on 30 November a similar meeting was presided over by Cardinal Cullen, with several former Zouaves sitting on the platform in their uniforms. Addresses were approved not only to the Pope, declaring the fidelity and veneration of the people of Dublin, but to the prime minister, asking that the government would extend its protection to the Holy See. During a meeting held at Thurles Cathedral, the MP for Tipperary, Denis Caulfield Heron, stated that 'the youth of our country are ready once more to don the uniform of the famous Papal Zouave (loud cheers) – and to join in a new crusade to recover for the Holy Father his ancient dominions (loud cheers)'.[13]

Two associations were formed in England during the immediate aftermath of events. The first was the Catholic Union, under the presidency of the Duke of Norfolk, exclusively consisting of Catholic laymen and 'chiefly directed towards the interests of the Holy See, which it will promote by all the moral means in its power'. This was soon broadened to represent all issues of Catholic interest.[14] Supporters of the restoration of papal sovereignty could also join the League of St Sebastian, which had branches across the English-speaking world and was spear-headed by 'soldiers of the Anglo-Irish Contingent of the late Pontifical Army'.[15] Its first honorary secretaries were the former Zouaves O'Clery, Kenyon and Teeling, and subscriptions were coordinated by Arthur Coombes, using as his address the Naval and Military Club, Piccadilly.[16]

---

11 Maisie Ward, *The Wilfrid Wards and the Transition* (London: Sheed & Ward, 1934), p.56.
12 AAW 'Resolutions for the Meeting at St James's Hall' in Letters to Clergy, Vol 2 (1869–1878); *The Tablet*, 17 December 1870, p.769.
13 *Evening Freeman*, 16 December 1870, p.2.
14 *The Tablet*, 18 February 1871, p.189.
15 *The Tablet*, 15 April 1871, p.463.
16 *The Tablet*, 8 April 1871, p.414.

A small deputation was granted an audience with the Pope on Good Friday 1871. They received his blessing and were reminded that for the present they 'must serve him in England and Ireland not by their arms but by their voices'.[17] The League produced *The Crusader*, 'a fortnightly journal devoted to the restoration of the Temporal Power',[18] organised masses and talks, sent loyal addresses to the Eternal City and promoted the collection of Peter's Pence. The first annual meeting, presided by Sir George Bowyer at Willis' Rooms, London, was attended by 12 former Zouaves. O'Clery expressed the hope that 'ere long the glorious standard of Pius IX would again wave over the dominions which had been so unjustly invaded'.[19]

The language of its chief organ was often forthright: 'Our work then is to help largely in restoring the temporal power of the Pope. It is not dead, as the age says; it is only buried alive. To get it out of its tomb of a prison, to take its grave clothes off it … this surely is a true Crusade.'[20]

The League gained the support of many notable Catholics, including the Duke of Norfolk, Lord Denbigh and several MPs. Members of the clergy were also enthusiastic. On addressing the League in January 1874, Archbishop Manning observed that, whereas revolutions in 1848 had been on the streets, they had now moved to the cabinets and thrones of Europe. He showed considerable foresight in predicting 'a large Continental war, which would far eclipse that under the First Empire' – the new world order could not last long and the Pope would eventually be restored to his rightful kingdom. Many of his listeners would be present on that joyful day 'in the old grey uniform of the Pontifical Zouaves' and perhaps act as officers when 'the time for action' arrived and large contingents of volunteers once again gathered in Rome.[21]

Understandably such organisations caused nervousness in many circles and filled the Protestant press with stories of conspiracy and a new Popish Plot. A correspondent in the *Dundee Courier* thought that both the Catholic Union and the League of St Sebastian were 'inimical to the well-being of this and of every free country'.[22] The United Kingdom Anti-Papist League wrote to Gladstone with their concerns in 1872 and to his successor as prime minister, Disraeli, two years later, denouncing the organisation as 'avowedly a military league for raising soldiers in every nation to fight for the restoration of the Pope's temporal power'.[23]

Gladstone had recently published a scathing attack on papal infallibility and used the opportunity given him by the anti-papists as best he could. He was assured by a member of the Scottish branch, G.L. Gordon Milne, that the League aimed 'to assist in any legal effort which may be made to restore the Holy Father to his legitimate rights as Sovereign of the Papal States'. Gladstone replied that the epithet 'legal' had seemingly only been added recently and that a perusal of *The Crusader* confirmed his suspicions that it was a purely 'nominal and colourable' term.[24] The League of St Sebastian continued the cause of the Zouaves and the Temporal Power, substituting the weapons of journalism for those of the battlefield, and stood in readiness for a new crusade, when the old grey uniforms could be dusted down. The League fizzled out during the 1880s.

---

17 *Ulster Examiner and Northern Star*, 26 April 1871, p.4.
18 *The Tablet*, 2 December 1871, p.736.
19 *The Tablet*, 27 January 1872, p.110. The former Zouaves were Messrs Coombes, Duke, Hansom, Kenyon, O'Clery, Pearson, Powell, Robinson, Sampson, Sellon, Tierney and Vavasour.
20 *Lancaster Gazette*, 11 January 1873, p.4, quoting *The Crusader*.
21 *Freeman's Journal*, 21 January 1874, p.3.
22 *Dundee Courier*, 25 October 1873, p.2.
23 *Downpatrick Recorder*, 28 November 1874, p.3.
24 *Freeman's Journal*, 22 December 1874, p.6.

Carrying the Flag in France, Spain and Central Africa

It is worth noting that some Zouave veterans continued to brandish the sword in the interests of Catholic truth and legitimacy. The most notable example could be found in France. The Zouaves returned from Rome to find that the Third Republic, which had replaced the Second Empire after the battle of Sedan, continued to fight against Germany for France's survival. Catholics interpreted France's misfortune as punishment for its ungodliness and its infidelity to the papal cause. Napoleon III had abandoned the Church and so God had abandoned France. The destinies of France and Rome became intertwined.

It is no surprise, then, that Athanase de Charette decided to continue the struggle, not so much against Prussia and its allies but against France's internal enemies. Many of the returning Zouaves joined a new unit under his command: the *Volontaires de l'Ouest* (Volunteers of the West). This irregular force was made up of three battalions and its officers were all former Zouaves. Recruitment was dependent on the recommendation of a priest and the uniform was identical to the pontifical regiment. Charette told the volunteers: 'This uniform is the property of the whole Catholic world whose belief we represent; it is the livery of Rome, it is not ours to be disposed of at will and linked to the fortunes of an unstable government.'[25] When the Volunteers were finally disbanded in August 1871, it was chiefly because Charette hoped they could one day serve the Pope again and wanted to break its bonds to the Third Republic. The Volunteers, however, were not Pontifical Zouaves under a different name and in a different context. As Patrick Nouaille-Degorce has argued, the unit had its own identity: the repatriated Zouaves only constituted a group within the Volunteers (including all the officers) and some former Zouaves joined other French regiments.

Many of the Volunteers, as suggested by the name, came from the traditionalist west of France, which had not only provided recruits for the Papal Army but had been the centre of the counter-revolution in the 1790s. A striking note of continuity with the Vendée could be found not only in the figure of Charette, the great-nephew of one of its heroes, but the symbol of the Sacred Heart of Jesus, which had been the counter-revolutionary emblem and could be found on the Volunteers' banner, embroidered by the nuns of Paray-le-Monial.[26] Imbued with Catholic piety, they fought for France's traditional identity as 'eldest daughter of the Church'. The irony was that the Volunteers, with their legitimist sympathies, not only fought for a republic but found themselves fighting alongside one of their great enemies, Garibaldi, who also supported the Third Republic and commanded the Army of the Vosges.

The Volunteers formed part of the Army of the Loire's 17th Corps under General Louis-Gaston de Sonis, himself a pious Catholic royalist who in his youth had considered a monastic vocation. At the end of 1870 the Army was involved in a number of actions against the Germans, including the battle of Loigny on 2 December. The previous day, the 16th Corps under Alfred Chanzy had been driven out of Loigny and Sonis, acting as the reserve, tried to recapture the village. It was a bitterly cold day and, despite being heavily outnumbered – 800 men (including 300 Volunteers) against 2,000 – Sonis charged from Villepion towards Loigny across open fields, his banner of the Sacred Heart replacing that of the French tricolour and cries of '*Vive Pie IX!*' alongside '*Vive la France!*'. The result was a bloodbath. At least five Volunteers fell while holding the banner, which was passed from one pair of hands to another. Theodore Wibaux remembered that 'the havoc in the ranks was frightful, it was like a scythe mowing down corn; mitrailleuses, grapeshot, shells came from all sides. The victims were so numerous that any attempt to enumerate them would be

---

25 Coëtlosquet, *Theodore Wibaux*, pp.288–289.
26 The Burgundian town was the centre of the devotion, having been the home of the seventeenth-century Visitation nun, St Margaret Mary Alacoque, who had received visions of the Sacred Heart. In 1873 Charette deposited the old Zouave banner at the shrine.

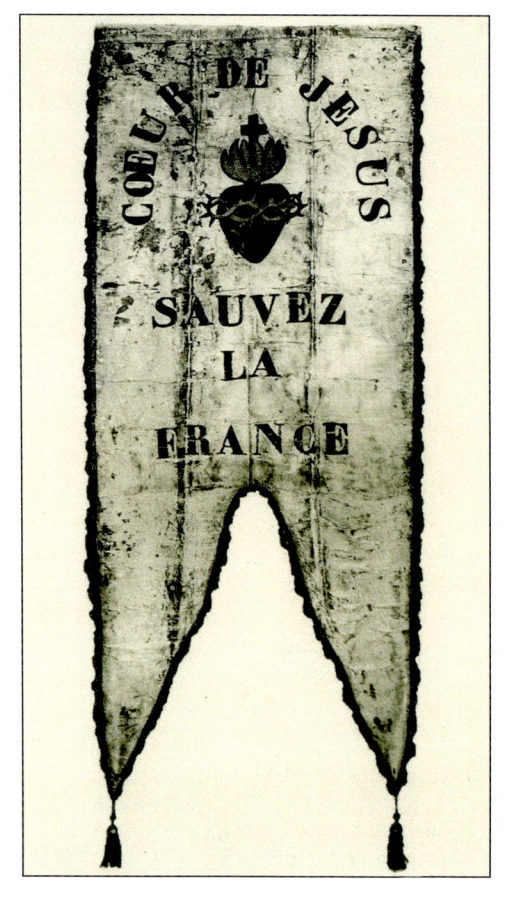

The Banner of the Sacred Heart carried by the Volontaires at Loigny. (Private collection, author's photograph)

useless; the ground seemed covered with the bodies of the fallen.'[27] Only three of 14 officers survived. Charette was injured and Sonis himself lost a leg.

Loigny was seen in the tradition of Castelfidardo and Porta Pia as a 'heroic failure' and an example of Christian self-sacrifice. Some writers referred to it as the Battle of Patay, a nearby village that had seen a significant French victory over the English in 1429 under the leadership of Joan of Arc, making the point that the fallen of 1870 were just as much martyrs for France. Sonis was presented as a new French saviour and his mutilated body seemed to act as a symbol for France in 1870. As Raymond Jonas has pointed out that, with his staunchly Catholic outlook, Sonis was aware that both victory or defeat at Loigny would aid the cause: victory would show the power of the Sacred Heart in the hour of France's need, defeat was a form of redemption through the shedding of blood: '[W]hen it was over, Catholic France had its heroes – Charette and Sonis – and proof that True France lived on.'[28]

In 1873 around 400 former Zouaves fought in the Third Carlist War, inspired by their old comrade Don Alfonso, the brother of the claimant to the Spanish throne, 'Carlos VII'. They wore the pontifical uniform, the kepi being replaced by the distinctive Carlist beret, and their banner once again featured the Sacred Heart. Prominent among their number were the Dutch brothers, Auguste and Ignatius Wils, and one of the first Canadian Zouaves (of Irish origin), Hugh Murray, who had been wounded at Mentana and eventually lost his life at the siege of Manresa in February 1874. Many of the Carlist Zouaves were Belgian and Dutch, although there were unsuccessful efforts to gain support in Britain and Ireland. Carlism represented another struggle for Catholicism and legitimacy. It was hoped that Don Carlos as king would stamp on liberalism and strongly support the Holy See. The campaign also struck an indirect blow at Victor Emmanuel since the war was partly caused by the chaos following the abdication of his second son, Amadeo I – briefly King of Spain between 1870 and 1873.

A final flurry of armed action could be found thousands of miles away in central Africa. Charles Lavigerie, Bishop of Algiers, founder of a prominent missionary congregation (the White Fathers) and a cardinal from 1882, organised a small unit made up of former Zouaves, under the command of Captain Léopold Joubert, a veteran of Castelfidardo, Mentana and the Siege of Rome (where he commanded a

---

27 Coëtlosquet, *Theodore Wibaux*, p.263.
28 Raymond Jonas, *France and the Cult of the Sacred Heart: An Epic Tale for Modern Times* (Berkeley, CA: University of California Press, 2000), p.166.

One of the Zouaves who worked with the White Fathers in Africa, the Belgian August Taillieu (1845–1883). (Zouavenmuseum, Oudenbosch, used with permission)

company at the Porta Salaria). They protected the missionaries as they worked around Lake Tanganyika, fortified their missions with palisades and ditches, trained the local militia and successfully combatted the Arab slave traders. Such militant missionary activity was closely linked to Lavigerie's dream of setting up a Christian Kingdom in the region and thus countering the influence of revolutionaries, Protestants, Muslims and slave traders. It might have been a quite different context but involved the same struggle for Catholic truth that had been fought by the Zouaves in Italy. Lavigerie even wondered, thinking of the loss of the Papal States: 'Was it not possible that ground lost in Europe might be made good in Africa?'[29] Joubert later married a Congolese woman and settled down with his large family as a model colonist and catechist. In that faraway outpost he kept alive the spirit of his old regiment; indeed, in the words of one recent writer, 'except for Joubert's campaign against the slavers, all of the Zouaves' ventures ended in failure'.[30]

Keeping the Memory Alive

There were regular reunions of Zouave veterans and, between 1892 and 1932, a French newspaper, *L'Avant Garde*. Charette was the magnet around which they gathered.[31] Closely linked to the cause of the Legitimists, there were ongoing suspicions that the French Zouaves would be resurrected to fight the Third Republic. In 1885 a Silver Jubilee celebration of the foundation of the Zouaves was held at Charette's home of La Basse Motte in Brittany. At the open-air mass the 'altar was surrounded by Pontifical trophies from Castelfidardo and Mentana' and, in imitation of St Peter's, silver trumpets were played at the consecration.[32] Among those present were veterans from England, Ireland and Canada, although the local bishop and the Papal Nuncio cancelled their attendance at the last minute, signifying an official cooling towards their cause. The Golden Jubilee was likewise commemorated in 1910, the menu including such dishes as sea bream with a 'Mentana glaze' and Castelfidardo tarts, while many Zouave *'anciens'* gathered at Loigny for Charette's requiem the following year.

---

29   Ian Linden, *Church and Revolution in Rwanda* (Manchester: Manchester University Press, 1977), p.30.
30   Charles A. Coulombe, *The Pope's Legion: The Multinational Fighting Force that Defended the Vatican* (Basingstoke: Palgrave Macmillan, 2008), p.213.
31   His second wife, Antoinette, was the great-niece of James K. Polk, 11th President of the United States.
32   *Portsmouth Evening News*, 30 July 1885, p.4.

The interior of the church at Loigny-la-Bataille as it appeared for Charette's requiem on 21 October 1911. On the catafalque can be seen his uniform, swords and decorations. (Private collection, author's photograph)

In the Netherlands a number of veteran organisations were founded, later united together in 1892. In the United States, the Papal Veteran Association organised an annual requiem in New York. The members, who attended in uniform and under arms, included not only Zouaves but those who had served in the Irish Battalion, such as the hero of Castelfidardo, Captain Kirwan, and Sergeant-Major Hynes, who had been presented with the *Bene Merenti* medal on the ramparts of Ancona.[33] Likewise Canadian veterans founded the Union Allet in 1871; 14 of them founded a small township on the banks of Lake Megnatic, not far from the American border, called Piopolis in honour of the Pope. In 1899 the Association des Zouaves du Quebec was founded by Charles-Edmond Rouleau to bring together veterans and their descendants as well as uphold the values of the cause. It became a branch of Catholic Action and a familiar part of Quebec life. Boasting at its peak some 2,000 members and 41 regional groups, Zouaves were present at many religious and civic events. The Association still exists as a social club, but its last military parade was during the visit of John Paul II to Quebec in 1984, when 100 Zouaves paid the pontiff military honours.

In London, an annual requiem Mass was sung for many years at the Church of St Etheldreda, Ely Place on the anniversary of Mentana 'for all those who, whether in Rome or elsewhere, had died in defence of right against might—principle against expediency'.[34] In Ireland, the parochial house at Magheracloone (County Monaghan) was given the name 'Mentana'. Whatever profession they followed, veterans showed great pride in their youthful experiences; some used the prefix 'Z.P.' after their name or were described as

---

33 *Dublin Weekly Nation*, 18 October 1879, p.10, reporting a requiem at the Church of St Francis Xavier on 20 September 1879, which featured a catafalque with the battle honours of Perugia, Spoleto, Castelfidardo, Ancona, Mentana and Rome.
34 *The Tablet*, 6 November 1875, p.595.

a 'Pontifical Zouave' on their tombstones. From his Australian home, George Collingridge often spoke of his 17 engagements and the battle scars received at Mentana. Photographs and uniforms were carefully treasured: Frederick T. Welman, the cricketer, even attended annual Fancy Dress Balls at Taunton in the late 1870s as a Zouave.[35] On the other side of the spectrum, there was an active society of Garibaldean veterans, both English and Italian, who organised a dinner each year in London to celebrate the anniversary of the fall of Rome.[36]

In Catholic circles the story of the Zouaves quickly passed into legend. Indeed, such was their glamour that some even boasted of belonging to the corps who had never enlisted, such as 'Commandant' George Hamilton-Browne, an Ulsterman raised in the established Church, who included five months with the Zouaves in his long list of military escapades.[37] In 1894 there was renewed interest in Julian Watts-Russell, largely thanks to the enthusiasm of a young ecclesiastic, Claud Reginald Lindsay, who was then studying in Rome at the prestigious Academia Ecclesiastica. Like Watts-Russell, he belonged to a wealthy convert family and was well-connected; his grandfathers were the Earl of Crawford and the Earl of Wicklow, while his sister-in-law was Cardinal Vaughan's niece. He was a keen historian and collected artefacts relating to the Zouaves, including Julian's bloodstained jacket and the diary kept by his brother Wilfrid. He visited Mentana and discovered that the little monument placed near the spot where he fell had been vandalised in 1870 and his heart, which had been buried there, saved by Signor Santucci from profanation and sent to his family in England. It was buried under the high altar of the Darlington Carmel, where his sister was a member of the community. Lindsay found the monument in the cellar of an *osteria* in the town. In February 1894 it was brought for safekeeping to the English College chapel, where it remains to this day: *The Tablet* judged it fitting that 'the last of the English martyrs will be vividly commemorated in the Church which is par excellence the Roman shrine of the martyrs of England'.[38]

Meanwhile, Julian's grave at Campo Verano was in a poor state since the vault had not been closed properly and rainwater had entered. Before being removed to a new grave, his remains were examined in the presence

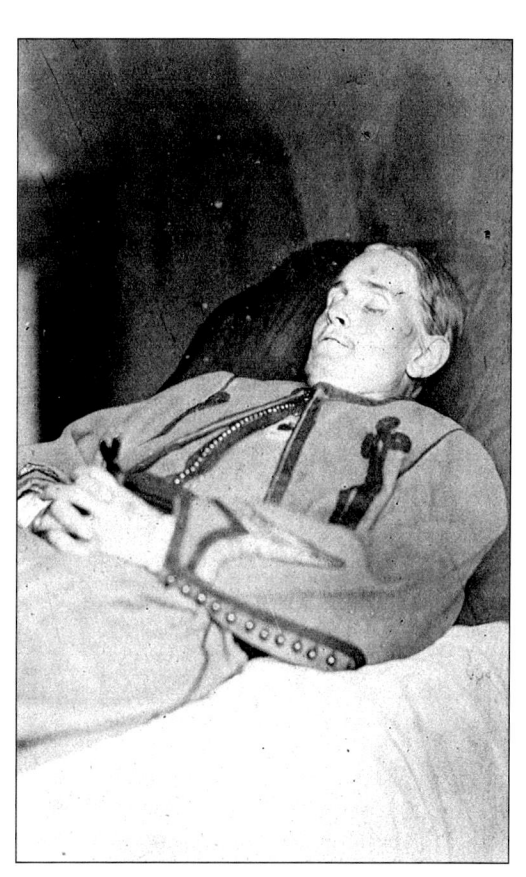

A French Zouave on his deathbed, dressed in his old uniform. (Private collection, author's photograph)

---

35 *The Tablet*, 6 November 1875, p.595.
36 Among the venues used was the 'Garibaldi Salon' of Haymarket's Central Restaurant.
37 See his *With the Lost Legion in New Zealand* (London: T. Werner Laurie, 1911). Using the pseudonym 'Richard Burke', it is hard to separate truth from fiction in his account, which focuses on the Maori Wars.
38 *The Tablet*, 3 March 1894, p.335.

of a small party. Despite hopes that his body might be incorrupt, a traditional indication of sanctity, only bones were found and the remains of a crown of roses that had been placed on his head, making him resemble 'the relics of so many Roman martyrs to whose life also Julian had borne so deep a resemblance'.[39] The costs were covered by donations from leading Catholics and former Zouaves. This tied in with the centenary celebrations of Julian's alma mater, Ushaw. When Monsignor Merry del Val asked Leo XIII for an apostolic blessing for this occasion, he reminded the pontiff of the College's glories including, 'amongst the many distinguished priests and laymen educated within her walls' not only Cardinal Wiseman but Watts-Russell, who had died 'to safeguard the rights and independence of the Holy See'.[40]

Old Zouaves were still represented at international events. At the Eucharistic Congress held in Lourdes in 1914, just before the outbreak of war, the banner of the Pontifical Zouaves was proudly carried in the closing procession by Captain Bartle Teeling and 'greeted with enthusiasm by those who are faithful to the memory of the past'.[41] At the Sydney Congress of 1928 it was the turn of George Collingridge and Ernest Burchett to take part in the procession.[42]

When the Lateran Treaty was signed in 1929, putting to rest the Roman Question and creating the Vatican City State, a group of Dutch veterans sent a telegram to Pius XI, stating that 'those who mourned in their youth over the Pope Bound, rejoice in their old age with the Pope Delivered'.[43] Around the same time, Wilfrid Clavering Robinson reflected on his experiences in the Zouaves and felt a sense of completion:

> The White Figure is still in the Vatican, no longer a Prisoner, but, even more than Pius IX, a Pope and King. That figure has shown itself to his people from the balcony of the Vatican basilica, and they have risen up, after their Sovereign Pontiff has blessed them, and cried: *Evviva il Papa Re! Evviva l'Italia!* And every old soldier like myself who served Pio Nono can echo their cries with heart and soul. We did not go out to Rome to fight Italy. We went to fight Pro Petri Sede, to fight those whom Mussolini has muzzled at last.[44]

By 1938, 32 Dutch Zouaves were still alive, many of whom received funding from the Dutch League of Papal Zouaves. The last died in 1947 and shortly afterwards the Government posthumously reinstated the Dutch citizenship of the Zouaves, which had been previously revoked. Oudenbosch became a particular centre for remembrance, with its Roman-style basilica. A monument to the fallen nearby features Pius IX with a dying Zouave at his feet. The town's streets include 'Zouavenladen', 'Porta Pia', 'Montelibretti' and 'Mentanalaan'. The Brothers of St Louis had a particular role in keeping their memory alive and one of them, Brother Christofoor van Langen, gathered a collection of documents and artefacts which formed the basis of a Zouavenmuseum, opened in 1947 and still running.

The final veteran died in 1952 at the age of 101: Octave Cossette of Velleyfield, Quebec, one of the 114 who had set out for Rome in September 1870 only to return home when they realised their efforts were too late.

---

39   *The Tablet*, 26 May 1894, p.814.
40   *The Tablet*, 20 October 1894, p.632.
41   *The Tablet*, 1 August 1914, p.192.
42   Information supplied by Winsome Collingridge, granddaughter of George Collingridge.
43   *The Tablet*, 23 March 1929, p.420.
44   *The Tablet*, 23 February 1929, p.251.

Conclusion

The 'Pontifical Army' seems something of an oxymoron in the twenty-first century. The campaigns described in this volume may embarrass some modern Catholics; in fact, a visitor to Rome will find few references to the Pope's transnational army of the 1860s. Today Popes are expected to be among the first to appeal for peace when conflict breaks out and any thought of military arms seems highly inappropriate. Even the famous Swiss Guard are seen as little more than an internal security force, who not only protect the person of the Pope but provide a photo opportunity for tourists at the Vatican's Bronze Doors.

If we normally associate the Middle Ages and the Renaissance with the 'warrior Popes', the dramas of the nineteenth century not only created the modern papacy but up until 1870 forced the Holy See to develop its military resources. Marked by recent experiences of revolution and aggressive secularism, the Church understandably displayed a siege mentality. The struggles fought out in Italy were part of a 'culture war' between tradition and modernity, faith and reason, legitimacy and usurpation. If the Pope was to maintain his kingdom, as many considered necessary, then he needed support not only from foreign powers but members of the faithful bearing arms. Called variously the 'crusaders of the nineteenth century' and 'cut-throat mercenary hirelings', they became either the heroes or villains of the vexed 'Roman Question'. Their presence was even used as a pretext for invasion of the Papal States in 1860 and 1870, Generals Fanti and Cialdini both stating their desire to rid Italy of foreign mercenaries and bring true protection and freedom to the people.

Substantial efforts were made by the Holy See to improve and reform its army during the period, especially under the visionary leadership of Monsignor Mérode and Generals Lamoricière and Kanzler. Discipline and training were improved, and use made of recent developments in military technology, including railways, telegraphs, breech-loading rifles and even an early machine gun. There is evidence that by 1870 military observers in other countries, including the Kingdom of Italy, were beginning to take note of the revitalised Pontifical Army.[1]

With hindsight, the transnational volunteers (constituting less than half of the Army's total strength) who fought under the papal flag may seem like 'heroic failures'. Most of them knew that the odds were heavily stacked against them, but they also understood the importance of standing up for their beliefs and the value, as they saw it, of sacrifice and martyrdom. 'For them,' writes David Alvarez, 'service in the Pope's army was a noble gesture in comparison with which concerns for personal advancement and financial reward were insignificant.'[2]

If the Pope was able to mobilise the more militant elements of Catholicism, every nation had its local contexts, which makes the subject of the British and Irish volunteers, hitherto largely ignored, particularly interesting. They should be seen alongside the several thousand subjects of the British monarch who volunteered to fight in overseas ventures during the long nineteenth century across Europe and South

---

1 Alvarez, *The Pope's Soldiers*, p.212.
2 Alvarez, *The Pope's Soldiers*, p.211.

America, though most of these involved liberal causes – not least of which were those who fought for Garibaldi. The United Kingdom was a predominantly Protestant state and the Risorgimento seen as a British cause. Nevertheless, within Victorian society there were strong elements of an Anti-Risorgimento, thanks largely to a revitalised and increasingly confident Catholic minority. Recruits for the Pontifical Army came from a variety of backgrounds, though the majority were middle class. Collections were widely taken for their maintenance and supporters existed at the highest levels of society. Even a sitting member of the House of Commons patrolled the walls of Rome in September 1870, gun in hand, ready to deter the army of the 'robber king'. The idea of British Catholics bearing arms for the Pope would, of course, have strengthened traditional anti-Catholic prejudices and confirmed the long held belief, held by many Protestants, that it was impossible to be a loyal subject of the British monarch and a true Catholic. To be Catholic was not to be English and to be under the sway of a foreign ruler.

Irish support for the Pope had its own dynamic, as much about scoring an indirect hit at the British Government, even though it paradoxically meant denying the Italians their desire for nationhood. It was a result of the 'convergence', to use the words of Donal Corcoran, 'of faith and fatherland, of religion and nationalism.'[3] The cause superficially united English and Irish Catholics but the Irish remained sensitive to English pretensions and any perceived insult to their national identity. The Irish Battalion of 1860 may have failed in its military objective but the energies behind its formation, as Emmet Larkin has argued, 'cumulatively resulted in the deepening of an Irish national consciousness' and 'intensified it in a way that made the Irish people even more aware of how very Catholic they were', in contrast to the Protestant English.[4]

The presence of British and Irish recruits – examples of the 'ideological volunteering' that had become widespread after the French Revolution – showed a desire to contribute to the ongoing struggles that were widely reported in the press and discussed at public meetings. It revealed a popular engagement in politics and religion that would have been less possible in a previous age. Their importance lay not in battle honours but as a visible expression of their cause: '[W]hat counted,' writes one historian of the papal recruits, 'was the not the shots they fired but the newspaper articles they could inspire, the signatures their example could elicit, the money they helped to raise for the Pope.'[5] Their presence in Rome showed that the British and the Irish could stand alongside their continental neighbours in defending the centre of Christendom and visible head of the Church. British and Irish Catholics, after years of persecution, surely felt they had come of age.

---

3 Corcoran, *Irish Brigade*, p.1.
4 Larkin, *Consolidation of the Roman Catholic Church in Ireland*, p.50.
5 Vincent Vaene, 'The Roman Question: Catholic Mobilisation and Papal Diplomacy during the Pontificate of Pius IX (1846–1878)' in Emiel Lamberts (ed.), *The Black International, 1870–1878: The Holy See and Militant Catholicism in Europe* (Leuven: Leuven University Press, 2002), p.145.

Appendix I

The Cast of Characters

For the ease of the reader, a brief biographical note is included for names mentioned frequently in the text. For English and Welsh Zouaves, see Appendix II.

Allet, Joseph Eugène (1814–1878), Swiss-born commander of the Pontifical Zouaves, 21 March 1861–20 September 1870.
Antonelli, Giacomo (1806–1876), Cardinal Secretary of State, 1848–1876.
Becdelièvre, Louis Aimé de (1826–1871), commander, first of the Franco-Belgian Tirailleurs in 1860 and then the Pontifical Zouaves (1 January–23 March 1861).
Bixio, Nino (1821–1873), associate of Garibaldi, Italian general and commander of the 2nd Division in 1870.
Cadorna, Raffaele (1815–1897), Italian general who captured Rome in 1870.
Cavour, Count (Camillo Benso) (1810–1861), prime minister of Piedmont, 1852–1859 and 1860–1861; first prime minister of Italy, 1861.
Charette de la Contrie, Athanse de (1832–1911), prominent French Zouave officer and a magnet for papal veterans up until his death.
Cialdini, Enrico (1811–1892), Piedmontese general and commander of IV Corps in 1860; created Duke of Gaeta in 1861.
Cullen, Paul (1803–1878), Archbishop of Dublin, 1852–1878, and first Irish cardinal, 1866.
Denbigh, 8th Earl of (Rudolph Feilding) (1823–1892), chairman of the Papal Defence Committee.
Derby, 14th Earl of (Edward Smith-Stanley) (1799–1869), British prime minister, 1866–1868.
Failly, Pierre Louis Charles de (1810–1892), commander of the French expeditionary force of 1867.
Fanti, Manfredo (1806–1865), commander of the Piedmontese forces in the 1860 campaign; regarded as the effective founder of the Italian Army.
Garibaldi, Giuseppe (1807–1882), Italian patriot and guerrilla leader.
Garibaldi, Menotti (1840–1903), eldest son of Giuseppe and fought at Mentana.
Gladstone, William Ewart (1809–1898), British prime minister, 1868–1874.
Kirby, Tobias (1804–1895), rector of the Pontifical Irish College, Rome, 1849–1891.
Lamoricière, Christophe Juchault de (1805–1865), French general; appointed commander-in-chief of the Pontifical Army on 8 April 1860.
Kanzler, Hermann (1822–1888), German-born commander-in-chief of the Pontifical Army and minister of arms from 27 October 1865.
Kavanagh (nee Clifford), Mary Constantia (1825–1898), mother of two Zouaves (the Vavasour brothers) and a keen supporter of the cause.
Manning, Henry Edward (1808–1892), Archbishop of Westminster, 1865–1892, and cardinal, 1875.

Mazzini, Giuseppe (1805–1872), Italian radical and political theorist.
Mérode, Xavier (1820–1874), Belgian-born papal minister of war, 1860–1865, and later archbishop, 1866.
Moriarty, David (1814–1877), Bishop of Ardfert and Aghadoe (Kerry) from 1856.
Napoleon III (1808–1873), nephew of Napoleon I; president of France, 1848–1852; emperor of the French, 1852–1870.
O'Clery, Patrick Keyes (1849–1913), Irish Zouave, 1867–1868, and historian.
O'Reilly De La Hoyde, Albert (1841–1903), Irish Zouave, 1861–1870, having previously fought with the Battalion of St Patrick.
O'Reilly, Myles (1825–1880), commanding officer of the Battalion of St Patrick and later Member of Parliament.
Palmerston, 3rd Viscount (Henry John Temple) (1784–1865), British prime minister, 1855–1858 and 1859–1865.
Pius IX (born Giovanni Maria Mastai Ferreti) (1792–1878), pope, 1846–1878.
Rocca, Enrico Morozzo della (1807–1897), Piedmontese general and commander of V Corps in 1860.
Russell, 1st Earl (John Russell) (1792–1878), British foreign secretary, 1859–1865; British prime minister, 1852 and 1865–1866.
Russell, Odo (1829–1884), unofficial British representative at the Vatican, 1858–1870.
Russell-Killough, Frank (1836–1935), member of a Franco-Irish family who served with the Battalion and Company of St Patrick, 1860–1862, the Zouaves, 1862–1864, and the Foreign Carabineers, 1864–1868.
Stone (nee Biddulph), Katherine Mary (1828–1892), journalist, poet and volunteer nurse in 1867 and 1870.
Stonor, Edmund (1831–1912), chaplain to the English Zouaves, later archbishop, 1889.
Talbot, George (1816–1886), monsignor and confidante of Pius IX.
Teeling, Bartholomew (1848–1921), Irish Zouave, 1867–1868; 'Bartle' returned to Rome in 1870 but arrived after the city was seized by the Italians.
Victor Emmanuel II (1820–1878), King of Piedmont-Sardinia, 1849–1861; King of Italy, 1861–1878.
Wiseman, Nicholas Patrick Stephen (1802–1865), Cardinal Archbishop of Westminster, 1850–1865.

Appendix II

A List of English and Welsh Zouaves

Abbreviations: M = Mentana Campaign; R = Fall of Rome; BM = Bene Merenti Medal

Name	D.O.B.	Birthplace	Matriculation	Enlisted	Corporal	Sergeant	Discharged	Remarks
Archdeacon, John	31/8/45	Wigan	9805	27/1/70			21/9/70	R
Barrier, Alfred	31/7/52	London	10658	18/8/70			21/9/70	R
Barnard, Thomas	1/2/42	London	9973	10/3/70			21/9/70	R
Barrett, George	1/11/45	????	8803	21/6/69	16/7/70		21/9/70	R
Bentley, Richard	1/6/35	Liverpool	9734	13/1/70			21/9/70	R
Berningham, George	20/7/50	Leek	10868	8/9/70			21/9/70	R
Bishop, Clement	22/10/39	Birmingham	6819	17/1/68			20/11/68	
Blair, Edward	25/12/50	London	4474	26/10/67			28/10/69	M
			9727	12/1/70			15/7/70	
			10828	8/9/70			21/9/70	R
Bologna, William	7/4/45	Newington	9560	12/12/69			21/9/70	R
Bradberry, Louis	26/8/48	London	6239	15/12/67	16/3/68		1/8/70	BM
Bradshaw, Arthur	22/8/52	London	8638	22/4/69			5/8/69	
Brennan, William	8/3/22	London	5921	6/12/67			23/12/69	
Brookes, Frederick	5/4/47	London	7792	9/7/68	21/3/70		14/7/70	
Brown, William	25/10/38	Andries	7659	10/6/68			16/6/70	
Burchett, Ernest	25/2/44	London	7532	7/5/68	21/4/70		21/9/70	R
Burton, John	4/5/43	Lancashire	9840	1/2/70			21/9/70	R
Butler, James	18/7/46	London	6507	22/12/67			8/1/70	
Carrigan, James	14/4/45	Wardour	8646	24/4/69			21/9/70	R
Carroll, Thomas	1847	Darrington	8588	10/4/69			21/9/70	R
Carter, George	10/10/48	London	10616	11/8/70			21/9/70	R

Name	D.O.B.	Birthplace	Matriculation	Enlisted	Corporal	Sergeant	Discharged	Remarks
Cary, Oswald	20/5/44	London	4043	18/5/67	21/12/67		28/5/69	M
Cavanagh, Martin	26/7/40	Liverpool	7588	12/5/68			12/5/70	
Chilton, William	2/11/42	Stone	8125	31/10/68			21/9/70	R
Cluskey, Patrick	29/11/50	????	8331	9/1/69			21/9/70	R
Collingridge, Alfred	1846	Oxford	2915	5/5/66			+18/10/67	M
Collingridge, George	29/10/48	Oxford	4165	22/6/67	21/11/67		22/6/69	M
Coombs, Arthur	30/3/37	Dorchester	7868	28/7/68			28/1/69	
Cotter, Patrick	12/7/50	Buxton	4848	9/11/67			11/11/69	
Coventry, James	26/2/49	London	7173	2/3/68			12/7/68	
Cremin, Patrick	14/3/41	London	10804	1/9/70			21/9/70	R
Cross, Joseph	22/12/48	Longton, Staffs	6662	1/1/68			1/7/68	
Curtis, George	7/5/46	Southampton	6959	1/2/68			+17/9/68	
Dalton, John Herbert	1844	Liverpool	2917	19/5/66			1/1/68	
D'Arcy, James	13/5/44	London	1/10/62	19/2/65				
			21/3/66	21/9/70				M R
D'Arcy, John	27/6/51	London	9558	12/12/69			21/9/70	R
De Coucy, Joseph	10/4/47	Worcester	6502	22/12/67			6/1/70	
De Graveroi, Henry	9/8/48	London	7093	15/2/68			23/8/68	BM
Dewe, George	25/6/51	Burntislande	8266	9/12/68			21/9/70	R
Dooley, Patrick	12/3/49	Norwood	7927	26/8/68	26/3/70	6/9/70	21/9/70	R
Duck, James	25/5/48	Liverpool	4948	11/11/67			14/11/69	
Duke, Philip	9/7/40	Hastings	6669	1/1/68			1/6/70	
Durant, Reginald Sydney	12/9/52	Chelmsford	9908	23/2/70			21/9/70	R
Evans, William	25/9/34	Levenshume	8090	17/1/68			25/10/69	
'Gallacher' [Gallagher], John	15/7/49	Liverpool	4847	9/11/67			31/1/68	
Godlehowski, William	8/5/49	London	10307	16/6/70			219/70	R
Gush, John Augustus Dominic	14/8/47	Bicton	9889	17/2/70			21/9/70	R
Hanrahan, John	8/6/40	Kilestone	6503	22/12/67			6/1/70	
Hansom, Joseph Stanislaus	29/6/45	York	4576	29/10/67			2/5/68	M
Harding, Robert	16/4/46	Redion	4379	16/10/67			28/10/69	M
Hinde, 'Eudes' [Jacob]	20/9/16	Ringwood	7487	16/4/68			31/12/68	
Holtham, Samuel	18/12/52	Liverpool	10143	28/4/70			21/9/70	R

Name	D.O.B.	Birthplace	Matriculation	Enlisted	Corporal	Sergeant	Discharged	Remarks
Hughes, Peter	16/3/46	Marlborough	7521	30/4/68			12/5/70	
Hyland, John	25/4/49	London	7978	15/9/68	6/2/70		21/9/70	R
Jacob, William	15/8/39	Cardiff	9701	6/1/70			21/9/70	R
Jerrard, George	28/2/47	London	6662	1/1/68			1/7/68	BM
Johnson, William	27/9/47	Preston	6880	22/1/68			22/4/70	
Judge, Edmund	23/3/30	London	9945	3/3/70			21/9/70	R
Kearney, William	26/8/48	Liverpool	8124	31/10/68			21/9/70	R
Keens, Ambrose	24/2/42	London	6234	15/12/67			15/12/69	
Keens, Christopher	25/5/37	London	6865	18/1/68			17/2/70V	
Keens, Henry	4/12/44	London	5967	7/12/67			31/12/69	
Kenyon, John George	11/10/43	London	?	9/70			21/9/70	R
Kinsella, James	20/3/42	Tongleton	7998	26/9/68			21/9/70	R
Little, Thomas	31/7/51	Hasley'	10139	28/4/70			11/9/70	
Livesey, Joseph	25/12/48	Piulton-le-Fylde	10140	28/4/70			21/9/70	R
Loton, Leonard	7/11/45	Cheadle	6237	15/12/67			31/12/69	
Lynch, James	17/3/49	London	6506	22/12/67			29/1/68	
Lyons, Patrick	1850	Liverpool	9944	3/3/70			21/9/70	R
'Mac Gallaghar', Hugh	18/5/46	Newcastle	5291	18/11/67			29/1/68	
MacGuiness, Joseph	25/1/46	Manchester	8415	8/2/69	26/6/70		21/9/70	R
MacKenna, Edmund	16/11/42	London	6633	29/12/67			8/1/68	
MacNeany, Andrew	28/9/45	Rugby	9842	1/2/70			21/9/70	R
Mandy, Francis	17/1/50	S. Africa	6820	18/1/68			19/10/68	
Maxwell, Walter Constable	15/8/50	*Everingham*	8140	10/11/68	26/4/70		21/9/70	R BM
Mitchell, Perceval	18/1/46	London	5326	22/11/67			21/9/69	
Mitchell, Thomas	20/5/46	London	6687	5/1/68			+1/8/68	
Muggeridge, Samuel	5/8/41	London	5947	6/12/67			20/9/68	
Nash, Francis	3/4/46	Bristol	10431	1/7/70			21/9/70	R
Newsham, Francis	2/12/48	Lytham	6881	22/1/68			16/8/69	BM
Nicholson, Thomas	4/10/45	Manchester	9382	8/11/69			12/5/70	
Norton, John	6/6/50	Wellington	8661	1/5/69			21/9/70	R
O'Donnell, John	20/6/49	Liverpool	8204	24/11/68	16/11/69		21/9/70	R
Pearson, Robert	1/9/50	Carlisle	9841	1/2/70			21/9/70	R

Name	D.O.B.	Birthplace	Matriculation	Enlisted	Corporal	Sergeant	Discharged	Remarks
Perkins, John	12/10/43	Clapham	9839	1/2/70			21/9/70	R
Petre, Oswald	8/9/48	Neyland	7980	15/9/68			2/7/69	
Powell, Joseph	17/12/38	Donington	7389	21/3/68	21/3/70		14/4/70	
Race, John	9/12/42	Gibraltar	5909	6/12/67			29/12/68	
Raymond, Thomas	21/2/48	Preston	7979	15/9/68	28/3/70		21/9/70	R
Richardson, Henry	26/12/45	Harlow	7977	15/9/68			+18/12/68	
Ricks, Désiré	2/3/47	Birmingham	7179	2/3/68			14/6/70	
Rily, Bernard	24/5/43	Crook	8092	17/10/68			21/9/70	R
Robinson, Wilfrid Clavering	4/10/48	Ramsgate	7501	24/4/68	21/3/70		26/5/70	
Ryall, Joseph	14/5/49	London	5928	6/12/67			26/12/69	
'Selton' [Sellon], Ernest	12/3/47	Brighton	9562	12/12/69			21/9/70	R
Shee, Daniel	4/4/46	London	4194	11/7/67	26/11/67		21/9/70	M R
Smith, Joseph	7/4/40	Wigan	9561	12/12/69			21/9/70	R
Stanley, Francis	15/1/50	Macclesfield	7999	28/9/68			21/9/70	R
Steen, Richard	14/3/52	London	9493	27/11/69			21/9/70	R
Stephens, James	18/11/51	Leeds	8416	8/2/69	26/7/70		21/9/70	R
Stourton, Arthur	21/2/41	York	7509	29/4/68	21/11/68		6/8/69	
Swift, Henry	27/11/38	Worcester	6509	22/12/67			14/7/70	
Tierney, James	23/8/49	London	5327	22/11/67			25/11/69	
Thornton, Edmund	18/7/45	Preston	6980	5/2/68	16/1/70		17/2/70	
Underwood, John	6/2/37	Madras	7169	26/2/68			26/2/69	
Van Sittard, Arthur	3/11/47	London	6526	22/12/67	1/1/69	16/1/70	21/9/70	M R BM
Vassar, Philip	6/7/50	Shiplam	8193	16/11/68	16/1/70		21/9/70	R
Vavasour, Oswald	3/6/48	York	10695	21/8/70			21/9/70	R
Vavasour, William	28/11/46	Hazelwood	4759	8/11/67			16/6/68	
			7989	22/9/68			16/4/69	
Vrain, Henry	22/11/46	Bath	6868	18/1/68			27/1/70	
			9992	17/3/70	16/7/70		21/9/70	R
Walker, Thomas	123/1/48	Preston	6913	28/1/68			10/8/69	
Walmsley, Thomas	20/3/49	Liverpool	7852	22/7/69			29/1/69	
Watman, Henry	6/1/50	St Neots	6960	1/2/68			17/2/70	
Watson, Joseph	17/11/42	New Malden	9559	12/12/69			21/9/70	R

Name	D.O.B.	Birthplace	Matriculation	Enlisted	Corporal	Sergeant	Discharged	Remarks
Watts-Russell, Julian	1850	Florence	4102	1/6/67			+3/11/67	M
Watts-Russell, Wilfrid	1846	Florence	4101	1/6/67			21/9/67	M
			10694	21/8/70			21/9/70	R
Wells, Joseph/Charles	16/3/43	London	637	16/2/61			1/7/61	
Welman, Frederick Tristram	19/2/49	Norton	7198	26/2/68			6/7/69	BM
Williams, Joseph	8/6/52	Shropshire	10141	28/4/70			21/9/70	R
Williams, Walter	12/7/50	Denby	7531	7/5/68			11/6/70	
Wilson, Alexander John	19/8/44	Inverurie	8123	31/10/68			21/9/70	R
Wood, Thomas	22/12/48	Bilston	6650	29/12/67			6/6/69	
Woods, Edward	31/8/46	Liverpool	7589	12/5/68			14/11/68	
			10803	1/9/70			21/9/70	R
Woodward, Charles	19/5/50	Bristol	4019	11/5/67	21/11/67	21/12/67	21/9/70	M R
Woodward, Frederick	28/6/41	Dunston	8519	6/3/69			21/9/70	R

NB. This list is based on *Régiment des Zouaves Pontificaux. Liste des Zouaves ayant fait partie du Régiment du 1er Janvier 1861 au 20 Septembre 1870* (Lille: Imprimerie Victor Ducoulombier, 1910 & 1920), 2 vols. This invaluable resource contains numerous errors, especially regarding the spelling of names and birthplaces (the presumably French compiler seems to have been unfamiliar with English) as well as some dates of birth. Where known, these have been corrected; otherwise, the details have been left as they are.

This table includes those who were born in England and Wales, as well as those who were born elsewhere but are likely to have identified as 'English Zouaves' (such as the Watts-Russell brothers, who were born in Florence; John Underwood, born in British India; and Alexander Wilson, born in Scotland but spent most of his life in Yorkshire). Don Alfonso de Borbone, born in London and a claimant to the Spanish throne, is for obvious reasons omitted. Some individuals do not appear in the *Liste des Zouaves*, especially some of those who volunteered in 1870 and arrived during the final chaotic days of Papal Rome (such as John Kenyon). Where known, these are included. It is also possible that a handful of those who claimed to have been Zouaves in later life never actually joined but wanted to be associated with the glamour of the regiment and its cause.

Appendix III

Note on Uniforms

The Battalion of St Patrick and Company of St Patrick

Most members of the Battalion of St Patrick did not receive the colourful green uniform that had been intended for them, making do with improvised (and often discarded) sets of uniforms and equipment from other infantry units. The designated uniform, which was adopted more successfully by the Company of St Patrick, consisted of a green shako (with yellow piping and crown) and single-breasted tunic (also with yellow piping and lace, stretching from the collar to the tails). The pointed cuffs and shoulder straps were similarly dark green with yellow piping. Full dress included a blue collar with yellow piping, a crossed keys and tiara brooch and ornate green and yellow shoulder rolls, nicknamed '*salsicciotti*' ('sausages'). The 'Zouave' trousers were green with yellow trimmings. The gaiters were white, leggings leather and belting black. Officers had double-breasted tunics with gold buttons and fringed epaulettes, and green kepis with gold piping.

According to an example preserved among the effects of Myles Keogh and described in an 1959 article in the *Irish Sword*, the badge worn on the shako featured a cross and Irish harp, superimposed on a Maltese cross and St

An officer of the Irish Battalion of St Patrick. (Drawing by Ralph Weaver, with permission)

The Badge of the Irish Battalion. (Private collection; author's photograph)

Peter's crossed keys, with the words PRO FIDE ('For the Faith'). The badge was mounted on an elliptical piece of yellow silk cloth, backed by silver braiding arranged as a rosette; a silver threadwork shamrock piped in green being superimposed on the back.[1]

The Pontifical Zouaves

The Zouaves originated in the Franco-Belgian Tirailleurs, who wore a uniform based on the French Chasseurs à Pied, with blue tunics (yellow piping), light greyish blue trousers and a black shako with green pom-pom. The epaulettes were yellow with green fringe. This was replaced by the distinctive Zouave uniform, which even in 1860 was worn by at least one company. It consisted of a short, collarless greyish-blue jacket, fastened at the top by one hook and decorated with red piping and a red trim clover design, a *veste* with small buttons and the characteristic baggy trousers, also with red piping. The square flat kepi was greyish blue with red piping and band, bearing a buglehorn badge. On the right breast there was a gold papal crossed keys brooch with a chain to which was attached a firing pin (purely ornamental after the adoption of the Remington rifle). The rear seam of the forearms and the trouser sides were red laced, the forearm also being decorated with multiple small round buttons from cuffs to elbow. A red wool sash and black belt was worn around the waist. The leggings were raw leather, edged with black, and gaiters were white. The greyish blue colour was deemed to be good camouflage.

An Officer of the Pontifical Zouaves. (Drawing by Ralph Weaver, used with permission)#

1 'The hat of an Irish soldier of the Papacy', *Irish Sword* IV (14), pp.2-4.

On 17 April 1867 a Kolpack was introduced for parade purposes – a black fur hat with a large tiara and crossed keys badge on the front and a white horsehair plume. This features in many *carte de visite* (CdV) images of Zouaves. Some wore a fez for more informal occasions.

In the summer and while in the *campagna*, rough canvas trousers were often worn. Powell reported that 'when we walk out in the heat we sometimes tie a white handkerchief on our kepi'.[2] A hooded coat or '*cappottella*' was used in colder weather. In the *campagna*, the coat and tent cloth were rolled and worn over the left shoulder.

Officers had black rather than red piping, a gold sword belt with red sash, and black boots with brown fold overs. Gold flowered chevrons on the sleeves denoted rank.

Initially the Zouaves and other Pontifical light infantry were armed with the M1853 carbine, of either French or Belgian manufacture, and other older firearms. The Zouaves were rearmed from 1868 with the M1867 'rolling block' Remington, of either British or Belgian manufacture (12.4 calibre, 130cm length). Officers had a sabre and revolver. The Zouaves who went on to fight in the Franco-Prussian War as the Volunteers of the West had use of the Chassepot rifle.

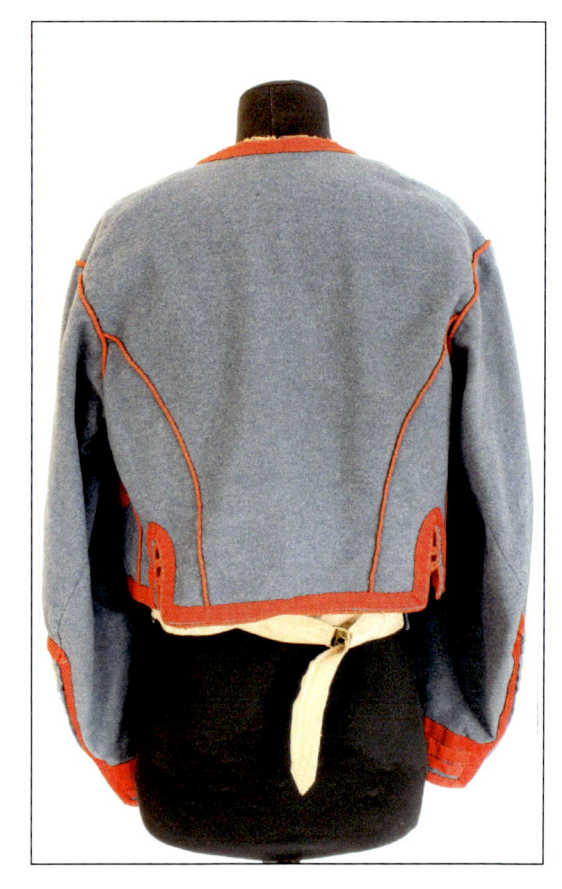

---

2   Powell, *Two Years in the Pontifical Zouaves*, p.106.

NOTE ON UNIFORMS   207

Details of a surviving Pontifical Zouave uniform. (Private collection; photograph by Alan Perry)

Appendix IV

Orders of Battles – Castelfidardo and Mentana

Castelfidardo, 18 September 1860[1]

Pontifical Forces
Pimodan's Attacking Column
- Six companies of Foreign Carabineers under Major Jannerat (820 men).
- Six companies of 1st Battalion, Indigenous Cacciatori under Major Ubaldini (720 men).
- Six companies of 2nd Battalion, Indigenous Cacciatori under Major Giorgi (750 men).
- Six companies of 2nd Battalion, Austrian Bersaglieri under Major Fuckmann (860 men).
- Four companies of Franco-Belgian Tirailleurs under Major de Becdelièvre (415 men).
- One company of St Patrick's Battalion under Captain Kirwan (105 men).
- Two Squadrons of Pontifical Dragoons under Captain Berzolati (215 men).
- 45 Austrian Cavalry under Captain Zichy.
- Mounted Guides under Captain de Bourbon Chalus.
- Mounted Volunteers and Gendarmes under Captain de Saintenac (60 men).
- 8th Mountain Battery (130 men).
- 11th Mountain Battery (130 men).

Total: 4,250 men and 12 artillery pieces.

Lamoriciere's Central Column
- Six companies of 1st Battalion, 1st Foreign Regiment (600 men).
- Six companies of 2nd Battalion, 1st Foreign Regiment under Major Dupasquier (600 men).
- Four companies of 2nd Battalion, 2nd Foreign Regiment under Major Bell (426 men).
- Five companies of 2nd Battalion, 2nd Regiment of Line under Major Sparagana (500 men).
- One squadron of Gendarmes under Captain Zampieri (120 men).
- Ambulance (24 men).
- Artillery support (40 men).

Total: 2,310 men.

---

[1] Based on Paolo Montinaro & Alberto Morera, *La Battaglia di Castelfidardo* (Rome: Edizioni Chillemi, 2019), pp.114-118.

Terrouane's Baggage Column
- Gendarmes and non-combatants (number unknown).
- 6th Mountain Artillery (100 men).

Total: approximately 150 men and 4 artillery pieces.

Total for Pontifical Forces: 6,710 men and 16 artillery pieces.

Piedmontese Forces
- Four companies of 26th Bersaglieri under Capitain Barbavara (434 men).
- Two companies of 12th Bersaglieri under Capitains Dalla Casa and Desperati (230 men).
- Four companies of 11th Bersaglieri under Major Lanzavecchia (443 men).
- Four companies each of the 1st, 2nd, 3rd and 4th Battalions, 10th Regiment of the Line under Colonel Bossolo (1,654 men).
- Four companies each of the 1st, 2nd, 3rd and 4th Battalions, 9th Regiment of the Line under Colonel Durandi (1,788 men).
- Three squadrons of Novara Lancers under Colonel Bovis (350 men).
- 2nd Battery of the 5th Regiment under Capitain Sterpone (112 men).
- Another battery of the 5th Regiment (50 men).
- 4th Battery of 8th Regiment under Captain Pizzetti (163 men).

Total: 5,224 men, 14 artillery pieces.

Mentana, 3 November 1867

Pontifical Forces
- Two battalions of Pontifical Zouaves under Colonel Allet (1,500 men).
- One battalion of Foreign Carabineers under Colonel Jeannerat (520 men).
- One battalion of the Roman (Antibes) Legion under Colonel d'Argy (540 men).
- One battery of six guns under Captain Polani (117 men).
- One company of Engineers under Captain Fabri (90 men).
- One squadron of Dragoons in four platoons under Captain Cremona (106 men).
- 50 Pontifical Gendarmes.

Total: 2,923 men, six artillery pieces.

Reserve made up mostly of sections of the French expeditionary force (Baron de Polhes)
- 2nd Battalion of Chasseurs à Pied (Comte).
- 1st Battalion of 1st Regiment of the Line (Fremont).
- 1st Battalion of 29th Regiment of the Line (Saussier).
- Two battalions of 59th Regiment of the Line (Berger).
- A platoon of 7th Chasseurs à Cheval (Wederspach-Tor).
- A half battery of three artillery pieces.
- A platoon of Pontifical Dragoons (Belli).

Total: 2,500 men, three artillery pieces.

Garibaldi's Forces[2]

- Three battalions of Bersaglieri (Stallo, Burlando, Missori), including a company of Livornese Carabiners under Captain Santini (700 men)
- Six columns of volunteers:
1. Colonel Salomone (four battalions, 1,000 men)
2. Colonel Frigyesi (four battalions, 800 men)
3. Major Valzania (three battalions, 800 men)
4. Major Cantoni (three battalions, 650 men)
5. Major Paggi (three battalions, approximately 825 men)
6. Colonel Elia (three battalions, approximately 825 men)
- Battalions under Majors Nisi, Ravizza and De Filippi and two companies under Major Andreazzi (850 men)
- A company of Engineers under Captain Aurelio Amici (40 men)
- A unit of Mounted Guides under Ricciotti Garibaldi (50 men)
- Two smooth-bore artillery pieces (with 70 balls)

Total: 5,760 men and two artillery pieces.

---

2   According to Pierluigi Romeo di Colloredo Mels, *Mentana 1867: La Disfatta di Garibaldi* (Bergamo: Luca Cristini Editore, 2020), p.109.

Bibliography

Archives

Archives of the Archdiocese of Birmingham – Oscott Papers
Archives of the Archdiocese of Dublin (IE/DDA) – Cullen Papers (Sections 274/2 and 333/3)
Archives of the Archdiocese of Westminster (AAW) – Wiseman and Manning Papers
Archives of the Birmingham Oratory (BO) – Newman Papers
Archives of the Pontifical Irish College, Rome – Kirby Papers (KIR)
Archives of the University of Hull – Papers of the Constable Maxwell Family of Everingham, Caerlaverock and Terregles
Archives of Ushaw College
Archives of the Venerable English College, Rome

Official Printed Sources

British Parliamentary Papers 1871. LXXII. Rome. No. I. *Correspondence Respecting the Affairs of Rome, 1870–1871* (London, 1871)
Hansard, Commons Debates, 1860

Contemporary Newspapers, Magazines and Journals

Advocate (Melbourne)
Atlas
Australian Star
Belfast Newsletter
Birmingham Daily Gazette
Bury Free Press
Carlow Post
Chelsea News and General Advertiser
Coleraine Chronicle
Congleton and Macclesfield Mercury
Cork Examiner
Crusader
Daily Post
Dalby Herald and Western Queensland Advertiser
Derry Journal
Downpatrick Recorder

Dublin Evening Packet and Correspondent
Dublin Evening Post
Dublin Weekly Nation
Dundee Courier
Edinburgh Evening Courant
Edmundian
Evening Freeman
Evening News Supplement (NSW)
Evening Standard
Falkirk Herald
Freeman's Journal
Glasgow Evening Citizen
Glasgow Free Press
Hartlepool Northern Daily Mail
Hull Packet
Illustrated London News
Illustrated Times
Irishman
Irish Times
Kendal Mercury
Kerry Evening Post
Kilkenny Journal
Kilkenny Moderator
Lancaster Gazette
Lancet
La Tribuna
Leeds Mercury
Liverpool Daily Post
London Daily News
Manchester Evening News
Morning Chronicle
Morning Post
Nation
Newcastle Guardian and Tyne Mercury
North Briton
Pall Mall Gazette
Portsmouth Evening News
Preston Chronicle
Punch
Reynold's Newspaper
Scotsman
Sheffield Daily Post
Sheffield Daily Telegraph
Staffordshire Advertiser
Stonyhurst Magazine
Sun

Tablet
Tamworth Herald
Times
Tipperary Vindicator
Ulster Examiner and Northern Star
Tralee Chronicle
Union Review
Universe
Venerabile
Weekly Register
Westminster Gazette
Wexford Chronicle
Worcester Journal

Contemporary Books, Memoirs, Novels and Poetry

Anon., *Album Storico–Artistico della Guerra d'Italia* (Torino: C. Perrin, 1860)
Anon., *Matricule du Bataillon des Tirailleurs Franco–Belges, Armée Pontificale 1860* (Lille: Imprimerie H. Morel, 1910)
Anon., *Régiment des Zouaves Pontificaux. Liste des Zouaves ayant fait partie du Régiment du 1er Janvier 1861 au 20 Septembre 1870* (Lille: Imprimerie Victor Ducoulombier, 1910 & 1920), 2 vols. Available online at: http://backup.diocese-quimper.fr/bibliotheque/files/original/b2321211594f72c8f9818ab-c7af1d0be.pdf
Althaus, Friedrich (ed.), *The Roman Journals of Ferdinand Gregorovius (1852–1874)* (London: G. Bell & Sons, 1911)
Bellefeuille, Edouard Lefebvre de, *Le Canada et les Zouaves Pontificaux. Memoires sur l'Origine, l'Enrôlement et l'Expédition du Contingent Canadien à Rome, Pendant l'Année 1868* (Montréal: Typographie du Journal *Le Nouveau Monde*, 1868)
Besson, Monsignor François-Nicolas-Xavier-Louis, *Frederick Francis Xavier de Mérode: His Life and Works* (London: W.H. Allen & Co., 1887)
Blakiston, Noel (ed.), *The Roman Question: Extracts from the Despatches of Odo Russell from Rome, 1858–1870* (London: Chapman & Hall, 1962)
Bresciani, Antonio, *Olderico: Ovvero Il Zuavo Pontificio, Racconto del 1860* (Rome: Coi Tipi della Civiltà Cattorica, 1862)
Bruneau, Antoine, *Frédéric De Saint-Sernin, Zouave au Service du Pape Roi* (Paris: Éditions Jourdan, 2020)
Busk, Rachel H. [published anonymously as 'Roman Correspondent of the *Westminster Gazette*'], *Contemporary Annals of Rome: Notes Political, Archaeological and Social* (London: Thomas Richardson & Son, 1870)
Cardella, Valerian, *Giulio Watts-Russell, Pontifical Zouave* (London: John Philp, undated)
Cler, Jean Joseph Gustave, *The Zouave Officer. Reminiscences of an Officer of Zouaves: The 2nd Zouaves of the Second Empire on Campaign in North Africa and the Crimean War* (Driffield: Leonaur, 2010)
Coëtlosquet, Reverend C. du, *Theodore Wibaux, Pontifical Zouave and Jesuit* (London: Catholic Truth Society, 1887)
Collingridge, George, 'Tales of the Papal Zouaves', *Austral Light* (Melbourne) (1899)
Crawford, F. Marion, *Sant' Ilario* (London: Macmillan & Co., 1895)

Daems, Reverend S., *The Double-Sacrifice; or, The Pontifical Zouaves. A Tale of Castelfidardo* (Baltimore, MD: Kelly, Piet & Co., 1870)

Disraeli, Benjamin, *Lothair* (London: Oxford University Press, 1975)

Erb, Peter C. (ed.), *The Correspondence of Henry Edward Manning and William Ewart Gladstone, 1833–1891* (Oxford: Oxford University Press, 2013), 4 vols

Gerlach, Eugenius de, *The Last Days of the Papal Army* (Birmingham: D. Kelly, 1870)

Hare, Augustus J.C., *Cities of Central Italy* (London: Smith, Elder & Co., 1884), 2 vols

Hare, Augustus J.C., *Days Near Rome* (London: Kegan Paul, Trench, Trubner & Co., 1907)

Herbert of Lea, Baroness Elizabeth, *Mentana; and What Happened Before* (London: J. Atkinson, 1868)

Jacob, W.J., *My Personal Recollections of Rome: A Lecture, Partly Delivered on the 9th of February 1871, at the Town Hall, Pontypool* (London: R. Washbourne, 1871)

McCaffery Michael J.A., *The Siege of Spoleto* (New York: P. O'Shea, 1864)

Nolan, Reverend J., *History of the Irish Pilgrimage to Rome; or, Notes on the Way* (London: Burns & Oates, 1893)

Nuyens, N., *Gedenkboek der Pauselijke Zouaven* (Roermond: Henri van der Marck, 1892)

O'Clery, Patrick Keyes, *The History of the Italian Revolution. First Period: The Revolution of the Barricades, 1796–1849* (London: R. Washbourne, 1875)

O'Clery, Patrick Keyes, *The Making of Italy, 1856–1870* (London: Kegan Paul, Trench, Trubner & Co., 1892)

O'Malley Baines, Thomas F., *My Life in Two Hemispheres* (San Francisco, CA: Henderson & Co., 1889)

Ozanam, Charles, *Une Ambulance a la Bataille de Mentana* (Paris: Imprimerie Adrien La Clere, 1868)

Pearson, Emma [published anonymously], *From Rome to Mentana* (London: Saunders, Otley & Co., 1868)

Powell, Joseph, *Two Years in the Pontifical Zouaves: A Narrative of Travel, Residence and Experience in the Roman States* (London: R. Washbourne, 1871)

Robinson, Wilfrid Clavering, *Under the Cross Keys* (publication details unknown)

Russell-Killough, Frank, *Dix Années Au Service Pontifical: Récits et Souvenirs par Le Cte Frank Russell-Killough, Ex-Captaine au Régiment de Carabiniers a Pied* (Mans: Typographie Edmond Monnoyer, 1871)

Ségur, Marquis A. de, *The Martyrs of Castelfidardo* (Dublin: M.H. Gill & Son, 1883)

Stone, Katherine Mary, *Our Flag: A Lay of the Pontifical Zouaves and Other Poems* (London: Burns & Oates, 1878)

Sullivan, Alexander Martin, *New Ireland* (Philadelphia, PA: J.B. Lippincott & Co., 1878)

Teeling, Bartle [writing as 'The Governor'], *My First Prisoner* (London: Roxburghe Press, undated)

Thérèse of Lisieux, *Story of a Soul: The Autobiography of Thérèse of Lisieux* (Washington, DC: ICS Publications, 1996)

Winn, C. Allanson, *What I Saw of the War: A Narrative of Two Months of Campaigning with the Prussian Army of the Moselle* (London: William Blackwood & Sons, 1870)

Wiseman, Nicholas, *Recollections of the Last Four Popes* (London: Hurst & Blackett, 1860)

Secondary Works

Altholz, Josef, *The Liberal Catholic Movement in England: The 'Rambler' and Its Contributors, 1848–1864* (London: Burns & Oates, 1962)

Alvarez, David, *The Pope's Soldiers: A Military History of the Modern Vatican* (Lawrence, KS: University Press of Kansas, 2011)

Anon., *Ai Vittoriosi di Castelfidardo* (Rome: Numero Speciale a Cura del 'Picenum' Autorizzato dal Comitato Pro Monumnto, 1932)
Berkeley, George Fitzhardinge, *The Irish Battalion in the Papal Army of 1860* (Dublin: Talbot Press, 1929)
Biondini, Renato, *I cannoni dell'Unità d'Italia. Le nuove artiglierie nelle campagne militari del 1859–1861* (Ancona: Edizioni Affinità Elettive, 2018)
Chadwick, Owen, *A History of the Popes, 1830–1914* (Oxford: Oxford University Press, 1998)
Coltrinari, Massimo, *Il Combattimento di Loreto detto di Castelfidardo, 18 Settembre 1860* (Rome: Edizioni Nuova Cultura, 2008)
Coltrinari, Massimo, *L'Investimento e la Presa di Ancona. La Conclusione della Campagna di Annessione delle Marche 20 Settembre–8 Ottobre 1860* (Rome: Edizioni Nuova Cultura, 2010)
Coltrinari, Massimo, *L'Ultima Difesa Pontificia di Ancona 7–29 Settembre 1860* (Rome: Edizioni Nuova Cultura, 2012), 2 vols
Colloredo Mels, Pierluigi Romeo di, *Mentana 1867: La Disfatta di Garibaldi* (Bergamo: Luca Cristini Editore, 2020)
Corcoran, Donal, *The Irish Brigade in the Pope's Army, 1860: Faith, Fatherland and Fighting* (Dublin: Four Courts Press, 2018)
Coulombe, Charles A., *The Pope's Legion: The Multinational Fighting Force that Defended the Vatican* (Basingstoke: Palgrave Macmillan, 2008)
Crociani, Piero, *L'Ultimo Esercito Pontificio* (Rome: Stato Maggiore dell'Esercito, 2020)
Crociani, Piero & Fiorentino, Massimo, *La Neuvième Croisade, 1860–1870: Histoire, Organisation et Uniformes des Unités Étrangères au Service du Saint-Siège* (Paris: Tradition Magazine, 2000)
Cryan, Mary Jane, *The Irish and English in Italy's Risorgimento* (Ronciglione: Etruria Editions, 2011)
Davis, John A. (ed.), *Italy in the Nineteenth Century* (Oxford: Oxford University Press, 2000)
De Cesare, Raffaele., *The Last Days of Papal Rome, 1850–1870* (London: Archibald Constable & Co., 1909)
Di Giovine, Fracesco Maurizio, *Gli Zuavi Pontifici e i loro Nemici* (Chieti: Edizioni Solfanelli, 2020)
Esposito, Gabriele, *Armies of the Italian Wars of Unification, 1868–70 (1): Piedmont and the Two Sicilies* (Oxford: Osprey, 2017)
Esposito, Gabriele, *Armies of the Italian Wars of Unification, 1868–70 (2): Papal States, Minor States and Volunteers* (Oxford: Osprey, 2018)
Guenel, Jean, *Le Dernière Guerre du Pape: Les Zouaves Pontificaux au Secours du Saint-Siège, 1860–1870* (Rennes: Presses Universitaires de Rennes, 1998)
Hamilton-Browne, George [writing as 'Richard Burke'], *With the Lost Legion in New Zealand* (London: T. Werner Laurie, 1911)
Hibbert, Christopher, *Garibaldi and His Enemies* (London: Penguin Books, 1987)
Hunter-Blair, David, *John Patrick Third Marquess of Bute, K.T.* (London: J. Murray, 1921)
Hunter-Blair, David, *In Victorian Days and Other Papers* (London: Longman, Green & Co., 1939)
Innocenti, Lorenzo, *Per il Papa Re. Il Risorgimento Italiano Visto Attraverso la Storia del Reggimento degli Zuavi Pontifici, 1860/1870* (Perugia: Casa Editrice Esperia, 2004)
Jonas, Raymond, *France and the Cult of the Sacred Heart: An Epic Tale for Modern Times* (Berkeley, CA: University of California Press, 2000)
Larkin, Emmet, *The Consolidation of the Roman Catholic Church in Ireland, 1860–1870* (London: University of North Carolina Press, 1987)
Levillain, Philippe (ed.), *The Papacy: An Encyclopaedia* (London: Routledge, 2002)
Linden, Ian, *Church and Revolution in Rwanda* (Manchester: Manchester University Press, 1977)
McAfee, Michael J., *Zouaves: The First and Bravest* (Gettysburg, PA: Thomas Publications, 1991)
Martino, Lucio, *The Irish against the Savoys* (Genova: Eldon Edizioni, 2011)

Mitchell, Adrian, *Plein Airs and Graces: The Life and Times of George Collingridge* (Kent Town: Wakefield Press, 2012)
Nouaille-Degorce, Patrick, *Les Volontaires de l'Ouest dans la guerre de 1870–1871* (Allaire: Editions Edilys, 2015)
Paoletti, Ciro, *A Military History of Italy* (Westport, CT: Praeger Security International, 2008)
Pemble, John, *The Mediterranean Passion: Victorians and Edwardians in the South* (Oxford: Oxford University Press, 1988)
Pichon, Alain, *Les Zouaves Pontificaux* (Paris: Éditions Hérault, 2017)
Riall, Lucy, *Garibaldi: Invention of a Hero* (London: Yale University Press, 2007)
Scirocco, Alfonso, *Garibaldi: Citizen of the World* (Princeton, NJ: Princeton University Press, 2007)
Taylor, A.J.P., *The Struggle for Mastery in Europe, 1848–1918* (Oxford: Clarendon Press, 1954)
Trevelyan, G.M., *Garibaldi and the Making of Italy* (London: Longmans, Green & Co., 1911)
Vigevano, Attilio, *La Fine dell'Esercito Pontificio* (Rome: Stabilimento Poligrafico per l'Amministrazione della Guerra, 1920)
Ward, Maisie, *The Wilfrid Wards and the Transition* (London: Sheed & Ward, 1934)
Wright, O.J., *Great Britain and the Unifying of Italy: A Special Relationship?* (Basingstoke: Palgrave Macmillan, 2019)

Articles

Anderson, Olive, 'The Growth of Christian Militarism in Mid-Victorian Britain', *English Historical Review*, 86:338 (1971), pp.46–72
Anon., 'Pontifical Zouaves: The Collingridge Brothers', *Vatican News: The Journal of the Vatican Philatelic Society*, 6:354 (2012), pp.20–27
Bacchin, Elena, 'Brothers of Liberty: Garibaldi's British Legion', *Historical Journal*, 58:3 (2015), pp.827–853
Buerman, Thomas, 'The Ideal Roman Catholic in Belgian Zouave Stories', in Carla Salvaterra & Berteke Waaldijk (eds), *Paths to Gender: European Historical Perspectives on Women and Men* (Pisa: Pisa University Press, 2009)
Buerman, Thomas, 'Lions and Lambs at the Same Time! Belgian Zouave Stories and Examples of Religious Masculinity', in Jan De Maeyer, Leen Van Molle, Tine Van Osselaer & Vincent Viaene (eds), Gender and Christianity in Modern Europe (Leuven: Leuven University Press, 2012)
Duffy, Eamon, 'Manning, Newman and the Fall of the Temporal Power', in British Embassy to the Holy See (ed.), *Britain and the Holy See: A Celebration of 1982 and the Wider Relationship* (Rome: British Embassy to the Holy See, 2013)
Dumont, Dora, 'The Nation as Seen from Below: Rome in 1870', *European Review of History*, 15:5 (2008), pp.479–496
Fyfe, Janet, 'Scottish Volunteers with Garibaldi', *Scottish Historical Review*, 57:164/2 (1978), pp.168–181
Gilley, Sheridan, 'The Garibaldi Riots of 1862', *Historical Journal*, 16:4 (1973), pp.697–732
Göhde, Ferdinand Nicolas, 'German Volunteers in the Armed Conflicts of the Italian Risorgimento 1834–70', *Journal of Modern Italian Studies*, 14:4 (2009), pp.461–475
Guenel, Jean, 'Service de santé, morbidité et mortalité dans le regiment des zouaves pontificaux en Italie (1861–1870), *Histoire des Sciences Médicales*, 29:3 (1995), pp.261–269
Harrison, Carol E., 'Zouave Stories: Gender, Catholic Spirituality and French Responses to the Roman Question', *Journal of Modern History*, 79:2 (2007), pp.274–305
Marraro, Howard R., 'Canadian and American Zouaves in the Papal Army, 1868–70', in *Canadian Catholic Historical Association (CCHA) Report 12* (1944–45), pp.83–102

O'Carroll, Ciarán, 'The Irish Papal Brigade: Origins, Objectives and Fortunes', in Colin Barr, Michelle Finelli & Anne O'Connor (eds), *Nation/Nazione, Irish Nationalism and the Italian Risorgimento* (Dublin: University College Dublin Press, 2014)

O'Connor, Anne, 'Triumphant Failure: The Return of the Irish Papal Brigade to Cork, November 1860', *Cork Historical and Archaeological Society*, 2:114 (2009), pp.39–50

O'Connor, Anne, 'The Pope, the Prelate, the Soldiers and the Controversy: Paul Cullen and the Irish Papal Brigade', in Daire Keogh & Albert McDonnell (eds), *Paul Cullen and His World* (Dublin: Four Courts Press, 2011)

O'Connor, Anne, '"Giant and Brutal Islanders": The Italian Response to the Irish Papal Brigade', in Colin Barr, Michelle Finelli & Anne O'Connor (eds), *Nation/Nazione, Irish Nationalism and the Italian Risorgimento* (Dublin: University College Dublin Press, 2014)

O'Driscoll, Florry, 'Confounding the Garibaldian Liars: The Letters of Albert Delahoyde, Irish Soldier of the Papal Battalion of St Patrick and Papal Zouave in Italy, 1860–1870', *Studi Irlandesi: A Journal of Irish Studies*, 6 (2016), pp.49–63

Pécout, Gilles, 'The International Armed Volunteers: Pilgrims of a Transnational Risorgimento', *Journal of Modern Italian Studies*, 14:4 (2009), pp.413–426

Riall, Lucy, 'Martyr Cults in Nineteenth-Century Italy', *Journal of Modern History*, 82:2 (2010), pp.255–287

Sarlin, Simón, 'The Anti-Risorgimento as a Transnational Experience', *Modern Italy*, 19:1 (2014), pp.81–92

Sarlin, Simón, 'Mercenaries or Soldiers of the Faith? The Pontifical Zouaves in the Defense of the Roman Church (1860–1870)', *Millars: Espai i historia*, 43:2 (2017), pp.189–218

Scott, Ivan, 'The Diplomatic Origins of the Legion of Antibes: Instrument of Foreign Policy during the Second Empire', in Nancy N. Barker & Marvin L. Brown Jr (eds), *Diplomacy in the Age of Nationalism* (Dordrecht: Springer, 1971)

Simpson, Martin, 'From Zouaves Pontificaux to the Volontaires de l'Ouest: Catholic Volunteers and the French Nation, 1860–1910', *Annales Canadiennes d'Histoire/Canadian Journal of History*, 53:1 (2018), pp.1–28

Simpson, Martin, 'Serving France in Rome: The Zouaves Pontificaux and the French Nation', *French History*, 27:1 (2013), pp.69–90

Sutcliffe, Marcella Pellegrini, 'British Red Shirts: A History of the Garibaldi Volunteers (1860)' in Nir Arielli & Bruce Collins (eds), *Transnational Soldiers: Foreign Military Enlistment in the Modern Era* (Basingstoke: Palgrave Macmillan, 2013)

Vaene, Vincent, 'The Roman Question: Catholic Mobilisation and Papal Diplomacy during the Pontificate of Pius IX (1846–1878)', in Emiel Lamberts (ed.), *The Black International, 1870–1878: The Holy See and Militant Catholicism in Europe* (Leuven: Leuven University Press, 2002)

Wentzell, Tyler, 'Mercenaries and Adventurers: Canada and the Foreign Enlistment Act in the Nineteenth Century', *Canadian Military History*, 23:2 (2014), pp.57–77

Whinder, Richard, 'Julian Watts-Russell and the Papal Zouaves', in Nicholas Schofield (ed.), *A Roman Miscellany: The English in Rome, 1550-2000* (Leominster: Gracewing, 2002)

Websites

<https://ajwpapalzouave.blogspot.com/>
<https://www.leftlion.co.uk/read/2018/november/giuseppe-garibaldi-nottingham-forest-freedom-fighter/>
<https://www.mugamentana.it/ilmuseo/>
<https://www.theosophical.org/publications/quest-magazine/3617-blavatsky-and-the-battle-of-mentana>

Index

Acerbi, Giovanni, 104
Acquapendente, 120 (fn)
Ahearn, Thomas, 145
Albini, Captain, 72
Allet, Joseph Eugène, 90-91, 117, 157, 161, 16, 192, 197
Altieri, Cardinal Lodovico, 96
American Zouaves, 87-88 (Civil War), 127 (Pontifical)
Ancona, xiv, xv, 27, 31, 42, 47, 50, 51, 53, 55, 56, 61, 62, 66, 67, 68, 69, 70-74, 77, 96, 103, 192
Antibes Legion, see French Army in the Papal States
Antonelli, Cardinal Giacomo, 21, 32, 38, 42, 43, 48, 49, 50, 53, 70, 75, 79, 80, 97, 98, 117, 160, 168, 172, 177, 197
Archdeacon, John, 135, 186, 199
Arquati, Giuditta Tavana, 103
Arundell, Lord, 119, 138, 139
Aspromonte, 94, 99, 165
Australia, 129, 130, 137, 138, 141, 153, 154, 184, 185, 193, 194
Azzanesi, Achille, 98, 104

Bach, Joseph Alois, 101
Bagnorea, 99, 120 (fn), 132
Bandiez, Alfred du, 65
Barre de Nanteuil, Alfred de la, 63, 68
Barrett, James, 82
Baye, Captain De, 58, 59
Becdelièvre, Louis Aimé de, 33, 63, 89, 90, 197
Bembo, Faustin, 93
Bernardini, Count, 113
Bernadette, St, 163
Bishop, Clement, xi, 124, 140, 143, 157, 185, 199
Bixio, Nino, 169, 174, 197
Blackney, James, 40, 51, 56
Blavatsky, Helen, 106
Blumensthil, Bernard, 33
Borbone, Alfonso de, 93, 105, 190, 203
Bourbon-Chalus, Comte de, 33, 105, 208
Bowyer, Sir George, 34, 38, 43, 45, 49 (fn), 147, 188
Boyle, General de, 74
Brennan, William, 138, 154, 199
Bresciani, Antonio, 91
Brignone, General, 57, 58, 59, 60, 77

British Army, Units: 10th Hussars, 40; 18th Regiment of Foot, 40; 40th Regiment of Foot, 186; 54th Regiment of Foot, 173; 63rd Regiment of Foot, 141; 64th Regiment of Foot, 141; 78th Highlanders, 141; 86th Regiment of Foot, 173; Lancashire Rifle Volunteers (64th), 141; Carlow Militia, 40; Cornish Militia, 45; King's (Liverpool Regiment), 186; Longford Militia, 186; Louth Militia, 51; Rifle Brigade, 186; Waterford Artillery, 40; West India Regiment, 89; Warwickshire Militia, 40; Welch Regiment, 186; Yorkshire Hussars, 186;
Browne, Henry, 148
British Legion (Garibaldi), 45-47
Burchett, Ernest, 141, 184, 194, 199
Busk, Rachel, 165
Bute, Marquis of, 138-139

Cadorna, Raffaele, 55, 71, 169, 173, 181, 197
Cairoli, Enrico, 103
Canadian Zouaves, 126-127
Cardwell, Edward, 43
Cary, Oswald, 102, 128, 143, 200
Castelfidardo, xi, xiv, xv, 42, 51, 53, 61-69, 70, 71, 73, 74, 77, 79, 81, 90, 91, 97, 98, 101, 102, 110, 113, 128, 133, 134, 135, 140, 144, 173, 178, 190, 191, 192, 208-209
Castella, Simon de, 72, 110
Castelli, Emilio, 68
Catholic Union, 187
Cavour, Count, (Camillo Benso), 17, 22, 26, 52, 69, 73, 75, 96, 196
Cialdini, Enrico, 52, 53, 61, 62, 68, 71, 195, 197
Chambers, Mr, 40, 58
Chambord, Count de, ('Henri V'), 92
Charette de la Contrie, Alain de, 90, 110
Charette de la Contrie, Athanse de, 33, 90, 91, 92, 98, 101, 102, 103, 110, 124, 141 (fn), 157, 160, 171, 173, 176, 178, 189, 190, 191, 192, 197
Charette de la Contrie, Ferdinand de, 90
Charette de la Contrie, Francoise Athanse de, 92
Charette de la Contrie, Louis de, 90
Chassepot, Alessandre, 120
Chérisey, Marquis de, 69

218

Chika, Heahim, 93
Chillaz, Captain de, 90
Città di Castello, 55
Civitavecchia, xiii, 32, 42, 55, 92, 98, 104, 126, 151, 168, 170, 172, 174, 181
Clarendon, Lord, 116
Claxton Gun, 125, 176, 181
Clausel, Bertrand, 86
Clement VI, 70
Clement XII, 70
Clifford, Sir Charles, 147
Collingridge, Alfred, 96, 101, 128-129, 132, 137, 140, 152, 153, 155, 164, 200
Collingridge, George, xi, 100, 102, 107, 120, 122, 128, 137, 140, 185, 193, 194, 200
Coombes, Arthur, 187, 188 (fn), 200
Coppinger, Dudley, 173
Coppinger, John, 40, 51, 59, 82
Costes, Captain, 103-104
Courcy, Joseph De, 142-143, 144
Courten, Raphael De, 55, 110
Courten, Victor de, 110
Coventry, James, 140, 141, 200
Crean, Michael, 59
Cropt, General, 51, 55
Crowley, Jeremiah, 146, 151,
Cullen, Paul, (Archbishop of Dublin), 24, 39, 49, 146, 163, 187, 197
Curtin, Daniel, 177, 180

D'Alessandri, Fratelli, 114
D'Arcy, James, 51, 66, 82, 140, 160, 200
Darlington Carmel, 133, 193
Della Rocca, Enrico, 53, 55, 56
Deady, Jerome, 58, 59
Delahoyde, see: O'Reilly, Albert De La Hoyde
Delany, William, 141, 159, 160, 163
Denbigh, Earl of, (Rudolph Feilding), xiii, 34, 119, 138, 144, 162, 166, 188, 197
Desclée, Jules-Louis, 100
Diamond, Peter, 40, 82 (fn)
Disraeli, Benjamin, 165, 188
Dixon, Joseph, (Archbishop of Armagh), 39, 80
Dominicans of San Clemente, Rome, 38
Drane, Mother Raphael, 157
Dufournel, Emmanuel, 133
Duke, Philip, 141, 154-155, 184, 200
Dumas, Arthur, 186
Dunn, James, 142-143, 144
Durrant, Reginald, 185, 200
Dunne, Edward, 60
Dunne, Henry, 51
Dunne, John, 45

Ellsworth, Elmer, 87-88

English College, Rome, xi, 23, 47, 79, 133, 135, 154, 155, 160, 168, 171, 173, 177, 187, 193
English, Louis, 79
Errington, John, 140

Faber, Frederick, 24, 129
Failly, Pierre de, 104, 105, 120, 198
Fanti, Manfredo, 52, 57, 59, 68, 71, 74, 195, 197
Fenians, 127, 147, 159-161
Fitzgerald, Major, 49, 50, 51
Forde, Laurence, 49
Foreign Enlistment Act (1819), 43, 44, 46, 126, 131, 143, 145, 149, 150
Formby, Henry, 149
Francis II, (King of the Two Sicilies), 93, 94
French Army in the Papal States: Antibes Legion, 98, 101, 102, 103, 110, 111, 126, 209; Failly's Expeditionary Force, 104, 105, 111-114, 120-122
Fuckmann, Major, 63, 208
Fulham, Thomas, 82
Furey, Nicholas, 68, 81
Furlong, Thomas, (Bishop of Ferns), 39

Gabrielli-Wiseman, Randolfo, 143
Gainsborough, Earl of, (Charles George Noel), 34, 138, 139
Garibaldi, Giuseppe, 17, 20-21, 24, 25, 26, 28, 35, 43, 44, 45, 46, 50, 51, 52, 55, 74, 87, 93, 94, 95, 99-122, 147, 165, 166, 169, 174, 181, 187, 188, 196, 197
Garibaldi, Menotti, 101, 102, 104, 106, 113, 164, 197
Garibaldi, Ricciotti, 99, 104, 210
Giorgi, Major, 98, 208
Giraud, Maximin, 93
Gladstone, William Ewart, 20, 21, 24, 168, 188, 197
Gordon, Charles Menezies, 146-147, 148, 186
Gordon, William Fletcher, 143, 146-147
Gorman, Daniel, 72
Grant, Thomas, (Bishop of Southwark), 119
Granville, Lord, 168
Gregory XVI, 24, 32y
Guérin, Joseph-Louis, 68, 133-134
Guillemin, Arthur, 101
Gurdon, Anselm, 163
Guttemberg, Franz Ferdinand, 42, 71
Guttemberg, Madame, 72

Hansom, Joseph, 34 (fn), 141, 185, 188 (fn), 200
Hazlewood Castle, 139, 184
Henquenet, 113
Herbert of Lea, Lady, xv, 23, 108, 114, 153
Heron, Daniel Caulfield, 187
Herries of Terregles, Lord, 138, 139
Heycamp, Nicholas, 100
Hinde, Jacob, 138, 141, 185, 200
Holtham, Benjamin, 144, 184, 186

Holtham, Samuel, 143, 144, 186, 200
Howley, Edward, 40
Hudson, Sir James, 75, 78
Hughes, John, (Archbishop of New York), 81
Hugo, Victor, 115
Hunter Blair, David, 177
Hynes, Sergeant Major, 192

Irish College, Rome, xi, 34, 41, 47, 51, 137, 144, 173
Irish Ladies' Papal Defence Fund, 161 (fn), 163-164
Italian Army, Units: Artillery, 171, 174; Bersaglieri, 73, 174, 176, 178, 180; Infantry, 173, 176, 178; Lancers, xiv, 171, 173, 209
Iturbide, Salvador, 93

Jacob, William, 136, 137, 144, 179, 180, 185, 201
Jannerat, Major, 62, 208
Jervoise, Henry, 169, 183
Johnson, William, 143-144
Jong, Pieter, iv, 101
Joubert, Leopold, 190-191

Kanzler, Hermann, 56, 97, 98, 101, 102, 104, 105, 106, 108, 110, 111, 113, 114, 119, 122, 124, 125, 127, 155, 164, 168, 169, 170, 173, 175, 177, 178, 181, 197
Kanzler, Laura, 97-98, 164
Kanzler, Rodolfo, 178
Kavanagh, Mary Constantia, 136, 155, 156, 164, 166-167, 197
Keens brothers, 143, 184, 201
Kenney, Paul, 42, 50
Kenyon, John, 141, 172, 184, 185, 186, 188 (fn), 201, 203
Keogh, Myles, 82, 204
Kerkhove, Paul van de, 174
Kiely, Daniel, 40, 81, 82
Kinsella, James, 143
Kirby, Tobias, 34, 40, 41, 116, 134, 137, 145, 146, 173, 197
Kirkham, William, 173, 174, 176-177
Kirwan, Mark, 51, 63, 192, 208

La Rocque, Alfred, 126, 144
Lamoricière, Christophe Juchault de, 30, 31, 32, 33, 39, 40, 48, 50, 51, 53, 55, 56, 57, 60, 61, 62, 66, 67, 68, 69, 70, 71, 72, 73, 77, 79, 89, 97, 195, 197
Lanasol, Hyacinth de, 65, 68
Langdale, Lord, 138
Langley, Charles, 59
Lavigerie, Charles, 190
L'Avant Garde, 191
Lazzarini, Colonel, 56, 57
League of St Sebastian, 187-188
Leahy, Patrick, (Bishop of Cashel), 41
Leo III, 108

Leo XIII, 194
Lewis, Ralph Fitzgibbon, 141, 173
Li-Kou-Win, Pierre, 93
Limminghe, Alfred de, 94
Lindsay, Claud Reginald, 193
Loreto, 61, 62, 63, 65, 68, 69, 73, 77, 78,
Luther, Michael, 40
Lynch, Charles Edward, 137

Maguire, John Francis, 24, 76
Maistre, Captain de, 105
Mandy, Francis, 140, 143, 201
Manning, Henry Edward, (Archbishop of Westminster), 24, 33, 78, 116, 118, 119, 134, 136, 146, 148, 149, 150, 161, 166, 168, 188, 197
Mario, Jessie White, 165
Mazzini, Giuseppe, 17, 26, 94, 116, 167, 169, 187, 198
Maxwell, Walter Constable, xi, 139, 140, 142, 143, 144, 185, 186, 201
McCaffery, Michael, 41
McClellan, George B., 86, 87
McDevitt, Dr, 78
McDonnell, Charles, 38-39, 48, 49, 50
McGarry, James, 42
McLoughlin, Bonaventure, 50
McSweeney, Eugene, 51, 68
Macerata, 50, 55, 61
Matthews, Henry, 147
Meaney, Joseph, 40
Mentana, xiv, xv, 91, 102, 105-122, 123, 124, 125, 126, 129, 131, 132, 134, 135, 136, 140, 144, 145, 148, 149, 156, 157, 160, 161, 164, 165, 167, 176, 178, 186, 190, 191, 192, 193, 194
Mérode, Xavier, 29, 30, 31, 32, 43, 49, 50, 58, 79, 80, 81, 83, 97, 98, 169, 195, 198
Milne, G. L. Gordon, 188
Minghetti, Marco, 96
Mitchell, Perceval, 142
Molloy, Bernard, 144, 184, 186
Mombello, Augusto, 121
Montelibretti, 101-102, 120 (fn), 128, 129, 132, 133, 194
Monterotondo, 90, 102, 103-104, 105, 107, 108, 120 (fn), 131, 134
Montgomery, George, 34, 144-145
Monti, Giuseppe, 103
Moreau, Father, 146, 147
Moriarty, David, (Bishop of Ardfert and Aghadoe), 25, 34, 39, 41, 44, 198
Mullins, Mr, 148, 151
Mundy, Rodney, 52
Murray, Hugh, 126, 190
Mustafa, Abdallah, 93

Napoleon III, 19, 20, 26, 27, 28, 30, 32, 42, 52, 53, 55,

70, 78, 79, 91, 92, 94, 98, 99, 104, 111, 116, 119, 120, 166, 189, 198
Naughton, Edward Patrick, 47
Nerola, 101, 102, 120 (fn), 128, 132, 164
Nevin, Private, 72
Newman, John Henry, 23, 25, 129
Newsham, Francis, 144, 184, 201
Nugent, Laval, 38, 44, 50
Nulty, Thomas, (Coadj Bishop of Meath), 116

O'Beirne, Andrew, 72
O'Brien, Dominic, (Bishop of Waterford), 41
O'Brien, William, 82
O'Callaghan, Henry, 160
O'Carroll, Patrick, 40, 50, 71
O'Clery, Patrick Keyes, 101, 103, 167, 172, 173, 174, 178, 184, 185, 186, 187, 188, 198
O'Connell, Michael, 82
O'Connor, Mr, 159-160
O'Connor, Charles, 160
O'Dwyer, Timothy, 39, 43-44
O'Donnell, John, 141, 201
O'Donoghue, Daniel, 43
O'Flynn, Philip, 81, 82, 155
O'Keeffe, Joseph, 82
O'Mahony, Francis, 40, 71
O'Neill, David, 59
O'Reilly, Albert De La Hoyde (or Delahoyde), 71, 73, 82, 174, 184, 198
O'Reilly, James, 82
O'Reilly, Ida, 49, 58, 77, 134
O'Reilly, Myles, 49, 51, 58, 59, 60, 77, 80, 81, 134, 184, 198
O'Shaugnessy, Thomas, 82
Oakeley, Frederick, 24
Old Hall Green (St Edmund's College), 144
Osimo, 61, 68, 134
Oudenbosch, xi, 93 (fn), 126, 127, 156, 194
Ozanam, Charles, 105, 106, 110, 113, 114

Palgrave, Francis, 115
Palmerston, Viscount, 20, 21, 23, 26, 27, 46, 78, 198
Papal Defence Committee, xiii, xiv, 138, 146-148, 184
Pas, Mizael de, 62, 68
Passo Corese, 90
Peard, John Whitehead, 45, 47, 106
Pearson, Emma, 95, 96, 102, 106, 114, 115
Pearson, Robert, 188 (fn), 201
Persano, Admiral, 71, 74
Perugia, xiv, xv, 27, 51, 53, 55, 56-57, 58, 61, 71, 74, 78, 192 (fn)
Peter's Pence, 22, 34-35, 144, 147, 188
Petre, Oswald, 139, 142, 185, 202
Petre, William, (Baron Petre), 49, 119, 138
Philip Neri, St, 135

Piedmontese Army, Units: Artillery, 53, 56, 58, 59, 67, 68, 70, 72, 209; Bersaglieri, 53, 56, 57, 58, 59, 63, 65, 72, 209; Infantry, 58, 59, 209; Lancers, 58, 61
Pimodan Georges de, 32, 55, 61, 62, 63, 65, 66, 67, 68, 69, 77, 198
Piopolis (Canada), 192
Pius VI, 21
Pius VII, 22
Pius IX, xiii, xiv, 19, 21-22, 24, 28, 29, 52, 72, 75, 79, 82, 90, 92, 96, 97, 118, 119, 120, 136, 146, 159, 166, 169, 174, 180, 182, 188, 198
Pius XI, 194
Poer, Edmond de la, 173
Pontifical Army, Units: Artillery, 31, 32, 33, 55, 56, 57, 62, 63, 65, 66, 68, 70, 80, 82, 98, 99, 101, 104, 110, 143, 151, 170, 271, 173, 208, 209; Austrian Bersaglieri, 63, 80, 208; 'Crusaders of Cathelineau', 33, 128, 134; Battalion of St Patrick, xiv, xv, 33, 38-77, 80, 128, 184, 192, 196, 198, 204-205, 208; Company of St Patrick, xv, 80-83, 198, 204-205; Dragoons, 40, 63, 80, 90, 93, 98, 104, 108, 110, 124, 151, 156, 169, 171, 173, 178, 180, 208, 209; Foreign Carabineers, 33, 40, 65, 80, 82, 98, 102, 103, 108, 110, 111, 113, 151, 170, 198, 208, 209; Franco-Belgian Tirailleurs, 33, 40, 51, 58, 59, 62, 63, 65, 67, 68, 69, 77, 86, 89, 90, 128, 134, 140, 197, 205, 208; Gendarmes, 31, 55, 80, 90, 93, 94, 98, 100, 102, 170, 171, 180, 181, 208, 209; Guides de Lamoricière, 33, 40, 62, 63, 80, 208, 210; Indigenous Cacciatori, 33, 63, 65, 67, 69, 208; Line Infantry, 31, 56, 67, 98, 99, 104, 208; Zouaves, xi, xiii, xiv, xv, 33, 40, 51, 66, 80, 81, 82, 83, 86, 89-194, 205-207, 209
Pope Hennessy, John, 77
Powell, Joseph, 103, 124, 125, 135, 137, 138, 151, 152-153, 154, 155, 157, 158, 159, 161, 162, 167, 185, 188, 202, 206
Power, John Talbot, 184
Puyo, Albert, 93

Quatrebarbes, Bernard de, 102, 103
Quatrebarbes, Théodore de, 33, 70, 72, 103
Quelen, Urbain de, 101, 133
Quirck, James, 82

Rattazzi, Urbano, 98
Renaud, Alfred, 144
Résimont, Zénon de, 170
Robinson, Wilfrid Clavering, 178, 180, 185, 188 (fn), 194, 202
Roche, Thomas, 137
Rosati, 120
Rospigliosi, Prince, 93
Ross, Sir Thomas, 43
Rouher, Eugene, 116
Russell, Lord John, 20, 21, 27, 75, 78

Russell, Odo, 27, 28, 32, 38, 42, 50, 55, 115, 117, 126, 159
Russell-Killough, Frank, 40, 50, 66, 71, 81, 82, 98, 108, 113, 198
Ryan, William. 186

Sampson, Donat, 143
San Martino, Gustavo Ponzo di, 168-169
Schmidt, Anton, 55, 56, 57
'Scholey', 106
Schuster, Johann, 89
Selby, Fauconberg, 40
Selby, Robert, 40
Sellon, Ernest, 185, 188 (fn), 202
Senigallia, 27, 55, 56, 61, 77
Seward, William, 81
September Convention, 96, 98, 104, 116, 166, 167, 168
Serra, Colonel, 172
Serristori Barracks, 102-103, 155, 159
Shanahan, Timothy, 39, 42
Shee, Daniel, xiv, 128, 167, 171, 184, 185, 202
Sheehan, Jeremiah, 184
'Sitting Bull', 82
Sonis, Louis-Gaston de, 189, 190
Spoleto, xiv, xv, 41, 51, 55, 57-60, 61, 71, 74, 78, 81, 134, 169, 181, 185, 192 (fn)
Stanley, Frank, 143
Stone, Katherine Mary, xi, 101-102, 105, 114, 128, 136, 144-145 (fn), 155, 164-165, 177, 181, 198
Stonor, Edmund, xiii, 128, 133, 139, 142, 146, 147, 158, 160, 162, 163, 164, 177, 180, 1812, 198
Stourton, Arthur, 139, 141, 202
Stonyhurst College, 126, 144
Straker, Catherine, 77-78
Styles, Edward, 45, 46 Sullivan, Alexander Martin, 38-39, 41, 42, 43, 76
Sullivan, Dennis, 82
Surratt, John, 93-94, 127
Swinburne, Algernon Charles, 115
Swift, Henry, 142-143, 144

Talbot, George, 24, 29, 40, 49 (fn), 75, 116, 117, 120, 133, 148, 149, 160, 198
Taillieu, August, 191
Taparelli, Luigi, 22
Teeling, Bartle, 137, 141, 143, 174, 185, 186, 187, 194, 198
Thérèse of Lisieux, St, 163
Thomalé, Jean, 110
Tivoli, 98, 107
Tognetti, Gaetano, 103
Troussures, Major de, 107, 111, 178

Ubaldini, Major, 63, 65, 208
Uhe, Lieutenant, 70

Upholland (St Joseph's College), 144
Ushaw (St Cuthbert's College), 133, 143, 144, 145, 157, 194

Vansittart, Clement, 140, 141, 157, 165
Vavasour, Oswald, 139, 143, 164, 174, 202
Vavasour, William, 139, 142, 143, 144, 151, 156, 157, 164, 184, 186, 202
Veaux, Arthur de, 110
Vespignani, Virginio, 120
Victor Emmanuel II, 17, 26, 39, 45, 61, 72, 73, 74, 116, 167, 169, 182, 187, 190, 198
Victoria, Queen, 21, 38, 75, 89, 116, 142
Volontaires d l'Ouest, 189-191
Vrain, Henry, 184

Wardour Castle, 139
Waterworth, Father, 142-143, 144, 147
Watts-Russell, Julian, xi, xii, 102, 106, 128, 129-135, 140, 141, 142, 144, 157, 193-194, 203
Watts-Russell, Michael, 129, 141, 186
Watts-Russell, Wilfrid, 102, 128, 131, 140, 141, 142, 167, 186, 203
Weetman, Henry, xi, 139
Wells, Joseph (or Charles), 128, 203
Welman, Frederick Tristam, 139, 142, 143, 144, 158, 193, 203
Wibaux, Theodore, 91-92, 189-190
Wils, Auguste & Ignatius, 190
Wilson, Alexander, xi, 139, 155, 203
Winchester, Elizabeth Lowther, 165
Wiseman, Nicholas, (Archbishop of Westminster), 23, 24, 25, 34, 41, 47, 78, 79, 140, 143, 149, 194, 198
Woodward, Charles, 40, 128, 140, 141, 143, 144, 186, 203
Woodward, Frederick, xiv, 203
Woodward, Henry, 40, 51
Worcester Workhouse, 142-143, 144, 146, 147
Wyndham, Percy, 45

Zappi, Giovan Battista, 55, 98, 178